The Limits of Symbolic Reform

The Limits of Symbolic Reform

The New Deal and Taxation, 1933–1939

MARK H. LEFF

DEPARTMENT OF HISTORY
WASHINGTON UNIVERSITY

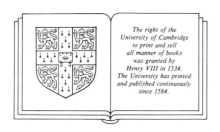

The right of the
University of Cambridge
to print and sell
all manner of books
was granted by
Henry VIII in 1534.
The University has printed
and published continuously
since 1584.

CAMBRIDGE UNIVERSITY PRESS

CAMBRIDGE
LONDON   NEW YORK   NEW ROCHELLE
MELBOURNE   SYDNEY

Published by The Press Syndicate of the University of Cambridge
The Pitt Building, Trumpington Street, Cambridge CB2 1RP
32 East 57th Street, New York, NY 10022, USA
10 Stamford Road, Oakleigh, Melbourne 3166, Australia

First published 1984

Printed in the United States of America

Library of Congress Cataloging in Publication Data
Leff, Mark Hugh.
The limits of symbolic reform.
Includes bibliographical references.
1. Taxation – United States – History – 20th century.
2. New Deal, 1933–1939.   I. Title.
HJ2377.L44   1984   336.2′00973   84–4325
ISBN 0 521 26268 2

To Barry D. Karl

"But what good came of it at last?"
  Quoth little Peterkin.
"Why that I cannot tell," said he,
"But 't was a famous victory."
    – Robert Southey, "The Battle
            of Blenheim"

Why not? None of us is ever going to make $100,000 a
year. How many people report on that much income?
    – Franklin D. Roosevelt, 30 July 1941, on
        proposal to impose 99½% tax rate
        on incomes exceeding $100,000

Contents

vii

Acknowledgments

One of the many drawbacks of a study representing more than a decade's work is that one accumulates more and deeper debts than can be acknowledged in a page of tightly rationed space. My colleagues in the Washington University History Department have been unfailingly and often unreasonably supportive. Their friendship means a great deal to me, and this is a better book because of their suggestions and encouragement. I am similarly indebted to Frank Freidel, Martha Ozawa, Arnold Heidenheimer, John Coatsworth, and Frank Zimring. Dora Arky, Carolyn Brown, Becky Bryan, and Marcia Skalnik went above and beyond the call of duty or the threshold of tolerance in typing various drafts. As friends and historians, Bill Kirby, Marc Hilton, Jamil Zainaldin, and Ray Solomon have been important to me and therefore to the development of this book. I'm also grateful for the competence and patience of everyone associated with Cambridge University Press, from the original readers to my copyeditor Alfred Imhoff, and especially my editor Frank Smith. Archivists and librarians from the District of Columbia to Columbia, Missouri, from Madison to Chapel Hill, were extremely helpful, especially the resourceful staffs of the Franklin D. Roosevelt Library, the National Archives, and the Library of Congress. During crucial stages of this enterprise, I also depended on the Ford Foundation and the National Endowment for the Humanities.

Carol Skalnik Leff was my main source of emotional and intellectual support, though this is hardly the place to count the ways. But she was also my most telling critic, saving the reader from much that was awkward or poorly conceived and some that was unforgivable. My daughter Alison and my son Benjamin have contributed an inestimable amount to my personal well-being, even if at the expense of adding months to this particular enterprise. Finally, Barry Karl, to whom I dedicate this book out of a personal and academic indebtedness that goes far beyond his guidance on New Deal taxation, has given me a respect for the creative power of historical analysis that this book could never fully reflect. All errors of fact and interpretation are of course my own, though I sure wish someone had caught them.

Introduction: Political Imagery and Financial Reality

Anyone venturing onto terrain as forbidding as the tax system should have a good excuse. This book began innocently enough in Barry Karl's graduate seminar in 1972. Taxes were then – as always – in the news, particularly an ill-fated proposal by presidential candidate George McGovern to redistribute income, labeled by the *New York Times* "a return to the initial thrust of Franklin Roosevelt's New Deal."[1] This loose popular notion that New Deal taxes "aimed at far-reaching social reform" and income redistribution, thus reflecting the broader "social democratic emphasis" of the New Deal, was an enticing one.[2] Franklin Roosevelt himself, after all, had called for "a wiser, more equitable distribution of the national income" and had denounced the privileged few "economic royalists" whose "hatred" he tauntingly welcomed.[3] I did not then anticipate the parallels I would later find between the symbolic functions of New Deal rhetoric and the most celebrated New Deal tax bills, each a triumph of form over content. It was clear, though, that tax policy – characterized by one author as "at the heart of the New Deal"[4] – could offer a direct measure of the validity of this popular image of the New Deal.

Yet there was good reason to be skeptical of the image of the New Deal that Franklin Roosevelt helped to project. The emerging historical understanding of the New Deal, one that has elaborated and entrenched itself in the dozen years since I began this study, emphasized the New

---

1 *New York Times*, 2 July 1972, sec. 4, p. 8.
2 Forrest McDonald, *The United States in the Twentieth Century*, 2 (Reading, Mass.: Addison-Wesley, 1970), p. 116; W. Elliot Brownlee, *Dynamics of Ascent: A History of the American Economy* (New York: Knopf, 1974), p. 307; Hubert H. Humphrey, *The Political Philosophy of the New Deal* (Baton Rouge: Louisiana State University Press, 1970), p. 114.
3 Samuel I. Rosenman, comp., *The Public Papers and Addresses of Franklin D. Roosevelt*, 1 (New York: Random House, 1938): 645 (22 May 1932); Ibid., 5: 234 (27 June 1936); Ibid., 5: 568 (31 October 1936).
4 Oliver Pilat, *Pegler: Angry Man of the Press* (Boston: Beacon Press, 1963), p. 142.

1

Deal's commitment to the essentials of the capitalist system, called into question the degree of redistribution of power and wealth in the New Deal, and denigrated the feeble impact of the New Deal tax system. Ellis Hawley, for example, highlighted the New Deal's coupling of "skirmishes" on the economic "flanks" (such as attacks on "widely hated," "vulnerable" groups) with its willingness to underwrite piecemeal corporate efforts to attain economic stability.[5] Paul Conkin, too, had pointed to the Rooseveltian tendency to substitute fighting words and symbolic deeds for more substantive action.[6] Even so, I was not fully prepared for the statistical picture emerging from my research. By no stretch of the imagination was the New Deal tax system a vehicle for broad income redistribution to lift up those at the bottom of the economic pyramid. For various reasons, only some of them relating to the broader health of the economy, the share of tax collections drawn from potential sources of redistributive taxation (mainly the personal and corporate income taxes) was considerably *lower* in the New Deal than in World War I, the 1920s, or the decades succeeding the New Deal.

Gradually I came to recognize that two federal tax systems operated in the United States between 1933 and the eve of World War II: one a revenue workhorse, the other a symbolic showpiece. Though occasioning only nominal political debate, it was the first system, relying primarily on taxes that bore disproportionately on lower incomes, that counted financially. FDR not only inherited this skewed tax system; it was an edifice that he helped build and maintain. There was also a second tax structure, full of sound and fury over income taxes and loopholes. But it signified almost nothing in revenue terms, registering instead the waxing and waning of political status. These two themes – the transformation of the functional tax system and the political role of symbolic tax policy during the Roosevelt years – are the focus of this study.

This analysis, therefore, represents an exploration of the economic and political determinants of the New Deal tax system. Taxation has been characterized as an X-ray, revealing the anatomy of political and social power.[7] Yet the potential of this characterization has not been fully tapped,

5 Ellis W. Hawley, *The New Deal and the Problem of Monopoly* (Princeton, N.J.: Princeton University Press, 1966).
6 Paul K. Conkin, *FDR and the Origins of the Welfare State* (New York: Crowell, 1967). Conkin later developed this theme in Paul K. Conkin and David Burner, *A History of Recent America* (New York: Crowell, 1974), pp. 236–7, 243, 248.
7 William A. Williams, *The Great Evasion* (Chicago: Quadrangle Books, 1964), p. 159.

for the volatile mixture of politics and economics that shapes the tax structure tends to be neglected in favor of circumscribed studies that focus on either one or the other. It is the confluence of economics and politics (not such traditional economic approaches as the building of economic models to estimate the tax system's actual impact on economic growth) that concerns me in this study. To interpret taxation within the framework of the power alignments of the 1930s and of the New Deal as a whole, it is necessary continually to cross over this artificial boundary between politics and economics: to ask why trifling imposts produced more political heat than remunerative ones, to integrate the implicit and explicit economic theories generated by the Depression with the political assumptions of the period, to analyze the political forces that shaped taxation's distributive impact, and to evaluate the gap between private assessments and public pronouncements on tax policy. Ultimately, it is through such questions that the tactics of the New Deal and the operating assumptions of its tax system can most fully emerge.

In pursuing these questions, and particularly in understanding the broader political impact of tax controversies that in retrospect can seem much ado about nothing, I found valuable political scientist Murray Edelman's perspective on "symbolic politics." Edelman shows how political symbolism helps to create and maintain the gap between appearance and reality, between popular perceptions and "actual gains and losses" in power and money. The "choice or creation of political enemies," a tactic that proved so important in Roosevelt's presidency, is an integral part of this use of symbolism. The result, Edelman points out in an observation directly relevant to an understanding of the relationship of the New Deal to the reformist forces it confronted, can be to divert and reassure people and thereby to deflect or undermine reform efforts.[8]

To the extent that tax policy colors understanding of the New Deal, it can do so in misleading ways. In particular, Franklin Roosevelt's slashing oratory in the colorful 1935 Revenue Act fight can encourage the supposition that New Deal taxes must have eased income inequality in favor of the "forgotten man." Such conclusions are extravagant at best; high rates on upper income brackets were counterbalanced by less glamorous taxes that obtained more impressive collections from the poor. To this extent, the government acted as a bourgeois Robin Hood, taking not only from the rich but also at times from the poor to rescue the merely comfortable

---

8 Kenneth M. Dolbeare and Murray J. Edelman, *American Politics*, 3d ed. (Lexington, Mass.: Heath, 1977), pp. 471–2, 475, 456.

from the tax man. Given the influence of this "middle-class" group on tax debates (one evidenced in congressional solicitude for the lower- and middle-income tax brackets, the stable social center in which "your friends and my friends are found"),[9] this result is not unpredictable. William Buckley puts forward the generalization that since "the principal leverage in democratic bourgeois societies" belongs to the middle class, the upper and lower classes will bear a heavier share.[10] Yet this peculiar brand of redistribution, amounting to the successful playing of the middle against both ends, was not merely an indicator of middle-class influence. It was also not the sole creation of the New Deal. The income tax had been introduced in the spirit of a populist-progressive impulse that vilified "malefactors of great wealth." The carriers of this soak-the-rich tradition saw the nation as a battleground for two contending forces: a coterie of opulent power grabbers and the mass of "plain folks." Concentration of wealth and privilege affronted the partisans of this tradition, especially because they associated the acquisition of the great American fortunes with dishonest methods and practices. Tax policy, by cutting the bloated few down to size, would be emblematic of a shift in social and economic power, a shift that could restore fair play to the system. Since the late nineteenth century, this symbolic thrust had exercised special appeal to agrarian, cheap-money, antitrust forces. Thus the income tax was sponsored mainly by Southerners and Westerners as a means of limiting the excessive power of rich Easterners. Not until the pruning of income-tax exemptions in World War II (which, unlike the New Deal, was a watershed for the tax system) did this scourge of "abnormal" incomes become routine and financially productive. Despite a cut in income-tax exemptions and a rise in tax rates directed at the so-called middle class in the year preceding the New Deal, the income tax in the 1930s never applied to more than 5 percent of Americans, and only a small minority of those shouldered most of the tax. The renowed American suspicion of concentrated power and concern with opportunity fanned hostility to "special privilege," directing attention to the richest taxpayers. However, this scarcely represented a national commitment to income redistribution; in fact, it clashed with the powerful sentiment that government had no business divesting a solid citizen of his or her earned income to compensate for shortcomings of the weak or untalented.

9 U.S., Congress, House, *Congressional Record*, 73d Cong., 1st sess., 1933, pt. 5: 4359, 4347.
10 William F. Buckley, Jr., *Four Reforms: A Program for the '70s* (New York: Putnam, 1973), p. 60.

The income tax thus was designed more to quell abuses than to shift income within the rest of society – hence its heavy weighting toward the opulent. Taxation has always lacked a certain legitimacy in this country; the government's right to expropriate even a part of someone's reasonable living expenses was suspect. At least until World War II, the federal government could openly seek to tax only those who had a surplus of income that permitted them substantial savings (i.e., the rich, the super-rich, and corporations). Obviously, this structure of *direct* taxation had little capacity to tap the incomes of the American public as a whole; it was deliberately designed to *avoid* taxing "the people." Even in the twentieth century, the federal government has imposed major general tax hikes only in national emergencies: wars and the 1929–33 Crash.

This injunction against taxing the people, however, was not quite as constraining as it sounds. Its emphasis on taxing extraordinary wealth had an underside. *Indirect* taxation could be sanctioned as a lower-profile component of higher-visibility social or economic programs, or as an excise on nonessentials such as liquor or tobacco. These indirect taxes, which tended ultimately to fall most heavily on poorer consumers, injected regressive elements into the tax structure. The paramount triumph of the relatively affluent was in positioning themselves on the right side of the dividing line between plutocrat and average citizen, keeping their distance from the excesses of the super-rich. Though a higher corporate tax could reach middle-class stockholders, they otherwise enjoyed a double immunity. The symbolic progressive tax crusade against the economic royalists exempted them. Similarly, the resort to alternative tax rationalizations, finessing the ban on taxing the people, spawned regressive indirect taxes that treated their incomes kindly.

The result, according to the most detailed (though by no means authoritative) economic study of who ultimately ended up paying taxes in the 1930s, was that the federal tax burden applied at virtually a flat percentage rate to all except the most well-heeled 1 or 2 percent of Americans (with the poorest sixth also chipping in a little extra).[11] FDR's

---

11 Helen Tarasov, *Who Pays the Taxes?*, Temporary National Economic Committee Monograph No. 3 (Washington, D.C.: Government Printing Office, 1940), p. 6; Helen Tarasov, *Who Does Pay the Taxes?*, Studies in Government Finance (New York: New School for Social Research, 1942), p. 44. See also Mabel Newcomer, "Effect of the Tax Burden on Different Income Classes," in Carl Shoup et al., *Studies in Current Tax Problems* (New York: Twentieth Century Fund, 1937), pp. 29–30, 5. Thomas Renaghan's "Distributional Effects of Federal Tax Policy 1929–1939" (*Explorations in Economic History* 21 [January 1984]: 40–63) came to my attention after this book was in proofs. Renaghan's findings are largely consistent with the other studies cited here: starkly higher taxes on the

reputation for raising taxes on corporate profits, estates, and personal incomes is not undeserved (though Congress and other "outside" pressures merit much credit for these "New Deal accomplishments," but such taxes tended to concentrate on the largest incomes. Only the group at the very top of the income pyramid, the lucky 1 percent drawing over $10,000 a year, experienced a markedly bigger percentage tax bite. And, as seen in Part II, the disinclination to move beyond this top 1 percent sharply limited both the redistributive and the revenue potentials of the 1930s tax system.

The detailed analysis of fiscal decision making during the 1930s offered in succeeding chapters demonstrates that the New Deal response served to perpetuate previous attitudes and approaches to taxation, while creating a tax system whose effects often diverged from the rhetoric accompanying it. Indeed, the Roosevelt administration repeatedly extended the regressive excise taxes enacted under the Hoover administration, while adding to the burden on low-income Americans with taxes on liquor, agricultural commodities, and wages covered by social security. Other New Deal taxes would raise tax rates for corporations and the wealthy, but would not dig deeply enough into the income stream to have a significant impact on the income shares of the great majority of Americans.

This does not in itself demonstrate a New Deal failure to secure a fairer distribution of economic resources. That can only be assessed through a much broader study than this one, encompassing an analysis of the government programs that these taxes helped finance. That is an interesting question, to be sure, but it is also perilously complex and difficult to quantify (who, for example, received the financial benefit from government-backed mortgages: homeowners? banks? the construction in-

top 1% and some regressivity at the bottom of the income scale once social security taxes are included. He concludes that the greatest relative tax increases between 1929 and 1939 were in these top and bottom brackets. For the top 10% or so, Renaghan offers mixed results, showing some progressivity throughout for 1933 and 1936, only to have this progressivity vanish (for the percentiles below the very top) in 1939. I should note that certain methodological/technical problems affect Renaghan's findings, especially the hazards of combining estimated income levels of consumer units with the far more restrictive figures on net income registered in tax returns. Renaghan's method of supplying missing data, for example, seems to lead to a great exaggeration of the differences between the 1936 and 1939 tax distributions, since his resort to more prosperous 1941 figures as a proxy for the distribution of income in 1939 produces a distortion for the top brackets. Renaghan also offers a comparison of the "post-fiscal" impact on income (as measured by the changing Gini coefficient), but its applicability to this book seems limited by the inclusion of government transfer payments in addition to taxes.

dustry? construction workers?); besides, it is too encompassing and would
have made it impossible to delve beneath the surface to examine the social
and political implications of the highly controversial tax policy of the New
Deal. One might similarly pursue the speculation that the New Deal's
narrowly based income tax yielded such sparse revenues that it constrained
the expansion of the welfare state, thus circumscribing the New Deal's
redistributive potential. This, however, would have to be counterbalanced
against the probability that a less popular and more "painful" tax policy
– by promoting what conservatives called "tax consciousness" – would
have broadened the base of resistance to New Deal expenditures.

Even the necessarily incomplete vista opened by this study is relevant
to the broader question of the New Deal's impact. By assessing the level
of awareness of tax incidence and the priority placed upon it, it brings
into focus the New Deal's commitment to income redistribution. In addition,
by locating New Deal taxes within their political context and by examining
alternative tax proposals, it becomes easier to determine whether the New
Deal took the nation to the border of reform possibility or whether it was
more inclined to moderate or coopt movements for broader change. Were
New Deal redistributive goals, in other words, articulated largely for public
consumption, or did they represent a sincere operational commitment?

Chapter 1 addresses this question by establishing the framework for
early New Deal nonprogressive taxes, whereas Chapter 2 analyzes the
parallel tax-reform "soak-the-rich" effort, which until 1935 centered in
Congress. But in 1935, the president shifted gears, a fundamental change
in strategy analyzed in Chapter 3. The liberal swing in the 1934 elections,
along with the famous "Thunder on the Left" from Huey Long and
others, represented an increasing challenge to Roosevelt. His initial efforts
to suppress this discontent and to salvage a middle way floundered as it
became clear that recovery had helped revive intense business opposition.
Roosevelt chose to stem the disintegration of his support by ceremoniously
drumming the "overprivileged" out of his coalition. Rhetoric was the most
direct way of dramatizing this rift and of binding together what was
essentially a negative coalition. The quintessence of this strategy was its
fearsome shadow, not its more limited substance. Thus the celebrated
Revenue Act of 1935, though financially frivolous, was politically crucial
to Roosevelt's broader strategy.

Chapter 4 traces the flowering of this approach toward taxation in 1936
and 1937, as FDR continued his sorties against "economic royalists." Yet,
by the last years of the decade, the New Deal tax position received stinging

setbacks. Part III chronicles this reversal, focusing particularly on the business ideology that played such an important role in setting the terms of the debate once the 1937 recession discredited New Deal economic leadership. Anxious to restore their tarnished status, businessmen targeted FDR's polarizing rhetoric and the tax legislation with which it had been associated. More substantive programs emerged unscathed, as the New Deal tax system drew hostile fire. Tax policy and the passions it evoked thus add a vital dimension to an understanding of Franklin Roosevelt's political appeal and the forces he confronted. Yet the tax structure itself exited the New Deal in much the same form it had entered it. The "forgotten man" – subject to a liquor tax, a social security tax, and renewed excise taxes – could derive only minimal concrete benefits from the new low-yield tax rates on upper-bracket incomes. The New Deal tax system illustrated the limits to symbolic reform.

Part I

Prelude to Reform: The New Deal Tax System, 1933–1935

1. Taxing the Forgotten Man

Compared to most Western Europeans, Americans are lightly taxed. But we have never taken our taxes lightly. From the Whiskey Rebellion to the Reagan tax cuts, tax and tariff policy have focused this nation's sectional, economic, and partisan conflicts, raising basic questions about the role of government itself. Yet the question of who ultimately pays taxes (what economists call "tax incidence") generates only limited public interest. Tax "dodges" by millionaires can rankle, but arcane disquisitions on the ultimate burden of specific taxes are beyond us. Most people live fruitful lives without grasping the distinction between a proportional tax and a progressive one.[1]

It is thus not surprising that New Deal debates skirted the issue of tax incidence. The public did show great sensitivity to inadequate sacrifices by the super-rich. Beyond that, however, the inchoate popular adherence to "ability to pay" yielded to more pressing matters of economic recovery: resuming production, restoring agricultural purchasing power, and providing security against old age and unemployment. Furthermore, the tax bite, by current standards, was modest. Federal revenues absorbed one-twentieth of the gross national product, as compared to one-fifth today.[2]

Inertia, too, crippled the cause of progressive taxation. The high exemptions and light middle-bracket rates of the U.S. income tax left it peculiarly vulnerable to economic fluctuations. In the prosperous late 1920s, the corporate and individual income tax provided two-thirds of all federal tax revenues (see Table 1), a proportion higher than in any other country in the Western world.[3] As the Depression erased corporate

---

1 Walter J. Blum and Harry Kalven, Jr., *The Uneasy Case for Progressive Taxation* (Chicago: University of Chicago Press, Phoenix Books, 1963), p. x.
2 U.S., Department of Commerce, Bureau of the Census, *Historical Statistics of the United States, Colonial Times to 1970* (Washington, D.C.: Government Printing Office, 1975), pp. 1106–7, 224 (hereafter cited as Census, *Historical Statistics*). U.S., Office of Management and Budget, *Budget of the United States Government, Fiscal Year 1984* (Washington, D.C.: Government Printing Office, 1983), pt. 9, p. 53.
3 Paul Studenski, ed., *Taxation and Public Policy* (New York: Richard R. Smith, 1936), p. 150.

11

Table 1. Components of the U.S. federal tax structure, 1925–80 (in percentages of annual collections)

Fiscal year (years ending June 30)	Total federal tax collections ($)	Individual income tax	Corporate income and excess profits tax[b]	Estate & gift tax	Customs	Excise taxes					Capital stock	Social insurance[c]
						Total	Alcohol	Tobacco	Manufacturers'	AAA processing		
1926–30 average	3,482,919,000	28	36	2	17	16	[a]	12	2	...	1	...
1931	2,806,653,000	30	37	2	13	19	[a]	16	[a]	...	...	...
1932	1,885,484,000	23	33	2	17	24	[a]	21	[a]	...	...	...
1933	1,870,589,000	19	21	2	13	45	2	22	13	...	...	...
1934	2,985,673,000	14	13	4	10	43	9	14	13	12	3	...
1935	3,642,789,000	14	16	6	9	37	11	13	9	14	3	...
1936	3,907,020,000	17	19	10	10	40	13	13	10	2	2	...
1937	5,139,512,000	21	21	6	9	34	12	11	9	...	3	5
1938	6,017,952,000	21	22	7	6	29	9	9	7	...	2	12
1939	5,500,411,000	19	21	7	6	32	11	11	7	...	2	13
1940	5,671,452,000	17	20	6	6	33	11	11	8	...	2	15
1941–5	25,702,302,000	38	37	2	1	15	6	3	2	...	1	6
1976–80 average	397,923,600,000	47	15	1	2	5	2	1	2	...	...	31

[a] Less than ½%.

[b] Excess-profits tax comprised 2% of corporate income-tax category from its revival in 1933 until fiscal 1940; from fiscal 1941–5, in a new form, it accounted for 58.5% of the category; the windfall-profits tax on oil companies for fiscal 1980 amounted to 2% of the corporate collections in 1976–80.

[c] Old-age payroll taxes account for the preponderance of this category, which also includes railroad retirement taxes and the federal share of unemployment insurance contributions.

Sources: U.S., Census, Historical Statistics, pp. 1105–7; Annual Report on the State of the Finances for the Fiscal Year Ended June 30, 1940 (Washington, D.C.: Government Printing Office, 1941), pp. 665–6; U.S., Office of Management and Budget, The Budget of the United States Government, Fiscal Year 1983 (Washington, D.C.: Government Printing Office, 1982), pt. 9, pp. 48–9.

profits, and as the stock-market crash produced capital-loss deductions that further ravaged the top incomes underwriting the American personal income tax, income- and profits-tax receipts dropped precipitously. These taxes provided less than one-third of federal tax revenues by 1934. Only in World War II would they again account for more than half of federal revenues.

This fiscal setback was international, but the United States suffered the direst collapse.[4] Without the finery provided by a flourishing upper class, the U.S. tax system had no clothes. Throughout the world, nations took the path of least resistance, concocting indirect taxes that disproportionately burdened the poor. The United States was a prime culprit. The "forgotten man at the bottom of the economic pyramid" did not escape the notice of federal tax collectors.

Why did this retrogressive tax trend – a redistribution produced by sagging tax collections and fresh levies on the poor – occasion so little stir? The public's inclination to ascribe the Depression to the depredations of the economic elite might have reinforced the traditional populist-progressive thrust against tax evasion and the super-rich; why did the president fail to exploit this sentiment? Why did the intensity and volume of public debate often vary inversely with the revenue productiveness of a tax, with excise taxes (levies on the sale of specific items) securing perfunctory passage, whereas symbolic forays against the top income brackets could produce a furor?

Temporarily setting aside idiosyncratic influences, five interrelated factors seem to account for the cast and insignificance of early New Deal tax laws. First, the Depression lent added unpopularity to taxes. Second, Franklin Roosevelt, relying on conciliation in taxation and other areas to encourage recovery, was initially reluctant to turn popular wrath on the super-rich. This reluctance highlighted a third constraining factor; the existing personal-income-tax structure, with its upper-bracket orientation, lacked the flexibility for major revenue expansion. Extension of this over-loaded tax apparatus to lower incomes was blocked by a fourth factor; amid an otherwise incoherent approach to tax incidence, public hostility to "taxing the people" held firm. Yet, despite these constraints, some tax increases appeared necessary, for the fifth and final factor was the demand of political and economic orthodoxy for at least occasional obeisance to

4 Ibid.; Paul Studenski, "Modern Fiscal Systems, Their Characteristics and Trends of Development," *Annals of the American Academy of Political and Social Science* 183 (January 1936): 29, 38.

budget balancing. These five factors need some elaboration. The following introductory section will deal with each of them in turn, erecting a scaffolding for the next two chapters, which consider specific tax laws and campaigns in 1932–5.

Although 1930s tax policy sustained past trends, shifting economic conditions also provide an essential backdrop. Whereas public-opinion polls indicate that only a bare majority deemed their tax bills excessive after 1935,[5] the sudden sense of deprivation in the early years of the Depression had produced a citizens' revolt against direct taxes. Particularly at the state and local levels – where budget balancing was a practical or constitutional necessity and where the inflexible property tax exacted burdens disproportionate to the shrunken incomes of some property owners – organized tax rebellions flared episodically. Taxpayers associations, often vehicles for substantial property owners and real estate interests, gained considerable strength. One partial count identified over 1,000 such organizations at the state, county, city, and neighborhood levels.[6] These groups primarily monitored state and local spending, although they also campaigned against property and income taxes, joined chambers of commerce in coordinating business efforts to publicize hidden tax burdens, and often lent support to proposals to meet deficits through sales taxes. Entrenched in local power structures, they had easy access to the media for antitax broadsides. Particularly in 1932–3, when tax strikes and marches on city hall betrayed a potential for violent tax revolt, these associations helped legitimize the desperation of farmers and the tightly squeezed middle class.

On the national level, the main taxpayers' association was the American Taxpayers' League, formerly the American Bankers League. This group had favored high-bracket income-tax reduction even in the palmy Republican days of 25 percent top rates and had formed local "tax clubs" to press for the repeal of the federal estate tax. Receiving free radio time for dozens of programs in 1932–3 from the National Broadcasting System, it continued through pamphlet campaigns in succeeding years to promulgate its demands for federal and state general sales taxes, a balanced budget through slashed expenditures, and the paring of income and estate tax rates to no more than 25 percent. Though claiming 735,000 active and

---

5 Hadley Cantril, ed., *Public Opinion 1935–1946* (Princeton, N.J.: Princeton University Press, 1951), pp. 851–2. This relationship held in all classes, with a widened gap among the prosperous.

6 "Taxpayers' Organizations Supplement," *Tax Policy* 6 (March 1939): 1.

affiliated members in the late 1930s, this group was dismissed as "one of the phoniest of Washington's many phony lobbying organizations." It apparently failed to mobilize support from the relatively affluent groups that brought success at state and local levels.[7] In the absence of a federal property tax or a broadly based income tax that could enlist wider concern outside wealthy circles, the very real popular emnity toward taxes cut least deeply in the federal sphere.

Any shortcomings in group influence were rectified by a calculated economic decision, implemented by Franklin Roosevelt in the 1933–5 period conceptualized as the First New Deal. Aiming to foster business confidence as the spearhead of economic advance, Roosevelt granted the economic elite a virtual veto over corporate and upper-bracket taxes. With these revenue alternatives blocked off, the quest for business confidence tended to paralyze the tax system or force it into regressive channels.

Major political groups, huddled at the brink of economic collapse, initially surrendered Roosevelt considerable maneuvering room, some even according tax initiatives the critical role in economic policy.[8] Instead, shunting aside such innovative staff recommendations as a tax on undistributed corporate profits,[9] FDR developed no New Deal tax program in his first two years in office. He apparently believed that to get along with business, it behooved him to go along with a policy of mild taxation.

The politics of ostracism, which FDR would practice on a symbolic level in 1935–6, had little to recommend it as an emergency recovery measure. Instead, Roosevelt talked of a "concert of interests" to promote recovery – and seemed inclined to regard corporate power as the conductor.[10] His earlier campaign pronouncement that "our people and our business cannot carry these excessive burdens of taxation"[11] was a tacit acknowledgment that few issues could enrage businessmen more than tax increases; even the relatively minor adjustments in 1933–4 loosed a flood of protests

---

7 Ruth Brindze, *Not to Be Broadcast* (New York: Vanguard Press, 1937), pp. 78–9; "Taxpayers' Organizations in the United States," *Tax Policy* 5 (September 1938): 3; Kenneth G. Crawford, *The Pressure Boys* (New York: Julian Messner, 1939), p. 165.

8 "Tax Profits!," *New Republic* 75 (24 May 1933): 32.

9 Elliot A. Rosen, "Roosevelt and the Brains Trust: An Historiographical Overview," *Political Science Quarterly* 87 (December 1972): 538.

10 Samuel I. Rosenman, comp., *The Public Papers and Addresses of Franklin D. Roosevelt*, 1 (New York: Random House, 1938): 632 (18 April 1932) (hereafter cited as *Addresses of FDR*).

11 Ibid., 1: 806 (19 October 1932).

against "soaking the rich." In early 1935, Secretary of Commerce Roper spoke for the administration when he stated that tax increases could some-day be levied on the profits of a healthy economy, but "it would be very unwise to burden business with additional taxes at this time, which would serve only to retard recovery."[12]

If stiffer corporate taxation was to be ruled out, the inflexibility of the existing personal-income-tax structure made its expansion an unpromising alternative revenue source. At the end of the 1920s, taxable incomes of $50,000 or more accounted for 24 percent of the *income* reported on tax returns, but provided four-fifths of the income *tax*. The Crash eroded these incomes; all through the 1930s, these top brackets contained less than 10 percent of the total income reported. Nevertheless, the top-heavy income tax still drew upon the $50,000-plus brackets for over half of its much-shrunken revenues. The problem was palpable. To make the income tax truly productive would have been politically hazardous. The New Deal would have had to transcend the history of the income tax by transforming it from a class tax to a mass tax. As Treasury Secretary Mills explained in 1932, "We have become accustomed to high exemptions and very low rates on the smaller taxable incomes. That is our fixed conception of an income tax, and it is very difficult as a practical matter to change fixed conceptions of this character."[13] Corporate chicanery and tax-shirking, not overall tax incidence or income redistribution, was the cardinal public issue. Concern with tax incidence focused on the super-rich; all else languished in the penumbra of public consciousness.

Four factors, then, straitjacketed the search for additional revenues: the Depression-induced antipathy to further taxation, the administration's reluctance to tap the incomes of corporations and the wealthy, its inability to build on the narrowly gauged personal income tax, and the traditional popular resistance to taxing the people. Prescriptions for budget balancing clashed with these inhibitory factors, but ultimately had a muted impact. In the upheaval of the 1932–3 emergency, the dictates of fiscal orthodoxy led to frantic efforts to narrow budget deficits. As in World War I, Congress and the president rushed to fiscal responsibility, in the process trampling even the moderately affluent taxpayers. This enthusiasm was short-lived. Except in the cataclysmic atmosphere surrounding the passage of the

12 Daniel Roper to Lawrence H. Sloan, 16 January 1935, "Business Advisory Council for Dept. of Commerce, January 1935" folder, box 35, Winthrop W. Aldrich Papers (Baker Library, Harvard University, Cambridge, Mass.)

13 U.S., Congress, Senate, Committee on Finance, *Revenue Act of 1932, Hearings on H.R. 10236*, 72d Cong., 1st sess., 1932, p. 3.

1932 Revenue Act, budget balancing prevailed mainly in token form, or in the guise of relatively unobjectionable taxes; Republicans sacrificed it to lower taxes, whereas New Deal adherents usually shelved it in favor of recovery expenditures. Lacking the legal restrictions or the threat of default that crippled state and local governments, federal officials were to sanction deficits averaging one-third of expenditures in the 1930s. Yet initial budget-balancing concerns left their mark, forcing revenue hikes upon a tax system already circumscribed by public and governmental perceptions of political possibility. These limitations on the flexibility of the tax system paved the way for revenue-raising measures with a more regressive cast to them.

Most importantly, the notion of taxing "luxuries" had broad appeal. Even the economics profession did not yet utilize the concept of "superior goods" – products absorbing an increasing share of income as one moved up the income scale. To the economists as to the public, luxuries were "nonessential" items – such as candy, liquor, cigarettes or yachts – whose absence would not induce material deprivation. The taxation of luxuries proved irresistible. "Here, my friends, is a simple 'out' that should appeal to every Member of this House," crowed one congressional advocate of higher liquor taxation. "Who would complain? Nobody has to buy whisky unless he wants it. It is a luxury."[14]

Luxuries, then, to use economist Henry Simons's felicitous phrase, were "commodities which poor people ought to do without and won't." Better than anyone before or since, Simons captured the essence of the New Deal tax system:

> It seems a little absurd to go around arguing that poor people could or ought to do without tobacco, especially if it is taxed, in the face of the facts that they simply do not do anything of the kind, that the commodity was selected for taxation because they are not expected to do so, and that the government would not get much revenue if they did. The plain fact, to one not confused by moralistic distinctions between necessities and luxuries, is simply that taxes like the tobacco taxes are the most effective means available for draining government revenues out from the very bottom of the income scale.[15]

Regressive taxes were supported by a number of other eclectic arguments. Alcohol and tobacco were only the prime examples of "sumptuary" taxes

14 A. Willis Robertson, in U.S., Congress, House, *Congressional Record*, 75th Cong., 3d sess., 1938, 83, pt. 3: 3192.
15 Henry C. Simons, *Personal Income Taxation* (Chicago: University of Chicago Press, 1938), p. 40.

on "demerit goods"; such goods, with their unsavory social reputations, were susceptible to economic penalties that had long furnished a major portion of government revenues. Sales or manufacturers' excise taxes on widely consumed goods enjoyed a record of easy enforcement and promised relatively stable returns as compared to the perilously top-heavy income-tax system of the 1920s. The gasoline tax was the most prominent and clear-cut levy to rely on the theory that it was a "user charge" or "benefit tax" that covered the expenses of some related special-purpose program (in this case roads). Social security and agricultural subsidy each had its own nonprogressive tax, a relationship that carried over, to some extent, in the National Industrial Recovery Act.

Looking at the resulting tax structure in 1936, liberal columnist Ernest K. Lindley was critical of the apparent disregard for socioeconomic impact shown by New Deal tax architects; Lindley accused the administration of finding it "easier to follow an opportunistic policy of getting a little here and there, whenever it could find an excuse for prodding Congress into action."[16] The public, however, generally supported regressive taxes assessed as part of the cost of gasoline, cigarettes, and beer; polls found citizens placing taxes on tobacco, luxuries, and liquor at the bottom of a list of "most unfair" taxes and designating them the preferred vehicle for a tax increase.[17] This positive attitude laid the groundwork for a great deal of political mischief. To mobilize against the tangible immediate burdens of income and property taxes was easy; to recognize and resist the cumulative effects of hidden taxes on daily purchases required a level of sophistication that few possessed. This kind of "painless" taxation on the installment plan was insidious; there was merit in the comment that "if the individual or the family were sent a bill for $10 and were told it was for cigarette taxes, there would be a tax rebellion."[18] Political leaders could have educated the public on these issues. They did not. Public-opinion leaders such as newspapers showed far more appreciation for the tribulations of the rich, whereas congressmen tended to identify with the problems of the affluent and vocal "middle class" from which they came.

It is ironic, though scarcely coincidental, that the very group that most needed tax relief suffered a multiple vulnerability from untutored economic

16 Ernest K. Lindley, *Half Way with Roosevelt* (New York: Viking Press, 1936), p. 248.
17 Cantril, *Public Opinion*, pp. 851, 325.
18 Francis Maloney, in U.S., Congress, Senate, *Congressional Record*, 76th Cong., 1st sess., 1939, 84, pt. 7: 7696.

understanding, hidden taxes with slippery incidence patterns, and political impotence. When in need of additional emergency revenue, politicians chose the path of least resistance. Tariffs offered no recourse; in fact, they declined from 17 percent of federal revenues at the end of the 1920s to 6 percent by the end of the 1930s, thanks to the sorry state of international trade and the traditional Democratic position that this was one "benefit tax" on which consumers and certain regional interests received a raw deal. Even so, social insurance and indirect taxes (tariffs; the excise taxes on liquor, tobacco, and selected manufactured items; and agricultural processing taxes) became the largest share of total tax revenue, jumping from 33 percent in the supposedly business-oriented New Era to 47–65 percent in the Forgotten Man's New Deal[19] (see Table 1).

The tax structure thus became more dependent on lower incomes. This shift did not emerge from some elite conspiracy; rather, it followed from a broader economic, political, and social dialetic. Operating within the multiple constraints of popular antipathy to direct taxes, the budget-balancing orthodoxy, the First New Deal ethos of business conciliation, the inflexibility of the income tax, and a historical legacy that granted legitimacy to taxing the super-rich but not "the people," the tax system gravitated toward ad hoc or regressive "luxury" taxes. These neglected, unglamorous, but dominant components of the 1930s revenue structure deserve individual attention.

Manufacturers' Excise Taxes: Honing the Legacy of 1932

Although the tax system was initially one of the sickest sectors of the American economy, excise taxes were a prime growth industry in the Depression. At the close of the 1920s, only the tobacco excise and the

---

19 If unemployment insurance contributions applied to the federal government rather than to the state governments coerced into levying the tax and depositing it in the federal Treasury, the share of indirect and social security taxes in Roosevelt's first two terms would never have dropped below half. However, it is also the case that the partial coverage of the social security system mitigated the exaggerated regressive effects of its high ceiling on taxable wages, whereas certain minor excise taxes – such as those on furs, cameras, and issues and transfers of capital stock – had a progressive impact. Subsuming the capital-stock tax, a proxy levy on expected corporate profits, progressive taxes surely exceeded regressive ones in the later part of the decade. See H. Dewey Anderson, *Taxation, Recovery and Defense*, Temporary National Economic Committee Monograph No. 20 (Washington, D.C.: Government Printing Office, 1941), pp. 91, 94.

stamp tax on corporate stock issues garnered as much as 1 percent of total federal taxes. During Roosevelt's first term, three other excises – those on liquor, regulated agricultural commodities, and selected manufacturers – assumed a controlling position in the revenue system.

Though the Revenue Act of 1932 lies outside the chronological focus of this study, it warrants examination here. As the progenitor of the New Deal tax system, it claims several distinctions. First, it had a marked deflationary impact, which at full employment would have practically doubled the tax yield.[20] Second, it extended the tax structure nearly to the limits of political possibility, allowing FDR to coast on its revenues while smothering outside pressures for tax increases. Third, and just as importantly, it resurrected the excise taxes on manufacturers. In a relatively prosperous period, the revenue act's boosts in the taxes on personal incomes, corporate profits, and estates and gifts would have yielded more new revenue than the selective excises.[21] Declining incomes, however, erased these advances, whereas manufacturers' excise taxes surged forward. For the remainder of the decade, these selective excises reached the pinnacle of their revenue role in U.S. history, accounting for over one-twelfth of federal tax collections (though only two-fifths as much as the combined liquor and tobacco excises).

In 1932, Depression fears of fiscal irresponsibility had created enormous pressure for a fundamental tax revamping. "We shall have to hit every individual in the United States," concluded Finance Committee Chairman Reed Smoot (R–Utah).[22] Treasury Secretary Mellon and his successor, Ogden Mills, advocated hikes in the income, corporate, and estate taxes, along with a cut in income-tax exemptions. However, the Treasury's primary emphasis was on an excise-tax package that remained basically intact in the final bill. This program invigorated the taxes on tobacco, admission to amusements, and issues and transfers of stock, while introducing excise taxes on motor vehicles and gasoline, radios and phonographs, long-distance telephone calls and telegrams, and checks. Fiscal conservatives were pleased to achieve this combination of broadly based excises and lower tax exemptions. Progressives also met with success. Their soak-

---

20 E. Cary Brown, "Fiscal Policy in the 'Thirties: A Reappraisal," *American Economic Review* 46 (December 1956): 868.

21 *Annual Report of the Secretary of the Treasury on the State of the Finances for the Fiscal Year Ended June 30, 1940* (Washington, D.C.: Government Printing Office, 1941), p. 3.

22 U.S., Congress, Senate, *Congressional Record*, 72nd Cong., 1st sess., 1932, 75, pt. 10: 11019.

the-rich ethos fostered hikes in upper-bracket income taxes and aimed excises at the playthings of the opulent: yachts, jewelry, cosmetics, furs, and cameras. Opposition from Hoover's Treasury Department had failed to block these "nuisance" excises, despite assertions that the paltry revenue yield would not justify the costs of enforcement and the harm to taxed industries.

Ideological differences, though, rarely ruled excise-tax debates. The economics profession gave such taxes a strong vote of confidence, even though it was moving toward a position that would confer theoretical superiority on broad-gauged direct taxes on income.[23] A popular consensus accepted the validity of taxing commodities "of wide use but not of first necessity" so as to yield "fairly substantial revenues" without complex or expensive administration.[24] Other criteria, such as preservation of competitive situations, gave way to the idea that "it is vastly more important to the United States that we should balance the Budget than that we should be fair to particular industries."[25] Ease of collection, revenue potential, and the firm's ability to withstand a loss in sales volume brought by the new exactions were paramount during consideration of the 1932 Revenue Act, according disproportionate influence to companies with the proper blend of political efficacy and precarious finances.

The major new manufacturers' excise taxes in the 1932 act, those on motor vehicles and gasoline, exemplify the terms of the debate. The motor-vehicle excise met the "wide use" standard, for most families owned a car or truck.[26] Its reimposition (after repeal in 1928) highlighted the curious relationship between corporate strength and political vulnerability, which surfaced in the Senate Finance Committee's feeling that "there is no industry in the United States that is in better condition to pay than the automobile industry."[27] Auto companies, spearheaded by multimillionaire

23 In a 1936 poll, senior professors of public finance split 47–5 in favor of "such luxury taxes as can be practically administered" and 50–2 in favor of a tobacco tax. "Tax Opinion Survey," *Tax Policy* 3 (May 1936): 5.

24 "Report of the Chamber of Commerce Committee on Federal Taxation," in U.S., Congress, House, Committee on Ways and Means, *Revenue Revision, 1932, Hearings*, 72d Cong., 1st sess., 1932: 213; U.S., Congress, Senate, Committee on Finance, *Revenue Bill of 1932*, S. Rept. 665 to Accompany H.R. 10236, 72d Cong., 1st sess., 1932, p. 11.

25 David Reed, in U.S., Congress, Senate, *Congressional Record*, 72d Cong., 1st sess., 1932, 75, pt. 10: 11035.

26 Census, *Historical Statistics*, p. 716; "The Fortune Survey," *Fortune* 12 (July 1935): 118.

27 Reed Smoot, in U.S., Congress, Senate, *Congressional Record*, 72d Cong., 1st sess., 1932, 75, pt. 10: 11028.

progressive Senator James Couzens (R–Mich.), a former major stockholder and organizational genius in the Ford Motor Company, waged a fierce fight against the tax. However, the argument of Michigan representatives and car dealers that such taxes would hobble the "key" American industry, a "tax patriot" upon whom the government and the economy relied, could not muster sufficient support to kill the 2–3 percent excise.[28]

Likewise, the federal entrance into gasoline taxation spawned a potent interest-group alliance, which nevertheless failed to block the 1-cent gas tax in 1932 and the temporary advance to 1½ cents in 1933. In early 1932, a letter campaign to Congress, directed by the American Petroleum Institute, helped snuff out this proposed levy in the House, and, initially, in the Senate.[29] The deepening revenue crisis, however, finally allowed this Treasury-supported measure to rout oil company opposition, though the industry exacted compensating taxes on imports of gasoline and other petroleum derivatives. Unwilling to accept failure, the oil industry pressed its case against the treatment of "Taxoline"[30] throughout the decade. Oil retail outlets, the American Automobile Association, farm organizations, and the auto industry pelted Congress with protests, and numerous memorials from state legislatures inveighed against federal tax competition. The endemic reluctance of governments to relinquish new productive revenue sources prevailed, however.

Excise taxes have fallen into disrepute for soaking consumers in inverse proportion to their incomes.[31] The presumption that the consumer pays

---

28 Arthur Vandenberg, in U.S., Congress, Senate, *Congressional Record*, 72d Cong., 1st sess., 1932, 75, pt. 10: 11616–17.

29 "A.P.I. Organizes Campaign Against 1-Cent Federal Gasoline Tax," *National Petroleum News* 24 (24 February 1932): 17.

30 "Taxoline! A Fitting Name," *National Petroleum News* 24 (29 June 1932): 13.

31 Popular economics offhandedly relegates excise taxes to a regressive status, but modern incidence theory concedes more complexity. In jargonese, "inelastic demand" and "elastic supply" shift consumption taxes to prices, whereas elastic demand and inelastic supply shift the burden to the profits of producers and their factor suppliers. In other words, for those rare taxed goods on which tax-induced price increases send consumers fleeing to other products, companies without the flexibility to transfer resources away from the taxed goods will bear the brunt of the tax. In the Depression this situation seemed most pressing for "declining-cost" industries operating at fractional capacity. Such firms could ill afford to spread their fixed costs among even fewer sales, forcing them into an inelastic supply situation in which they absorbed part of the excise tax as a trade-off against slashed production. Monopolies also provide an interesting case, for their method of calculating prices muffles the effects of excise taxes on production. It can be shown that, given demand and supply conditions, excise taxes bring greater price increases (and thus consumer burden) in competitive industries

luxury taxes has dominated economic orthodoxy throughout the history of excises. Historically, though the regressivity issue rarely surfaced, the paradox of the poor absorbing "luxury" taxes did not escape attention.

Such concerns, however, carried little weight in the tax debates of the early 1930s, for the drawback of regressivity had become an asset. Excise taxes targeted consumers. The imposition of a gas tax, for example, upon an overproducing industry was predicated on an inelastic consumer demand that would maintain gas purchases despite price hikes. Even the liberal *New Republic* celebrated this consumer excise tax burden, noting that otherwise excise taxes would constitute capital levies on floundering industries, triggering the very cuts in employment, wages, and investment that political leaders sought to avoid.[32] The surest way of averting a manufacturer burden was to tax items on which buyers assumed the added tax rather than fled to other products. Commodities subject to such an inelastic demand tend to be those on which the poor concentrate their purchases. This quirk of fate was socially lamentable but politically opportune, for poorer consumers were less likely to mobilize in opposition to taxes.

In fact, in the looking-glass world of excise-tax disputes, industries proved the champions of the silent consumer. As the House Ways and Means Committee observed in response to tobacco industry and grower pressure in 1934: "The tobacco-consuming public, as other classes of consumers, are unorganized and, generally speaking, inarticulate when taxes and tariffs are concerned."[33] But taxed industries raced to their consumers' defense. Organized industry groups, often formed expressly to counteract excises, hired lobbyists to remonstrate before Congress. Excise taxes generated far more congressional mail than any other tax.

The assault of businessmen upon excise taxes was nothing if not wide ranging. At times they charged that levies like the "iniquitous excise tax on candy" were "a direct capital tax" that they could not pass on to consumers.[34] Often these same complainants would reverse the charges,

than in monopolies. See Richard A. Musgrave and Peggy B. Musgrave, *Public Finance in Theory and Practice* (New York: McGraw-Hill, 1973), p. 437. In any case, these immediate corporate burdens diminish in the long run as resources retreat to untaxed products.

32 "The Tax Bill," *New Republic* 71 (29 June 1932): 166.

33 U.S., Congress, House, Committee on Ways and Means, *Reduce Internal-Revenue Taxes on Tobacco Products*, H. Rept. 1882 to Accompany H.R. 9441, 73d Cong., 2d sess., 1934, p. 4.

34 P. M. Allen to Carter Glass, 1 May 1934, "Tax—1934" folder, box 318, Carter Glass Papers (University of Virginia Library, Charlottesville).

claiming that the consumer paid the entire tax, though still rather inconsistently forecasting ruin for their industries. They also sternly resisted the "luxury" justification of the excise, asserting either that the commodity was good for you or that the rich were not its sole consumers (the fact that consumption patterns were skewed toward the upper-income ranges weakened their case not a whit, for the tax was deemed retrogressive merely for bearing on the "people" rather than on surplus incomes). Even more potent, in an age with more concern for sacrosanct groups than for overall regressivity, was the emphasis on the inequities of taxing children. Thus, chewing-gum manufacturers and sporting-goods retailers declared their excise "a penalty tax to those who are least able to pay it."[35] Finally, a common refrain of taxed industries was indignation at being singled out for excise taxation when they were in "no better position than other industries to stand a special tax of this kind."[36] At least, some groused, complementary goods should receive stiffer taxes (cotton manufacturers, for example, worked for rayon taxes, and the liquor industry opposed the repeal of the excises for home-brewed beer).[37] Mainly, however, taxed industries moved to advocacy of a broad sales tax. As consumer representatives, these industries had their limitations.

This final argument elucidates an important theme: Excise taxes revealed wide rifts in the solid front formed by businessmen on most other tax issues. Corporate and individual income taxes posed a redistributive threat against which corporate leadership could unite. Excise taxes, on the other hand, fostered the same "every man for himself" psychology that suffused tariff controversies. Political scientist Theodore Lowi labels these issues "distributive," for they entail discrete costs and benefits, forcing Congress to accommodate the resultant fragmentation in committee.[38] Individual interests jockeyed for position, whereas the rest of the corporate community,

35 E. S. Hurd to Robert L. Doughton, 31 March 1936, folder 541, Robert L. Doughton Papers (Southern Historical Collection, University of North Carolina Library, Chapel Hill). A similar argument justified taxes levied on alcohol and tobacco, because these taxes supposedly fell "heaviest on those most able to pay; at least the children escape by not indulging." T. Jefferson Coolidge, "Unwarranted Pressure," *Vital Speeches* 4 (1 December 1937): 125.

36 L. B. Whitehouse to Carter Glass, 1 December 1937, "Tax – November 15, 1938" folder, box 363, Carter Glass Papers (University of Virginia Library, Charlottesville).

37 "Compensating Tax on Rayon Sought By Cotton Industry," *Tax Magazine* 12 (August 1934): 439; U.S., Congress, House, Committee on Ways and Means *Revision of Revenue Laws, Hearings,* 75th Cong., 3d sess., 1938, p. 981.

38 Theodore J. Lowi, "American Business, Public Policy, Case-Studies, and Political Theories," *World Politics* 16 (July 1964): 677–715.

confident that consumers footed most of the bills anyway, kept their distance. The Chamber of Commerce of the United States, whose strong retailer component soured it on a federal sales tax in the 1930s, went so far as to repeatedly recommend substantial use of excise taxes that could be passed on to the consumer.[39] The chamber construed this issue in terms of its redistributive effects, contending that, since most people paid no income tax, "they should consequently be called upon to contribute through excise taxes."[40] This stance was atypical; organizations like the National Association of Manufacturers avoided excise-tax issues, while backing demands for a sales-tax alternative. But, when the real revenue-raising excises came before Congress, the affected industries generally stood alone, isolated by a climate of business opinion that found excise taxes less objectionable than other levies.

The New Deal's record on excise taxes lacked the ambivalence of the business community's consumer-advocacy stance. Casting aside the hopes of 1932 that the new excises would only be of a temporary "emergency" nature,[41] the administration repeatedly shepherded extensions through Congress at one- or two-year intervals. Each committee report carried basically the same disclaimer: "It is recognized that some of these excise taxes are objectionable or contain objectionable features, but obviously, we cannot afford to lose the revenue provided for by these excise taxes at this time."[42] Even in the late 1930s, FDR sublimated his enhanced skepticism toward regressive taxes, arguing that "their collection has been perfected, our economy is adjusted to them, and we cannot afford at this time to sacrifice the revenue they represent."[43]

39 Chamber of Commerce of the U.S., "Referendum Number Sixty: Federal Taxation 1932," Special Bulletin (Washington, D.C., 22 April 1932), p. 2; Committee on Federal Finance, Chamber of Commerce of the U.S., *Federal Revenue Legislation* (Washington, D.C.: Chamber of Commerce of the U.S., "Referendum Number Seventy: Federal Taxes and Expenditures," Special Bulletin (Washington, D.C., 28 February 1936), p. 2. These pamphlets are all available at the library of the Chamber of Commerce of the U.S., Washington, D.C. Chamber representatives assailed low-revenue "nuisance" excises, but they generally steered clear of positions on specific excises.

40 Chamber of Commerce of the U.S., "Referendum Number Seventy on the Report of the Special Committee on Federal Taxes and Expenditures" (Washington, D.C., 11 December 1935), p. 26.

41 U.S., Congress, House, Committee on Ways and Means, *Revenue Bill of 1932*, H. Rept. 708 to Accompany H.R. 10236, 72d Cong., 1st sess., 1932, p. 43.

42 U.S., Congress, Senate, Committee on Finance, *Extension of Certain Excise Taxes and Postage Rates*, S. Rept. 920 to Accompany H.J. Res. 324, 74th Cong., 1st sess., 1935, p. 2.

43 *Addresses of FDR*, 8: 47 (5 January 1939).

Congressional Democrats performed as rubber stampers on this "distributive" issue. Excise-taxation extension sailed through Congress with minimal floor debate, whereas less remunerative income-tax adjustments dominated the congressional discussion. In 1935 and 1936, some New Deal critics charged that tariffs, sales taxes, tobacco taxes, and excise taxes betrayed the New Deal's shallow commitment to income redistribution, saddling "the great mass of people living below the American standard of decency" with a burden that "should be borne by the rich."[44] Yet these charges never caught fire. Only a small minority of liberal Democrats – almost none of them from the Northeastern and Middle Atlantic regions, which always tended to favor consumption taxes over levies on their disproportionate wealth – joined their third-party colleagues in opposing the extension of excise taxes.[45]

Republicans, however, joined the campaign of selected businesses to defend the consumer against the perpetuation of the 1932 excise taxes. Each extension, they declared, was a "breach of faith on the part of the Administration," because the 1932 Revenue Act had marked these taxes for early elimination.[46] An integral role of an opposition party is to prick the inconsistencies of government programs, to inject arguments into the political debate that policymakers prefer to avoid. Republicans performed this function, exploiting the gap between the New Deal rhetoric of helping the poor and the reality of extending taxes on consumption items. Even as GOP spokesmen talked up a general sales tax, they dressed down all excise taxes – even the luxury-directed ones – as discriminatory burdens "which fall most heavily on the poor and those least able to pay."[47] Excise-tax extension bills pitted 90 percent of the Democrats against 90 percent of the Republicans.[48] Despite their closer rhetorical ties to budget balancing, Republicans took the understandable – if perhaps irresponsible – view that they should not have to bite the political bullet twice by first opposing spending measures and then supporting the taxes to finance them.

44 Charles E. Coughlin, *Series of Lectures on Social Justice* (Royal Oak, Mich.: Radio League of the Little Flower, 1935), p. 234; Charles Truax, in U.S., Congress, House, *Congressional Record*, 74th Cong., 1st sess., 1935, pt. 9: 9546.

45 U.S., Congress, House, *Congressional Record*, 74th Cong., 1st sess., 1935, 79, pt. 9: 9451–2.

46 U.S., Congress, House, Committee on Ways and Means, *Extension of Certain Excise Taxes and Postage Rates*, H. Rept. 935 to Accompany H.J. Res. 375, 75th Cong., 1st sess., 1937, p. 21.

47 Ibid., p. 21. Republicans, too, sometimes equated "consumers" with the "poor."

48 Edward F. Hanlon, "Urban – Rural Cooperation and Conflict in the Congress: The Breakdown of the New Deal Coalition, 1933–1938" (Ph.D. diss., Georgetown University, 1967), pp. 189, 293.

Certain excises – generally the so-called nuisance taxes on such items as yachts, candy, cameras, sporting goods, and jewelry – went by the boards in the New Deal. This was not unexpected. Arising out of a desperate need for revenue, many of these taxes also did a similarly limited tour of duty in both World War I and World War II. As one senator noted at their birth in 1932: "Those upon whom they are visited are highly organized; they are sensitive, class conscious, tax conscious. They will get rid of these taxes when the present exigency shall have passed."[49]

One basic factor distinguished the repealed excise taxes from most of the survivors: Most garnered minimal revenues, and only one (the two-cent charge on bank checks and drafts, which clashed with the administration's expansionary monetary policy) collected more than 8 million dollars annually. The administration's opposition to cutting tax receipts limited the excise-tax revenues that could be sacrificed; thus Congress generally felt compelled to repeal only those excises "yielding comparatively small returns."[50]

On the face of it, the administration's excise-tax position became more sophisticated in the late 1930s than this division might suggest. Even FDR himself, in 1939, warned that higher consumer taxes would garrote purchasing power[51] and referred in a press conference to the regressive effects of cigarette taxes.[52] A couple of years earlier, in a study that laid the foundation for tax excisions in 1938, the Treasury's Division of Research and Statistics evinced similar distress over the consumer burden from excise taxes – which it noted was greatest under nonmonopoly conditions

49 Thomas Gore, in U.S., Congress, Senate, *Congressional Record*, 72d Cong., 1st sess., 1932, 75, pt. 10: 11619.

50 "Report of the Subcommittee of the Committee on Ways and Means Relative to Proposed Tax Revision," in U.S., Congress, House, Committee on Ways and Means, *Revision of Revenue Laws, 1938, Hearings*, 75th Cong., 3d sess., 1938, p. 71.

51 Franklin D. Roosevelt, *Complete Presidential Press Conferences* (New York: DaCapo Press, 1972), 17 January 1939, 13: 67; *Addresses of FDR*, 8: 348 (22 May 1939). The Fiscal and Monetary Advisory Board – a quasi-Keynesian stronghold despite the moderating influence of Morgenthau, Hanes, and other skeptics – may have influenced FDR's seeming conversion. At the close of 1938, it presented him with a memorandum arguing against new "processing taxes, taxes on payrolls, excise taxes," and other levies "which operate to reduce substantially consumer purchasing power." Estate and gift taxes, along with higher income taxes on the middle brackets (partly implemented by gradually eliminating the personal exemption as income rises) received a stamp of approval. Morgenthau Diaries, 19 December 1938, book 157, pp. 113–14, Henry A. Morgenthau, Jr., Papers (Franklin D. Roosevelt Library, Hyde Park, N.Y.; hereafter cited as FDR Library).

52 Roosevelt, *Press Conferences*, 4 January 1939, 13: 35.

or where buyers maintained purchases of products despite higher prices. The Treasury established five criteria for evaluating excise taxes: revenue returns, ease of collection, incidence, economic damage, and effect on other taxes.[53] In practice, these criteria reduced to a much simpler calculation. If an excise tax had a small yield, and if the taxed firms made enough of a stink to complicate enforcement, the Treasury usually backed repeal. The Treasury, organizationally biased toward smooth operation, felt that such low-yield taxes were more trouble than they were worth. If, in addition, the tax truly impaired an industry's health, or if it could be shown that a wide group of consumers did not view the taxed good as a luxury, that was gravy. In such cases, the alliance of the affected industry and the Treasury was a formidable one, leaving a vacuum in opposition.

One can appreciate the Treasury's criteria more fully by examining and contrasting two taxes on the borderline of revenue insignificance, the excises on fur articles (collecting $3–8 million annually) and on cosmetics (collecting roughly $7–12 million annually).[54] Industrywide challenges to both taxes exploited the ambiguities inherent in the concept of widely used luxuries. Yet the fur tax was repealed in 1938, whereas the cosmetics tax dured.

The Depression crushed fur sales even more severely than it hit many other luxury industries. "This ruinous tax" of 10 percent on fur articles proved a ready scapegoat,[55] as furriers saw consumers shifting to complementary items to escape the tax. Terminological obfuscations abounded. A strong Northern contingent questioned whether fur coats could truly be considered a luxury in their frigid climates.[56] The core of the plea was for "the poor woman who has to have a fur coat." In a typical example of the confusion surrounding the notion of necessities, one lobbyist testified: "if a woman wants a coat that costs $20,000, it would be a luxury to the woman who could not afford to pay $20,000 for a fur coat, but it is not a luxury to the woman who can afford to pay it, to her it is a necessity."[57] Industry never had to confront the conception of the fur tax as a progressive tax that raked off a rising percentage of income as it moved up the income

53 Morgenthau Diaries, "The Economics of Excise Taxes," books 85–6.

54 H. Dewey Anderson, *Taxation, Recovery and Defense*, Temporary National Economic Committee Monograph No. 20 (Washington, D.C: Government Printing Office, 1941), pp. 141, 145.

55 Carl Laabs to Thomas Amlie, 5 January 1935, "1935, Jan. cont." folder, box 13, Thomas R. Amlie Papers (Wisconsin Historical Society, Madison).

56 Barth Chudik to Thomas R. Amlie, 30 January 1935, "1935, Jan." folder, box 14, Thomas R. Amlie Papers.

57 E. Fillmore, in U.S., Congress, House, Committee on Ways and Means, *Revenue Revision, 1934, Hearings*, 73d Cong., 2d sess., 1934, p. 810.

scale, for the nebulous concept of "luxury" left open too many other avenues for attack.

Fur-trade representatives were divided in their response to the excise tax. In 1934, pressure from the fur-trimmed-garment business culminated in a successful Senate floor amendment to exempt items costing under 75 dollars. But this siphoned away demand from the big-profit expensive furs.[58] Most importantly, the Treasury was inconvenienced. Revenues plummeted, and enforcement problems mounted in an industry already riddled with evasion. In 1936, the Treasury ended the 75-dollar exemption and reduced the tax from 10 percent to 3 percent. This formula hiked prospective revenues, but it revealed the shallowness of the rhetorical commitment to the common consumer. In 1938, amid discouraging profit reports and continued pressure from the National Fur Tax Committee, Congress jettisoned the excise entirely.

One would think that cosmetics could better resist the "luxury" label than furs. Industry representatives hastened to establish that almost all American women used taxed products such as cold cream or face powder.[59] The Treasury, now more sensitive to questions of overall incidence of the tax system, had moved by 1937 to join certain liberals, radicals, economists, and business leaders in attacking the "common use" criterion that had formerly underpinned excise taxes. The five female members of the House, representing the concerns of consumers as well as affected women employees, futilely wielded this argument to assail this discriminatory excise. "More and more the women of the United States feel that they are the forgotten man," concluded Edith Nourse Rogers (R–Mass.).[60]

As early as 1932, beauty-industry periodicals urged readers to get "the prominent women in your immediate vicinity, the heads of women's clubs, civic organizations, etc., to tell their representative at Washington that they can't afford to pay 10 percent extra for their toilet goods."[61] An unbroken chain, extending down to the industry's largely female work force, backed this proconsumer position.

Why, given the forces and arguments for repeal, including enforcement problems, did the cosmetics tax survive? The simplest answer is probably

58 "Fur Trade Again Asks for Tax Relief," *Fur Trade Review* 63 (February 1936): 6.

59 U.S., Congress, House, Committee on Ways and Means, *Revision of Revenue Laws, 1938, Hearings*, p. 661.

60 U.S., Congress, House, *Congressional Record*. 75th Cong., 1st sess., 1937, 81, pt. 5: 5620.

61 S. W. Swift, "The Cosmetics Tax," *Toilet Requisites* 17 (July 1932): 19.

the primary one: In the biggest repeal year, 1938, the Treasury had clamped a limit on lost excise-tax revenue, and was loath to substitute cosmetics-excise repeal for the elimination of several less productive levies. Also, although the cosmetics industry had dropped from the position of profitability that assured the retention of the radio and mechanical refrigerator excises, it failed to shed its 1920s reputation as a boom, glamour industry. It was thus burdened by riches to a greater extent than the fur industry, which had only recently gotten on its feet after being decked by the Crash.[62] Finally, the cosmetics excise tax could not overcome the American notion of luxuries. Even furs retained a tenuous link to survival by adding warmth to coats and clothing, but cosmetics could readily be viewed as nonessentials, particularly by male decision makers.

The guidelines for excise taxation in the 1932 Revenue Act – selecting items "of wide use but not of first necessity," choosing industries that could survive any adverse effects of the tax, and securing significant receipts without administrative complications – incurred little challenge from the New Deal. Minor excises, often imposed through liberal pressure to burden the consumption pattern of the upper class, were the ones to go, for they failed the revenue test. The New Deal lopped off the rough edges of the 1932 Revenue Act's excise-tax system, bringing it into closer harmony with the Hoover administration's rationale.

Alcohol Taxes: Through the Glass Darkly

In addition to perpetuating inherited excise taxes, the New Deal made its own contribution to the structure of indirect taxation. Large alcohol tax collections, the Agricultural Adjustment Act (AAA) processing taxes, and the social security payroll taxes – all levies with the remotest connection to the ability-to-pay standard – were the principal New Deal contributions to the revenue system. To some extent, each of these exactions can be dismissed as taxation by inadvertence, for each took second billing to the popular program with which it was paired. Yet oftentimes issues not played to the grandstand are precisely those that best reveal the operating principles of the political system.

---

62 U.S., Department of Commerce, Bureau of the Census, *Biennial Census of Manufacturers 1935* (Washington, D.C.: Government Printing Office, 1938), pp. 711, 1203; U.S., Department of Commerce, Bureau of the Census, *Biennial Census of Manufacturers 1937*, part 1 (Washington, D.C.: Government Printing Office, 1939), pp. 1156, 1162.

The tax on alcoholic beverages fits this bill perfectly. This tax had always been the federal government's first line of defense when tariff collections proved inadequate, for the tenuous social status of drinking made alcohol a readily taxable "luxury." By the twentieth century, the legitimacy of liquor taxation was beyond dispute. Just prior to the tremendous expansion of income taxes in World War I, alcohol taxes had overtaken tariffs as the prime federal revenue source. Tax collections on beer, wine, and spirits came back strongly after the end of Prohibition. At the federal level, they reached a high of 13 percent of annual tax collections (see Table 1). Though federal taxes dominated the field, most states, now in dire revenue straits, invaded this formerly federal province. By the end of the decade, state and federal alcohol taxes annually gleaned over three quarters of a billion dollars.[63] Yet Congress imposed alcohol taxes in an astoundingly offhanded manner, and the question of who paid them never really entered the political arena.

Liquor taxes did not sneak into the tax structure; they paraded in. The Association Against the Prohibition Amendment (the AAPA), the forerunner of the reactionary American Liberty League, used the prospect of substituting liquor taxes for "the burdensome corporations tax and income taxes" to good effect in the 1920s.[64] The Depression catapulted these prospective alcohol tax revenues into preeminence. If only given a chance, Americans might drink themselves into a balanced budget. The Democratic platform pledged to repeal the Eighteenth Amendment and to legalize nonintoxicating beer in the meantime, in order "to provide therefrom a proper and needed revenue."[65] In the 1932 campaign, Franklin Roosevelt made much of this theme, ignoring the Prohibition Party's platform claim that it was "a scheme to tax the poor and exempt the rich."[66] Taxes on alcoholic beverages could finance public works and restore fiscal integrity without necessitating an income-tax hike.[67] One advocate of high liquor taxes later proclaimed his firm conviction that "if we had not had the opportunity of using that

63 Census, *Historical Statistics*, pp. 1106–7, 1129.
64 W. M. Stayton memorandum to Mr. Ewing, 26 October 1926, in U.S., Congress, Senate, Committee on the Judiciary, *Lobby Investigation, Hearings* before a subcommittee of the Committee on the Judiciary, pursuant to S. Res. 20, 71st Cong., 2d sess., 1930, pt. 9: 4166.
65 Donald B. Johnson and Kirk H. Porter, *National Party Platforms 1840–1972* (Urbana: University of Illinois Press, 1973), p. 332.
66 Ibid., p. 338; *Addresses of FDR*, 1: 810 (19 October 1932).
67 "Repeal Would Cause Large Income Tax Cut," *American Federation of Labor Weekly News Service* 23 (3 June 1933): 1.

argument, that repeal meant needed revenue for our Government, we would not have had repeal for at least ten years."[68]

This potential revenue seemed a politician's dream. Everyone would win, and only the bootlegging trade would lose. Jouett Shouse, a leading figure in both the AAPA and the Democratic National Committee, predicted a revenue bonus of at least a billion dollars from the repeal of Prohibition: a massive revenue transfer from bootleggers to the government, without any cost to American consumers.[69] In this limited sense, liquor taxation did not seem to burden the urban lower class, who, at worst, had made a cheap bribe to the political system in order to secure the repeal of Prohibition. In fact, the lower cost of legal liquor offered net benefits to many consumers. By "taking this money," Senator Tydings (D–Md.) explained, "we would be plucking the goose without making him squawk, so to speak."[70]

Alcohol taxation, then, was a natural concomitant of Prohibition repeal, made all the more automatic by the fact that alcoholic-beverage taxes were technically still on the books. When FDR redeemed his platform pledge to legalize and tax nonintoxicating beer, Congress rushed the bill through in only a week. Isolated Prohibition supporters repeated charges that the beer tax burdened the poor, and a few legalization advocates validly observed that the tax had been set well in excess of its traditional level (though the five-dollar-per-barrel rate actually represented a one-dollar reduction from the inflated 1919 tax that nominally remained in effect during Prohibition). But congressmen far more commonly viewed the beer tax and the windfall it was intended to produce as integral parts of the legalization plan. The Democratic-urban advocates of Prohibition repeal supported the combined bill, whereas the more Republican-rural forces rejected it.[71] The tax issue was incidental to this basic division.

68 John O'Connor, in U.S., Congress, House, *Congressional Record*, 73d Cong., 2d sess., 1934, 78, pt. 1: 113.
69 David E. Kyvig, *Repealing National Prohibition* (Chicago: University of Chicago Press, 1979), pp. 175, 177. This argument did not die in the post-Prohibition period. John J. O'Connor (D–N.Y.), who contended that the tax would somehow come out of the "extortionate" monopoly profits of the "Whisky Trust," used this claim to bolster his campaign for higher liquor taxes. In 1933, when two distillers cornered the scarce supply of legal liquor, this argument had some appeal, but even O'Connor intermittently bowed to the orthodoxy that drinkers would ultimately bear the tax. U.S., Congress, House, *Congressional Record*, 73d Cong., 2d sess., 1934, 78, pt. 1: 116–17.
70 U.S., Congress, Senate, *Congressional Record*, 72d Cong., 1st sess., 1932, 75, pt. 9: 10439.
71 Hanlon, "Urban–Rural Cooperation," pp. 57, 86–7.

With the repeal of Prohibition, taxes on liquor had to stand on their own. This posed no problem. Despite its regressive consequences, alcohol taxation degenerated into a technical issue. Experts calculated the maximum tax that could be imposed upon liquor consumers without sending them to the untaxed bootleg concoctions. Thus the House Ways and Means Committee promised that its liquor-tax schedule would "return the maximum amount of revenue without incurring the danger of perpetuating illegal liquor traffic by excessive rates."[72] This desire to maximize the alcohol-tax yield was practically universal. Certain liquor-reform "experts" had hoped to use the tax for social control of liquor usage (by imposing steeper taxes on beverages with higher alcoholic content). However, the revenue-bootlegger standard prevailed. A swarm of economists petitioned Roosevelt in early 1933 to maximize revenues from the beer tax.[73] Even when attacking indirect taxes for their disproportionate burdens on the poor, economists usually defended the liquor and tobacco taxes, which accounted for the bulk of indirect tax collections.[74] University of Chicago economist Henry Simons, who mounted a full-scale attack upon the regressivity of these levies, suffered the loneliness of the doctrinal purist.[75]

The liquor tax thus occupied a position of political invincibility. In 1936, the *New Republic* rejected the Republican crusade against "hidden" taxes as manifestly unfair, for "it fails to mention that the biggest addition to indirect revenues under Mr. Roosevelt is derived from liquor taxes, which constitute a special case."[76] "No one," the *New York Post* pointed out, "considers the liquor tax a typical 'consumer tax,' like a concealed tax on food or fuel. We have always had a liquor excise and it has always been considered as a completely justifiable special tax."[77] Even on the far

72 U.S., Congress, House, Committee on Ways and Means, *Liquor Taxing Bill of 1934*, H. Rept. 271 to Accompany H.R. 6131, 73d Cong., 2d sess., 1934, p. 1.
73 Marion K. McKay et al., to FDR, 19 January 1933, box 1, Official File 21, Franklin D. Roosevelt Papers (FDR Library).
74 Twentieth Century Fund, Committee on Taxation, *Facing the Tax Problem: A Survey of Taxation in the United States and a Program for the Future* (New York: Twentieth Century Fund, 1937), p. 434.
75 Simons, *Personal Income Taxation*, pp. 39–40. The Rockefeller Foundation's Liquor Study Committee also assailed the regressivity of alcohol taxes, with no greater political impact. Noting that "the question of incidence is often overlooked in the discussion of the taxation of alcoholic beverages," the committee proposed a special liquor-profits tax to lift part of the tax burden from consumers. Raymond B. Fosdick and Albert L. Scott, *Toward Liquor Control* (New York: Harper & Brothers, 1933), pp. 115, 128.
76 "Mr. Landon on Taxes," *New Republic* 88 (9 September 1936): 116.
77 *New York Post*, in "The Press Comments," *Roosevelt Record* 1 (8 September 1936): 9.

left of the political spectrum, where nonprogressive taxes generally received considerable abuse, such diverse figures as Benjamin Marsh of the People's Lobby, a writer in the *American Socialist Quarterly*, and Huey Long could all acquiesce in the alcohol tax without reference to its regressivity.[78]

The alcohol industry and its congressional allies, fretting that the tax reduced sales of legal liquor, valiantly came to the defense of overburdened drinkers. Brewers in particular depicted their product as a poor man's drink whose tax weighed "heavier on the poor than on the rich."[79] Outside the industry, however, the regressivity of the liquor tax did not prevent it and other so-called luxury taxes from assembling a supportive popular consensus.[80] Business spokesmen, including the National Association of Manufacturers and the Chamber of Commerce of the United States, were particularly enthusiastic. Business periodicals bubbled that alcohol taxes might bring 2 billion dollars in increased federal, state, and local revenues – enough to allow a let-up in exactions on business.[81] Among business executives polled by *Fortune* just prior to FDR's third term, the liquor tax topped thirteen other forms of taxation as the levy whose rates should rise, while it trailed all other tax categories in the percentages of executives feeling that its rates were too high or that it was "wrong in principle."[82]

This wide consensus initially extended to Congress. Republicans, whose strong Prohibitionist wing had earlier opposed a combined legalization-tax plan, now swung behind alcohol taxation. Immediately after the repeal of the Eighteenth Amendment, Congress virtually unanimously enacted the basic alcohol taxes of the 1930s.[83] A minor twenty-five-cent hike in

78 Benjamin Marsh, in U.S., Congress, House, Committee on Ways and Means, *Revision of Revenue Laws 1938, Hearings*, p. 200; David P. Berenberg, "Roosevelt," *American Socialist Quarterly* 2 (Summer 1933), in Loren Baritz, ed., *The American Left* (New York: Basic Books, 1971), pp. 247–8; and Huey Long, in U.S., Congress, Senate, *Congressional Record*, 72d Cong., 1st sess., 1932, 75, pt. 10: 10517.

79 J. F. Shadgen, "Beer – Taxes and Markets," *Modern Brewery* 12 (November 1934): 57.

80 See "The *Fortune* Survey," *Fortune* 18 (August 1938): 72; and "The *Fortune* Survey: XXIX," *Fortune* 21 (Spring 1941): 122.

81 Linda K. Brown, "Challenge and Response: The American Business Community and the New Deal, 1932–1934" (Ph.D. diss., University of Pennsylvania, 1972), pp. 118–19.

82 "Fourth *Fortune* Forum of Executive Opinion," *Fortune* 23 (February 1941): 66.

83 The bill passed the House 388–5. U.S., Congress, House, *Congressional Record*, 73d Cong., 2d sess., 1934, 78, pt. 1: 159. *New York Times*, 11 January 1934, p. 1, reported that the Senate's voice vote was unanimous, though other major

the impost on hard liquor encountered a bit more difficulty, passing the House in 1938 by votes of 160–34 and 290–96.[84] Interestingly, this opposition reunited most representatives from the two constituencies primarily responsible for Prohibition repeal: distilling industries and metropolitan centers, the latter suggesting an undercurrent of ethnic and urban-consumer resistance to higher liquor prices.

With the exception of this small liquor-tax increase and a cut in the fiscally insignificant wine tax designed to buck up the feeble and overstocked U.S. wine industry, alcohol-tax rates were stationary during the New Deal. Inertia and concern over bootlegging appear primarily responsible. The administration and its congressional leadership stressed that squeezing out bootleggers (by allowing legal dealers to undersell the massive inventories of illegal liquor) was a federal priority that outranked liquor-tax collections.[85] A disappointing yield from the liquor tax soon bore out the alarm over bootlegging competition, though the shortfall also derived from overoptimistic revenue predictions by campaigners for repeal, a decline in habitual liquor-consumption patterns brought by Prohibition and intensified by poverty, and the low quality of unaged legal whiskey.[86] By the late 1930s, however, the decline of bootlegging had begun to undermine this argument; one witness proclaimed the bootlegger "a bogeyman to scare Congress."[87] Perhaps the liquor industry and its allies, bolstered by some urban dissatisfaction, had blunted the drive for maximizing alcohol-tax revenue in the late 1930s. The mammoth increase in alcohol taxes and collections in World War II (the distilled-spirits levy rose from its New Deal level of $2.00–$2.25 per gallon to a rate of $9.00) certainly casts doubt on the degree of earlier adherence to the "maximum revenue" standard. World War II provided an ideal environment for alcohol taxes – the demand for liquor far outstripped the supply, because distilling facilities had been converted to the production of grain alcohol, while manufacturers hoarded their meager liquor supplies in expectation of

newspapers failed to comment on the extent of opposition. In committee, however, the alcohol-tax rates faced strong challenges. See *Washington Post*, 9 January 1934, p. 2.

84 *New York Times*, 11 March 1938, p. 3; U.S., Congress, House, *Congressional Record*, 75th Congress, 3d sess., 1938, 83, pt. 3: 3267.

85 *New York Times*, 12 December 1933, p. 1.

86 Tun Yuan Hu, *The Liquor Tax in the United States 1791–1947* (New York: Columbia University Press, 1950), pp. 84–6.

87 Yandell Henderson, in U.S., Congress, Senate, Committee on Finance, *Revenue Act of 1938, Hearings* on H.R. 9682, 75th Cong., 3d sess., 1938, p. 218.

massive profits after the lifting of price controls[88] – but the hikes also reflected the evaporation of the bootlegging threat and the greater war demands for revenue.

One factor had changed little. Politicians could afford to be cavalier about the fact that alcohol taxes shifted the tax burden toward the poor. Few, even the taxpayers themselves, were inclined to protest.

Tobacco Taxes: The One that Got Away

Given this tolerance for regressivity, why weren't tobacco taxes raised in the New Deal? They, too, seemed to have broad expert and popular support, though, in the early 1930s, popular sentiment against state and local taxation swept them to defeat in referenda.[89] Like liquor, tobacco retained an unsavory social reputation; in fact, the first state cigarette taxes emerged under an agricultural-Southern aegis in the 1920s as part of the rural anticigarette campaign.[90] In addition, tobacco taxes, like levies on alcohol, possessed a heritage of tax legitimacy that went directly back to the Civil War and intermittently to the colonial period. Yet despite the Depression revenue crunch that accelerated state adoption of cigarette taxes, and despite Treasury Secretary Mellon's 1932 proposal for a tobacco-tax increase, a federal cigarette-tax hike never received serious consideration during the New Deal. In fact, cigarette taxes (the increasingly dominant component of tobacco taxes) remained fixed from 1919 to 1940.

The failure to raise tobacco taxes becomes more comprehensible when one considers the relative severity of the existing tobacco tax. Unlike most of the major tax levies of World War I, the enormous increase in cigarette taxes had not been repealed in the 1920s. The cigarette industry, diverted by a postwar boom in profits, did not join other industries in pressing for excise-tax reduction. Congress and the Republican administration were quite content to watch this easy money continue to roll in.

In the context of the lax U.S. tax system, the cigarette levy was stiff. It worked out to six cents on a pack of cigarettes that generally sold for fifteen cents and often sold for a dime in the Depression years. A married person with two children paid less income tax on the then-substantial sum of $4,000 annually than the average smoker contributed to the federal

88 Hu, *Liquor Tax*, p. 112, Appendix II.
89 Virgil Chapman, in U.S., Congress, House, Committee on Ways and Means, *Revenue Revision, 1932, Hearings*, 72d Cong., 1st sess., 1932, p. 588.
90 Warren A. Law, "Tobacco Taxation in the United States" (Ph.D. diss., Harvard University, 1953), pp. 124–5.

coffers for his pack-a-day habit![91] Even without a tax increase, tobacco-tax collections (which held up reasonably well in the Depression) easily surpassed yields for either the alcohol or manufacturers' excise taxes (see Table 1). If the revenue seekers were looking for slackness in the tax system, there were better places to find it.

Narrower factors also account for the tobacco-tax freeze. Both the House Ways and Means Committee's chairman, Robert Doughton (D–N.C.), and its tax subcommittee chairman, Fred Vinson (D–Ken.), represented tobacco interests (hence the epigram "the only tax Fred Vinson ever opposed was that on tobacco").[92] Only far more pressing revenue needs could have induced that committee to raise tobacco taxes, especially on top of the new tobacco-processing taxes.

Indeed, the central tobacco-tax debate of the 1930s focused on efforts by the "Big Four" tobacco manufacturers to forestall administration plans to graduate cigarette-tax rates. Such differential taxation would have benefited producers of the cheaper "dimey" brands. The "Big Four" countered by proposing across-the-board tobacco-tax cuts, and succeeded in producing a standoff. Throughout this debate, the regressivity of tobacco taxation carried little weight with the political system. The administration was able to reap symbolic returns from the attempt to protect industry competition through differential taxation. But it knew that any general hike might hobble the economy brands, which held 15 percent of the market until rising consumer incomes, costs, and taxes finished them off in World War II.[93] Even if the administration could have overcome the staunch opposition of the House Ways and Means Committee leaders, it is doubtful if it would have so jeopardized its image as to raise the tax.

Processing Taxes: Agricultural Adjustment and the Wages of Starvation

In a list of New Deal humanitarian initiatives, the Agricultural Adjustment Act would not rank high. This law was expressly designed to boost farm

91 After deducting the earned-income credit allowed by the 1934 Revenue Act, the $2,500 married exemption, and the $800 credit for two dependents, a $4,000 annual income – even before deductions – was subject to no more than a $16.00 tax. At six cents a pack, a pack-a-day smoker annually contributed $21.90 to the federal till.

92 John H. Hatcher, "Fred Vinson: Congressman from Kentucky: A Political Biography: 1890–1938" (Ph.D. diss., University of Cincinnati, 1967), p. 374.

93 Law, "Tobacco Taxation," p. 107.

income by reducing the availability of basic necessities. While many suffered from exposure or starvation, it taxed bread, pork, and cotton clothing.

Good intentions can excuse the worst unforeseen consequences. The AAA processing tax, however, lacks the pretext of shortsightedness. Its advocates generally realized that consumers would have to carry the load. The lower incomes, disproportionately allocated to necessities, shouldered the heaviest relative burden.

If the processing tax was a mistake, it was a lucrative one. Though collections amounted to under a billion dollars during the measure's short life, the processing tax accounted for one-eighth of total tax revenues at its height in the early New Deal – almost as much as either the personal or the corporate income tax (see Table 1).

On the face of it, this method of financing the AAA was something more than a standard sales tax. It applied only to staple products on which the AAA disbursed bonuses (benefit payments) for curtailing production.[94] In line with the AAA's goal of boosting farmer purchasing power back to the 1909–14 level, the processing tax was used to jack up the commodity's price to this "fair-exchange value." The tax was assessed upon the "first domestic processing" of the item (e.g., the milling of flour).

This general concept was not a new one. The agricultural cause célèbre of the 1920s, the McNary-Haugen Bill, had depended on a similar "equalization fee" for its funding. AAA author Milburn L. Wilson included in his 1932 program a form of the processing tax suggested to him by U.S. Chamber of Commerce president Henry Harriman.[95] Adjustments were made in this tax, but it survived basically intact into the New Deal.

Why did the Roosevelt administration embrace this particular tax mechanism? The readiest explanation is that a processing tax was a comparatively painless way to extract substantial revenues from an unwitting public. Less sinister causes, however, should not be slighted. The coalescence of farm interests around the processing tax left a dearth of developed alternatives. By granting its imprimatur to a program that evolved within a narrow framework of farm relief, the New Deal inevitably shortchanged consumers.

94 Kingman Brewster et al., *Taxation under the AAA* (New York: Baker, Voorhis, 1934), p. 269. Competitive items also were taxed if the processing tax on the basic commodity left untaxed items at too great a competitive advantage. A compensating tax also applied to imports, whereas exports qualified for refunds.
95 Gilbert C. Fite, *George N. Peek and the Fight for Farm Parity* (Norman: University of Oklahoma Press, 1954), p. 231.

Sorely lacking was the counsel of future Federal Reserve Board chairman Marriner Eccles, who would later lead an administration contingent that criticized the processing tax for regressively sapping consumer purchasing power. George Peek and future Treasury Secretary Henry Morgenthau, top agricultural advisors whose skepticism toward the restrictionist philosophy behind the AAA soured them on the processing tax, offered some resistance. Peek favored supplemental financing through steep agricultural tariffs. Throughout the New Deal, Morgenthau found the processing tax anathema. Almost anything – one suggestion was a sales tax on the finished product – would be better, he told Roosevelt. FDR rejected such options, declining to relinquish the political and administrative advantages of collecting the tax from the none-too-popular middlemen.[96]

The alternative of supporting the AAA through general revenues and higher deficits seemed even more politically unpalatable in March 1933. In the presidential campaign, Roosevelt had publicly committed himself to the idea of a balanced budget and a self-financed program. He joined Secretary of Agriculture Wallace, a confirmed advocate of the processing tax throughout the 1930s, in the recognition that the tax freed the agriculture program from the restraint of the congressional appropriation process. The rationale for a processing tax that would raise costs of food and clothing came easily. The processing tax was "the farmer's tariff."[97] Depressed market conditions resulted in fire-sale staple prices that could not cover the costs of production. Consumers were thus effectively exploiting farmer impoverishment. Government, it was argued, had better ways of meeting urban want than sustaining social parasitism. Also, since the New Deal banked so heavily on using an agricultural upturn to forge the path to general recovery, consumers were theoretically beneficiaries of the total AAA program.

Despite the undeveloped state of tax-incidence theory, there were few illusions over who ultimately paid most of the processing tax. "Of course," explained AAA architect M. L. Wilson, "the processor cannot bear the

---

96 George N. Peek, "Diary," 12 March, 11 March, and 15 March 1933, George N. Peek Papers (Western Historical Manuscripts Collection, University of Missouri, Columbia). Morgenthau Farm Credit Diary, 3 May and 15 May 1933, pp. 10, 23, Henry A. Morgenthau, Jr., Papers. Morgenthau's Farm Credit Diary does not reveal any specific Morgenthau alternative to the processing tax. Van L. Perkins [*Crisis in Agriculture: The Agricultural Adjustment Administration and the New Deal, 1933* (Berkeley and Los Angeles: University of California Press, 1969), p. 38] accepts Peek's assertion that Morgenthau favored a sales tax.

97 Henry A. Wallace, *New Frontiers* (New York: Reynal & Hitchcock, 1934), p. 213.

tax, which means that the tax will be passed on to the consumer."[98] In congressional testimony on the agriculture bill, Secretary of Agriculture Henry Wallace readily conceded this point. So did the agriculture committees conducting the hearings. The consumer received little sympathy from them, for they enthusiastically ratified the desire of Roosevelt and his advisers to surmount the Depression by shifting purchasing power to their farmer constituents. Defenses of the consumer were dismissed with the calculation that few wage earners would get worked up over the tiny taxes hidden in their commodity prices; even the expected 15 percent rise in the price of bread only amounted to a penny a loaf. "We are going to collect it from somebody you say can't pay it," jibed one committee member to a witness asserting consumer hardship.[99] Wallace showed more sensitivity. In his 1934 annual report, he observed that "the most serious objection to the processing tax" – one that he deemed "an important and legitimate criticism" – was "that the greatest burden falls on the poorer people."[100] Yet the AAA only concerned itself with preventing middlemen from "pyramiding" the processing tax into even greater price increases; it was taken for granted that the processing tax itself should be paid by the consumer. "It is only fair," Roosevelt announced in October 1933, "that I should give credit to the sixty or seventy million people who live in the cities and larger towns of the Nation for their understanding and their willingness to go along with the payment of even these small processing taxes."[101] Though this transformed public incognizance into volition, the commendation was well deserved.

The public, in fact, put up surprisingly little resistance to the processing tax. The AAA raised more pressing issues, consigning tax regressivity to the backwater of legislative consideration. Conservatives recited the consumer argument, but usually placed it in a negativistic framework that revealed greater concern for taxed processors. To most liberal journals and radicals, however, the absence of an anti-super-rich orientation convicted the tax. It seemed retrogressive to "pay farmers, with public money – in

98 Milburn L. Wilson, *Farm Relief and the Domestic Allotment Plan*, The Day and Hour Series of the University of Minnesota, No. 2 (Minneapolis: University of Minnesota Press, 1933), p. 27.
99 U.S., Congress, Senate, Committee on Agriculture and Forestry, *Agricultural Emergency Act to Increase Farm Purchasing Power, Hearings* on H.R. 3835, 1st sess., 1933, p. 162.
100 U.S., Department of Agriculture, *Report of the Secretary of Agriculture 1934* (Washington, D.C.: Government Printing Office, 1934), p. 36.
101 *Addresses of FDR*, 2: 425 (22 October 1933).

part, hungry people's money – to grow less food."[102] The *Nation* declared the processing tax "the most indefensible tax ever levied by any government in modern times" and suggested that any farm subsidy be financed through increased income, inheritance, and corporation taxes, rather than by this "sales tax" on necessities.[103]

If lower-income groups failed to act upon the consensus that consumers paid processing taxes, some farmers mobilized to act because they failed fully to share this consensus. Hog-corn farmers, in particular, found that they were absorbing much of the pork-processing tax; it could not be shifted to consumers, because buyers changed to other products when prices rose. Overall, however, farmers seemed more satisfied. When FDR refused to substitute relief funds for processing taxes (an option provided in a 1935 rider offered by Senate conservatives), the president of the American Farm Bureau Federation congratulated him. "Farmers feel processing tax is heart of adjustment act," he wired Roosevelt, "and it is rightfully theirs under our tariff system. We will heartily support you in retaining the processing tax."[104] Farmers were understandably less concerned with the general incidence of the tax than with its role as guarantor of farm subsidies.

As was the case with other excise taxes, the most stalwart public defender was the industry on which the tax was assessed. Processors repeatedly chided the administration for rejecting an explicit sales tax while imposing a hidden one on the necessities of the urban poor. The AAA, they pointed out, affixed "a huge sales tax to the lowest-priced food and clothing items which are in most common use." The tax thus fell most heavily on "city dwellers" and "those least able to bear it."[105] This charge of regressivity made little impression during legislative consideration, but it was the best argument they had. Representatives from textile and other processing-tax districts adopted this strategy, chastising this sales tax "on the bread and plain food of the poorest of our people."[106]

102 Harold Loeb, "The Stupidity of Poverty," in Alfred M. Bingham and Selden Rodman, eds., *Challenge to the New Deal* (1934; reprint ed., Freeport, N.Y.: Books for Libraries Press, 1971), p. 158.
103 "The Farm Subsidy," *Nation* 136 (12 April 1933): 387.
104 Edward A. O'Neal to FDR, 11 April 1935, "Processing Taxes 1933–42," folder, Official File 137C, FDR Papers.
105 U.S., Congress, Senate, Committee on Agriculture and Forestry, *Agricultural Adjustment Relief Plan: Hearings* on H.R. 13991, 72d Cong., 2d sess., 1933, pp. 70–1; *New York Times*, 23 March 1933, p. 3.
106 David I. Walsh, Statement on processing tax, 11 April 1938, "1938 Press Releases/ Statements" folder, David I. Walsh Papers (Holy Cross College, Worcester, Mass.).

The bitterness of the processors' attack on the AAA taxes would make little sense if their own consumer argument fully convinced them. At minimum, processors objected to the costly administrative inconvenience of paying the tax. More importantly, acreage quotas and processing taxes sliced earnings by curtailing production, while processors, railroads, and other middlemen pinned their profit hopes on increased sales volume.[107] The processing tax also threatened to more directly compress profit margins. When processors failed to bounce back from the crash as rapidly as they hoped, they were quick to blame the processing tax for their problems.

From the inception of the agricultural adjustment bill, processors – particularly meatpackers, who seemed to have the most to lose – lobbied in force against the processing tax during both administration and congressional consideration. When Roosevelt finally sent the bill to the House, George Peek observed: "Processors wild – all kinds of dire mutterings."[108] Textile manufacturers later launched one of the fiercest and best-coordinated campaigns against any New Deal tax. Climaxing in April 1935, this bitter no-holds-barred dispute showed the desperation of a dying industry. This effort to repeal the processing tax gained the support of Southern cotton mills and many Southern politicians such as Eugene Talmadge, though the general support of cotton farmers for the AAA brought major splits within Southern congressional ranks.

Processing-tax repeal, however, was largely a New England regional issue; in fact, it was *the* regional issue. The New England mills had virtually the complete support of local opinion leaders. Government regulation itself was not the problem; in fact, Northern mills led the effort for restrictionist National Recovery Administration (NRA) controls to curb chronic overproduction and Southern cheap-labor competition. The processing tax, however, was a fine scapegoat for an industry in desperate need of more buyers. Edith Nourse Rogers (R–Mass.), the congresswoman from the textile town of Lowell, helped lead the repeal effort in the House, depicting the processing tax as a boa constrictor that "sapped and squeezed the operations of our cotton mills until one by one they are dying from lack of orders and from inability to function properly."[109] Despite a full-scale lobbying effort (luncheons, petitions, letters, resolutions, and mass rallies), the Roosevelt administration would not capitulate.

107 Peek, "Diary," 9 March 1933, George N. Peek Papers.
108 Peek, "Diary," 16 March 1933, George N. Peek Papers.
109 *Boston Daily Record*, 12 April 1935, p. 7, in Scrapbook, vol. 70, Edith Nourse Rogers Papers (Schlesinger Library, Radcliffe College, Cambridge, Mass.)

The processing tax, having survived this political challenge, succumbed to a legal one. On 6 January 1936, the Supreme Court struck it down, holding that it was not a constitutionally valid tax, since it was an integral part of an improper regulatory scheme that expropriated money from one group to benefit another.[110]

Undeterred, FDR immediately began to consider a new processing tax to fill the revenue vacuum. Eccles and the Treasury Department tried to dissuade him. Secretary Morgenthau, realizing that "sixty percent of the taxes today are consumer taxes," urged against adding another "consumer's tax" to this dismal New Deal record. This method of burdening lower incomes was "inconsistent with the policies of this Administration," Treasury adviser Jacob Viner asserted, grousing that even "Mellon or Hoover would not do that."[111] Roosevelt rejected Morgenthau's alternative of an income-tax hike as politically infeasible. Secretary of Agriculture Wallace's criticism was perhaps most telling. In search of easy money to finance autonomy for farm subsidies, Wallace even considered a sales tax. He argued that "if you shift over to the income tax basis you will stop the farm program in the very near future because the boys have too much pressure on the Hill. I mean the farmer would be kicked out in a very short time because those boys in the final analysis have more pressure than the consumer."[112] Wallace was correct. In observing that the consumer was more compliant than the organized interests, he spotlighted a prerequisite for the regressive components of New Deal tax policy. Treasury advisers had prevailed upon FDR to forgo primary reliance on a new processing tax, but a remnant remained. In a 3 March 1936 address that featured the undistributed-profits tax, Roosevelt proposed that a new processing tax be imposed over the next two or three years. Designed to offset the money that would be lost before new taxes could replace the old processing tax, this was to be a temporary, scaled-down version, levied at much lower rates and upon many more items. Again the main opposition came from processors rather than consumers. But things were now more complicated; this time the processing-tax debate took place outside the womb of narrow agricultural self-interest. Chairman Robert Doughton triumphantly reported to the president of Cannon Towels and other processor constituents that the Democratic Ways and Means Committee members had quashed the

110 *U.S. v. Butler*, 297 U.S. 61 (1936).
111 Morgenthau Diaries, 27 January 1936, book 16, pp. 66, 63, 68.
112 Ibid., pp. 51, 66.

administration's processing-tax proposal.[113] As one trade periodical noted, this was "a source of real gratification to the entire industry."[114] The administration went along, though it did offer a revised processing-tax plan to the Senate Finance Committee, only to see it rejected out of hand for injecting new controversy into an already unpopular bill.

The administration, however, still had a score to settle with the processors. Taxes held in escrow during the processors' judicial assault on the AAA now reverted to them. In this March 1936 tax package, Roosevelt recommended a "windfall profits tax" to recapture taxes earlier passed on to consumers. Wallace argued that anything less would be "a sheer gift," a position so sensible that the tax easily cleared Congress.[115] Yet the U.S. Chamber of Commerce and the processors took their customary stance in favor of tax inequity which favored business. The processors facilely changed their tune on the question of who ultimately paid the tax. In earlier years, all but the meatpackers had usually argued that consumers footed the processing-tax bill. Now processors did a volte-face, contending that the tax came out of their profits, whereas the savings from impounded taxes had been passed on to other middlemen. Tax-incidence contentions continued to be less of a science and more of a debating strategy.

Despite its setback in 1936, the processing-tax issue lingered for a few years. In 1937–8, FDR continued to suggest processing taxes to balance the budget and to fund farm subsidies. In 1938, a processing-tax amendment proposed by Senator Pope (D–Idaho) was crushed by a vote of 24–53. Secretary Wallace bent over backward to further it, but an election-shy administration did nothing to forestall defeat.[116] The processing tax had become a purely agricultural interest-group position; all of its Senate supporters had rural constituencies, whereas its opponents decried it as a sales tax on urban workers.[117]

113 Robert L. Doughton to Charles A. Cannon, 25 March 1936, folder 540, Robert L. Doughton Papers.
114 "New Processing Tax?" Cotton Textile Institute, Inc., *Current Information* 2 (8 April 1936): 38.
115 U.S., Congress, Senate, Committee on Finance, *Revenue Act, 1936: Hearings*, 74th Cong., 2d sess., p. 843.
116 U.S., Congress, Senate, *Congressional Record*, 75th Cong., 3d sess., 1938, 83, pt. 5: 5145. By 1939, FDR had soured on the notion of processing taxes, for he recognized that consumption taxes depressed needed purchasing power. However, the policy implications of this are ambiguous. He may have merely shifted tactics, because it became clear that congressional leaders could not be twitted into carrying through an earlier commitment to cover parity payments with new revenues from processing taxes. See *New York Times*, 14 June 1939, p. 1.
117 Hanlon, "Urban–Rural Cooperation," p. 380.

The most retrogressive New Deal tax was dead. It had taken a Supreme Court decision, a processor revolt, and urban opposition to kill it. At least in the 1933 emergency, when the Roosevelt administration – with its eyes open – proposed this sales tax on necessities, it seemed that equity must be subordinated to recovery. When Roosevelt tried to revive the tax in 1936, he betrayed a national set of priorities that downgraded concern over the tax burden on lower incomes.

Social Security Payroll Taxes as a Paradigm for New Deal Tax Policy

Payroll taxes for social insurance are the cardinal New Deal contribution to our current tax system. They are an ambiguous legacy. Most tax experts today agree that workers bear both the employee tax and the tax nominally levied on their employers. Though the social security tax basically applies at a flat rate on all covered wages, the lid on wages subject to tax and the exemption of nonwage income allow effective rates to plummet for upper-income recipients. As the social insurance system expands to account for nearly one-third of federal tax receipts (several times the share of corporate income taxes), it undermines the progressivity of the U.S. tax system.[118] The employee payroll tax for old-age insurance now siphons more income from many Americans than does the personal income tax.

As I have demonstrated in some detail elsewhere, Franklin Roosevelt – egged on by Treasury Secretary Morgenthau – bears primary responsibility for exclusive payroll-tax financing of social security.[119] He maintained this position despite certain objections from within his own administration, from the social insurance experts who drew up his old-age and unemployment-insurance programs, and from left-wing forces in Congress and elsewhere. The social security tax, many admonished, was inequitable and deflationary – overburdening the poorly paid, treating the well-to-do too kindly, and diverting needed purchasing power from the masses through a projected $47 billion reserve fund that would pile up as old-age payroll taxes exceeded benefit payments during the first thirty years of the program. Even the complex state-administered mechanism for

118 U.S., Office of Management and Budget, *The United States Budget in Brief FY 1985* (Washington, D.C.: Government Printing Office, 1984), p. 70.
119 This section is amplified in Mark H. Leff, "Taxing the 'Forgotten Man': The Politics of Social Security Finance in the New Deal," *Journal of American History* 70 (September 1983): 359–81.

unemployment insurance, primarily designed to sidetrack constitutional challenges, came under fire for failing to draw on more progressive federal general revenues.[120] Foreign social insurance programs used payroll taxes too, but usually supplemented them with government contributions.

Complaints about the failure of social security's financial scheme to redistribute income, however, cut no ice with FDR. The social security tax squared with FDR's use of the private insurance model in conceptualizing the program. The tax, whose similarity to an insurance premium was widely noted, was designed to safeguard the recipient's dignity and self-reliance. It differentiated social security from demeaning means-tested poor-relief programs by establishing an individual's "earned right" to a pension, something that FDR would later note offered the program political insulation from any future conservative Congresses inclined to dismantle it.[121] Besides, income redistribution was hardly a major objective of FDR's social security proposal. And even if it were, other tax increases were problematic; the narrow base of the income-tax structure, for example, limited its expansion and thus prevented it from covering a major share of the social security obligations. Given Roosevelt's undeniable malaise over large budget deficits, he was irresistibly drawn to payroll taxes, which

120 Few in fact denied the regressivity of the social security tax, which was commonly equated with a sales tax. Undoubtedly, the opulent paid less than an equal share of the payroll tax, because more of their income fell within exempted nonwage categories such as dividends or property income. This seemed similar to the way in which sales taxes bypassed savings by the rich, and many Americans were content to stop here in their analyses of tax burdens. Yet this was only part of the story – a revealing part in coming to an understanding of 1930s tax debates. Though the payroll tax only applied to the first $3,000 of annual wages, it taxed wages below this ceiling at a constant rate. Little realized now and less appreciated then is that this formula was quite inclusive. Only 3% of covered workers earned more than $3,000, and 93% of combined wages of social security participants were subject to tax. Michael Resnick, "Annual Earnings and the Taxable Minimum for OASDI," *Social Security Bulletin* 29 (November 1966): 39–40. Certain low-paid occupations were excluded from the social security program, so that they and the unemployed paid no payroll tax. Only a peculiar set of blinders could obscure the distinction between a sales tax, which hit the poorest hardest, and an employee-payroll tax, which exempted many of the poor, exacted a proportional share from most workers, and only tailed off on the affluent. It should be noted, however, that this comparison is more apt to the extent that social security taxes were passed along to the consumer (an especially common assumption for the employer's payroll tax).

121 "Memorandum on Conference with FDR concerning Social Security Taxation, Summer, 1941," Luther Gulick file, Franklin D. Roosevelt Foundation Papers (FDR Library).

not only could project an image of fiscal responsibility but actually would accumulate a large reserve fund that would reduce the government's borrowing needs.

A similar calculus applied to broader tax policy in the early New Deal. Anxious to stay in the good graces of the business community on whom recovery depended, the administration initially needed to display both "fiscal responsibility" and respect for the financial well-being of corporations and the super-rich. The popular distaste for open taxes on "the people" also limited the New Deal's options. The administration thus portrayed social security not as a tax but as the basis of a cut-rate insurance policy. It gravitated, then, toward two alternate revenue approaches: levies that could be rationalized as necessary adjuncts to popular programs and hidden taxes that engendered little consumer complaint. Lacking the organization, information, inclination, or sophistication to mobilize against burdensome consumer taxes that often amounted to only pennies per purchase, the broad public – anaesthetized to the regressive direction of New Deal tax policy – never forced that policy into center stage. Congressional debates, far from clarifying the tax-incidence effects, often became confused, particularly over such misleading conceptions as "luxuries" or "ability to pay." The administration thus inevitably fooled most of the people a good part of the time. A 1939 survey discovered that 25 percent of Americans polled, mostly those in the lower-income brackets, responded that "they did not happen to pay any taxes."[122] Of course, they were wrong. The New Deal had renewed excise taxes on widely consumed items, it had revivified alcohol taxes, and it had imposed new processing and social security taxes. In pursuit of more pressing problems, the administration gave short shrift to tax-incidence concerns.

Yet this regressive result, though still a subordinate issue to protection against dependent old age and unemployment, engendered unprecedented controversy. In the period bracketing the drafting and enactment of social security, from mid-1934 to mid-1935, the diminished fear of economic collapse had thawed an undercurrent of dissent. Popular inertia was giving way to an atmosphere conducive to liberal and radical activism. Pressures that would lead to a redirection of New Deal tax policy in mid-1935 were already mounting.

122 *New York Times*, 21 June 1939, p. 5.

2. The Congressional Origins of Soak-the-Rich Taxation

The regressive drift of taxation in the early 1930s can give an impression of inevitability. Most of the political and economic elite either sought regressive taxes or shared the public's ignorance or indifference.

Although the public countenanced regressive taxes in 1932–4, however, it also provided fertile soil for assaults on the super-rich. FDR temporarily exploited popular outrage by threatening to move against exorbitant salaries, but he generally drew back from the more advanced efforts to make taxes more progressive. It was Congress, not the executive branch, that led the effort for tax reform. The two main themes of this chapter, congressional initiative and progressive alternatives to the regressive cast of early New Deal taxes, thus inextricably merge.

This chapter makes much of this legislative–executive dichotomy, an oversimplification on both sides of the equation. In Congress, the rural–urban split that had plagued the Democratic Party continued to cut deeply on tax issues. The comparatively wealthy Northeast manifested almost solid opposition to progressive tax reform. Time and again, rural congressmen – particularly non-Southerners – broke away from their urban colleagues to take up the old populist-progressive-Democratic chant against concentrated wealth. The sectional rhetoric of earlier income-tax debates had abated, but it died hard. Faced with the charge that "over 50% of the Federal taxes are collected from six States," a Mississippian parried that "most of the wealth that is now in those particular six States came from the people in the poor States and that it is now in the hands of the very few in this country."[1] This chapter focuses on such regionally based congressional assertiveness on programs to tax or penalize the super-rich.

The Revenue Act of 1932

The roots of this congressional assertiveness can most directly be traced to the Revenue Act of 1932. Many congressmen shared neither the Mellon-

---

1 Jack Houston and A. L. Ford, in U.S., Congress, House, *Congressional Record*, 74th Cong., 1st sess., 1935, 79, pt. 5: 5560.

Mills-Treasury solicitude for rich investors nor the Roosevelt entourage's nonchalance toward tax reform. They thus rebelled against the 1932 revenue bill, signaling a deep and enduring congressional break from President Hoover.

At first, it seemed that the primary desire of Democrats was to demonstrate that they could be just as fiscally responsible as Republicans. Though the Hoover administration's tax proposal primarily relied on a broad package of excise taxes on manufacturers, Treasury Secretary Mills and President Hoover were less than fully disappointed when all but one (Robert Doughton) of the House Ways and Means Committee Democrats – upon urgings by financier Bernard Baruch – joined with the minority contingent of Republicans to substitute a general sales tax. With the nomination of Al Smith, the urban-business wing of the Democratic Party had captured a strong foothold in party leadership, which helped give the party a conservative cast on taxation. A sales tax meshed well with the hostility to income redistribution and income taxes of John Rascob and Jouett Shouse, leaders of the Democratic National Committee. The three most recent Democratic presidential nominees all endorsed the sales-tax proposal. Speaker of the House John Nance Garner had hitched his wagon to the star of publisher William Randolph Hearst, who led the campaign for a sales tax in hopes that it would snuff out the income tax. Garner thus reversed his past opposition to the tax, as did House Majority Leader Rainey (D–Ill.).[2]

The Hoover administration had earlier been hesitant to propose a tax increase, for fear that congressional firebrands would substitute taxes on the rich, thereby crippling the "investment brackets" upon whom Hoover and Mellon relied to pull the nation out of the economic trough. Yet the administration had so successfully defined the fiscal emergency in its own terms that commentators on all sides predicted smooth sailing for the proposed $2\frac{1}{4}$ percent sales tax.

It is too easy to overlook the strong foundation on which the sales-tax movement rested. Its main appeal was that it was in consonance with the prime criterion of 1930s taxes. It promised to be relatively painless. Because it was levied in the form of a general excise tax on the final stage of manufacturing (in contrast to a sales tax on retailers, which states used to forestall the exodus of local industry), and because consumers bore it in daily droplets, it would scarcely impinge on the average citizen's consciousness. The Ways and Means Committee concluded that no other

2 Jordan A. Schwarz, *The Interregnum of Despair: Hoover, Congress, and the Depression* (Urbana: University of Illinois Press, 1970), pp. 132, 114.

tax would "yield the amount imperatively required with as little protest, as little annoyance, and as little disturbance to business."[3]

Other factors also favored the sales tax. Although lacking the diversionary veils that obscured the regressivity of other indirect taxes (only in World War II was it sold as an inflation fighter), the sales tax could still exploit the prevailing unsophisticated grasp of tax incidence by basing its fairness on the fact that the rich would pay more tax than the poor since they bought more. The sales tax also had impressive international credentials. Over the past fifteen years, it had spread through Canada, Australia, much of South America, and continental Europe. Particularly in the financial crunch following World War I, such easy pickings had proved irresistible.[4] Finally, a U.S. sales tax had vigorous industrial support. A phalanx of manufacturers, led by the National Association of Manufacturers (NAM) and firms that otherwise would face selective excises, formed the backbone of the sales-tax movement. Although some smaller manufacturers and some groups with strong retailer influences registered their dissent, much of the articulate business community sublimated their antagonism to taxation and weighed in for the sales tax. Once World War I had made the income tax a real threat, business leaders were inclined to use financial crises (1921, 1932, and World War II) to press for such a redistribution of the tax burden.

Though most of the political, journalistic, and economic establishment had rallied to the sales tax, many liberals were appalled at the Democratic Party's abject surrender to the forces of fiscal conservatism. An article in the *Nation* declared that this Democratic tax bill made "the Mellon plan look like a capital levy."[5] To progressive Governor Gifford Pinchot of Pennsylvania, the sales tax proved that the moneyed interests dominated both party organizations, using them "to take money from the people and put it into the hands of the magnates."[6] Within the House, Southern

---

3 U.S., Congress, House, Committee on Ways and Means, *The Revenue Bill of 1932*, H. Rept. 708 to Accompany H.R. 10236, 72d Cong., 1st sess., 1932, p. 10.

4 Robert M. Haig and Carl Shoup, *The Sales Tax in the American States* (New York: Columbia University Press, 1934), p. 5. A common device was a turnover tax. Though the famous Townsend old-age pension plan relied on a variant of this mechanism, the turnover tax does not seem to have been taken seriously in the United States. The imagery would have been inappropriate, for the tax would have squeezed smaller businesses and fostered corporate consolidation by imposing greater levies on items going through multiple stages of production.

5 Paul Y. Anderson, "The Crazy Democrats," *Nation* 134 (16 March 1932): 303.

6 *New York Times*. 3 April 1932, p. 4.

Democrats [led by Doughton and John Rankin (D–Miss.)] and Republican progressives [led by Fiorello La Guardia (R–N.Y.)] organized a revolt against the tax.

To some extent, redistributive issues may rely for success on a conspiracy of silence, in which political leaders can freely take a "responsible" position in opposition to shadowy public preferences. But once so-called demagogues exploit the emotionally charged themes inherent in such proposals, the frame of reference shifts. Because the sales tax was so clearly designed to favor Eastern wealth, the super-rich, and the corporations that much of the public blamed for the Depression, it could easily become an emblem of a discredited approach toward government.[7] Before the sales tax reached the floor, a favorable reception was widely anticipated. Instead, the House reacted like a supersaturated solution. An organized rebel bloc introduced the seed crystal that solidified it into majority opposition.

The congressional rebellion rested on the belief that the super-rich should shoulder more responsibility for the consequences of the Depression. Luxuries and excessive incomes were particularly offensive in this time of mass deprivation and sacrifice, and the stagnant savings of the bloated few took the blame for strangling mass purchasing power. The traditional scapegoating role of taxation put a premium on such sentiments. To Illinois Democrat Ham Lewis, appropriate targets of steeper death taxes included "the putrid sons of the financial scion" and men "who spend their time capering upon their yachts in distant waters, accompanied with their diamond-bedecked Delilahs as their companions of joy."[8] Senator Clarence Dill (D–Wash.) took up the cudgels for the middle class, which he depicted as insecurely perched between the rich and the down-and-outers (farmers, the unemployed, and ruined depositors). Highlighting

---

7 One does get the impression that the sales tax brought home a rudimentary public appreciation of unfair tax incidence. Congressmen received a tremendous amount of mail on this subject. In a 1938 poll, one-third of the sample designated the sales tax as the "most unfair" tax, easily leading the pack. Public-opinion polls between 1937 and 1942 repeatedly found that the public preferred some sort of income-tax increase (either extending it to lower-income groups or raising its rates) to a new national sales tax. Only in World War II, when the expansion of the income tax and advancing conservatism made people more amenable to the unprecedentedly unified business crusade for sales taxation, did a majority of the public respond that they preferred a national sales tax to higher income taxes. Schwarz, *Interregnum*, p. 134; Hadley Cantril, ed., *Public Opinion 1935–1946* (Princeton, N.J.: Princeton University Press, 1951), pp. 325–6.

8 U.S. Congress, Senate, *Congressional Record*, 72d Cong., 1st sess., 1932, 75, pt. 9: 10196.

stock-market manipulation, he claimed that "those who accumulated these vast fortunes in days of prosperity took more than their fair share of the profits of production" and should now pay "the major part of the increases in taxes."[9]

Other writers have dealt with this revolt in greater detail than is necessary here.[10] A brief overview, however, is worthwhile, for the revolt reflects the same pressures for progressive tax reform that Roosevelt would soon confront.

In the House, a series of income-tax amendments broke the back of the Hoover administration–Democratic leadership alliance. The Ways and Means Committee claimed that its own tax hikes already approached the point at which higher income taxes would only diminish revenue yields. Yet by an astounding 153–97 vote, the House accepted progressive California Republican Phil Swing's proposal to boost the surtax rate on incomes above $100,000 from the 20 percent ceiling in the current law to a maximum of 65 percent. Whistles, applause, and a total absence of decorum reigned as a Democratic–progressive alliance took charge for a few mad days. Asserting that "the greatest menace this country faces is the accumulation of wealth in the hands of a few individuals," they wielded the income tax as "a social tax" to combat that threat.[11]

To newspapers, Democratic leaders, and sympathizers with the Hoover administration, the House seemed bent on a deranged, anarchic assault on wealth and stability. A tally of 236–160 ultimately crushed the sales tax.[12] The House divided along partisan, regional, and urban–rural lines. Democrats, disregarding their party helmsmen, opposed the sales tax by three to one. Although Republicans favored the sales tax by a clear margin, it failed to break even among Western, Southern, and Midwestern GOP congressmen. The Northeast (especially New York City, in the Democrats' case) provided most of the sales-tax supporters in each party. Congressman La Guardia claimed "complete victory."[13] However, inspirational pleas

9 Ibid., pt. 9: 10184.
10 In my account, I have relied primarily on two secondary sources: Schwarz, *Interregnum*, pp. 106–41; and Roy G. Blakey and Gladys C. Blakey, *The Federal Income Tax* (New York: Longmans, Green, 1940), pp. 302–34. Coverage in the *St. Louis Post Dispatch* was superb, though slanted from the left. Also see Walter K. Lambert, "New Deal Revenue Acts: The Politics of Taxation" (Ph.D. diss., University of Texas at Austin, 1970), pp. 1–103.
11 *St. Louis Post-Dispatch*, 19 March 1932, p. 2A.
12 U.S., Congress, House, *Congressional Record*. 72d Cong., 1st sess., 1932, 75, pt. 7: 7324.
13 Arthur Mann, *La Guardia: A Fighter Against His Times, 1882–1933* (Chicago: University of Chicago Press, 1959), p. 310.

for responsibility by Speaker Garner, and a compromise package hammered out in the Ways and Means Committee and endorsed by Doughton and La Guardia, deflated the rebellion. In a new spirit of fiscal responsibility, the House discarded the Swing surtax on super-incomes and accepted a weighty system of excise taxation.

The struggle for more steeply graduated income taxes then resumed in the Senate. An intense administration lobbying effort initially prevented the Senate Finance Committee from reporting out an income-tax schedule patterned by Senator Tom Connally (D–Tex.) on the higher tax rates of 1922. Maverick progressive Senator James Couzens (R–Mich.), who lifted his even more stringent tax amendment from the 1918 Revenue Act, also met with a 31–49 failure on the Senate floor. Business tax clichés – compactly presented in Hoover's warning to the Senate that "it may well be that the income taxes have already been raised to the point of diminishing returns through avoidance which will ensue by the use of tax-exempt securities and are already so high as to approach the danger point in retardation of enterprise" – seemingly still reigned supreme.[14] But though Hoover held out hope until the last, Congress was in no mood to enact a sales tax. Ranking Senate Finance Committee Democrat Pat Harrison helped humiliate it in committee and floor votes. When the government's financial position required that the Senate's tax package be beefed up, Hoover and the Treasury backed down. With their acquiescence, the Senate, which had earlier acceded to administration demands to defeat the Connally income-tax schedule in the interests of preserving business confidence, passed it by 86–3. The normal income-tax rate rose to 4 percent on the first $4,000 taxed and 8 percent on income above that, and surtaxes climbed to a maximum of 55 percent.

Congressional activism on progressive tax reform thus met with some success. The final bill adopted the Senate's stricter income-tax schedule, boosted estate-tax rates and restored the gift tax, hiked the tax on corporate profits, and introduced certain "luxury" excise taxes. However, Treasury Secretary Mills, a master of persuasion, had by no means come away empty-handed; the act also removed the hefty tax credit for an individual's "earned" income, followed the Treasury's recommendation to end the $3,000 corporate tax credit (a severe blow to many small firms), and imposed the regressive excise taxes originally offered by the Treasury. Most importantly, the administration had plucked a mammoth tax increase from a devastated economy. Still, Hoover and the Democratic leaders

14 *St. Louis Post-Dispatch*, 31 May 1932, p. 1.

had failed to ram through a sales tax. Though Hoover would revive this proposal in late 1932 and early 1933 (when revenue predictions failed to materialize), he was talking mainly for the record. The federal sales tax had become a symbol of Hoover's supposed insensitivity to suffering. Only someone with stronger humanitarian credentials might have successfully championed a revenue scheme so clearly favorable to the rich.[15]

In the Beginning: Roosevelt, Taxation, and the NIRA

FDR came into the presidency with an ambiguous position on taxes. As governor, his primary initiative had been the imposition of a tax on gasoline to relieve the property-tax burden on Upstate New Yorkers. Also, after proposing a small across-the-board income-tax cut in 1929 (the legislature instead raised exemptions to confer greater benefits on smaller-income taxpayers), he met rising welfare demands in 1932 by doubling income-

15 Schwarz (*Interregnum*, pp. 109, 129–32, 214–15) also attributes the death of the manufacturers' sales tax to a desire to safeguard state retail- sales-tax revenues. Though several congressmen used this argument, I am not convinced. Although a number of states had a gross-receipts tax, this was a form of franchise tax that was imposed at low rates, usually collected little revenue, and targeted businesses rather than consumers. During consideration of the 1932 Revenue Act, only Mississippi had the sort of general retail-sales tax that would spread to other states in the 1930s (West Virginia, though, had a close relative directed at extractive industries).

   If Congress had blocked other taxes, a states' rights explanation would have been more compelling. Every state employed a gas tax, the leading state revenue source throughout the 1930s. Yet the 1932 Revenue Act initiated a one cent federal gas tax, albeit over considerable opposition. Over one-third of all states imposed a personal income tax, a levy destined to spread in the 1930s. Yet the 1932 Revenue Act cut the federal exemption and roughly doubled the federal rates. Virtually all states levied a death tax, which – like the income tax – accounted for about 8% of state revenues in 1932. Yet the 1932 Revenue Act halved the estate-tax exemption, more than doubled estate-tax rates, and then provided that the credit for state death taxes (which wiped out up to 80% of the federal tax bill) would not apply to any of this increase. Clearly, federal revenue demands ran roughshod over state tax systems.

   Perhaps the causality is reversed. The federal rejection may have catalyzed the mushrooming state adoption of the sales tax in 1933–5. At this point, protective state efforts reinforced the existing roadblocks to federal sales taxation. In any case, the failure to safeguard more vital state revenue sources in 1932 suggests that the states' rights argument was then a weak reed. Neil H. Jacoby, *Retail Sales Taxation* (New York: Commerce Clearing House, 1938), p. 68; Tax Institute, *Tax Yields: 1940* (Philadelphia: Tax Institute, 1941), p. 48.

tax rates. On the national level, the denunciation of Treasury Secretary Mellon's favoritism toward the wealthy played a large role in dissenting Democratic-progressive rhetoric, and FDR joined in. In both the 1932 campaign and within his advisory councils, however, tax reform never received top priority.

It is easy to slight Roosevelt's real faith in a balanced budget and his conservative approach toward taxation. He mirrored the consensus of the political and economic establishment that taxes put a damper on recovery. In an October 1932 Pittsburgh attack on Hoover that Republicans would later quote more often than the New Testament, Roosevelt warned:

> Taxes are paid in the sweat of every man who labors because they are a burden on production and are paid through production. If those taxes are excessive, they are reflected in idle factories, in tax-sold farms, and in hordes of hungry people, tramping the streets and seeking jobs in vain. Our workers may never see a tax bill, but they pay. They pay in deductions from wages, in increased cost of what they buy, or – as now – in broad unemployment throughout the land. There is not an unemployed man, there is not a struggling farmer, whose interest in this subject is not direct and vital.[16]

FDR, however, did not deny a governmental responsibility to promote some income redistribution. His presidential campaign themes of opportunity for the forgotten man, the abolition of special privilege, and the shoring up of mass purchasing power to underwrite recovery – all complemented his demand for "a wiser, more equitable distribution of the national income."[17] Roosevelt also had some appreciation for the notion of tax regressivity. As governor, he denounced certain proposed state excise taxes on "so-called luxuries" for bearing "relatively far more heavily upon the poor than upon the rich," though this never became much of an issue.[18] In a radio speech during the presidential campaign, he described the Democratic platform commitment to "a system of taxation levied on the principle of ability to pay" as "a declaration in favor of graduated income, inheritance and profits taxes, and against taxes on food and clothing, whose burden is actually shifted to the consumers of these necessities of

16 Samuel I. Rosenman, comp., *The Public Papers and Addresses of Franklin D. Roosevelt* 1 (New York: Random House, 1938): 798 (19 October 1932) (hereafter cited as *Addresses of FDR*).

17 FDR, 22 May 1932, in Daniel R. Fusfeld, *The Economic Thought of Franklin D. Roosevelt and the Origins of the New Deal* (New York: Columbia University Press, 1956), pp. 205, 245.

18 *New York Times*, 13 January 1932, p. 20.

life on a per capita basis rather than on the basis of the relative size of personal incomes."[19] When Roosevelt embarked on the regressive tax spree of 1933, it was neither out of ignorance nor lack of humanitarianism. Overall tax incidence never broke through the consciousness of most Americans as a major social issue, particularly when desperate problems of economic recovery crowded out other concerns.

Roosevelt's first plunge into federal tax legislation gratified the progressive forces that had propelled him to the presidency. In December 1932 and January 1933, Roosevelt's open repudiation of support for a sales tax was instrumental in waylaying Hoover's revived sales-tax proposal; the bill subsequently failed even to clear the Ways and Means Committee. Displaying a sensitivity to tax incidence that would not grace later New Deal tax proposals, he charged in private correspondence that a sales tax "distributes the tax burden inequitably – people with less money have to pay a greater proportion than people with more money."[20]

FDR's tax stance was not as clear-cut as it then appeared. Despite the Southern and Western sponsorship that carried Roosevelt to his nomination and election, it is not irrelevant to note that he was a New Yorker (albeit from Upstate), from an environment that could breed fiscal conservatism and special hostility to federal taxes on wealth. In a stroking session on 10 January 1933 with an emissary of sales-tax champion William Randolph Hearst, FDR reportedly confided that "I am not opposed to the sales tax," explaining that he preferred to extend current excise taxes "until we had a broad base which would be tantamount to a general sales tax."[21] From his advisers, FDR received divided counsel. Hoping at least to cover regular government expenditures, Adolf Berle broached the possibility of a sales tax in November 1932. Other advisers proposed various progressive taxes to compress loopholes, to penalize retained corporate profits (Tugwell's pet proposal, designed to "liberate" purchasing power by rechanneling sterile corporate surpluses to stockholders), and to dip into upper incomes. Brain Truster Schuyler Wallace's plan to cut income-tax exemptions and hoist normal tax rates received serious consideration in FDR's meeting with establishment Democrats in early January, but strident protests from

19 *Addresses of FDR*, 1: 661–2 (30 July 1932).
20 Frank Freidel, *Franklin D. Roosevelt*, vol. 4: *Launching the New Deal* (Boston: Little, Brown, 1973), p. 53.
21 Edmond D. Coblentz, ed., *William Randolph Hearst* (New York: Simon and Schuster, 1942), p 149.

Congress against such an assault on the middle class punctured this trial balloon.[22]

Roosevelt thus drifted into the presidency without a tax policy, but with an inclination to get revenue wherever he would encounter the least resistance. The National Industrial Recovery Act (NIRA) posed a thorny problem, for it lacked a natural companion tax (such as alcohol taxes for prohibition repeal and processing taxes for agricultural subsidies). Yet FDR was determined to make at least a gesture toward budget balancing by covering the $220 million in interest and sinking-fund requirements for the $3.3 billion bond issue for public works. His solution was to propose a manufacturers' sales tax of a little over 1 percent and to call it a "re-employment tax." Budget Director Lewis Douglas, whose fiscal conservatism rivaled that of Carter Glass (FDR's first choice for Secretary of the Treasury), thought it a smashing idea. Certain labor leaders also acquiesced in a sales tax, reasoning that any friend of the public-works and labor provisions of the NIRA was a friend of theirs.[23]

Roosevelt's congressional helmsmen were less impressed. Though tax reform ranked near the bottom of FDR's agenda, it had long been a primary rallying point for Democrats and progressives. With business conciliation and a sure revenue stream as two of FDR's main objectives, soaking the shriveled incomes of the rich lost some of its appeal. Still, FDR had to contend with the fact that many congressional Democrats had pledged themselves against the sales tax.

As an alternative, congressional leaders persuaded FDR (it was not difficult) to let them hammer out the unpopular financial arrangements. In testimony before the House Ways and Means Committee, Budget Director Douglas offered two basic revenue packages: a sales tax with no exclusions, or a combination of higher normal tax rates, full taxation of corporate dividends (which were exempt from the normal tax), and a motley choice of excise taxes on gasoline, coffee, tea, cocoa, admissions,

22 Berle to Moley, 10 November 1932, in Freidel, *FDR: Launching*, p. 73; Robert F. Himmelberg, *The Origins of the National Recovery Administration* (New York: Fordham University Press, 1976), p. 186; Elliot A. Rosen, *Hoover, Roosevelt, and the Brains Trust* (New York: Columbia University Press, 1977), pp. 140, 142; "Memorandum of May 19, 1932," box 1/safe, Raymond Moley Papers (Hoover Institution, Stanford University); Freidel, *FDR: Launching*, p. 55.

23 At all other times, the sales tax was the one levy that mobilized labor opposition. The NIRA sales tax, however, even garnered support in testimony from William Green, the president of the AFL. U.S., Congress, House, Committee on Ways and Means, *National Industrial Recovery*, Hearings on H.R. 5664, 73d Cong., 1st sess., 1933, pp. 125–8.

or long-distance phone calls. The Ways and Means Democrats could either embrace a sales tax that had come to represent callous Republican favoritism toward the privileged, or they could hike the tax bill of the so-called middle class.

The Ways and Means Committee (minus its Republican members, who reveled in the Democrats' predicament) chose the latter course. From today's vantage point, their choice had much to recommend it. The income-tax changes affected a relatively affluent group, for less than 3 percent of the population was then covered on taxable returns.[24] If there was slack in the income-tax system, the "lower" and "middle" brackets may have been the place. No income-tax schedule in the 1930s exacted more than 3 percent of the income of a married person earning $7,500 a year after deductions, a comparatively princely sum that placed him well within the top 1 percent of income recipients.[25]

Yet the howl from Congress was immediate. The NIRA almost failed to obtain the procedural rule that would have brought it to the House floor, as most progressives and Republicans joined to block its tax plan.[26] Lacking any symbolic thrust against the top brackets, the tax program was vulnerable. Taxes belonged on "those who by their unbounded greed have brought this curse upon the country," not on "the man of modest means," whose tax bill had already just been increased by the 1932 Revenue Act.[27] Sales-tax advocates were quick to goad administration loyalists. "The opposition to a general sales tax," one congressman chided, "always promises, as a substitute, to collect the needed tax off the rich, and yet the bill itself answers that statement. This bill which the committee has brought in does not collect it from the incomes of the rich, but collects it from the earnings of the great middle class in this country."[28]

To make matters worse for the committee bill, the investigation of J. P. Morgan by the Senate Committee on Banking and Currency (dubbed the Pecora investigation, after the unrelenting committee counsel) unfolded

24 Lawrence Seltzer, *The Personal Exemptions in the Income Tax* (New York: Columbia University Press for the National Bureau of Economic Research, 1968), p. 62.
25 Adolph J. Goldenthal, *Concentration and Composition of Individual Incomes, 1918–1937*, Temporary National Economic Committee Monograph No. 4 (Washington, D.C.: Government Printing Office, 1940), p. 26.
26 *New York Times*, 26 May 1933, p. 1.
27 Theodore Christianson, in U.S., Congress, House, *Congressional Record*, 73d Cong., 1st sess., 1933, 77, pt. 5: 4352.
28 Harold McGugin, in U.S., Congress, House, *Congressional Record*, 73d Cong., 1st sess., 1933, 77, pt. 5: 4355.

a startling tale. No partner – not even J. P. himself – in Morgan's famed investment-banking house had paid a cent in U.S. income taxes for either 1931 or 1932.[29] Their huge salaries and other gains were wiped out by losses on securities, losses that could be carried forward to erase further income in 1933. In a country that taxed capital gains, such a manipulation of capital losses might have been expected. Roosevelt himself had used various deductions – including a substantial capital loss, a larger than usual deficit on his gentleman farm, bad debts, charity, tax-exempt bonds, and state taxes – to pare his 1932 federal tax bill on his $19,000-plus income (not including his governor's salary, which was exempt from federal income tax) to $31.31.[30] But J. P. Morgan and his ilk had traditionally been the prime targets of the income tax. At a time of popular and congressional protests that the super-rich escaped public hardships and sacrifices, the fact that they also escaped taxes forged a constituency for tax reform. It is a commentary on the early conservatism of the New Deal that FDR exploited this popular dissatisfaction without succumbing to its anti-super-rich ethos.

The final NIRA bill, however, did make certain concessions to this ethos. Just before the bill reached the floor, in immediate response to the Morgan revelations, the House Ways and Means Committee squeezed in a ban on using net business losses from one year to write off income in the subsequent year (the so-called loss carryover). The Senate Finance Committee, after narrowly rejecting a sales tax, offered a thoroughly revised tax plan. It levied a 5 percent tax on corporate dividends paid to individuals. It eliminated the rise in normal tax rates and truncated the gas tax hike from ¾ cent to ½ cent. To compensate for the consequent revenue loss, it dipped into corporate taxes, a field politicians had avoided to facilitate recovery. At Chairman Harrison's instigation, it instituted a complex twin levy on capital stock and excess profits.[31] Finally, the Morgan

---

29 U.S., Congress, Senate, Committee on Banking and Currency, *Stock Exchange Practices*, S. Rept. 1455 pursuant to S. Res. 84, S. Res. 56, and S. Res. 97, 73d Cong., 2d sess., 1934, p. 321.
30 "Individual Income Tax Return for Calendar Year 1932," "Income Tax Returns-Federal" folder, "Papers Pertaining to Family, Business and Personal Affairs, 1882–1945," box 140, Franklin D. Roosevelt Papers (Franklin D. Roosevelt Library, Hyde Park, N.Y.; hereafter cited as FDR Library).
31 The federal government had imposed a capital-stock tax from 1916–26, and many states taxed corporations in this manner. However, obtaining an accurate estimate of a company's assets posed insuperable administrative problems. To quell a company's temptation to minimize taxes by undervaluing its assets, the committee defined excess profits as anything above 12½% of this self-assessed

disclosures led the committee to make a number of technical changes.[32] Effective 1 January 1933, short-term net capital losses (on stocks and bonds held less than two years) could no longer be carried forward to the next year, partners could no longer subtract a partnership's net losses on short-term securities from their individual incomes, and private bankers lost their exemption from the ban on deducting short-term capital losses from other income. This Senate bill prevailed in conference committee. Congress had taken the initiative in closing tax loopholes and had replaced the administration's alternatives of a sales tax or middle-bracket taxation with a corporate tax.

The NIRA was one of the outstanding legislative departures in this nation's history. Yet its relatively minor tax provisions had generated the most debate and heat. Taxation was clearly a potent symbolic issue. Congress had boarded the tax-reform train, leaving the Roosevelt administration at the station.

Except as they reflect the administration's conservatism on taxes vis-à-vis its congressional supporters, the NIRA taxes scarcely deserve a footnote in the history of New Deal taxation. Anticipating a revenue geyser from the alcohol-tax spigot, Congress – following up on FDR's suggestion – mandated that the new NIRA taxes would lapse if the budget balanced or if the Twenty-First Amendment were ratified. The repeal of Prohibition terminated the 5 percent dividends tax and the ½ cent boost in gas taxes

estimate. It also pointed to "abnormal profits" as a "secondary" target of an excess-profits tax. Treasury rulings, along with future opportunities to make new capital-stock declarations (rather than merely adjusting the old one for deficits, retained profits, etc.), would vitiate these objectives of "fair" valuation and reasonable profits (instead, companies were free to value their capital stock at the minimum level that would avoid the excess-profits tax on future profits). Yet several proposals emanated from Congress and the administration in 1933–6 to put teeth in the excess-profits tax by boosting and graduating its rates while slicing its exemption – without allowing a redeclaration of capital stock. Thus, the excess-profits tax, surprisingly enough, retained some independent if tenuous connection with excess profits. U.S., Congress, Senate, Committee on Finance, *National Industrial Recovery Bill*, S. Rept. 114 to Accompany H.R. 5755, 73d Cong., 1st sess., 1933, p. 6. See U.S., Treasury Department, Bureau of Internal Revenue, *Regulations 64 (1934 Edition) Relating to the Capital Stock Tax Under Section 701 of the Revenue Act of 1934* (Washington, D.C.: Government Printing Office, 1934), pp. 11, vii. The fullest historical treatment is Kenneth James Curran, *Excess Profits Taxation* (Washington, D.C.: American Council on Public Affairs, 1943), pp. 156–65, which rides herd on the ambiguities in the role of the excess-profits tax between 1933 and 1936.

32 U.S., Congress, Senate, Committee on Finance, *National Industrial Recovery Bill*, S. Rept. 114, 73d Cong., 1st sess., p. 7.

on 31 December 1933, while the capital-stock/excess-profits tax was slated to expire in mid-1934.

The 1934 Revenue Act

The 1934 Revenue Act was a somewhat more important battlefield, but the same forces were involved. Again, Congress took the lead on tax reform. Again, the Roosevelt administration acted as a drag on legislation to penalize the super-rich.

The Pecora investigation, having electrified the debate over the NIRA, provided the backdrop for the 1934 Revenue Act. The debased reputation of the banking fraternity took a further beating.[33] On tax matters, business ingenuity had survived the crash. Such banking luminaries as Otto Kahn, Charles Mitchell, and Thomas Lamont transformed paper capital losses into immediate tax benefits by selling stock to a relative and then buying it back. Another tax dodge troubling the committee was the personal holding company or "incorporated pocketbook." By effectively incorporating himself and accumulating income in this corporation, a taxpayer could avoid income taxes, flouting the unenforceable federal law directed against such practices.

Hoping to curb this evasion, the House on 10 June 1933 authorized a Ways and Means Committee investigation to fortify and simplify the tax system.[34] In December 1933, the investigatory subcommittee (working with the staff of the Joint Committee on Internal Revenue Taxation) offered extensive recommendations to close loopholes, even at the expense of inequities to wealthy taxpayers.

The Treasury was not amused. One business commentator claimed that the Treasury's role in the subcommittee's report amounted to "practically nothing" (though FDR soon went on record as advocating "stringent preventive or regulatory measures" against "individuals who have evaded the spirit and purpose of our tax laws"), leading to recommendations that were "more soak-the-rich than Treasury wishes."[35] Although it is not practical to examine every technical revision that aroused the Treasury Department's ire, its basic argument was that, although many of the

33 U.S., Congress, Senate, Committee on Banking and Currency, *Stock Exchange Practices*, S. Rept. 1455, 73d Cong., 2d sess., pp. 321–3.
34 U.S., Congress, House, *Congressional Record*, 73d Cong., 1st sess., 1933, 77, pt. 6: 5701.
35 *Kiplinger Tax Letter*, 11 December 1933, p. 1; *Addresses of FDR*, 3: 12 (3 January 1934); *Kiplinger Washington Letter*, 23 December 1933, p. 3.

recommendations moved in the proper direction, the subcommittee's swashbuckling approach was unfair, difficult to enforce, and fraught with unforeseen consequences that might reduce expected revenue. In the final committee report, the Treasury carried the day. It blocked the proposed abolition of consolidated returns (which had allowed corporations under the same ownership to pool their incomes onto one form, thus diminishing taxes by counterbalancing the gains of one firm against losses incurred elsewhere). It squelched the recommendation to discard the reorganization provisions and to bar partners from deducting their share of net partnership losses from their individual returns (a particularly unjust suggestion, because gains were taxed in this manner). It successfully opposed the proposal to substitute a foreign tax *deduction* for the foreign tax *credit* (which allowed taxes paid foreign governments to be fully credited against the American tax, rather than merely deducted from taxable income, as was done with state income taxes), arguing that it would cripple foreign trade. Finally, the Treasury vehemently denounced the "inherent unfairness" of the subcommittee's radical plan to arbitrarily lop off one-quarter of all depreciation and depletion deductions. Angered by "alarming" and rising depreciation deductions that dwarfed reported profits (it was common practice to claim greater depreciation losses on income-tax returns than in corporate reports), and attracted to this easy method of inflating reported corporate profits, many congressmen proved difficult to budge on this issue. The Treasury's visionary proposal that all discovery and depletion allowances be scrapped as an unjustified subsidy never had a chance in committee or on the floor, given oil-industry pressure. The Treasury finally pledged to achieve roughly an "equal" overall reduction by tightening its depreciation regulations (shifting the burden of proof to the taxpayer and upping the IRS's guideline periods for writing off investments).[36] Though this change phased in slowly and was never as drastic as promised, depreciation allowances generated much complaint from businessmen (particularly small ones, who lacked the resources to fight Treasury assessments) and probably discouraged corporate investment.

Treasury Secretary Morgenthau eagerly embraced this Ways and Means Committee bill, affirming that it brought about "a more equitable distribution

---

36 U.S., Congress, House, Committee on Ways and Means, *Revenue Revision, 1934, Hearings*, 73d Cong., 2d sess., 1934, pp. 25, 78; U.S., Congress, House, Committee on Ways and Means, *The Revenue Bill of 1934*. H. Rept. 704 to Accompany H.R. 7835, 73d Cong., 2d sess., 1934, pp. 8–9.

of the tax burden over those persons who are best able to sustain it."[37] Although the House capitulated to this voice of reason, the Senate, and particularly its progressive bloc, was less tractable. The Senate Finance Committee made few changes, though Chairman Harrison resuscitated the capital-stock/excess-profits tax. On the Senate floor, however, major contests developed on the income and estate taxes, as well as over certain technical provisions. Without denying the soak-the-rich bias that permeated these amendments, it is important to recognize that potential revenue contributions from the "middle" brackets did receive some attention. The surprising previous optimism that liquor taxes, expenditure cuts, and economic growth would balance the budget began to evaporate when Congress overrode FDR's veto of an appropriations increase in late March. Many old progressives had a deeper commitment to fiscal responsibility through higher taxes than did the administration or most recovery-oriented congressional conservatives. Senator La Follette (Progressive–Wis.), whose eagerness to stabilize national finances was cut with an appreciation of overall tax incidence, and Senator Couzens (R–Mich.), whose opposition to the auto-excise tax on his state's major industry conditioned his advocacy of a productive income tax, had assumed leadership of the progressive bloc on tax questions. They led it to maintain a broader view of tax incidence than individual members might otherwise have taken. La Follette's amendment, which kicked up levies on all income taxpayers and hoisted the maximum tax from 63 percent to 77 percent, only failed by a 36–47 tally.[38] Couzens's amendment to impose a temporary 10 percent surcharge on each income-tax payment eventually squeaked through the Senate on a 43–36 vote.[39] Both amendments gained disproportionate support from rural Democrats and Republicans, whereas urban Senators from both parties were predominantly hostile.[40] At least among progressives and rural Senators, middle-bracket taxation seemed acceptable if sweetened with tax penalties upon the super-rich.

The deconcentrator role of estate taxes was even less ambiguous than for the income tax, and progressives achieved a clear victory here. The

37 Morgenthau to Doughton, 12 February 1934, in U.S., Congress, House, *Congressional Record*, 73d Cong., 2d sess., 1934, 78, pt. 3: 2512.
38 U.S., Congress, Senate, *Congressional Record*. 73d Cong., 2d session, 1934, 78, pt. 6: 6091.
39 Ibid., pt. 6: 6402.
40 Edward F. Hanlon, "Urban–Rural Cooperation and Conflict in the Congress: The Breakdown of the New Deal Coalition, 1933–1938," (Ph.D. diss., Georgetown University, 1967), p. 135.

Senate Finance Committee, which mirrored the general fear that income-tax hikes would impede recovery, had boasted that its increase in estate taxes would "tend to prevent undue accumulation of wealth."[41] The $50,000 exemption for the estate tax (plus an additional $40,000 exclusion for life insurance) was generous to a fault, especially when compared to the $500 exemption for British death taxes. In 1934, for example, upward of 99 percent of decedents owed no estate tax; of the remaining unlucky fraction, 98 percent (those with humble estates worth less than $1 million after deductions) usually paid less than a tenth of their net estates in federal death taxes.[42]

Senator La Follette's estate- and gift-tax amendments, like his income-tax proposals, recognized the twin attraction of higher rates and a broader tax base. The Senate Finance Committee had boosted rates only on net estates worth over $1 million and jacked up the maximum rate only from 40 to 50 percent. La Follette's amendment clipped the estate-tax exemption to $40,000 ($25,000 was his original proposal, but he upped that figure to help gain Finance Committee acquiescence to his amendment) and elevated tax rates (up to a maximum of 60 percent) on estates worth over $120,000 before subtracting the exemption. This amendment carried the Senate by 64–14[43] and found its way into the final law (though the $50,000 exemption was restored).

The attempt of progressives to rewrite the 1934 Revenue Act on the Senate floor met with mixed success, but one should rather be impressed with the breadth of their efforts. Proposals to bar corporate deductions of high salaries, to penalize holding companies by disallowing deductions for intercorporate dividends, and to end tax exemption for all government securities were defeated on the floor, and the House disposed of Couzens's 10 percent income-tax surcharge. However, successful Senate amendments to abolish consolidated returns, to boost estate taxes, and to open up income-tax information and corporate salary payments to public inspection all cleared the conference committee in modified form.

The 1934 Revenue Act was clearly another case of congressional initiative. It was primarily the product of innovative proposals from Senate progressives and a House subcommittee. In addition to provisions already mentioned,

41 U.S., Congress, Senate, Committee on Finance, *Revenue Bill of 1934*, S. Rept. 558 to Accompany H.R. 7835, 73d Cong., 2d sess., 1934, p. 7.
42 U.S., Treasury Department, Bureau of Internal Revenue, *Statistics of Income for 1933* (Washington, D.C.: Government Printing Office, 1935), pp. 52–5.
43 U.S., Congress, Senate, *Congressional Record*, 73d Cong., 2d sess., 1934, 78, pt. 6: 6416.

the statute graduated the taxation of capital gains and limited all capital losses to the amount of gains plus $2,000.[44] It reshuffled the tax schedule by granting a 10 percent "normal" tax deduction for the first $14,000 of "earned" (wage) income and by simultaneously reducing the normal tax to a flat 4 percent and raising the surtax. This package tended to increase taxes on people receiving over $9,000 a year, while offering a slice of tax relief to most income-tax payers earning less than that.[45] It also revived the capital-stock/excess-profits tax, imposed a special penalty tax on personal holding companies, and disallowed losses in intrafamily sales of property.

The 1934 Revenue Act was not a major piece of legislation, for it collected too little additional revenue (roughly a third of a billion dollars annually) and left too many major loopholes unplugged.[46] Yet it confirmed the administration's fear that a rise in corporate or upper-bracket individual taxes would antagonize the economic elite. The unpopularity of the temporary NIRA dividends tax had already given some indication of that. In response to the Ways and Means subcommittee proposals for the 1934 revenue bill, business groups mobilized in opposition and were gratified (though far from satisfied) by the "constructive" changes made in the final House bill. "Then," raged Fred Clausen, the U.S. Chamber of Commerce's chief tax lobbyist, "to the consternation and discouragement of the business men of the nation, we witnessed the spectacle of a political

---

44 This graduation worked in two ways. The longer the seller had held the security, the smaller the proportion of gain or loss that was taxable (thus all but 30% of a stock held over ten years was on the house, whereas the whole thing was taxable if held less than one year). This fraction was then treated as regular income, taxable at whatever graduated income-tax rate applied to the taxpayer.

   Capital losses had sharpened the drop in income-tax receipts between 1929 and 1933. These losses had been used to cancel out huge chunks of taxable income. The 1932 Revenue Act and the NIRA had sheared this allowance for stocks held less than two years, and the 1934 Revenue Act finished the job.

45 U.S., Congress, House, *Congressional Record*, 73d Cong., 2d sess., 1934, 78, pt. 7: 7838. Because dividends were exempt from the normal tax, the conversion of normal tax to surtax was a backhanded tax on dividends. The calculation of a $9,000 dividing line takes into consideration the differing share of dividends at varying income levels, along with a new rule that allowed the personal exemption to be subtracted from net income in calculating the surtax. For taxpayers receiving all salary income (no dividends), the cutoff point rises to $19,000 for single taxpayers and $26,000 and up for families.

46 U.S., Congress, Senate, *Congressional Record*, 73d Cong., 2d sess. 1934. 78, pt. 7: 7832. The prevailing estimate was $417 million, but this included $85 million for stricter control of depreciation allowances, because the Treasury had pledged to use administrative means to approximate the revenue from the Ways and Means subcommittee's straight 25% cut.

holiday. Senators with radical aspiration to use the powers of taxation to confiscate and redistribute private capital began their shooting." The chamber joined other businessmen in assailing publicity of income-tax information, the jump in levies on dividends, the double cross on the capital-stock/excess-profits tax (which had been introduced in 1933 as a temporary emergency measure), the plan to restrict depreciation allowances, and the shift from the "original purpose of a corrective measure" to a package that sought significant revenue through an "excessive burden" on incomes.[47] "Business," reported the *Kiplinger Tax Letter*, "attacks the new law as a deterrent to recovery when the 'road to plenty' should be unimpeded. The government is charged with inconsistent acts by helping business with one hand and placing burdens in its way with the other."[48] The administration could promote a recovery policy that relied upon cooperation and concessions from businessmen, or it could sponsor substantive progressive tax reform, but it might have required more skill than even Roosevelt possessed to do both at once. Even administration sponsorship of the temperate 1934 Revenue Act might have precipitated an open break between FDR and business leaders. As Fred Clausen ominously concluded, "When you are seeking causes for the hesitancy of business to renew its courage and reestablish industrial activity, charge this ill-considered modified program with its fair share of the blame."[49]

Publisher William Randolph Hearst, who loathed the "punitive" 1934 Revenue Act for "soaking the thrifty," echoed other antagonists in ascribing it to the "nitwits and ignoramuses" who were "in the majority in Congress."[50] He had properly pinpointed the responsibility. It was a triumph of Senate progressives. The administration, though supportive of the mild loophole restrictions in the House bill, erected barriers to more sweeping tax reform. Roosevelt had ducked the rising discontent on his right, but at the expense of allowing Congress to make political points with more liberal forces. More than a year would pass before FDR showed that he had absorbed the congressional message.

47 Chamber of Commerce of the U.S., "Revenue Bill of 1934," March 1934, p. 7; Chamber of Commerce of the U.S., "Minutes of Twenty-Second Annual Meeting May 2 to 4, 1934, and Twenty-Ninth Meeting of National Council May 1, 1934," pp. 445–6. Both of these are available at the library of the Chamber of Commerce of the U.S., Washington, D.C.
48 *Kiplinger Tax Letter*, 14 April 1934, p. 4; *Kiplinger Tax Letter*, 12 May 1934, p. 1.
49 Chamber of Commerce of the U.S., "Minutes of Twenty-Second Annual Meeting," p. 445.
50 "Soaking the Thrifty," *San Francisco Examiner*, 3 May 1934, p. 14.

One of the more demanding historical feats is to penetrate the mindset of a past generation. Although debates over income, estate, or corporate taxation in the 1930s can have a deceptively modern ring, one encounters no such problem with the final two subjects of this chapter: income-tax publicity and salary limitation. Both are alien to today's political agendas. Both provide a window to past concerns with income-tax revision, corporate abuses, and excessive affluence.

Income-Tax Publicity

The notion of opening up everyone's income-tax returns to public scrutiny is today almost unthinkable. Yet in the 1930s, an age less solicitous of civil liberties, this idea had special appeal. Feasts in the midst of famine were galling enough, but sleazy tax dodges to avoid a "fair" share of public responsibility received still less sympathy. The public had a right to know. Income-tax publicity, in this sense, was a prototypical progressive reform. By the 1920s, it had become a rallying point for farm-bloc Senators, who warned that "secrecy is of the greatest aid to corruption" and urged that "to-day the price of liberty is not only eternal vigilence [sic] but also publicity."[51] The 1924 Revenue Act required that the name, address, and tax payment of every income-tax payer be made available to the public. If seamy practices were subjected to public attention, progressive dogma provided, they would somehow go away. Though some newspapers refused to publish this information, coverage was extraordinarily comprehensive. Whole pages were devoted to lists of payments by local citizens. Feature stories reported on the biggest corporate assessments and the tax payments of prominent out-of-towners like Babe Ruth or Standard Oil. Teasers told of divorcees who were investigating their husband's income and wealthy taxpayers who escaped with paltry tax payments. When the vehement opposition of Andrew Mellon and President Coolidge culminated in the repeal of publicity in the Revenue Act of 1926, it was a sign that the tax code had drifted from its progressive moorings.

The next big break for income-tax publicity came during consideration of the NIRA, when the Pecora investigation catapulted income-tax evasion onto the front page. Senator Robert La Follette, Jr., had taken up the fallen standard of income-tax publicity from his father. Had publicity been in effect over the past decade, he declared, the "unconscionable

---

51 Robert Howell, in U.S., Congress, Senate, *Congressional Record*, 68th Cong., 1st sess., 1924, 65, pt. 8: 7690.

evasions and understatements of income revealed by the investigation of the Senate Banking and Currency Committee would never have taken place."[52] His amendment for full publicity coasted through the Senate on a 56–27 vote.[53] However, the conference committee, informed by Treasury experts that publicity would be administratively "cumbersome," left such disclosure to presidential discretion.[54] This change, along with the removal of a Senate provision to deny government securities a tax-exempt status, infuriated progressives, who joined en masse with Republicans to nearly sink the NIRA conference package (which passed, 46–39).

Progressives might have not been up in arms had they not been aware of the Treasury's stalwart opposition to publicity and skeptical of Roosevelt's inclination to avail himself of this discretionary power. When FDR predictably failed to act, the Senate, by a vote of 41–34, attached La Follette's full publicity amendment to the 1934 revenue bill.[55] Remembering the NIRA revolt, the conferees relented. They refused to publicize full income-tax returns, but they authorized the release to the public of each taxpayer's name, address, total gross income, total deductions and credits, and tax payment.

As with earlier publicity votes, the dominant division was along urban–rural lines.[56] Except in highly urbanized states, a substantial majority of Democrats and most Republicans favored publicity; although only one Northeasterner supported La Follette's amendment, Midwestern and Western Senators turned out strongly in its support, though the South split almost evenly (for Democratic Party stalwarts opposed the change).

To advocates of income-tax publicity, tax evasion was the paramount issue. Always a transcendent moral question to progressives who set a high standard for relations between a citizen and his government, tax evasion assumed added importance when economic calamity fanned popular resentment toward the rich.[57] In a letter to Roosevelt, old progressive

---

52 U.S., Congress, Senate, *Congressional Record*, 73d Cong., 1st sess., 1933, 77, pt. 6: 5852.

53 Ibid., pt. 6: 5420

54 Heartsill Ragon, in ibid., pt. 6: 5694.

55 U.S., Congress, Senate, *Congressional Record*, 73d Cong., 2d sess., 1934, 78, pt 6: 6554.

56 Hanlon, "Urban–Rural Cooperation," p. 135.

57 This is not to imply that the public overwhelmingly backed income-tax publicity. Clearly the House would not have passed this legislation had it not been part of a conference report. Popularity may not even be an important question, for publicity itself never received the amount of public discussion that would have made it a salient issue. A Gallup Poll was conducted on this question, but

Josephus Daniels spoke of vast increases in tax payments by the wealthy once publicity in his state incited public indignation.[58] Faith in this magical elixir was unbounded: "Publicity," proclaimed George Norris, "is the greatest cure for evils which may exist in government."[59] Publicity advocates directed their barbs at wealthy tax evaders and clearly would not have hesitated to use publicity information to discredit this group (one congressman looked forward to getting his hands on the returns of local corporations who were "stealing the constituents of my district blind"), but their moral concern with tax evasion incorporated a more encompassing demand that taxpayers pay their fair share.[60] Again, they proved willing to inconvenience the relatively affluent if the super-rich were also called upon to sacrifice.

Income-tax publicity, then, had two major functions. The first was deterrence; if someone "knows that his return is a matter of public record, he will hesitate a long time before he will resort to any device designed to relieve him of his fair share of the tax."[61] The second was a kind of automatic self-correction in which "loopholes will be discovered immediately and legislation passed to correct evasions" – a process that seemed to be validated by the disclosures from the Pecora investigation.[62] Publicity proponents doubted the impartiality of Internal Revenue Bureau employees, and clearly hoped that opening the tax records to public scrutiny would keep bureau officials honest.[63]

unfortunately not until April 1938 (after the public, no longer considering tax evasion a big issue, had soured on government reform and criticism of businessmen). The result of that poll, though inapposite and ambiguous, is interesting: Although a majority opposed making income-tax reports public, the figures reversed themselves on the question of publicizing income tax reports of "rich men." Cantril, *Public Opinion*, p. 316.

58 Josephus Daniels to FDR, 14 April 1934, "Daniels, Josephus: 1934" folder, Official File 237, FDR Papers.

59 U.S., Congress, Senate, *Congressional Record*, 74th Cong., 1st sess., 1935, 79, pt. 4: 4511.

60 Frank Hook, in U.S., Congress, House, *Congressional Record*, 74th Cong., 1st sess., 1935, 79, pt. 3: 3410; George Norris, in U.S., Congress, Senate, *Congressional Record*, 74th Cong., 1st sess., 1935, 79, pt. 4: 4511.

61 Robert La Follette, Jr., in U.S., Congress, Senate, *Congressional Record*, 73d Cong., 2d sess., 1934, 78, pt. 6: 6553.

62 Wright Patman, in U.S., Congress, House, *Congressional Record*, 73d Cong., 2d sess. 1934, 78, pt. 3: 2600.

63 Robert La Follette, Jr., in U.S., Congress, Senate, *Congressional Record*, 73d Cong., 2d sess., 1934, 78, pt. 6: 6546; Robert La Follette, Jr., in U.S., Congress, Senate, *Congressional Record*, 74th Cong., 1st sess., 1935, 79, pt. 4: 4512.

This "pink slip" law (so called because taxpayers submitted the publicity data on a separate pink form) applied to corporations, partnerships, and the 7¼ percent of the population that was covered on the 4 million taxable and nontaxable personal returns.[64] But this relatively small group was politically influential enough to wield the ultimate veto power. Income-tax publicity never had a chance to fall short of its sponsors' expectations. Less than one year after its Senate passage, it was repealed.

Fundamentally, antagonism toward income-tax publicity stemmed from a natural reluctance to submit one's financial dealings to the tender mercies of gossips, acquaintances, competitors, and the public. But this case was considerably embellished for political consumption. With the country still in the throes of a terrible crime wave, many opponents voiced concern that pink slips would be red flags for criminals. Income-tax information would provide " 'fingers' for the underworld" and sucker lists for high-pressure salesmen."[65] Racketeers and con artists would let their fingers do the walking in a government directory that seemed tailored to their special needs. The rival argument that criminals could identify the wealthy in other ways did not suffice; Robert Doughton argued that it was in-appropriate even to appear to aid "that bunch" at the same time that "many good people in the country are lying awake at night in constant dread and constant fear of that criminal element."[66]

The *New Republic* charged that the only good reason why any person would object to the release of his income-tax return was "because he is ashamed of its size or source" – "a good reason from his point of view, but certainly not from that of the community."[67] Opponents of publicity disagreed. This "innovation in snoopery" would allow gossips to pry "into their neighbor's affairs" and "sordid-minded people in any community to go and look up your tax return and publish it."[68] "We are so insensate to the finer feelings of people, so wantonly ruthless," lectured Senator Louis Murphy (D–Iowa) "that we have taken the curtains and shades from the homes of our taxpayers and pulled out the walls of the bathroom to assure

64 Simon Kuznets, *Shares of Upper Income Groups in Income and Savings* (New York: National Bureau of Economic Research, 1953), pp. 245, 252.

65 *New York Times*, 21 February 1935, p. 18.

66 U.S., Congress, House, *Congressional Record*, 74th Cong., 1st sess., 1935, 79, pt. 3: 3407.

67 "The Week," *New Republic* 82 (20 March 1935): 143.

68 Robert Bacon, in *New York Times*, 24 February 1935, sec. 4, p. 5; Allen Treadway and Bertrand Snell in U.S., Congress, House, *Congressional Record*, 73d Cong., 2d sess., 1934, 78, pt. 7: 7839, 7829.

that the Peeping Toms shall have full and unobstructed opportunity to feast their eyes on the 'pink slip.' "[69]

By thus debasing individual privacy, publicity would also destabilize society. The publicity effort had "been boiled in the cooking pots of demagogues whose ulterior motives are not the public interest, but class cleavage and the creation of class hatreds."[70] "There is a lot of feeling against a merchant at this time who is making some profit," wrote the president of a lumber company to Senator Norris, "and as we see it to make these 'pink slips' public would make our farmer customers hate the merchant more than ever, while what we need is a live and let live spirit."[71]

The tenor of some of these arguments is suggestive of the many futile assaults on the New Deal from its right flank. Progressives responded with the majoritarian, antielitist defenses of the underdog that had usually served them well. Radical congressman Charles Truax (D–Ohio) proclaimed himself "fed up on this pink-slipped, silk-stockinged propaganda," adding that "I am fighting for the 123,000,000 people who do not pay income taxes."[72]

Why did this rebuttal fail to dent the publicity-repeal juggernaut? The answer lies not only in self-preservation ("when the first income-tax payments were made public," one House member recalled, "the names of the Congressmen were the first ones most eagerly published and scanned"),[73] though that too might have played some part. Most importantly, the antipublicity campaign was transformed into a defense of the middle class. Seeing one's business affairs laid out on the local front page might be embarrassing for a successful businessman, but for less successful ones this possibility, or even the somewhat less remote possibility of competitors requesting this information, might be a humiliating and ruinous warning to creditors. Even the group that spearheaded the anti-pink-slip forces – the reactionary Sentinels of the Republic – used small-business imagery

69 U.S., Congress, Senate, *Congressional Record*, 74th Cong., 1st sess., 1935, 79, pt. 4: 4508.
70 Robert Bacon in *New York Times*, 27 February 1935, p. 5.
71 W. H. Adams to George Norris, 13 March 1935, "Publicity of Income Tax Returns" folder, tray 6, box 6, George W. Norris Papers (Library of Congress, Washington, D.C.)
72 U.S., Congress, House, *Congressional Record*, 74th Cong., 1st sess., 1935, 79, pt. 3: 3394.
73 Charles Gifford, in U.S., Congress, House, *Congressional Record*. 75th Cong., 3d sess., 1938, 83, pt. 3: 3058.

that obscured its dependence on wealthy conservatives.[74] Industrialist Raymond Pitcairn, a seasoned practioner of single-issue politics who directed this campaign as the Sentinel's national chairman, allowed that "income taxpaying citizens are a minority group," but added, "recovery will fail without the leadership and efforts of these income taxpaying citizens working in large industry and in small industry, in big business and in little business and in agriculture throughout the whole nation."[75]

Although even congressional leaders and other sympathizers saw little hope for repeal as late as February 1935, the repeal forces had begun to assemble an unbeatable coalition. Naturally, income-tax publicity was opposed by merchants' associations, chambers of commerce, and other conservative or business groups. Then Speaker Byrns and Ways and Means chairman Doughton announced their opposition to publicity. That Bureau of Internal Revenue and other Treasury officials would look kindly upon repeal was one of Washington's worst-kept secrets. Though Treasury Secretary Morgenthau refused urgent requests to endorse repeal, he was imposing neutrality on a department that was anything but neutral.[76] FDR's apparent caution, conservatism, and drift in early 1935 made income-tax publicity even more vulnerable.

Meanwhile, the Sentinels of the Republic laid the groundwork for a massive taxpayer protest. Special anti-pink-slip packets furnished taxpayers with propaganda sheets and a petition to Congress, urging them to write Secretary Morgenthau, their congressmen, and their local newspapers. When the Treasury sent out the pink slips and the filing date for income taxes approached, an avalanche of indignant telegrams and letters, many of them identical, inundated Congress. In addition, many people apparently affixed to their pink slips a sticker – available in the Sentinels packet and at some banks – declaring "I protest against this outrageous invasion of

74 Thomas Cadwalader to Alexander Lincoln, 15 May 1935, "Sentinels . . . Social Security Bills, etc. 1935–1936" folder, box 1, Alexander Lincoln Papers (Schlesinger Library, Radcliffe College, Cambridge, Mass.); also see U.S., Congress, Senate, Special Committee to Investigate Lobbying Activities. *Investigation of Lobbying Activities, Hearings* pursuant to S. Res. 165 and S. Res. 184, 74th Cong., 2d sess., 1936, pt. 6: 2049–51, 2094.

75 Raymond Pitcairn, "Petition to the Congress of the United States," Raymond Pitcairn to "All Income Taxpayers," 1 March 1935; Raymond Pitcairn to Henry Morgenthau, Jr., undated mimeographed telegram; all in "Publicity of Income Tax Returns" folder, tray 6, box 6, George W. Norris Papers.

76 Morgenthau Diaries, 26 February 1935 and 27 February 1935, book 3, pp. 406, 408, 416; Morgenthau Diaries, 11 March 1935, book 4, pp. 66D, 66E.

my right of Privacy."[77] Congressmen were impressed, and they often commented that the bulk of the protests came from "the small taxpayers."[78] In the House, a last-ditch amendment to confine publicity to people earning over $25,000 a year was easily turned back (it was too late for that now; besides, progressives deemed evasion a moral issue that cut across income levels).[79] Then, only a month after the pundits had discounted the chances of repeal, it swept through the House, 301–99. Republican representatives, who by 1935 enjoyed extraordinary cohesion on virtually every issue, balloted almost unanimously for repeal. All third-party congressmen stuck with publicity, but even rural Democrats split slightly against it, and Southern Democrats – whose innate conservatism often surfaced when party loyalty was not involved – balloted for repeal by almost two to one.[80] The Senate division was similar, except that Republicans from farm states divided evenly. No Northeasterners voted for publicity, but this only confirmed the pattern of the 1934 vote. More striking was the erosion of support from rural conservative Democrats. La Follette's bid to revive his publicity amendment succumbed to a 25–51 tally – a startling turnaround from the 41–34 count a year earlier.[81]

Faced with implicit administration opposition and open rumblings from the politically influential lower- and middle-bracket income-tax payers, the rural-reform coalition had been stripped to its progressive core. In taking charge, Congress had gone too far on its own, and it hastened to retreat to safer ground. On salary limitation, a more economically radical concept, success was less complete but more durable. This success flowed partly from a clearer orientation toward the higher ranges of income. Also, the administration never smothered it with indifference or veiled hostility. Instead, Franklin Roosevelt, well aware of the ground swell upon which this reform rose, worked to coopt the salary-limitation movement.

---

77 The George W. Norris Papers (tray 6, box 6, "Publicity of Income Tax Returns" folder) include the Sentineis packet and much constituent correspondence. *New York Times*, 15 March 1935, p. 23.

78 M. M. Logan, in U.S., Congress, Senate, *Congressional Record*, 74th Cong., 1st sess., 1935, 79, pt. 4: 4506.

79 U.S., Congress, House, *Congressional Record*, 74th Cong., 1st sess., 1935, 79, pt. 3: 3410.

80 Hanlon, "Urban–Rural Cooperation," p. 189; U.S., Congress, House, *Congressional Record*. 74th Cong., 1st sess., 1935, 79, pt. 3: 3411.

81 Hanlon, "Urban–Rural Cooperation," p. 217; U.S., Congress, Senate, *Congressional Record*, 74th Cong., 1st sess., 1935, 79, pt. 4: 4526.

Salary Limitation

Because most forms of salary publicity and limitation are not taxes, it may not seem necessary to consider this issue in a study on taxation. Although it is certainly possible, however artificially, to segregate tax-based salary-limitation schemes from the broader effort to limit excessive compensation, this approach would not be desirable; salary limitation, as part of the panoply of attacks on superfluous wealth, goes to the core of the American search for rich scapegoats in the early New Deal. It thus supplements and sharpens the lessons of New Deal tax policy.

The obsession with corporate salaries in the early New Deal is an interesting one. Doctors, lawyers, and small businessmen were quite deliberately excluded from consideration, partly because such incomes were difficult to regulate. But also, a populace that had traditionally cast a wary eye on "middlemen" found it easy to view corporate executives and other bureaucrats as an extraneous, unproductive layer that soaked up an extravagant share of the shrunken consumer dollar. The widely bruited gap between a corporation's dispersed ownership and its actual control cast corporate directors as a specially privileged, self-regulating group that selfishly hoarded outrageous salaries and bonuses. Though the point should not be overdone, corporate salary limitation could be viewed as a transitional stage in the public's hunt for a scapegoat for the economic collapse. For example, the fact that huge corporations – soon the object of much abuse – devoted an even more minor portion of their total incomes to large executive salaries than small corporations rarely entered the debate until the later 1930s.

The popular consensus against high corporate salaries is striking. In early 1936, well past the peak of this movement, a five-to-two majority in a *Fortune* poll agreed that officials of large corporations were generally overpaid.[82] In 1933, people in high places – both in and out of the administration – demanded government action out of fear "that continued maintenance of the high salaries might have an unhappy public reaction."[83] Even establishment conservatives such as the *New York Times* counseled a strategic retreat on this issue, and the *Hartford Courant* warned: "In times of prosperity such evidences of prodigality may be glossed over, but in times of depression they sink in and sow more seeds of social

82 Cantril, *Public Opinion*, p. 1010.
83 *New York Times*, 20 October 1933, p. 8.

revolution than can ever be sown by soap-box orators of communistic persuasion."[84]

Themes of sacrifice, fraud, frugality, revolution, and stockholder rights permeated the debate on salary limitation. Under Roosevelt's economy program, federal salaries had temporarily been cut 14 percent, and many were loath to use government corporate aid to prop up executive salaries that exceeded those of congressmen, cabinet members, or even the president. When the Pecora investigation uncovered million-dollar bonuses and finagling by corporate officers to further their personal interests, the prestige of business ebbed still lower. Even stockholders, who had tolerated secrecy on this subject in the 1920s, now withdrew their passive sanction for officers to determine their own compensation; it scarcely seemed proper for executives to pull in salaries and bonuses of over $100,000 while their companies slashed dividends and verged on bankruptcy.

The business community, still in disarray after the Depression panic, could not maintain a solid defense against this thrust. Although the current clearly ran against them, however, conservative businessmen and certain allies in the press did not fold up their tents when confronted with this challenge. Their position was not as weak as it might appear. Though reformers could point to individual industries (insurance was a favorite, for top salaries in the biggest companies continued to rise until 1933) in which salaries had remained at exorbitant levels, bonuses had shriveled up. Although salary reductions came grudgingly, the average drop in total compensation of executives was comparable to wage cuts for others.[85] Besides, affected industries pointed out, bloated corporate salaries had no discernible broad economic effect, because these large salaries comprised only the tiniest fraction of 1 percent of sales.[86] At the same time, companies needing government aid were often the very ones most in need of the managerial talent that high salaries could attract. Furthermore, they snapped, a government running huge deficits had little standing to instruct them

84 *Hartford Courant*, quoted in "The Federal Government and High Salaries," *Literary Digest* 116 (11 November 1933): 9.

85 Robert A. Gordon, *Business Leadership in the Large Corporation* (Berkeley and Los Angeles: University of California Press, 1961), pp. 281, 286, 287; Buel W. Patch, "Control of Corporate Salaries," *Editorial Research Reports* 2 (10 Sept. 1935): 240–1; John G. Baker, *Executive Salaries and Bonus Plans* (New York: McGraw-Hill, 1938), p. 25.

86 See Baker, *Executive Salaries*, pp. 143, 238. Combined compensation to executives in small companies loomed relatively larger, rising as high as 4% of sales in smaller steel companies. Also, of course, top-executive salaries could appear astronomical if compared to a company's vanished profits.

on how to run their businesses.[87] Government policy should neither be influenced by "envy of economic success" nor dictated by "radical politicians and the radically minded class of persons with small incomes upon whom these politicians rely for votes."[88]

By depicting salary limitation as a symbol with little economic impact, opponents had perhaps isolated the key to its success. The political system was running scared in 1933, and publicity and denunciations of lavish salaries proved a ready outlet. Politicians could get considerable mileage out of castigating the "greedy pigs" who were "getting a million or more a year in salaries and bonuses and other robberies of the business they control."[89] The government thus attacked high salaries across such a broad front that it is difficult to give a coherent rendering of the programs put forward. There were three basic approaches toward curbing executive compensation: investigation and publicity, ceilings on corporate salaries in government programs, and tax penalties on high salaries.

Salary Publicity

The publicity-investigation effort owed much to Felix Frankfurter, the Harvard law professor who became one of FDR's leading sycophants and advisers. Frankfurter harbored a Brandeisian suspicion of giant corporations and their leaders. Certain corporate salaries, he believed, were "absurdly disproportionate to service performed and . . . constitute quite frequently a form of graft."[90] In mid-1932, in search of a congressional champion for the cause, he asked Senator La Follette to sponsor a resolution ordering the Federal Trade Commission (FTC) or similar organizations to investigate salaries conferred by banks, public utilities, and large industrial or mercantile corporations.[91] Frankfurter saw the economic collapse as an opportunity to get a maximal impact from salary exposure "before we are again drugged into indifference by a period of recovery."[92] He ultimately found a sponsor

87 David Lawrence, "The High Cost of Presidents," 21 October 1933, in *The Editorials of David Lawrence*, vol. 1: *The Era of the New Deal* (Washington, D.C.: U.S. News and World Report, 1970): 40.
88 "Concerning 'Excessive' Salaries," *Railway Age* 113 (10 June 1933): 818.
89 Kent Keller, in U.S., Congress, House, *Congressional Record*, 73d Cong., 1st sess., 1933, 77, pt. 4: 4132.
90 Felix Frankfurter to Robert La Follette, Jr., 13 July 1932, "La Follette, Robert M., Jr." folder, box 74, Felix Frankfurter Papers (Library of Congress, Washington, D.C.)
91 Ibid.
92 Felix Frankfurter to James Couzens, 23 February 1933, "Couzens, James" folder, box 50, Felix Frankfurter Papers.

for his concerns in another Senate progressive, Edward Costigan (D–Colo.). Costigan bought the issue from top to bottom, introducing a resolution authorizing the compilation and release to the Senate of salary information on corporate executives and directors by the Federal Reserve Board (for banks), the Reconstruction Finance Corporation (for banks outside the Federal Reserve system), the Federal Power Commission (for public utilities), and the Federal Trade Commission (for corporations operating in interstate commerce with over 1 million dollars in assets). After a couple of false starts, the Senate adopted the Costigan resolution without recorded opposition on 29 May 1933. This was minor legislation, to be sure. The substitution of study for action should never be overrated, even if salary questionnaires intimidated and angered corporate leaders. But one should not disregard the impetus to congressional soak-the-rich forces from the salary data released in 1934. The masses were "aroused" against such salaries, declared Senator Wheeler, "at this time when wage earners are out of employment and hungry. For these captains of industry to be drawing down large salaries is unconscionable and unpatriotic. The practice must be curbed by legislation, through taxation and publicity."[93]

As Wheeler's statement suggests, one of the fruits of publicity was more publicity. In 1934, the issue was not controversial. Like its income-tax counterpart, salary publicity was a Senate contribution to the 1934 Revenue Act, passed in what one conservative columnist termed "a savage 'soak the rich' atmosphere."[94] Its sponsor, Tennessee Democrat Kenneth McKellar (then on the fringe of the progressive camp on tax issues, though he earned a reputation in World War II as one of the New Deal's nastiest, most parochial critics), introduced it only after the Senate had rejected more substantive salary measures. After Finance Committee Chairman Harrison gave it his assent, it cleared the Senate without debate on a perfunctory voice vote and was retained in conference. Although newspapers all but ignored the initiative, the basic issues – public irritation over excessive executive salaries and bonuses and a stockholder's right to know of such abuses – had already been hashed out in earlier debates. Henceforth, corporation income-tax returns included a list of names and total compensation of employees receiving over $15,000 annually. The Treasury submitted to Congress a cumulative list, which was then made public.

93 Burton Wheeler, quoted in Patch, "Control," p. 246.
94 Frank Kent, "Weather Signs," 11 February 1935, in Frank R. Kent, *Without Grease* (New York: Morrow, 1936), p. 87.

Because the salaries of top corporate executives were already widely publicized through the Securities and Exchange Commission (SEC) (albeit in a far less complete and more cumbersome form), the case for salary publicity appears weaker than for income-tax publicity; it was merely a symbolic index of distaste for excessive corporate salaries. The $15,000 salary cutoff meant that it only affected a tiny fraction of 1 percent of the population. Naturally, organizations like the Chamber of Commerce of the U.S., the New York Board of Trade, and the Commerce Department's Business Advisory Council opposed both income-tax and salary publicity.[95] But lacking a broader popular revolt, conservative spokesmen failed to convince Congress to piggyback salary-publicity repeal on income-publicity repeal in 1935; a repeal amendment for the former failed in the Ways and Means Committee and was shouted down by the House in 1936.

In 1937, however, a 230–114 vote passed a salary-publicity repeal amendment advocated by the House Democratic leadership. The vote breakdown basically replicated the 1935 income-tax-publicity conflict. Third-party members unanimously backed publicity, Republicans preponderantly rejected it (though a few more rural members from the West Coast region voted in support), Southern Democrats opposed publicity by a sizable margin, and other rural Democrats were its defenders (they split slightly against repeal). The only change was among urban Democrats. The infusion of a new breed of urban liberals had shattered the past unanimity against publicity (though urban Democrats still divided against it by a five-to-two ratio).[96]

If the vote breakdown was familiar, parts of the debate seemed like a recurring nightmare. The evaporation of the kidnapping scare toned down the crime argument somewhat. Still, the Chamber of Commerce registered the complaint that the list of names "has been a veritable gold mine for salesmen of all kinds, blackmailers, kidnappers, and others compiling lists

95 U.S., Congress, Senate, Committee on Finance, *Revenue Act of 1938, Hearings on H.R. 9682*, 75th Cong., 3d sess., 1938, p. 475; *New York Times*, 15 April 1937, p. 32; Committee on the Revenue Act to the Business Advisory and Planning Council for the Department of Commerce, "Desirable Changes in the Revenue Act of 1934," 10 April 1935, p. 12, "1933–1935" folder, box 19, Official File 3Q, FDR Papers.

96 Hanlon, "Urban – Rural Cooperation," p. 193; Julius Turner, *Party and Constituency: Pressures on Congress*, Johns Hopkins University Studies in Historical and Political Science, vol. 69 (1951), no. 1 (Baltimore: Johns Hopkins University Press, 1952): 91, 157; U.S., Congress, House, *Congressional Record*, 75th Cong., 1st sess., 1937, 81, pt. 4: 3889.

of prospects or victims for doubtful purposes."[97] By attributing "ill feeling between employers and employees" to the publication of bosses' salaries, foes of publicity also capitalized on malaise over the recent wave of strikes. As a spokesman for the National Retail Dry Goods Association pointed out, "the workman at the bench," who "fails to appreciate the knowledge, the experience and the skill and personal qualifications of leadership modern business requires of executives," sometimes comes to "regard such compensation as excessive" – an observation borne out by the AFL's advocacy of corporate-salary publicity and its exploitation in bargaining sessions of the disjunction between wage cuts and huge executive salaries.[98]

Privacy continued to be the underlying argument for repeal, but administrative inconvenience now assumed an important role. Because most salary information was already available from the SEC, critics pointed out, the nugatory additional "benefits" of salary publicity could not justify the time and expense for corporations, the Treasury, and the Ways and Means Committee to submit, compile, and distribute the salary list.

This case was strong enough to carry repeal through the Senate Finance Committee and the House in 1937. Although it failed to reach the Senate floor near the end of the session, prospects for 1938 looked good, especially after the 1937 recession rocked Congress into an enhanced attentiveness to corporate demands.

Several factors undercut the strength of this case for the repeal of salary publicity, however. First, popular suspicion of the super-rich persisted, albeit in diluted form. A March 1938 Gallup Poll on the question of publicizing corporate salaries above $15,000 a year split the public in half along economic lines, but a considerable majority thought that corporate salaries over $75,000 should be made public.[99] Second, members of the middle class, who had so vigorously condemned income-tax publicity, could not get equally incensed over a salary-publicity law that left most of them untouched. Third, providing an additional salary list was far less threatening to corporations than releasing income-tax figures. Finally, Franklin Roosevelt, having broken with business leaders in 1935, was

97 U.S., Congress, Senate, Committee on Finance, *Revenue Act of 1938, Hearings*, p. 475.
98 Allen Treadway, in U.S., Congress, House, Committee on Ways and Means. *Revision of Revenue Laws 1938, Hearings*, 75th Cong., 3d sess., 1938, p. 282; Jay Iglauer, in U.S., Congress Senate, Committee on Finance, *Revenue Act of 1938, Hearings*, pp. 128–9; "Salary List Repeal Opposed by A. F. of L.," *American Federation of Labor Weekly News Service* 28 (12 February 1938): 1.
99 Cantril, *Public Opinion*, p. 1010.

now free to indulge his proclivities for any battle with excessive wealth. In May 1937, he commented that he thought he would veto the repeal of salary publicity if it passed the Senate.[100] Then, in March 1938, as the House began to consider a 1938 revenue bill that had dropped salary publicity, Roosevelt grasped this issue as a way to moralize his political position. Alleging public indignation over the 1 million dollars paid to the president of Bethlehem Steel, he announced himself "100% in favor" of retaining salary publicity. Proclaiming that a "private office is also a public trust," he attacked family corporations for reducing their profits by paying themselves excessive salaries.[101]

The Congress did succeed in 1938 in truncating salary publicity, limiting it to salaries above $75,000. Still, salary publicity had remained on the books, long after the curbing of executive salaries had ceased to be a live public issue. It was not until 1949, when the Treasury testified it considered the extraction of 1,000 names from 600,000 returns a waste of time, that this form of salary publicity quietly died.[102] An exercise in symbolic politics whose time had passed, salary publicity had been a congressional measure that FDR later coopted. This reversal of congressional and executive roles was an object lesson in the history of New Deal taxation.

Salary Ceilings

That was the view from 1937–8. In 1933–4, however, the congressional and executive roles were not so clearly distinguishable, though congressional interest in salaries usually dominated. Congress was most inclined to act in cases in which the government offered direct support to corporations. A special urgency surrounded the irony of taxing poor people to fund immense salaries that "could not be paid if the taxpayers of the United States did not supply the money."[103] Top salaries in public-service corporations had long drawn ire from state legislatures, a combination of penny-pinching and antielite urges that simultaneously guided efforts at

---

100 FDR, quoted in K. (Henry Kannee) to Mr. Forster, 14 May 1937, "Aug. 1936–1937" folder, box 2, Official File 962, FDR Papers.
101 Franklin D. Roosevelt, *Complete Presidential Press Conferences* (New York: Da Capo Press, 1972), 4 March 1938, 11: 202–4; FDR to Robert Doughton, 8 March 1938, "1938" folder, box 2, Official File 962, FDR Papers.
102 *New York Times*, 18 August 1949, p. 33.
103 Hugo Black, in U.S., Congress, House, *Congressional Record*, 72d Cong., 1st sess., 1932, 75, pt. 14: 15120.

reducing government pay. It was not a long step to regulating salaries in the government's client corporations. Hugo Black (D–Ala.), whose labor sympathies and populist suspicions of big corporations pulled him toward the forefront of the effort to shift the tax burden from the poor to the rich, generally led this cause. In 1932, he vainly tried to prevent the Reconstruction Finance Corporation (RFC) from lending money to any firm that paid its executives more than $15,000 a year (subsequent amendments, lifting the barrier to $100,000, also failed).[104] In succeeding years, he scored a series of small triumphs: an amendment prohibiting the government from granting air- and ocean-mail contracts to firms paying salaries above $17,500 in 1933; the extension of that salary ceiling to all contracts under the new Air Mail Act in 1934; and, in 1936, the prohibition of salaries above $25,000 as allowable costs on government ship contracts.[105]

Though the effort to put a cap on salaries thus extended over several years, the iron was hottest in 1933 and 1934. In Congress, the partial success in 1933 of the campaign to restrict salaries of corporations borrowing from the Reconstruction Finance Corporation was probably the greatest triumph. The huge salaries of insurance executives became a national scandal, and the Pecora investigation was raking the nation's financial establishment over the coals. In the Senate Banking and Currency Committee's hearings on an RFC proposal to allow the corporation to purchase the stock of insurance companies or use that stock as security for loans (a method of financial aid that had already been authorized for banks), Senator Couzens challenged RFC Chairman Jesse Jones to battle high insurance salaries by restricting such aid to insurance companies willing to hold down annual compensation for executives to not more than $25,000. Jones claims to have "countered" with a $10,000 figure, and the committee compromised on $17,500.[106] This was scarcely a major breakthrough for salary limitation; the insurance industry's need for aid had largely been saturated in 1932 and early 1933, and one congressman estimated that only "four or five" companies were "likely to take advantage" of this new

104 Virginia Van Der Veer Hamilton, *Hugo Black: The Alabama Years* (Baton Rouge: Louisiana State University Press, 1972), p. 199.
105 George T. Washington and V. Henry Rothschild, *Compensating the Corporate Executive*, 3d ed., 2 vols. (New York: Ronald Press, 1962), 2: 774; Hamilton, *Hugo Black*, p. 233; Washington and Rothschild, *Compensating*, 2: 786.
106 Jesse H. Jones with Edward Angly, *Fifty Billion Dollars* (New York: Macmillan, 1951), p. 110; Duncan Fletcher, in U.S., Congress, Senate, *Congressional Record*, 73d Cong., 1st sess., 1933, 77, pt. 3: 2852.

assistance (the actual figure for the 1930s was only double that).[107] On the Senate floor, despite warnings against caving in to public alarm during this "dangerous period" when people "believe the worst," the Senate accepted the $17,500 ceiling for insurance companies receiving this new form of aid from the RFC.[108] But the Senate also took a more radical step; it applied a $17,500 limit on salaries in *all* corportions receiving new or renewed loans from the RFC – a proposal that promised to have a punishing effect on railroads, mortgage companies, and banks seeking further loans.

Because assistance to the insurance industry played a relatively small role in the future growth of the RFC, Jesse Jones might well have been eager to use salary-limitation measures in that area to appease limitation sentiment and skepticism about government support of business. In any case, he was not at all pleased with the new broader Senate amendment. When the bill came to the House Banking and Currency Committee, he announced that he had conferred with President Roosevelt, who preferred a discretionary power to declare when such remuneration was unreasonable.[109] He assured committee members that he would meet their desire to scale down what he conceded to be excessive salaries. A close committee vote thus rejected a strict limit, instead accepting a provision affirming the power of the RFC (not the president) to prescribe reasonable salaries for borrowers.[110] Challengers on the House floor, who had "no confidence in the Reconstruction Finance Corporation reducing these big salaries," were beaten back.[111]

Several days later, the RFC used a loan to the Southern Pacific Railroad to establish its new policy. The agreement mandated salary cuts on a grand scale ranging from 10 to 60 percent (resulting in a top salary of $60,000).[112] Jesse Jones announced that "it will be the policy of the Corporation to impose similar conditions in all future loans to railroads or other corporations paying excessive salaries" – a prediction as extravagant

107 Robert Luce, in U.S., Congress, House, *Congressional Record*, 73d Cong., 1st sess., 1933, 77, pt. 4: 4133; Reconstruction Finance Corporation, *Seven Year Report* (n.p., 1939), p. 12.
108 U.S., Congress, Senate, *Congressional Record*, 73d Cong., 1st sess., 1933, 77, pt. 3: 2852, 2866.
109 U.S., Congress, House, *Congressional Record*, 73d Cong., 1st sess., 1933, 77, pt. 4: 4130–1.
110 Ibid., pt. 4: 4129.
111 Thomas Blanton, in ibid., pt. 4: 4127; ibid., pt. 4: 4129, 4134.
112 Minutes, vol. 16, pt. 3, 25 May 1933, pp. 1510–12, 1520, 1522, Record Group 234, Reconstruction Finance Corporation (National Archives, Washington, D.C.).

as the salaries Jones would later approve.[113] Though some congressmen were not satisfied by this token of good faith, the more lenient House version prevailed in conference committee. Thus the final law clamped a $17,500 limit on salaries of insurance companies whose stock was purchased (or used as collateral for loans) by the RFC, and it required applicants for new or renewed loans to whittle down executive compensation to "what appears reasonable to the Reconstruction Finance Corporation."[114]

This salary limitation, as a critical editorial conceded, was "clearly adapted to the dominant temper of the times."[115] But, as with so many reforms of the New Deal, particularly those involving a curbing of wealth, the effect was primarily symbolic. Much of the credit for taming this legislation belonged to the administration. During the course of congressional consideration, RFC chairman Jones had continuously maneuvered, first to focus limitation efforts solely on insurance companies, and then to make broader salary limitation discretionary, with a well-timed grandstand play on railroad salaries to impress the congressional conference committee.

The RFC was predictably lax in enforcement, though salary restrictions had already been used to firm up the finances of marginally solvent clients and to deflate receivership expenses by slashing remuneration of receivers. It did not ignore the law: Special forms were provided for listing salaries above $4,800, agency managers were required to attest to the reasonableness of salaries paid by applicants, applications from insurance companies required board-of-director resolutions freezing remuneration at $17,500 while the RFC held their stock or notes, and even old borrowers seeking discounts on loans were obliged to work out new salary agreements and to promise not to increase salaries without RFC permission.[116] But the RFC never extended the railroad-salary-reduction campaign to other areas.

Thus the administration did not distinguish itself in the effort to curb the salaries of RFC borrowers. On the other hand, the salary-limitation campaign, unlike most tax-reform efforts, did not bypass the administration.

113 "Limitation on Salaries Imposed by the R.F.C." *Railway Age* 94 (3 June 1933): 809–10.
114 *Statutes at Large*, vol. 48, pt. 1: 120.
115 *Baltimore Sun*, "R.F.C. Salary Strings," in *New York Times*, 11 June 1933, sec. 4, p. 4.
116 Loan Agency Bulletin No. 170, 24 June 1933, p. 1, and Loan Agency Bulletin No. 185, 28 July 1933, pp. 1–2; Record Group 234, Reconstruction Finance Corporation; "Provisions of Public Act 35 Authorizing Subscriptions to Preferred Stock of Insurance Companies," *Eastern Underwriter* 34 (8 Dec. 1933): 14.

The RFC's crackdown on the railroads' most generous salary paymaster, Southern Pacific, was only a first step in pruning executive compensation throughout the industry. Beginning in June, the carrot of a ½ percent reduction in RFC interest rates was used as an inducement to reduce railroad salaries. Then, in July, Joseph Eastman, the newly installed federal coordinator of transportation, called together railway leaders and urged them to sharply reduce the pay of their top corporate management. Eastman declared that the public considered top-level railroad salaries to be "excessive and unjustified," according salary limitation "a psychological importance which much exceeds its money significance." He even pressed his case on economic grounds, warning that self-perpetuating boards of directors easily developed a tendency to be overly generous in compensating their colleagues in management.[117]

Eastman's comments were warmly received outside the industry.[118] He had the railroads over a barrel, particularly because the RFC was already weeding out some of the twenty-six executives who had been paid over $60,000 as of March 1933. Declaring a personal preference for a $50,000 ceiling, Eastman settled for $60,000 in late August.[119] Railroad executives were in no position to buck the government on this hot public issue, and they fell in line.

The railway-salary cutback may have been the primary concrete accomplishment of the salary-limitation effort, but it was Franklin Roosevelt himself who catapulted this issue to the peak of its political prominence. The opportunity presented itself on 17 June 1933, with the appearance before the Pecora investigation of Albert Wiggin, the former president of the Chase Manhattan Bank. Forced to account for the continuance of his astronomical salaries during a period in which his bank was sustaining huge losses, he explained that pay decisions emerged from a cozy group in which "we all sat together" and determined each other's salary.[120] This was scandalous enough. But when he admitted that he himself had suggested his $100,000 "retirement pay," he unleashed a furious reaction from public and stockholder alike (which soon forced him to decline the pension).

117 *New York Times*, 15 July 1933, p. 6; *Commercial and Financial Chronicle* 136 (2 September 1933): 1699.
118 "The High Salaries of Railroad Executives," *Literary Digest* 116 (29 July 1933): 7.
119 L. H. Robbins, "Inquiry into High Salaries Pressed by the Government," *New York Times*, 29 October 1933, sec. 8, p. 3; "General Atterbury's Salary Reduced to $60,000 at Own Request," *Railway Age* 94 (23 September 1933): 447.
120 *New York Times*, 18 October 1933, p. 1.

The government's response was immediate. On 18 October, the day after Wiggin's testimony, the FTC announced that it had sent out salary questionnaires to interstate corporations the previous week (after sitting on the Costigan resolution for over four months).[121] The week before, Roosevelt had also begun to examine excessive salaries. Then, on 19 October, in a meeting with Attorney General Cummings that was billed as a four-star attraction, he discussed the question of salary control. Roosevelt, the newspapers explained, fully embraced the concern with excessive industrial salaries that had generated the salary investigations authorized by the Costigan resolution, and it was "understood" that this and other data would be used in the near future to formulate legislation curbing executive compensation.[122] This seemed to be an indication of a redistributive thrust on FDR's part, to "push wages up and salaries down."[123] "Shivers coursed up and down spines of highly paid executives," reported *Newsweek*.[124]

For all the hoopla, Roosevelt appears to have taken the salary issue more seriously than did most congressmen. Pecora's probe in the Senate Banking and Currency Committee had whipped up public outrage against corporate abuses, but aside from limiting salaries in government-aid programs, congressmen devoted little thought to specific remedies for exorbitant executive compensation. In contrast, Roosevelt had received an outline from Cummings on 12 October 1933 on various methods of curbing salaries, with primary emphasis on Roosevelt's bugbear, the movie industry. FDR then brought this memorandum to the attention of the NRA hierarchy.[125] Cummings also examined the salaries of insurance executives for FDR. Roosevelt forwarded this memo to RFC Chairman Jesse Jones for his response.[126]

Hopes for any salary legislation from the Executive Department were ultimately dashed. But in one area there was at least the appearance of action. Roosevelt, who was remarkably adept at squeezing the maximum symbolic impact from the minimum systemic consequence, lighted upon

121 *New York Times*, 19 October 1933, p. 1.
122 *New York Times*, 20 October 1933, p. 1; "The Federal Government and High Salaries," *Literary Digest* 116 (11 November 1933): 9.
123 *Chicago Tribune*, 20 October 1933, p. 6.
124 "Salaries: New Deal Axe Being Sharpened to Cut Big Incomes," *Newsweek* 2 (28 October 1933): 22.
125 FDR to General Johnson, 20 October 1933, "1933–34" folder, box 5, Official File 98a "Salaries 1933–1945," FDR Papers.
126 FDR to Jesse Jones, 13 November 1933, in ibid.

AT LEAST THE REST OF US MIGHT SHOW OUR SYMPATHY

Source: St. Paul *Pioneer Press* (24 October 1933): 8. Reprinted by permission of the Saint Paul *Pioneer Press*.

the salaries of movie stars.[127] He declaimed "the size of earnings of – I hate to be impolite, but immature persons who, perhaps, are making more money than is reasonable in good conscience," and he questioned "whether it is conscionable" for producers and directors to make "four or five or six or eight times the salary of the President of the United States."[128] Attorney General Cummings had suggested that the NRA codes offered the best method of curbing these salaries, though he had conceded that legal problems also made "moral suasion" a desirable recourse.[129] A revision of the motion-picture code imposed a $10,000 fine for companies offering "unreasonably excessive inducement" to employees, but the questionable legality and economics of this provision led to its immediate, and ultimately permanent, suspension.[130] That was the closest that salary restriction came to inclusion in an NRA code; in fact it was the closest that the administration came to fulfilling the pledges made in October from high atop the salary-limitation wave.

Salary Penalties

The third category of salary limitation, income-tax penalties, also received consideration from the administration. In his 12 October 1933 memorandum to Roosevelt, Cummings had broached the possibility of curbing salaries by stepping up personal income taxes or by amending the corporate income tax to disallow deductions for salaries above a certain benchmark. But these proposals got nowhere. Cummings had dismissed the personal tax hike as difficult to confine to salaries, and he noted that the restricted corporate tax deduction, at the current tax rate on profits, only represented a penalty of 13¾ percent.[131]

127 An opposite viewpoint, I suppose, also has merit. Salary limitation only zeroed in on the compensation of executives, partly because it was felt that this closed elite group had subverted the system by inflating its own salaries far beyond reason. An attack on Hollywood salaries, however, represented a clearer challenge to the system itself, for movie contracts were presumably determined by "free market" forces. Roosevelt, of course, was not rejecting capitalist principles; he merely resented flagrant demonstrations that the system produced glaring inequities.

128 Roosevelt, *Press Conferences*, 11 October 1933, 2: 324–5.

129 Homer Cummings to FDR, 12 October 1933, pp. 3, 5, "1933–34" folder, box 5, Official File 98a "Salaries 1933–45," FDR Papers.

130 "Code of Fair Competition for the Movie Industry" (#124), in U.S., National Recovery Administration, *Codes of Fair Competition*, vol. 3 (Washington: Government Printing Office, 1934): 235; Buel W. Patch, "Control of Corporate Salaries," *Editorial Research Reports* 2 (10 September 1935): 247.

131 Homer Cummings to FDR, 12 October 1933, pp. 3–4, "1933–34" folder, box 5, Official File 98a "Salaries 1933–45," FDR Papers. Actually, Cummings com-

The real push to use taxation for salary limitation came from Congress. In a last-minute addition to its report on the 1932 Revenue Act, the Senate Finance Committee subjected compensation in excess of $75,000 to a special personal tax rate of 80 percent and provided that such excesses would not be deductible as business expenses in calculating corporate tax liabilities. The committee declared "that the large amounts of compensation, particularly in the form of bonuses, emoluments, and rewards frequently paid to the officials of corporations are greatly in excess of reasonable compensation for the services actually performed."[132]

This attempt to curb extravagant salaries through taxation was quashed in conference committee, but it did not die there. In drawing up the reform package that formed the basis of the Revenue Act of 1934, the Ways and Means investigatory subcommittee "debated at length the amount of deduction allowed a corporation on account of salary or other compensation received by any officer of the corporation." But despite "numerous examples of excessive officers' salaries," the subcommittee declined action, claiming that such a change would reduce total revenue yield (since the corporate tax rate, even in addition to the tax paid by individuals on an increase in dividends, fell far below the personal surtax on mammoth salaries).[133] Despite the protest of the American Farm Bureau Federation that "general social and economic benefit" rather than revenue justified

---

mitted the grievous error of claiming a 13½% corporate-tax rate.

Further administration involvement in salary limitation also deserves mention. The administration-sponsored Securities Act of 1933 prescribed a salary list for the registration statement for stock issues, but this was added in Senate committee at the suggestion of the chairman. The required salary information in the Securities and Exchange Act of 1934, however, derived from the administration's Corcoran draft. Also, the Treasury disallowed certain corporate deductions of salaries as "unreasonable" (based on a provision that has been on the books since 1918). This, however, was and is standard procedure, and its narrow application should be recognized. Though thinly veiled gifts have sporadically been disallowed, this provision was not a weapon to curb executive compensation per se; the courts would not permit that. Instead, the Treasury during the New Deal, as at other times, primarily used this provision to combat tax evasion by closely held corporations that tried to attain a business deduction by paying stockholders large salaries and bonuses in lieu of dividends. Washington and Rothschild, *Compensating* 2: 758–73.

132 U.S., Congress, Senate, Committee on Finance, *Revenue Bill of 1932*, S. Rept. 665 to Accompany H.R. 10236, 72d Cong., 1st sess., 1932, pp. 13–14.

133 U.S., Congress, House, Committee on Ways and Means, *Prevention of Tax Avoidance, Preliminary Report*, by Subcommittee of the Committee on Ways and Means, House Committee Print, 73d Cong., 2d sess., 1933, p. 2.

such salary penalties, the House went along.[134] In the Senate, however, Kenneth McKellar (D–Tenn.) put forward an amendment to bar corporate deductions for salaries over $50,000. Again the revenue argument prevailed over the desire to counteract "innumerable scandals about the high salaries paid corporation officers."[135] Protests over lavish salaries were an excellent outlet for frustration over economic failure, but the legislative returns from the salary-limitation effort were paltry. Unlike other apparent dead ends, it had a revival in 1942–3, when FDR vainly tried to limit annual salaries to $25,000 after taxes, under the flag of equalization of war sacrifices. But like other dead ends, it has vanished from the historical picture of the New Deal. That is unfortunate, for it obscures the key place of the villainous rich in the New Deal tax philosophy.

Conclusion

Except for a foray into salary limitation (enough to storm the front pages and the magazines, but not enough to have any substantive effect outside the railroad industry), Franklin Roosevelt had held back from the more advanced ranks of the soak-the-rich campaign in the early New Deal. It was Congress that played to the grandstand with investigations, publicity, salary ceilings for government aid programs, elimination of certain business-tax deductions, and rhetorical demands that the opulent too join in tax sacrifices; all these measures had a symbolic impact that far surpassed the limited effect on overall distribution of wealth. FDR never publicly opposed such efforts, but rarely did he endorse them. However trampled the reputation of business, he still relied on business collaboration to secure recovery. Not only was the ethos of collaboration inherent in the NRA, but FDR had painted himself into a corner in terms of his economic objectives. Historian John Braeman has noted that FDR's commitment to saving the capitalist system, combined with his rejection of such alternate mechanisms for expansion as full-scale national planning or bold coun-tercyclical government spending, mandated the avoidance of measures

---

134 Chester Gray, in U.S., Congress, House, Committee on Ways and Means, *Revenue Revision, 1934, Hearings*, p. 200.
135 Kenneth McKellar, in U.S., Congress, Senate, *Congressional Record*, 73d Cong., 2d sess., 1934, 78, pt. 6: 6243. Upon the release of the FTC's salary study, Thomas Gore also revived the salary-restriction amendments that he had guided through the Finance Committee and the Senate in 1932. U.S., Congress, Senate, *Congressional Record*, 73d Cong., 2d sess., 1934, 78, pt. 3: 3371.

that might further depress the "business confidence" needed for self-generated recovery.[136]

This task of bolstering confidence was a delicate one, however. Businessmen could take alarm over the most minor of rhetorical challenges or tax changes. They were a community in search of an excuse; in July 1934, the U.S. Chamber of Commerce's *Nation's Business* had wailed that with the muckraking of business it was no wonder "that commerce and industry, so misrepresented, preached at, blamed for every shortcoming of human nature, have failed to respond, when the principal factor in such response lies in the faith and confidence of the people themselves in the very institutions and processes to which they look for recovery."[137] Until 1935, Roosevelt generally refrained from providing this excuse. But then, when business cooperation proved chimerical and when the threat from his left seemed greatest, Roosevelt proved that he could vilify concentrated wealth with the best of them. In its own "reform" efforts, Congress had shown that this was what the public demanded.

136 John Braeman, "The New Deal and the 'Broker State': A Review of the Recent Scholarly Literature," *Business History Review* 46 (Winter 1972): 428.
137 "Through the Editor's Specs," *Nation's Business* 22 (July 1934): 7.

Part II

One Part Revenue, Two Parts Rhetoric: The Reform Impulse in the Ascendant, 1935–1937

Prior to 1935, even a blind partisan of the New Deal would have had difficulty making the case that Franklin Roosevelt had used the tax system to redistribute income toward the forgotten man. Falling incomes and new taxes had saddled the New Deal with an inequitable revenue system that relied less on direct taxation (taxes assessed on individual or corporate income or wealth) than at any time since World War I. Yet in its first two years, the New Deal redistributive tax machine operated in reverse; alcohol tax collections, processing taxes, and renewed manufacturers' excise taxes were its primary contribution to the revenue structure, and social security taxes were on the way. When a revenue package had to stand on its own rather than hide under the skirts of a more important recovery or reform measure, Roosevelt was less inclined to shift the tax burden to the poor. Even so, the primary antiplutocrat emphasis of the NIRA taxes and the Revenue Act of 1934 came at Congress's instigation.

If the tax policy of the first two-plus years of FDR's presidency seems at odds with the traditional image of New Deal concern for the forgotten man, the tax policy of the next two-plus years carves out a more positive image. The so-called Wealth Tax, the Revenue Act of 1935, dominates the scene. It hoisted the top personal income-tax rate from 63 to 79 percent, graduated the corporate income tax to penalize big corporations, and boosted estate taxes.[1] Continuing this reformist

---

1 Whenever possible, I have combined the normal tax and the surtax in income-tax statistics. Everyone owing a personal income tax paid the normal tax rate; higher incomes paid graduated surtaxes in addition. For the Revenue Act of 1935, the normal tax rate was 4%, and surtaxes ranged from 4% on net incomes of $4,000–$6,000 to 75% on net incomes over $5 million. The use of these separate taxes was anachronistic. It harked back to the pre–World War I income tax, when there was still hope that a flat tax would facilitate collection-at-the-source as in Britain, and when, as in the British system, the normal tax and corporation tax were set at identical rates, so that the exemption of dividends from normal taxation would fend off double taxation of corporate profits.

Though I cannot afford to become enmeshed in technical jargon, one other definitional point should be broached. Figures delimiting income-tax brackets are taxable net individual incomes (as used here, this equals gross income minus

91

thrust was the Revenue Act of 1936, which introduced a tax penalty on corporations that retained profits rather than distributing them as dividends, and the Revenue Act of 1937, which closed tax loopholes for individuals. This section examines each of these laws. As a structural or redistributive reform, it turns out, only the 1936 Revenue Act is of any importance. But taxation was one of the nation's paramount political concerns. Perhaps no other issue so clearly revealed the nature of interest-group conflict and the transformation of political tactics, priorities, and coalitions in the mid-1930s.

Historians cannot be accused of ignoring the political significance of taxation in the 1930s. Yet the emphasis is sometimes misplaced. Though historians today are well aware of the limits of Franklin Roosevelt's commitment to structural economic change, even someone as discerning as John Blum leads in the wrong direction in his conclusion that "Roosevelt meant to soak the rich to help the poor" through his 1935–7 tax-reform surge.[2] This formulation reflects the crucial problem of the 1930s. By only "soaking" the rich, and the very rich at that (allowing the slightly less affluent to enjoy low tax rates on incomes that cumulatively were considerable), Franklin Roosevelt's fleeting onslaughts against "economic royalists" produced minimal revenues and thus were of negligible assistance in redistributing income to the nation's poor.

New Deal taxation in 1935–7 thus offers an opportunity to better define the limits of Franklin Roosevelt's commitment to a more equitable income distribution. Even more importantly, these limits are themselves the product of a political process and an image that tax policy was designed to project. It is that process to which we now turn.

> the total of exemptions and deductions). This is the figure used in arriving at the income subject to surtax; for the 4% normal tax, a special credit was also allowed for "earned" income. This becomes complicated, for before 1934 the personal exemption and the credit for dependents were not deductible in calculating the surtax – a fact best disregarded.
>
> 2 John M. Blum, " 'That Kind of a Liberal': Franklin D. Roosevelt after Twenty-five Years," *Yale Review* 60 (October 1970): 17.

3. The Paradox of Symbolic Reform: Enacting a Wealth Tax without Sharing the Wealth

Only one piece of New Deal legislation, the Revenue Act of 1935, made even a pretense of using personal income taxation to redistribute wealth. Yet even this tax package collected too little revenue to supply any significant relief to the "forgotten man"; the administration itself predicted an added annual revenue yield of only $250 million, a mere $45 million of which derived from the personal income-tax increase for the over-$50,000 brackets.[1]

To understand why the 1935 Revenue Act was so financially insignificant, one must move beyond current historical explanations (most prominently, the misguided claim that Congress diluted Roosevelt's original proposals) to examine the economic and social environment that prevented the income tax from collecting more money. Our perceptions of income levels are distorted by Depression-wracked earnings and by prices under a seventh of today's. Even by a generous accounting, 38 percent of families had incomes lower than $1,000 in the 1930s, 74 percent earned under $2,000, less than 10 percent received as much as $3,200 (the minimum subject to income tax for a couple with one child), and 1 percent drew over

---

1 Historians today are well aware of the limits of the New Deal's redistributive efforts. No analysis of the New Deal is complete without reference to the sluggish income- and wealth-distribution statistics of the New Deal years. The richest 1% accounted for roughly an eighth of personal income (almost as much as the total share of the poorest 40%), and the top 5% received a bit over one-quarter. Though these figures had declined in 1929–33, and plunged again during World War II, they stabilized during the New Deal. Wealth concentration showed a similar pattern, though the figures did register a slight increase betwen 1933 and 1939 in the share held by the top 1% of adults (from 28.3% of personal wealth to 30.6%). U.S., Department of Commerce, Bureau of the Census, *Historical Statistics of the United States, Colonial Times to 1970* (Washington, D.C.: Government Printing Office, 1975), pp. 301–2 (hereafter cited as Census, *Historical Statistics*); Robert J. Lampman, *The Share of Top Wealth-Holders in National Wealth, 1922–1956* (Princeton, N.J.: Princeton University Press, 1962), p. 24.

  These statistics are less damning than they appear. Especially in a time of economic flux, broader economic forces – rather than a federal-government sector that, until World War II, never captured as much as a tenth of the national income – tend to be the dominant determinants of the way income is distributed.

93

$10,000. In 1982, 5 percent of American households pulled in over $60,000; in the 1930s, the cutoff point for the top 5 percent came at less than $4,000.[2]

Superimposed on this income distribution was a misleading social self-conception, which must be examined in order to avoid confusion. In a 1939 poll, 88 percent of Americans located themselves in the middle "social" class, not a surprising figure in itself. When asked for a self-definition in terms of "income class," the drop-off was less than might be expected. Two-thirds chose middle and 1 percent classified themselves as upper class, while only 31 percent conceded that they belonged to the "lower" income class.[3]

The first point to recognize is that, although Americans stubbornly placed themselves in the middle of any "class" spectrum, they still suffered a gnawing sense of deprivation at the widening gap between achievement and expectation. Assessing the depth of need in the world's richest country was a hazardous process; one study makes the dubious claim that wages above $1,000 in the 1930s denoted a "middle-income family" possessing "a fairly comfortable standard of living." But by the definition of the time, there were minimal social standards that were not being met. Welfare department estimates placed the minimum "subsistence" or "adequacy" budget at roughly $800–$1,300 for a family of four. Public-opinion polls, probing for the somewhat more exacting standard of the minimum required to live "decently," or in "health and comfort," set the figure at $1,500–$2,000. Most commonly bandied about was the Brookings Institution's postulate that the minimum income required for a family's "basic necessities" was $2,000 – a level beyond the reach of most Americans in the 1930s.[4]

2 Census, *Historical Statistics*, p. 299; U.S., Bureau of Census, Current Population Reports, Series P-60, No. 142, *Money Incomes of Households, Families, and Persons in the United States: 1982* (Washington, D.C.: Government Printing Office, 1984), p. 16. These 1930s income figures would have been lower had they excluded nonmoney income (such as home-grown food or the rental value of a home). The data I cite from *Historical Statistics* are a revision of the National Resources Committee's Consumer Purchases Study for 1935–6. The unrevised figures, still occasionally used, would show even lower income levels. Note: A $3,200 income would be wiped out by the exemption for the couple ($2,500) and the child ($400) plus the 10% earned-income credit (at least $300, because the first $3,000 of income was assumed to be earned).

3 George H. Gallup, *The Gallup Poll: Public Opinion 1935–1971*, vol. 1 (New York: Random House, 1972), p. 148.

4 Winifred D. Wandersee Bolin. "The Economics of Middle-Income Family Life: Working Women During the Great Depression," *Journal of American History* 65 (June 1978): 63–4; Oscar Ornati, *Poverty Amid Affluence* (New York: Twentieth

Americans, therefore, do not appear to have seen any inconsistency in defining themselves as middle class when their living standard fell below a "decent" income level. Aspiration replaced concrete circumstance as a guideline to class status. As a result, there was a discrepancy between class self-identification and the perception of economic adequacy. But there was an even greater discrepancy between the income levels of those who defined themselves as middle class and the income levels that were deemed middle class in political parlance. Indeed, for political purposes, the middle and upper classes were often defined to encompass an astonishingly small proportion of the population. Stripping these terms of any generic meaning, the middle class was reduced to an idealized picture of independence, stability, and comfort – a pernicious attitude because taxes lacked a certain legitimacy until that level had been reached. Huey Long mourned the withering away of the middle class and stated that 96 percent of Americans fell below the poverty line. The upper middle class was delimited by a business analyst at $10,000 – $50,000. One economist even seemed to define middle class as those earning between $5,000 and $500,000, whereas the "wealthy" drew incomes above this. When this loose terminology was superimposed on the myopia of those more affluent Americans who determined political decisions or actively lobbied for them, the debate could become rather parochial. One witness unselfconsciously explained that "while an income of $10,000 may seem a large amount in small towns, in the larger cities ... the widow with children will find careful planning necessary for comfortable living and educational advantages." Even Franklin Roosevelt, perhaps as deserving of the term "patrician president" as anyone in our history, could unblushingly include himself with the reporters at his press conference in talking of "comparatively poor people like us."[5]

These differing political, sociological, and economic conceptions of what it meant to be middle class forged a crucial ideological chain in the tax philosophy. Identifying themselves as middle class, Americans were

Century Fund, 1966), p. 148; Hadley Cantril, ed., *Public Opinion 1935–1946* (Princeton, N.J.: Princeton University Press, 1951), pp. 138, 140; Maurice Levin, Harold G. Moulton, and Clark Warburton, *America's Capacity to Consume* (Washington, D.C.: Brookings Institution, 1934), p. 56.

5 Huey Long, letter, in U.S., Congress, Senate, *Congressional Record*, 74th Cong., 1st sess., 1935, 79, pt. 7: 8041; *Kiplinger Washington Letter*, 1 February 1936, p. 3; Maxine Yaple, "The Burden of Direct Taxes as Paid by Income Classes," *American Economic Review* 26 (December 1936): 709; Franklin D. Roosevelt, *Complete Presidential Press Conferences* (New York: Da Capo Press, 1972), 4 January 1939, 13: 35.

all too easily able to respond to the plight of others who could effectively lay claim to that status, including the rarefied middle class often championed in political debate. Given a willingness to pay fealty to middle-class aspirations, the $15,000-a-year man in the top 1 percent income bracket could wear his middle-class status like political armor; in it, he could merge with the agglutinous "us" – the mass of the people – to become a victim rather than a specially privileged predator. He was thus immunized from contributing to efforts to redistribute income away from the special interests. The elastic conception of the middle class, then, was more than a curiosity; it was a crippling constraint on meaningful tax reform.

Sympathy for the poverty of all but the super-rich informed the income-tax system. Between 1933 and 1939, 2½ – 5 percent of the population (as compared to well over half since World War II) was included on taxed income returns, due mainly to high personal exemptions ($1,000 for single individuals, $2,500 for married couples, and $400 deducted for each dependent). Even in the Depression, members of this upper crust were not just scraping by; a family unlucky enough to owe income tax was usually affluent enough to hire household help or to add to savings. The ratio of income-tax collections to personal income stood at about 1 percent (today's level is roughly 12 percent). Approximately 6–7 percent of the income tax between 1933 and 1939 was paid by the 33–61 returns reporting net incomes exceeding $1 million, whereas over half was usually collected from the 8,000–18,000 households reporting net incomes over $50,000.[6]

Although a vague "ability to pay" criterion enjoyed wide theoretical acceptance, its impact upon the overall taxation scheme was slight. The middle class and lower upper class were secure enough in the driver's seat to be exempted from this standard. The maximum conceivable federal income tax (assuming no deductions and the worst possible mix of salary versus other income – otherwise, payments would have been far lower)

6 Lawrence H. Seltzer, *The Personal Exemptions in the Income Tax* (New York: Columbia University Press for the National Bureau of Economic Research, 1968), p. 62; Richard Goode, *The Individual Income Tax*, rev. ed., (Washington, D.C.: Brookings Institution, 1976), pp. 4, 302; U.S., Department of Labor, Bureau of Labor Statistics, *Family Expenditures in Selected Cities, 1935–36* (Washington, D.C.: Government Printing Office, 1941), 1: 303–52; Joseph A. Pechman, *Federal Tax Policy*, 4th ed. (Washington, D.C.: Brookings Institution, 1983), pp. 60–1; U.S., Treasury Department, Bureau of Internal Revenue, *Statistics of Income for 1942*, pt. 1 (Washington, D.C.: Government Printing Office, 1945), pp. 232, 238, 239.

on a $4,000 income received by a couple with two children was $16. Even if that same family received $12,000 (placing it in the richest 1 percent), it owed less than one-twentieth of that amount in taxes. Because the exemption for singles was so much lower, their tax bite was deeper – but not much. A bachelor's $1,500 income (placing him in the twentieth income percentile for singles) subjected him to an income tax of no more than $14, whereas tax collectors soaked his $4,000 income (the second percentile for singles) for less than $108. Wealthier groups had a greater ability to pay than poorer citizens, but they also had a greater ability and opportunity to avoid payment. Higher tax rates for the top 1 percent became a veil for the favored treatment of the relatively affluent.

This soak-the-rich fallacy, once placed in its political context, provides a framework within which the Revenue Act of 1935 may be understood. To facilitate the development of such a framework, this chapter will begin with the identification of two competing approaches in tax-reform politics: the popularly and historically grounded soak-the-rich philosophy and a more comprehensively redistributive approach. It will be seen that Roosevelt's 1935 tax proposal has greater affinities with the former. Following this inquiry into the economic assumptions of the Wealth Tax, an additional reinforcing dimension will be added. This dimension is the broader political context, encompassing the shift in 1935 toward a politics of polarization that targeted the same overprivileged enemies as the soak-the-rich tradition. With this background, it will then be possible to turn to the specific development of the 1935 Revenue Act and the controversies surrounding it.

Redistributive Taxation: The Alternatives

To grasp the basic economic realities of the New Deal tax system, it is important to appreciate the theoretical underpinnings of the tax-reform position. This task appears deceptively simple. After one cuts through the obligatory cliches about taxing according to "ability to pay," one common theme rises to unite the diverse groups on the "left" in the 1930s: a fixation on "our fundamental malady, the maldistribution of wealth and income."[7] Taxes, the most direct means of righting this imbalance, thus held an honored place in the left's gallery of panaceas. The inherent inequities of capitalism naturally excited opposition; taxes could respond

7 Benjamin Stolberg and Warren J. Vinton, *The Economic Consequences of the New Deal* (New York: Harcourt, Brace, 1935), p. 73.

to this discontent without altering the mode of production. From Henry George's demand in 1883 for a "radical" solution to the distribution of wealth (which he placed at the center of the nation's "political and social problems") to Stuart Chase's advocacy in 1932 of "drastic redistribution of the national income through income and inheritance taxes," the drumbeat of protest continued.[8]

Only in the 1930s, with the evaporation of the lure of rising production, did such concerns become preeminent. Impelled by a nagging concern or reasoned "belief that the depression was permanent," many felt that the returns from harnessing and more equitably distributing existing economic resources could dwarf benefits from attempting to replicate past investment and expansion.[9] The frequent solution was simple: Take from the rich and give to everybody else.

Despite this theoretical imperative, taxation had been a trivial component of New Deal legislation before mid-1935. Opposition to Roosevelt's slighting of tax reform was thus intense – so intense that it has obscured a fundamental difference among the tax reformers themselves. One man's redistribution, it turns out, was another man's tokenism.

On one side were the carriers of the populist-progressive soak-the-rich tradition that had shaped the tax system so decisively in the past. Soak-the-rich initiatives had long derived strength from the classic American concern with "opportunity." This had a redistributive component, but a strictly limited one. It has been capsulized in Theodore Roosevelt's dictum that "we stand for equality of opportunity, but not for equality of reward." "We must set our faces against privilege," he argued in 1909, "just as much against the kind of privilege which would let the shiftless and lazy laborer take what his brother has earned as against the privilege which allows the huge capitalist to take toll to which he is not entitled."[10] Grounded in this outlook was the prescription that freer opportunity required taxes on the rich. These taxes could unblock the highways of mobility, mitigating the class rigidification brought about by the restraining impact of great fortunes. At the same time, however, any more comprehensive program of redistribution was suspect, for it would unfairly confiscate earnings from some of the people to give special privilege to others.

8 R. Alan Lawson, *The Failure of Independent Liberalism 1930–1941* (New York: Putnam, 1971), pp. 22, 82.

9 Upton Sinclair, *We, People of America, and How We Ended Poverty* (Pasadena, Calif.: National End Poverty in California League, 1936), p. 12.

10 Theodore Roosevelt, "Socialism," *Outlook* 91 (27 March 1909): 664.

Such themes still resonated in the 1930s. The widely recognized need for more direct aid to the Depression's impoverished had attenuated this circumscribed conception of redistribution but did not transcend it. The economic crisis had only intensified the symbolic value of taxation, turning the desire to penalize the rich into an urge to exact retribution from them. The "opportunity" theme had somewhat less prominence, but could readily be found in FDR's Wealth Tax address (in fact, he quoted his cousin Theodore on the subject) or in the statement of one supporter of Roosevelt's inheritance-tax proposal that its purpose was "only secondarily to relieve financial dynasties of the burden of riches" – "its primary purpose is to increase economic opportunities for the millions of young men and women reared under more modest circumstances."[11]

This intention, however, was not all encompassing. Even in developing the argument that "the redistribution of wealth is a necessity if we wish to preserve our civilization," Senator Norris hastened to explain that "this does not mean we should take the property of A and give it to B." "It only means," he went on, "the taking of money from the estates of the very wealthy" and giving it "to all the people, from whom it was originally taken."[12] On its face, this is a disingenuous formulation; A's property, after all, does end up in the hands of all the Bs. But A, the representative of the few plutocrats, is not really a part of "our civilization." He is an interloper, who drains the community of its resources and blocks normal channels of opportunity.[13] Leveling off the apex of the wealth pyramid thus only returns things to a more natural state. The idea that "redistribution of wealth" might require the government to take from the corner grocer to give to his happy-go-lucky delivery boy was foreign to this classic "people-versus-the-interests" viewpoint. By thus subdividing the indivisible "people," the government would only have been imposing another form of oppression on them.

This view dominated the tax-reform thrust. But on the other side, perched upon a much scantier popular base, was a group with a broader

11 Samuel I. Rosenman, comp., *The Public Papers and Addresses of Franklin D. Roosevelt,* 4 (New York: Random House, 1938): 273 (19 June 1935) (hereafter cited as *Addresses of FDR); New York World-Telegram,* 21 June 1935, p. 22; "Taxation: Federal, Printed Matter, News Clippings" folder, box 185, Felix Frankfurter Papers (Library of Congress, Washington, D.C.).

12 U.S., Congress, Senate, *Congressional Record,* 74th Cong., 1st sess., 1935, 79, pt. 2:2181.

13 This mindset – especially the notion of defending "the independence of the community against encroachments" (p. xi) – has been most systematically analyzed in Alan Brinkley's *Voices of Protest* (New York: Knopf, 1982), esp. pp. 143–68.

commitment to income redistribution. For the government to benefit the poor, they argued, it would have to move beyond the mountainous holdings of the outrageously rich (the wealthy elite could not have agreed more, which accorded such proposals a sympathetic hearing that the lack of popular support would not otherwise have permitted). Full of their own altruism, the affluent middle-class cadre of intellectuals who spearheaded redistributive tax plans readily conceded that they themselves were woefully undertaxed. The lower ranges of the income tax would have to be beefed up to put sufficient monies at the government's disposal.

Though not as neat as a historian might wish, this division is critical to understanding the left in the 1930s. Huey Long, William Borah, the Union Party, Miles Reno's Farmers' Holiday Association, and other soak-the-richers had little tolerance for the "college professor" mentality of the intellectual left.[14] The intellectual left, in turn, held many of their populist counterparts in contempt. The *New Republic* dismissed the Every Man a King plan as the economics of "a naive utopian" and depicted Long as a "clever, unscrupulous and ruthless politician," who used empty promises to play "upon the emotions of the rabble."[15] Benjamin Marsh of the People's Lobby challenged Long to propose a true revenue-raising tax package "instead of bamboozling the masses of innocents."[16] As of 1935, this branch of the left – often young, usually college educated, and always earnest – berated Long, Coughlin, and their ilk as incipient fascists. Unless one recognizes this mutual antagonism and discards the assumption that the left was monolithic on taxes, New Deal tax politics cannot be put in proper perspective.

Soaking the Rich

Never at a loss for words, Huey Long had a ready retort to the charge that he had failed to introduce a Share Our Wealth plan in his home state: "There are no big fortunes in Louisiana."[17] Huey Long was often outrageous, but he was never stupid. In confining the victims of tax reform to freaks and outlanders, he was appealing to a popular prejudice against

14 Monetary Committee of the National Farmers' Holiday Association, "Another Professor Speaks Out," *Plain Talk* 12 (November 1935): 33.

15 "Huey Proposes," *New Republic* 82 (20 March 1935): 147.

16 "People's Lobby in Challenge to Sen. Long on Taxation," *Progressive* 4 (20 July 1935): 1.

17 U. S., Congress, Senate, *Congressional Record*, 74th Cong., 1st sess., 1935, 79, pt. 9:9909.

villainous plutocrats. Franklin Roosevelt himself could smugly assert his firm belief that "I don't think people ought to be *too* rich" or could casually argue that fortunes as great as Henry Ford's "should be abolished."[18] Louis Brandeis, as midwife of the deconcentration philosophy, put top priority on taxes to cut down the economic and political power of the "super-rich."[19] Other Americans blamed their current depressed condition on the "uncalled for and useless accumulation of wealth in high places," agreeing with George Norris that "the control by a few men of untold millions of property" had "brought starvation and misery into the land."[20]

Thus myriad tax proposals focused on the "filthy rich." Huey Long's Share Our Wealth plan, for example, would not have touched the first million dollars of a family's fortune.[21] Father Coughlin, the Farmers' Holiday Association, the editors of *Common Sense*, and numerous others sought taxes that would put an absolute ceiling on wealth or income.[22]

Of course, it was easier to suggest confiscatory tax plans than to implement them. Public opinion polls in 1935–7 indicated that most Americans opposed limits on the amount of money one could inherit, though a substantial minority favored a ceiling on private fortunes (generally of 1 million dollars or more). By 1939, as the business-tax message reached new heights of persuasiveness, the public rejected by a wide margin the suggestion that heavy taxes on the rich or confiscation of all wealth above "what people actually need to live on" be used to redistribute wealth. The notion of "taking money from those who have much and giving money to those who have little" commanded majority assent except among the prosperous, but the public kept a tight rein on the application of this principle.[23]

One point seemed clear: Tolerance for income redistribution evaporated as the taxed income brackets approached a level to which one might

18 Frances Perkins, *The Roosevelt I Knew* (New York: Harper & Row, 1946), p. 124; Thomas H. Eliot to Frances Hopkinson Eliot, 10 June 1934, "Thomas Eliot's letters to his parents 1933–1937" folder, series 1, Thomas H. Eliot Papers (Washington University Archives, St. Louis) (Used by permission of the author).

19 Bruce A. Murphy, *The Brandeis/Frankfurter Connection* (New York: Oxford University Press, 1982), pp. 105, 159.

20 William J. Engle to George Norris, 22 March 1935, folder 6-F, tray 6, box 5, George W. Norris Papers (Library of Congress); *New York Times*, 16 February 1935, p. 14.

21 Huey P. Long, "Share Our Wealth is Coming," *American Progress* 2 (April 1935): 1.

22 Mark H. Leff, "The New Deal and Taxation, 1933–1939: The Limits of Symbolic Reform" (Ph.D. diss., University of Chicago, 1978), pp. 174–5.

23 Cantril, ed., *Public Opinion*, pp. 1040–1.

aspire. The striking common ground of most radical tax plans was the exemption of 99 percent of the population from increased income taxes.[24] For most Americans, redistribution of wealth meant deconcentration of wealth. Fostered in some cases by the desire to alienate as few people as possible, the progressive tradition of income taxation still flourished on the left. International practice to the contrary, the income tax remained a tool to extract revenue from abnormally high incomes.

The "Intellectual" Alternative: Broadening the Tax Base

An alternative, one that would have invigorated the income tax by building up its base rather than by decorating its summit, did exist. It is a forgotten New Deal alternative, partly because Franklin Roosevelt – both an exploiter and a partisan of the soak-the-rich tradition – variously chose to ignore or suppress it. Yet it had a strong ideological base, and it remained a live political issue throughout the New Deal, ultimately to triumph under entirely different circumstances in World War II. To a sizable slice of what might be called the "intellectual left" – liberal economists, journals of progressive opinion, "public interest" (read middle class) lobbies – tax broadening seemed a fiscally responsible way to extend government services and to redistribute a significant share of the national income. This section will examine these tax objectives and then follow the winding legislative history of the effort to implement them.

The campaign to broaden the tax base by slicing exemptions and/or raising taxes on the lower brackets was founded on a central precept of the left: "What we need is a new distribution of wealth – and a mighty radical one."[25] Advocates of redistributive taxation parted company with

24 Speakers on the left commonly contended that 1% of adults owned 59% of the wealth (double the best estimate available today), and that 4% owned at least 80 or 87% of the wealth. Although the reputable and reasonably accurate Brookings Institution study of the 1929 income distribution should have tempered this claim, the estimation of wealth distribution was a rudimentary art. This left the door open for advocates to select figures that suited their purposes. They commonly chose the succulently high concentration statistics in a 1926 Federal Trade Commission study based on probate records in 24 countries between 1912 and 1923. The legitimacy of outdated figures was enhanced by the assumption that the Crash had accentuated concentration; actually, the reverse was the case. Lampman, *Share of Top Wealth-Holders*, p. 202; and U.S., Federal Trade Commission, *National Wealth and Income* (Washington, D.C.: Government Printing Office, 1926), p. 58.
25 Clarence Darrow, quoted in *Progressive*, 30 March 1935, p. 2.

their populist counterparts in their belief that soaking the rich was a narrow, inadequate, and unsystematic solution. John Flynn, the *New Republic* financial columnist whose isolationism would later lead him into the radical right, saw the political process as mired in inconsequential issues:

> One of them wants to throw a teacup of water on the blaze, and the other thinks he shouldn't do it. I can't help asking – what difference does it make which one wins the argument? I think it would be a very good idea if these gentlemen down in Congress would put their teacups away and start getting out the hose.[26]

Thus, Flynn urged, if one were to balance the budget and bring about "a more intelligent distribution of income," "just soaking the rich" was not enough. No fan of regressive hidden taxes, Flynn supported Senator La Follette's program to expand the income-tax pool and to raise rates on the subplutocrats. Income taxes would have to "soak everybody," starting with the lowest exemptions feasible.[27]

Others on the left touched a bit more lightly on fiscal integrity, but they made similar points. Seeing tax reform as a prerequisite to national survival, the *Nation* chastised Roosevelt for not taking "hold of taxation as the best tool with which to rebuild society."[28] In 1935, the journal advanced a program of lower income-tax exemptions; stiffer levies on personal incomes, corporations, and inheritances; and a phaseout of virtually all indirect taxes.[29] In supporting La Follette's tax-reform package, it rejected the notion that lower income-tax exemptions taxed the poor. Given the income distribution, it pointed out, income-tax payers were "a favored few."[30] Interestingly, by 1937, when much of the right had come to embrace lower income-tax exemptions, the *Nation* had soured on this idea. Still, it continued to reject soak-the-rich precepts. The very rich, it noted, "pay a reasonably fair share of the total taxes, but the moderately

---

26 Frank H. Buck, John T. Flynn, and Allen T. Treadway, "Let's Face the Tax Problem," *Town Meeting*, bulletin of America's Town Meeting of the Air 2 (23 April 1936): 18.

27 Wright Patman, Merryle S. Rukeyser, and John T. Flynn, "Which Way Out– Inflation or Taxes," *Town Meeting*, bulletin of America's Town Meeting of the Air 2 (20 February 1936): 28, 23; Frank H. Buck, John T. Flynn, and Allen T. Treadway, "Let's Face the Tax Problem," *Town Meeting*, bulletin of Americas Town Meeting of the Air 2 (23 April 1936): 18, 23; "Mr. Flynn Discusses Bob's Tax Plan," *Progressive* 4 (16 May 1936): 8.

28 "Mr. President, Begin to Tax!" *Nation* 140 (6 March 1935): 264; "Wanted: A Philosophy of Taxation." *Nation* 141 (3 July 1935): 4.

29 "Mr. President, Begin to Tax!" *Nation* 140 (6 March 1935): 264.

30 "Editorial Paragraphs," *Nation* 141 (21 August 1935): 197.

well-to-do get off more lightly than in any other country."[31] Thus, to soak up excess savings that would otherwise remain outside the investment or consumption streams, the *Nation* keyed on higher taxation for the "middle brackets," variously defined as $4,000 to $75,000, or $5,000 to $100,000.[32]

Of all the groups that put forward redistributive tax plans, the People's Lobby was the most enthusiastic and persistent. It is difficult, though, to know how seriously to take it. Boasting a small, largely middle-class membership of a little over 2,000; hawking a program of "elimination of profit" through a variation of Henry George's land tax and an eventual government takeover of essential industries; operated on a wealthy woman's shoestring; and dominated by a freewheeling abrasive professional gadfly – Benjamin Marsh – who used his reform pipeline to the Roosevelt administration to accuse it of "handing out ballyhoo and blah to the American people"; this group nevertheless cranked up an efficient publicity machine for redistributive taxation.[33] From Roosevelt's entrance into the presidency, correspondents John Dewey (the lobby's president until 1936) and Benjamin Marsh (its executive secretary) chided him that no extant or pending legislation could significantly combat the Depression unless the tax system were changed "to achieve an adequate, equitable distribution

---

31 "Ripe for Taxation," *Nation* 145 (6 November 1937): 494. Such reference to foreign tax practices was common. Part of the impetus for tax reform was the desire to modernize the U.S. tax system, to bring it up to foreign standards. Even after a much-trumpeted and envied reduction in Britain's lower income-tax brackets in the spring of 1935 (and even though Britain was less inclined to tax middle or lower incomes and more inclined to tax giant ones than, say, France or Germany), Britain still imposed far heavier taxes than the U.S. on incomes below $100,000. Though one suspects that British statistics were used more as a foil than as a model, they figured prominently in the arguments of La Follette and others. Vito Marcantonio, the radical congressman from New York, even proposed to put teeth in the 1935 Revenue Act by substituting the British rates on inheritances, corporate profits, and incomes above $5,000. Alan Schaffer, *Vito Marcantonio, Radical in Congress* (Syracuse, N.Y.: Syracuse University Press, 1966), p. 37; U.S., Congress, House, *Congressional Record*, 74th Cong., 1st sess., 1935, 79, pt. 11: 12403.

32 "Who Should Pay Taxes," *Nation* 144 (15 May 1937): 552–3; "Ripe for Taxation," *Nation* 145 (6 November 1937): 494.

33 "Report of Benjamin C. Marsh, Executive Secretary for 1938," and "Report of the Executive Secretary to Annual Meeting, People's Lobby, Inc., Jan. 4, 1937," in Minutes of the Meeting of Stockholders and Directors of The People's Lobby, Inc., Benjamin C. Marsh Papers (Library of Congress); "Program," *People's Lobby Bulletin* 5 (June 1935): 2; "Redistribution of Income Now," *People's Lobby Bulletin* 5 (June 1935): 1; Benjamin Marsh to Harold L. Ickes, 5 March 1935, box 1, Benjamin C. Marsh Papers.

of consuming and purchasing power."[34] The People's Lobby program directed to this goal provided for a heavy tax on undistributed corporate profits, higher estate and gift taxes "in the lightly taxed lower as well as higher reaches," and steeper income taxes for everyone receiving over $3,000.[35] In a lobby-sponsored petition that spotlighted the replacement of taxes on consumption by broad-based progressive taxes, this tax approach gained 900 signatures, including an honor roll of the intellectual left (John Dewey, Stuart Chase, George Counts, Paul Douglas, and Reinhold Neibuhr, among others), along with scattered social-service, labor, farm, women's, and social-work leaders.[36] In meetings with congressional leaders, speeches, and repeated testimony to congressional committees, the lobby hammered at the theme that the lower- and middle-income-tax brackets could better bear taxes than the oppressed victims of consumption taxes. Benjamin Marsh lamented that this country lacked "the guts to tax people." Chiding that the United States, in contrast to Britain, was "afraid to tax the middle class," Marsh and the People's Lobby moved to the front lines of the campaign for redistributive taxation.[37]

Meanwhile, behind the lines, the redistributive-tax position received support from the economics profession. Moving beyond symbolic politics to actual revenue figures, economists usually recognized that the super-rich were too small a group to make a significant dent in the revenue deficit (a pleasing conclusion for a profession that viewed the super-rich as engines of economic growth). At the same time, many of the poor were clearly too near the subsistence level to justify their role as the Peter who

---

34 Benjamin Marsh to Franklin Roosevelt, 10 April 1933, box 1, Benjamin C. Marsh Papers; John Dewey to the President, 10 January 1934, box 1, Benjamin C. Marsh Papers.

35 Colston E. Warne, "Taxation and Socialization," *People's Lobby Bulletin* 6 (May 1936): 1–2; "Redistribution of National Income Now," *People's Lobby Bulletin* 5 (June 1935): 1; Benjamin Marsh, in U.S., Congress, House, Committee on Ways and Means, *Proposed Taxation of Individual and Corporate Incomes, Inheritances, and Gifts, Hearings*, 74th Cong., 1st sess., 1935, p. 101; Benjamin Marsh, in U.S., Congress, House, Committee on Ways and Means, *Revision of Revenue Laws 1938, Hearings*, 75th Cong., 3d sess., 1938, p. 198.

36 *Daily Worker*, 8 June 1937, p. 3; *New York Times*, 11 June 1937, p. 7; "Suggested Statement on Changes in the Revenue Act," "1937" folder, box 60, Amos Pinchot Papers (Library of Congress).

37 U.S., Congress, House, Committee on Ways and Means, *Proposed Taxation, Hearings*, 74th Cong., 1st sess., p. 102; U.S., Congress, House, Committee on Ways and Means, *Revenue Revision–1939, Hearings*, 76th Cong., 1st sess., 1939, p. 272.

was supposed to pay Paul. Taxation of middle incomes seemed to be the answer. The proclivity of economists for neat mechanistic schemata, in this case the notion that the tax system should take an ever-higher percentage of income as it rode up the income scale, only enhanced the logic of challenging the favored position of the middle class.

Thus even before Roosevelt took office, a position paper approved by 101 economists counseled him to slash income- and estate-tax exemptions and to elevate rates on "moderate-sized incomes" of $5,000–$30,000.[38] In 1937, a detailed analysis of the U.S. tax system by the economic research staff of the corporate liberal Twentieth Century Fund advocated stiffer middle-bracket rates and lowered exemptions for both estate and income taxes as an adjunct to lower consumption taxes.[39] The whole concept of lower-, middle-, and upper-income tax brackets was misleading, declared a Twentieth Century Fund economist. *All* income-tax payers belonged in "the upper brackets when the general distribution of family income in the United States is considered." "The gold is in the foothills, not in the mountains," he concluded.[40]

By the late 1930s, even maverick liberal economists, who had often focused on the need to tax giant incomes, were ready to embrace steeper levies on the middle brackets. The prospect of gleaning a revenue bonus from these affluent savers meshed well with the economists' accent on the redistributive and antisavings role of taxation. David Cushman Coyle, a leading advocate of measures to wrest power and idle funds from the rich, felt that higher taxes on $3,000–$50,000 incomes should allow this middle range to carry the bulk of the revenue load.[41] Adherents of countercyclical spending such as Marriner Eccles, Walter Heller, Richard Gilbert, Lauchlin Currie, and Harry White applauded higher income or

38 Marion K. McKay et al. to FDR, 19 January 1933, box 1, Official File 21, Franklin D. Roosevelt Papers (Franklin D. Roosevelt Library, Hyde Park, N.Y.; hereafter cited as FDR Library).

39 Twentieth Century Fund, Committee on Taxation, *Facing the Tax Problem: A Survey of Taxation in the United States and a Program for the Future* (New York: Twentieth Century Fund, 1937), p. 414. For lack of a better label, I use the much-abused term "corporate liberal" to denote an ideology that sees government initiative in improving social welfare as conducive to the long-term welfare and stability of large corporations.

40 J. Frederic Dewhurst, "What Can the Government Do," *New Republic* 93 (2 February 1938, pt. 2): 385.

41 David C. Coyle, *Why Pay Taxes* (Washington D.C.: National Home Library Foundation, 1937), pp. 171, 130.

estate taxes on these middle brackets.[42] When the *New Republic* sponsored
a forum of liberal economists in 1938, a majority favored cuts in income-
tax exemptions and higher middle-bracket rates.[43] Keynesianism had begun
to infiltrate and polarize the profession, but on the question of administering
a middle- and lower-bracket income-tax antidote to a top- and bottom-
heavy tax system, left-wing economists stayed with their colleagues.

University of Chicago economist Henry Simons, a forceful advocate
of combining the repeal of most regressive taxes with a stiff rate increase
in the lower ranges of the income tax, put the position of the profession
most boldly. Current income taxes, he maintained, were "absurdly low in
the case of what conventional discussion strangely refers to as the lower
and middle-sized incomes." "For the future, the main question is whether
our taxes shall fall mainly on people with incomes ranging from $3,000
to $20,000 or largely on people below the $2,000 level. What happens
to the rates beyond $20,000 is not of major importance."[44]

The tax-broadening campaign, then, appealed to a segment of the left,
usually middle-class intellectuals, who advocated a systematic effort to
direct income toward the lower class. Imbued with a faith in directed
intelligence and government planning, but often uneasy with the inflationary
potential of budget deficits, these reformers believed that the super-rich
alone could not finance the needed redistribution of income.

Though it is hazardous to put forward any "Great Man" theory of
taxation, this does appear to be a case in which personality shaped political
events. James Couzens (R–Mich.) and Robert La Follette, Jr. (R–Wis.),
members of the Senate Finance Committee, had staked out a position of
expertise and special interest in tax reform. They had paid their dues,
compiling impeccable progressive credentials; La Follette, particularly,
could be trusted to share his father's belief that concentrated wealth

42 "Telephone Conversation with Chairman Eccles, Jan. 8, 1936," "Personal and
  Confidential Notes, 1932–1942" folder, box 7, Emanuel A. Goldenweiser Papers
  (Library of Congress): Walter W. Heller and Merlyn S. Pitzele, "Organized Labor
  and Tax Policy," *American Federationist* 46 (April 1939): 377; Richard V. Gilbert
  and others, *An Economic Program for American Democracy* (New York: Vanguard
  Press, 1938), pp. 53–5; Morgenthau Diaries, 9–10 December 1938, book 155,
  pp. 174, 241, Henry A. Morgenthau, Jr., Papers (FDR Library).
43 "Economic Authorities Discuss the Depression," *New Republic* 93 (2 February
  1938, pt. 2): 386.
44 Henry C. Simons, *Personal Income Taxation* (Chicago: University of Chicago Press,
  1938), p. 219.

undermined democracy.[45] These two respected and influential senators, whose desire to tax middle incomes was not generally shared by their colleagues, slipped into the leadership of the tax-reform forces in the U.S. Senate.

This leadership became crucial when operating upon another political fact. In 1932–4, the mad rush to recoup government revenue losses threatened to trample everything in its path, including a soak-the-rich movement that could not yet fend for itself. Although not enthusiastic, most progressives were willing to raise lower- and middle-bracket taxes if the only alternative was a regressive sales or excise tax. Thus the 1932 Revenue Act hoisted income-tax rates all along the scale, for – in Couzens's words – it was "in the medium income groups that we find the reliable incomes from which we would get the revenue."[46] Even Huey Long argued that the middle incomes had gotten off too lightly. "The average American," he said, "would be tickled to death if he could make enough to get inside the taxable class."[47]

This pattern of support persisted in 1934. On La Follette's and Couzens's amendments to boost income-tax rates from top to bottom, the progressive bloc turned out in force. The amendments broke even in the South, were virtually blanked in the urban states, but cleaned up in rural areas – the home of the soak-the-rich philosophy. In the House, by way of contrast, such proposals as Couzens's amendment for a temporary 10 percent income-tax surcharge never had a chance despite Senate passage. Although a younger, more liberal crew of urban congressmen offered something less than the solid opposition shown by their old conservative Senate counterparts, Southern support vanished. Other rural congressmen, hostile to such taxes on the "people," turned against the amendment by a margin of two to one.[48]

To Raymond Moley, the Senate voting pattern was consistent with the historical role of the income tax as an impost on urban industrial America. A dearth of taxable constituents explained why "even very progressive

45 Robert La Follette, Jr., 9 April 1934, quoted in U.S., Congress, Senate, *Congressional Record*, 73d Cong., 2d sess., 1934, 78, pt. 7: 7199.
46 U.S., Congress, Senate, *Congressional Record*, 72d Cong., 1st sess., 1932, 75, pt. 10: 11031.
47 *St. Louis Post-Dispatch*, 14 May 1932, p. 1. See U.S., Congress, Senate, *Congressional Record*, 72d Cong., 1st sess., 1932, 75, pt. 9: 10396, 10398.
48 Edward F. Hanlon, "Urban–Rural Cooperation and Conflict in the Congress: The Breakdown of the New Deal Coalition, 1933–1938" (Ph.D. diss., Georgetown University, 1967), pp. 135, 100–1.

members of Congress from agricultural states are willing to impose larger tax burdens upon small incomes."[49] This rural group, he implied, might soon put across lower-bracket income taxation.

This analysis had several limitations. First, by neglecting the historical development of a rural anti-super-rich ideology, it slighted evidence that only the increases in higher brackets had made taxation of smaller incomes palatable to rural congressmen. Only in the Senate could such plans even get off the ground, for there they were shielded from immediate election pressures, promoted by influential sponsors, and polished with a budget-balancing veneer that signified moral integrity to the old Senate insurgents. An additional shortcoming of Moley's analysis is that it is misleading. Perhaps as relevant as the number of income-tax returns per capita (a measure, incidentally, that placed Robert La Follette's home state of Wisconsin just above the national average) was the ratio of high-income to low-bracket taxpayers. By this measure, agricultural representatives had proportionately less to lose by assailing giant incomes than by tampering with the lower incomes of their local elites.[50] Finally, and most importantly, Moley's prediction was incorrect. Once Roosevelt's Wealth Tax message cleared the way for heavier upper-bracket taxation, rural enthusiasm for across-the-board tax increases diminished.

One can too easily lose the trees for the forest, confusing the carefully defined objectives of that segment of the left that formulated and sponsored tax broadening with the contrary hopes of many who merely supported it. At this point, the focus must shift to Robert La Follette, who, beginning in 1935, was the dominant figure in the redistributive-tax movement.[51]

From his father, Robert La Follette inherited an incisive analytical mind, a progressive constituency, and a Senate seat. Yet he was no carbon copy; he shared neither his father's flashiness nor, in the 1930s, his central aversion to concentrated power. "Of all the progressives of that time," Rexford Tugwell says, Young Bob "had made the most complete transition to modernism."[52] It is characteristic of La Follette that his tax forms were

49 Raymond Moley, "What Can America Afford?" *Vital Speeches* 2 (1 September 1936): 742.

50 U.S., Treasury Department, Bureau of Internal Revenue, *Statistics of Income for 1935*, pt. 1 (Washington, D.C.: Government Printing Office, 1938): 73, 102–26.

51 Plagued by a deteriorating political position and poor health (he died a month after his defeat in the 1936 Republican Senate primary), Couzens faded out of the tax-reform picture.

52 Rexford G. Tugwell, *The Democratic Roosevelt* (Baltimore: Penguin Books, 1957), p. 220. Patrick J. Maney [*"Young Bob" La Follette* (Columbia: University of Missouri

models of scrupulous simplicity; perhaps just as characteristic is his stock and bond portfolio, a collection of blue chips, such as Reynolds Tobacco, Standard Oil, and General Electric.[53] Disregarding the search for panaceas and plutocratic villains, La Follette moved to the forefront of the campaign for public works, relief, and a stronger role for government in bringing about a more equitable distribution of income and purchasing power.

La Follette's tax plan meshed well with this philosophy. It turned the spotlight from the super-rich to "middle" incomes, transforming the income tax into a more productive redistributive tool. The plan, as offered annually between 1934 and 1939, cut exemptions by one-fifth, boosted tax rates, and began applying the surtax at lower income levels.[54]

An intriguing blend of traditional and modern arguments underpinned this package. La Follette perceived a desperate need for more government spending, but he feared that "uncontrolled printing-press inflation" might be the consequence.[55] He did not seek an immediate balanced budget, but he nonetheless urged that the government maintain its credit by obtaining "as large an amount of revenue from taxes as possible."[56] His income-tax package, he pointed out, would also safeguard revenue yields (by moving away from a narrow-based hair-trigger income tax that collapsed when economic distress deflated returns from the super-rich).

The traditionalism of La Follette's tax rationale is noticeable. Towering wartime deficits and the spacing of public-works expenditures to tide the

Press, 1978), pp. 130–2] points out, however, that La Follette embraced neither Tugwell's brand of collectivism nor a "fundamental challenge to the basic structure of capitalism."

53 "Income Tax Returns and Income Tax Data" folders for 1935–43, boxes 640–41, Robert M. La Follette, Jr., Papers, La Follette Family Collection Series C (Library of Congress). In all fairness to La Follette, it should be noted that these securities appear to derive primarily from a bequest in millionaire progressive Bronson Cutting's will. *New York Times*, 26 August 1937, p. 19. La Follette bent over backward to give the government a fair share; not until World War II (when higher rates and the redirection of civic consciousness rendered such altruism anachronistic) did he bother to compile a charity deduction.

54 Even this program was scarcely draconian. For a couple with no dependents, the maximum tax bill under La Follette's plan would only have risen from $80 to $100 on a $5,000 salary, and from $415 to $600 on a $10,000 salary (Britain would have taxed such salaries at $662.50 and $1,787.50 respectively, and assessments in France and Germany would have been considerably higher than that). U.S., Congress, Senate, *Congressional Record*, 75th Cong., 1st sess., 1937, 81, pt. 6: 6279.

55 U.S., Congress, Senate, *Congressional Record*, 73d Cong., 2d sess., 1934, 78, pt. 6:5977.

56 U.S., Congress, Senate, *Congressional Record*, 74th Cong., 1st sess., 1935, 79, pt. 6:6277.

nation over economic downturns had gained some acceptance even before the Depression. But despite the New Deal's sleight of hand in balancing the "ordinary budget" while borrowing to cover "emergency" expenditures, supporters of the New Deal often found its continuing deficits embarrassing. Imprisoned by the fiscal conservatism of a pre-Keynesian world, and paralyzed by fear of the economic and political fallout of higher taxes, Congress and the president drifted uneasily into deficits and regressive hidden taxes. Many spenders – La Follette among them – ridiculed the restorative powers of an annually balanced budget, but few possessed a coherent theory of recovery to take its place. In a world that accepts the notion that higher taxes in a Depression stifle demand and thus impede recovery, La Follette's tax-raising scheme might seem a foolish and economically destructive slave to principle. But, above all, it *was* principled, reflecting La Follette's inclination to systematically confront problems that liberals preferred to forget and that conservatives submerged in vague demands to slash unspecified wasteful government expenditures.

If La Follette's tax plan looked back to budget-balancing dogma, it also looked forward to a tax system that truly redistributed income. Some income equalization would be needed to create the balanced mass purchasing power that could rekindle and fuel economic engines. La Follette declared his adamant opposition to the "vicious indirect excise and sales taxes," but warned that they could not be dispensed with unless alternative revenue sources were found. Hence his strategy: "Build the income tax system to the point where it demonstrates its effectiveness as a revenue tax, and then it will be possible to get rid of the other forms of taxation which are depended upon at present."[57]

Thus La Follette's ultimate goal was to obtain federal revenue almost entirely from a progressive "graduated-tax system."[58] It is important to note, however, that La Follette never presented his income-tax plan as an immediate substitute for other taxes; his desire to fund greater government expenditures (on which he pinned his main hopes for recovery and redistribution) and to keep the deficit in check held a higher short-term priority. To this extent, La Follette's tax proposal could have been fought

57 U.S., Congress, Senate, *Congressional Record*, 76th Cong., 1st sess., 1939, 84, pt. 7:7696; Robert M. La Follette, Jr., "Taxation – A Vital Issue," *Progressive* 4 (9 May 1936): 1; U.S., Congress, Senate, *Congressional Record*, 75th Cong., 3d sess., 1938, 83, pt. 5: 5167; "Vested Interests Fight Bob's Tax Plan with Campaign of Falsehood, Misrepresentation," *Progressive* 4 (24 August 1935): 2.
58 "Bob Explains Ability to Pay Principle to Senate Voting on Tax Amendment," *Progressive* 4 (24 August 1935): 1.

over the question of whether new taxes were necessary. It was not. What kept La Follette's amendment in the limelight was the question of whether the tax system would target a new group.

The issue boiled down to one of raw social power. For the income tax to take a leading role in the tax system, for it to truly expand its revenue-raising capacity, it would have to move beyond the super-rich to the merely affluent and middle-class. "The important brackets that must be made to carry their fair share of the tax burden," said La Follette, "are those below $50,000 annual taxable income," because those classes accounted for under half the yield from the income tax, while pulling in a whopping nine-tenths of the net income reported by taxpayers.[59] Even those who would be blanketed into the income-tax system through lower exemptions, to say nothing of current taxpayers who would be subject to higher rates, were "relatively so much better off than other citizens" that they could more easily bear the burden.[60]

La Follette was playing with "political dynamite."[61] "Vote-fear" gripped congressmen at the idea of adding an estimated 1 million names to the tax rolls (which would have meant a 70 percent increase in the number of taxable returns for 1935) while simultaneously boosting taxes on an affluent group that comprised "the most articulate part of the voting public."[62] Congressmen did not get where they were by playing fast and loose with their political futures, especially in an election year. "The boys are not going home and tell their folks that they are going to reduce exemptions and make them pay more taxes," mused an old-guard Republican. "That is not going to be done."[63]

The assumption that such tax hikes would be "hopelessly unpopular" was all but universally accepted.[64] It is hazardous, however, to interpret public-opinion surveys on this question. Polls were unsophisticated, and answers from a poorly informed public were extremely sensitive to the wording of a question (public attitudes toward a tax could best be determined by questions comparing alternate means of garnering revenue; people

59 Robert M. La Follette, Jr., "Broadening the Income Tax Base," *Tax Magazine* 15 (May 1937): 254.
60 U.S., Congress, Senate, *Congressional Record*, 75th Cong., 3d sess., 1938, 83, pt. 5:5164.
61 *New York World-Telegram*, quoted in *Progressive* 4 (31 August 1935): 3.
62 Ibid., p. 3; "Tax Proposals," *Current History* 53 (June 1941): 29.
63 Frank Crowther, in U.S., Congress, House, Committee on Ways and Means, *Revision of Revenue Laws 1938, Hearings*, 75th Cong., 3d sess., 1938, p. 170.
64 *New York Herald Tribune*, quoted in *New York Times*, 2 June 1937, p. 16.

were inclined to turn down a tax increase standing on its own). On tax philosophy, the public seemed confused, inconsistent, or indifferent. In late 1937, for example, polls revealed that a plurality favored a shift from "hidden taxes" to direct taxes on earnings; that a majority rejected the suggestion that income-tax rates should rise or that more people should pay income tax; and that, when forced to choose between higher rates, a lower exemption, or a national sales tax, the public split roughly in quarters ("no opinion," appropriately, was the fourth category).[65] But on La Follette's proposal to cut exemptions to $2,000 for couples and $800 for singles, the answer was a ringing "no" – by a margin of four to one.[66]

One thing was certain. La Follette was no tribune of the people. They still seemed to view the income tax as a bludgeon against "abnormal incomes." This, combined with the fact that his plan would have exacted immediate sacrifices from a politically potent group, crippled his effort. Attempts to boost lower- and middle-bracket income taxes always elicited paeans to the "great middle class" – the "substantial class of the citizenry of any country," the "bulwark of sound and substantial government," the "class that takes care of relatives and friends who are less fortunate economically," the victims of higher real-estate and other local taxes, the "average persons who have climbed up the ladder of economic and social life."[67] Congress felt ungrudging sympathy for the predicament of the relatively affluent (many of whom, it should be noted, were small businessmen or self-employed professionals who considered themselves deprived, because their incomes had plummeted when former customers and clients could no longer afford their services, leaving them with onerous debts and property taxes). Besides, the middle class spent its money on items that could better be described as necessities than as frivolities; when "surplus income" was the main legitimate source of taxes, the ability to blanket the middle class in with "consumers" counted heavily. As economist Henry

---

65 Cantril, *Public Opinion*, pp. 852, 315, 325.
66 Ibid., pp. 315–16; *New York Times*, 12 March 1939, sec. 3, p. 5. Because $1,000 was considered barely enough to live on, the public was especially hostile to applying the federal income tax to single men earning less than that. It was considerably more inclined to reach below the $2,500 exemption for married men (between a fifth and a third of the sample supported this). Because the survey questions failed to explain that couples also received a $400 exemption for each dependent, the divergence of support for married as opposed to single people's exemption reductions may have been even greater than it appears.
67 David Walsh, in U.S., Congress, Senate, *Congressional Record*, 72d Cong., 1st sess., 1932, 75, pt. 9: 10121; John McCormack, in U.S., Congress, House, *Congressional Record*, 73d Cong., 1st sess., 1933, 77, pt. 5: 4347.

Simons acidly observed, congressmen and Treasury experts ignored the actual income distribution, reflecting instead "on their own conceptions of a modest living."[68] Alben Barkley (D–Ken.) in his attack upon La Follette's amendments, illustrates this point. He opposed such a tax increase on "the average citizens and the average families in our country," arguing that the "large proportion of the burden of local taxation is borne by the average man, whether we consider the average man as the one who receives less than $5,000 a year or the one who receives less than $10,000 a year – *we can make up our own average to suit our own view of what an average ought to be.*"[69]

La Follette considered such generous definitions of average men and the middle class ludicrous. The new taxpayers brought into the system by lower exemptions – who were "so much better off" than the many "citizens who have been stripped of everything they had" – could well afford a maximum tax bill of only four to ten dollars.[70] Or perhaps they could not, judging from the attack on La Follette from the left. Huey Long, who had defended tax increases proposed by Couzens and La Follette in 1932–4, now called the tax "a dig down into the pockets of the little people and robbing them in a legal way of the meager earnings and relief allowances they are presently granted."[71] Beginning in 1935, George Norris and William Borah, who had likewise supported the earlier across-the-board increases (and who would support later La Follette proposals to kick up surtaxes on families earning $6,000–$100,000) joined in attacking La Follette's plan to broaden the tax base. Mirroring the feelings of most of their progressive colleagues, these men claimed that the "small incomes" affected by the lower exemption and higher rates were already too tightly squeezed by the Depression and would be forced "to deny themselves in proportion to the increase."[72] Norris spoke of "the poor man who has an income of $2500 a year."[73] Borah, too, was fearful that an exemption reduction "will take from the persons who have the

68 Simons, *Personal Income Taxation*, pp. 218–19.
69 U.S., Congress, Senate, *Congressional Record*, 74th Cong., 1st sess., 1935, 79, pt. 12:13208. Emphasis added.
70 U.S., Congress, Senate, *Congressional Record*, 75th Cong., 3d sess., 1938, 83, pt. 5:5164.
71 U.S., Congress, Senate, *Congressional Record*, 74th Cong., 1st sess., 1935, 79: pt. 12:13058.
72 *New York Times*, 12 August 1935, p. 1.
73 U.S., Congress, Senate, *Congressional Record*, 75th Cong., 3d sess., 1938, 83, pt. 5:5166.

small incomes the possibility of maintaining themselves upon American standards."[74]

Outside of Congress, the idea of tax broadening also brought indignation from some liberals who backed La Follette on other issues. Nowhere was this dilemma clearer than in the *Progressive*. Though Robert La Follette, Jr., was its president, both the journal and its readers hewed closely to the anticoncentration, pro-small-business, soak-the-rich line of Robert Sr. Therefore, when Robert Jr.'s tax scheme received national coverage, certain columnists were chagrined, and many subscribers were mortified. One letter writer could barely contain himself. He labeled La Follette's plan "reactionary," asserted that public servants "who are after the poor man's taxes" should be "ruled out of the synagogue," and went so far as to declare Progressives no better than Democrats or Republicans. For any further subscriptions, he suggested that the *Progressive* "try the millionaires," for the working class could not support such a tax plan.[75]

La Follette realized that he was fighting an uphill battle. His Washington office urged the *Progressive* to communicate Young Bob's long-term objective of replacing indirect taxes with an income tax.[76] Among other things, it planted a statement on taxes to be used with a "Washington date line or a by-line with some *fictitious* name."[77] The *Progresssive* dutifully featured this counterattack. Under a banner headline, subtitled with the assurance that "Small Taxpayers Would Really Benefit," the article denied the charge that La Follette's was a "'soak-the-poor' plan." It was impossible to finance the government, it said, by taxes on incomes over $50,000, "because there are not enough of those incomes to tax." Senator La Follette "knows it is an unpopular question." "He will have to fight the misguided and ignorant opposition of the very people he is trying to befriend, but he has faith in their ultimate judgment when they have had an opportunity to learn the real facts of the situation."[78]

The *Progressive*'s heart, though, was plainly not in it. Only one month before its August 1935 defense of La Follette's plan, an editorial explained

74 U.S., Congress, Senate, *Congressional Record*, 75th Cong., 1st sess., 1937, 81, pt. 6:6285.
75 H. T. Porer, "Letter to the Editor," *Progressive* 4 (24 August 1935): 2.
76 Norman Clapp to William Evjue, 17 August 1935, "1935 W. T. Evjue" folder, box 12, Robet M. La Follette, Jr., Papers (Library of Congress).
77 Norman Clapp to William Evjue, 19 August 1935, "1935 W. T. Evjue" folder, box 12, Robert M. La Follette, Jr., Papers.
78 "Vested Interests Fight Bob's Tax Plan with Campaign of Falsehood, Misrepresentation," *Progressive* 4 (24 August 1935): 1–2.

that "broadening the tax base means to tax those who have the least so those who have the most will have to pay little."[79] By 1936, the *Progressive* wielded the same statistics employed by La Follette to move in precisely the opposite direction. It complained that "in 1933 incomes under $5,000 paid 10% of the total tax," and half the income tax was paid "on incomes of $55,000 or less" – facts that helped give the *Progressive* "a picture of a grossly overtaxed little man and a tax-evading big man."[80] Even on his own turf, Robert La Follette could not release taxation from its fixation on the super-rich "big man," for he could not shatter the vast sloppy category called the "little man," "the consumer," or "the people."

To the populist left, then, the very philosophy of La Follette's brand of tax reform was misguided. But this crucial liability became an asset in dealing with other groups. The central irony of the tax-broadening effort is that it drew its strength from groups who did not share its redistributive objectives. La Follette's tax plan struck a chord among many conservative opponents of taxing the rich. Business leaders, bankers, corporate lawyers, and some conservative congressmen – eager to push taxes down the scale and enamored with the notion that "tax consciousness" would swell the ranks of opponents of federal spending by belying "the myth that it is only the very rich that pay for governmental extravagance" – showered praise upon the exemption-reduction proposal.[81] Arthur Vandenberg (R – Mich.), who stood with the La Follette amendments through thick and thin, also spoke for many conservatives in his assertion that "we are never going to *legitimately* economize until *all the folks* realize (in their tax bills) that there is no Santa Claus."[82] Middle-bracket taxes seemed less desirable than exemption reductions (not surprisingly, for any transfer of the tax onus from the "top" brackets to the $10,000–$50,000 middle brackets would only reshuffle the burden among the richest 1 percent of Americans), but, even here, the allure of budget balancing for certain newspapers and conservative legislators engendered some support.

It was this conservative support that gave the legislative history of the La Follette amendments its peculiar flavor. By an extraordinary confluence of circumstances – a Senate resistant to popular pressures, a Finance Committee with an overload of fiscal conservatives, a tax proposal that

79 "The Grass Rooters Again," *Progressive* 4 (20 July 1935): 4.
80 "Tax Paying Power," *Progressive* 4 (4 January 1936): 7.
81 "Your Income Tax," *New York Times*, 15 March 1938, p. 22.
82 Arthur Vandenberg to James Couzens, 16 August 1935, box 112, James Couzens Papers (Library of Congress).

could serve as a symbolic vehicle for budget-balancing concerns, a lowering of expectations on the left as the prospects for top-bracket taxation tapered off, the separation of La Follette's exemption amendment from his surtax proposal, the inclination of the press to give big play to middle- and lower-bracket taxation – the La Follette tax scheme remained a live public issue.

La Follette's proposal to cut exemptions does not, however, have a stirring legislative history. Only once did it gain even a fleeting victory. The Senate Finance Committee, which contained a disproportionate delegation of conservative budget balancers, was a center for discontent with Roosevelt's soak-the-rich Wealth Tax plan in 1935. La Follette's tax proposals seemed a good vehicle for registering that discontent; they could inject a real revenue capability into the bill; they might enlarge the constituency that felt most threatened by mounting New Deal expenditures; and they might even weigh the bill down enough to prevent its passage. Apparently (the vote was not recorded), most of the conservatives – Chairman Harrison included – joined with certain progressives to put over La Follette's amendments to cut exemptions and to increase surtaxes.[83] "We simply turned the bill into a revenue measure," Chairman Harrison proudly explained. "If the administration does not want these rates, then it can say so."[84]

It is hard to tell what game Harrison was playing. Perhaps committee members, having received little guidance from the administration, took a flyer. In any case, the message did not take long to reach them. Alben Barkley, fresh from a yachting trip with FDR, seems to have learned that the president vehemently opposed the La Follette changes.[85] In Congress, also, the uproar was immediate. Little less than a miracle could force Congress to jack up the income-tax burden on such a large group of influential constituents. As Congressman McReynolds, a Wealth Tax supporter, commented on the Senate committee action, "ice will be a foot thick on the Potomac before that ever gets through the House."[86] McReynolds never had to get out his ruler. The Senate Finance Committee beat a quick retreat. By an 8–7 vote (with the New Deal loyalists – Harrison, Connally, Barkley, and Guffey – all in the majority), the committee

---

83 This amendment accepted the House's surtax increases on brackets above $100,000, but raised the House rates below that level.
84 *New York Times*, 11 August 1935, p. 2.
85 Martha H. Swain, "Pat Harrison and the New Deal" (Ph.D. diss., Vanderbilt University, 1975), p. 235.
86 *Washington Post*, 13 August 1935, p. 7.

deleted the La Follette revisions, substituting a schedule that only struck at millionaires.[87]

This two-day wonder appears to have deflated the exemption-cutting campaign. After this, La Follette just went through the motions. He annually brought the amendment to the floor, only to watch it die on a one-sided voice vote, or without any vote at all. La Follette declined to press matters, for in the political revulsion against taxing the middle class, even his customary allies deserted him.

La Follette's surtax amendments, on the other hand, were spirited affairs, fraught with political intrigue. The one constant was opposition from the Democratic leadership, but the amendments gained support from fiscal conservatives in the Senate Finance Committee and often from rural progressives on the Senate floor, who halfheartedly embraced the higher "middle-bracket" surtaxes once the prospects for further top-bracket increases had eroded.[88] La Follette's proposal thus split the Senate Finance Committee and received serious consideration in the Senate, though leadership pressures immediately reversed its fleeting victories there in 1937 and 1939 before the final votes. Yet even here, the unusual supporting coalition scarcely represented an endorsement of La Follette's redistributionist critique, and the prospects of La Follette's amendments in the House were dim in any case.[89] The populist-progressive soak-the-

87 *Washington Post*, 13 August 1935, p. 1.
88 These labels may seem a bit arbitrary. My definition of the "left" in the next section of this chapter may be used as a guideline. To characterize conservatives, this definition may simply be inverted. Conservatives were usually opposed to an overall expansion of government, skeptical of measures to redistribute income away from the super-rich "investment brackets," sympathetic to dominant business opinion, and hostile to current activities of organized labor. It would be nice if current liberals and conservatives could be distinguished so simply.

Conservatives and liberals may also be defined in terms of their response to specific issues. James W. Hilty ["Voting Alignments in the United States Senate, 1933–1944" (Ph.D. diss., University of Missouri-Columbia, 1973), pp. 143–5], in a well-executed mammoth research effort, has scaled individual senators according to hundreds of roll-call votes on "substantive domestic issues" between 1933 and 1944. Those on the liberal end of his composite scale were most likely to favor La Follette's surtax amendments except in 1935, when the Wealth Tax alternative temporarily soured them on the idea. Along the rest of the political spectrum, no clear pattern emerges, though the more conservative senators were slightly more likely to favor the amendments than their moderate counterparts. This issue cuts through traditional liberal–moderate–conservative distinctions, a reflection of the apparent confusion on this issue. In fact, between 1935 and 1939, the votes of many senators, of all ideological persuasions, fell on both sides of the La Follette surtax question.
89 See Leff, "New Deal and Taxation," pp. 204–6.

rich tradition that had forged the income tax remained the dominant one in the 1930s.

The Revenue Act of 1935 and the Politics of Polarization

Politicians abhor a vacuum, particularly a vacuum of support. This alone might explain Roosevelt's abandonment of his earlier politics of accommodation with business leaders. But another, more compelling, factor was at work. The mood of the country was changing. The paralyzing desperation that had stilled radical movements at the nadir of the Depression lifted once the worst was over.

Much of Congress – on the floor if not in committee – had shown a progressive inflationist bent in 1933–4. The traditional progressive contraposition of the people and the monopolistic interests structured many congressional debates. FDR would appropriate this vocabulary later in the New Deal, but this approach temporarily left him behind. The AFL-supported 30-hour spread-the-work bill, the federal guarantee of bank deposits, and the Thomas amendment to balloon the money supply – all measures enacted or passed by one House over FDR's opposition – seemed to be only a foretaste of congressional assertion from a rural progressive bloc.

The 1934 election, a smashing vote of confidence in the New Deal and a reform-minded Congress, paradoxically promised more trouble. The conventional wisdom had held that Democrats were in for the customary midterm drubbing; typically cocksure was the concession of a conservative columnist "that if the Democrats lose fewer than fifty seats it will be a real Roosevelt victory, a vindication of his policies."[90] When the returns came in, conservatives were thunderstruck. The Democrats picked up 7 seats in the House and 9 in the Senate. The Republican Party, outnumbered by 3 to 1 in Congress and retaining only 7 governors' chairs, was in tatters.[91] Radical pressure, on the other hand, was on the rise. Many new Democrats had been elected on platform pledges of recovery through public ownership or income redistribution, and third parties now held two governors' mansions, 10 House seats, and 2 Senate chairs. The election, although in one sense a vote of confidence in FDR, seemed to

90 Frank R. Kent, *Without Gloves* (New York: Morrow, 1934), p. 302.
91 Donald R. McCoy, *Coming of Age* (Baltimore: Penguin Books, 1973), pp. 227–8; Hanlon, "Urban–Rural Cooperation," p. 151.

reveal heightened popular pressure for greater New Deal redistributive efforts and brought to power a free-spending Congress that threatened to push Roosevelt further left than he had expected to go.[92] Thanks to the growing strength of congressional and share-the-wealth forces, it was predicted that the president "probably can't or won't stop some additions to tax burdens on the wealthy."[93] At the least, Roosevelt had a go-ahead for a new reform push. "Boys – this is our hour," confided a jubilant Harry Hopkins. "We've got to get everything we want – a works program, social security, wages and hours, everything – now or never."[94]

This was what conservatives feared and expected: "a move leftward by the administration."[95] They realized, for example, that a sales tax (the administration's moderate tax stance had kept that alive as a possibility) was now doomed.[96] Though some merely raised the barricades of business fundamentalism, others saw their best hope in an alliance of convenience "to try to 'build up' the President in opposition to radical Congressional policies."[97]

Indeed, Roosevelt at first seemed more inclined to repress the leftward threat than to take advantage of it. In his 4 January 1935 annual message, he did propose to replace the dole by a public employment program, though some liberal critics viewed this reform as "a morbid substitute for relief, making certain that able-bodied persons who cannot find work in a crippled capitalist system shall not draw help from the government without toiling for it at depressed wages in a federal work gang."[98] As a whole, the message bucked up conservatives. The *Hartford Courant* took heart that it revealed a trend "toward the right," despite a triumphal election result that had given "the President carte blanche to move in any

---

92 Robert S. McElvaine, *The Great Depression: America 1929–1941* (New York: Times Books, 1984), p. 229; William Leuchtenburg, *Franklin D. Roosevelt and the New Deal 1932–1940* (New York: Harper & Row, 1963), p. 117.

93 *Kiplinger Tax Letter*, 27 October 1934, p. 1.

94 Robert E. Sherwood, *Roosevelt and Hopkins* (New York: Harper & Brothers, 1948), p. 65.

95 Henry E. Everman, "Herbert Hoover and the New Deal, 1933–1940" (Ph.D. diss., Louisiana State University, 1971), p. 92.

96 *Kiplinger Tax Letter*, 24 November 1934, p. 2. The National Association of Manufacturers endorsed the sales tax anyway in December 1934. Thomas C. Longin, "The Search for Security: American Business Thought in the 1930s" (Ph.D. diss., University of Nebraska, 1970), p. 180.

97 Ibid., pp. 177–8; Rinehart J. Swenson, "The Chamber of Commerce and the New Deal," *The Annals* of the American Academy of Political and Social Science 179 (May 1935): 137.

98 "Our Surrendering President," *Nation* 140 (13 February 1935): 172.

direction that he might choose in order to promote recovery." The *Los Angeles Times*, in noticing this "tendency toward the right," joined most other papers in expressing satisfaction that the administration had turned a deaf ear to "its radical fringe."[99]

The House Democratic leadership, reportedly with White House approval, delivered a parallel message. When the Democrats had regained control in 1931, they had reduced from 218 to 145 the number of discharge-petition signatures needed to pry a bill loose from an unwilling committee. This decision had already encouraged congressional insurgents to challenge the House leadership on such popular causes as the Patman soldier's bonus bill; Congress's deeper radical tint in 1935 only seemed to reinforce the prognosis for what "responsible" Democrats viewed as "demagogic" bills that could not be publicly opposed without political sacrifice. Thus the Democratic leaders kicked the required discharge signatures back to 218 (half the House, rather than one-third). Republicans opposed this change as an attempt to streamline one-party rule. More pressing complaints were registered by third-party members and the 67 Democrats who bucked a 225–60 Democratic caucus endorsement.[100] Representative William Connery (D–Mass.) charged that the "only result" of the rise from 145 to 218 signatures "will be that progressive legislation on the Democratic side will be hamstrung."[101] To Republican taunts that the purpose was to block reform, stalwart Democrats could only reiterate their commitment to "orderly procedure and to proper functioning of a party majority."[102] The 1934 election had lost some of its radical sting. "Actuated by the fear of insurgents in their own camp," the *New York Times* reported, the Democratic leaders had minimized the possibility of radical legislation reaching the floor.[103] By providing that only a majority of the House could prevent a committee from bottling up a bill, they had succeeded in virtually neutralizing the discharge petition; between 1935 and 1939, only five petitions received the necessary signatures.[104]

Thus from the beginning of the 1935 congressional session, the administration arrayed itself against the liberal forces that seemed on the political

99 "Views of Press on President's Message," *New York Times*, 5 January 1935, p. 3.

100 U.S., Congress, House, *Congressional Record*, 74th Cong., 1st sess., 1935, 79, pt. 1:21; *Washington Post*, 3 January 1935, p. 1.

101 U.S., Congress, House, *Congressional Record*, 74th Cong., 1st sess., 1935, 79, pt. 1:18.

102 Hamilton Fish and Lindsay Warren, in ibid., pt. 1: 17.

103 *New York Times*, 13 January 1935, sec. 8, p.1.

104 Congressional Quarterly, *Guide to the Congress of the United States,* 3d ed. (Washington, D.C.: Congressional Quarterly, 1982), p. 426.

ascendant. Within the Executive Department, it pursued a similar policy. In only a few weeks of January and February 1935, the administration estranged these potential reformist allies. A rebellious reform clique in the Agricultural Adjustment Administration was purged for their efforts to aid the tenant-farm victims of the feudal Southern agricultural system; the purge was expected to quell any agency tendency toward " 'business baiting' or sharp criticism of middleman practices."[105] Roosevelt alienated the labor movement by vigorously upholding the payment of cut-rate wages on public work projects, by rebuking the AFL for not acquiescing in either an NRA auto code or an Auto Labor Board that killed the organization of auto workers, and by siding with newspapers against the National Labor Relations Board. Reform advocates were despondent, and their support for the New Deal hit bottom. Progressives complained that only conservatives retained easy access to FDR.[106] Rexford Tugwell concluded that "the President is slipping and that the big business interests have him stopped."[107]

Roosevelt seemed to be banking everything, a popular theory went, on allowing businessmen to initiate a wave of recovery that could ride him to reelection. In Congress, his legislative program had stalled, but Roosevelt stayed in the shadows. Speculation soon pictured him as gearing up for a "Save the country from radicalism" campaign.[108] Newspapers freely theorized about why FDR had veered "sharply towards the right."[109] Whatever the reason, it was not helping politically. His popularity disintegrated with "staggering rapidity." "Not even the shrewdest analyst," wrote Charles Beard in April 1935, imagined that within four months of a crushing victory, "defeat for 1936 would loom ominously on the horizon."[110] Indecision had allowed Roosevelt to drift into open seas; battered by the political waves, he stood isolated, rudderless, and seemingly vulnerable

105 *New York Times*, 6 February 1935, p. 2
106 Harold L. Ickes, *The Secret Diary of Harold L. Ickes*, vol. 1: *The First Thousand Days 1933–1936* (New York: Simon and Schuster, 1954): 300. Roosevelt did hold an alcoholic session with a small group of Senate liberals in early March, in which he apparently hinted that tax legislation was in the works and told them that progressives should stick together. Felix Frankfurter, "Memorandum on Tax Message," 24 June 1935, "Taxation: Federal, Miscellany" folder, box 185, Felix Frankfurter Papers; Morgenthau Diaries, 18 March 1935, book 4, p. 113.
107 Rexford Tugwell, 17 February 1935, paraphrased in Ickes, *Secret Diary*, 1: 303.
108 Paul Mallon, "The Washington Notebook," *Chicago Daily News*, 15 April 1935, p. 13.
109 *Washington Post*, 10 March 1935, p. B5.
110 Charles Beard, "The President Loses Prestige," *Current History* 42 (April 1935): 64.

to attack. The same banking and business leaders who had talked of Roosevelt as "the bulwark between the country and the 'wild men' of Congress" now rallied in opposition once FDR's tremulous appeasatory stance crippled him politically.[111] On the left, third-party prospects had never looked brighter.

It is difficult to gauge the strength of the political left in the spring of 1935. Part of the problem is definitional. Whatever people called themselves – liberals, progressives, radicals, or "the left" – they incorporated at least three of these four concepts: an enhanced government role (with major new spending programs), a redistribution of income and power from the "super-rich" to the "masses," a desire to curtail the influence of the "business community," and, perhaps, a better deal for organized labor.[112]

The diversity and fragmentation of the left makes impossible any definite overview of its activities. A good place to start is Huey Long. Only one year after his February 1934 formation of the predominantly Southern Share Our Wealth movement, his staff reckoned the number of clubs at over 27,000, and the total membership at well in excess of 4.5 million people.[113] Long's plan, in a late incarnation (he gradually lowered the allowable wealth ceiling) envisioned the use of taxation to limit family wealth to $1.5–5 million and family income to about 1 million. Rates were only raised for a small group of super-wealthy. Flawed by the American misconception of income distribution, the plan proposed a family-income floor of $2,000 to $2,500, justifying this high level by asserting – wrongly

111 Frank R. Kent, *Without Grease* (New York: Morrow, 1936), p. 110.
112 It may seem odd that I have not explicitly defined the left in terms of its position on tax questions. Thomas R. Amlie, for example, in *Let's Look at the Record* (Madison, Wis.: Capital City Press, 1950, p. 25), claims that "if you will tell me how a congressman has voted on the subject of taxation, I will tell you whether that congressman is a liberal or a conservative." Amlie may be correct. Certain votes on closing loopholes or on raising corporate or top-bracket income taxes do reveal a deep liberal–conservative division. But my definition picks up such votes with the "redistribution" and "responsiveness to business opinion" standards. Roll-call votes on other taxes – excise taxes, alcohol taxes, lower- and middle-bracket income taxes, etc. – are of little use in differentiating liberals from conservatives.
113 Robert E. Snyder, "Huey Long and the Presidential Election of 1936," *Louisiana History* 16 (Spring 1975): 123. Even a generous discounting of these obviously inflated figures would overstate the organizational support behind the Every Man a King program. Alan Brinkley (*Voices of Protest* [New York: Knopf, 1982], p. 186) points out that the Share Our Wealth organization was so diverse and loosely structured that "the imperatives of local politics, not the needs of national leadership . . . determined the shape of the Long organization."

– that it was a third of the national average.[114] The Every Man a King program also provided for old-age pensions; an eventual thirty-hour work-week; a veterans' bonus; free higher education; and a $5,000–$6,000 homestead comprising a house, a car, and a radio. It was nice if you could afford it. However, even the confiscation of every U.S. estate worth over $40,000 would not have yielded anything close to the $165 billion that Long expected to collect from the multi-million-dollar fortunes alone.[115] Likewise, even if current personal incomes had been flattened out to absolute equality, each consumer unit would only have received $1,631.[116] Other trifles, such as the difficulty of converting nonmonetary wealth (such as paintings) into distributable goods, received similarly rigorous attention in Long's scheme.

Rural progressives could summon no more than 18 Senate votes for variants of the Every Man a King package.[117] But Long himself transformed this panacea into a magnet for the dispossessed. As he toured the country in early 1935 to spread the word, his flamboyant irreverence had an almost cathartic effect. A cheering Georgia House gave Long a typical reception, complete with shouts of "pour it on, Huey," and "don't stop now, Kingfish!"[118]

A third-party presidential bid by Long was a leading topic of speculation. With Roosevelt already on a political slide, Republicans licked their lips at the prospect of a divided Democratic vote.[119] Though Roosevelt doubted that the left could unify behind Long or any alternative in the 1936 election, he recognized a sizable opposition element "who are flirting with the idea of a third ticket anyway with the knowledge that such a third ticket would be beaten but that it would defeat us, elect a conservative Republican, and cause a complete swing far to the left before 1940."[120] In no uncertain terms, he reiterated that Long was to be denied federal

114 T. Harry Williams, *Huey Long* (New York: Knopf, 1969), p. 693; Huey Long, in U.S., Congress, Senate, *Congressional Record*, 74th Cong., 1st sess., 1935, 79, pt. 7: 8042.

115 Lampman, *Share of the Top Wealth-Holders*, table A19.

116 Census, *Historical Statistics*, p. 301.

117 U.S., Congress, Senate, *Congressional Record*, 74th Cong., 1st sess., 1935, 79, pt. 9: 9911.

118 "Huey Long Draws Cheers of Georgia House Members," *Progressive* 4 (16 February 1935): 1.

119 *New York Times*, 14 April 1935, sec. 4, p. 7.

120 FDR to Edward M. House, 16 February 1935, in Elliott Roosevelt, ed., *FDR: His Personal Letters 1928-1945*, 2 vols. (New York: Duell, Sloan, and Pearce, 1950), 1: 452.

patronage and largesse.[121] Knowing Roosevelt's mood, Hugh Johnson unleashed a savage personal attack on the demagoguery of Long and Father Coughlin.[122] Democratic chairman Farley, painfully aware of Long's following, tried to lead FDR in a different direction. An up-front presidential identification with liberal forces, the Democratic party leaders counseled, would cut the ground out from under the burgeoning third-party movement. Thus, while beating the drums against "medicine men" who dispensed empty promises, Farley also denounced business desires to recapture control of the government.[123]

Even Huey Long would have posed a less immediate threat had numerous other signs of discontent not burst through the political seams at the same time. 1934 had been a banner year for labor militancy; general strikes in such cities as Minneapolis and San Francisco, farmworker uprisings, a massive textile walkout, and other crippling and violent strikes and riots seemed to usher in an assertive new spirit of class conflict. The Reverend Charles Coughlin, whose Sunday afternoon fulminations against international bankers attracted a larger weekly radio audience and more mail than anyone in the country,[124] mobilized his supporters in a National Union for Social Justice, dedicated to a contradictory inflationary program for uplifting the laboring class through whatever crusades or homilies currently appealed to Coughlin's sense of the main chance. On the West Coast, the Townsend movement's $200 monthly old-age pensions and Upton Sinclair's End Poverty in California (EPIC) movement provided politically diverse but persuasive evidence of the pressures for change.

Third-party movements also showed considerable strength. The Minnesota Farmer-Labor party, led by the self-proclaimed radical governor Floyd Olson, had easily retained control of that state in the 1934 election, and its ideological neighbor, the Progressive Party, swept into a dominant role in Wisconsin. The Farmers' Holiday Association, after a ripsnorting address by Huey Long, pronounced a plague on both traditional party houses. Bridging the gap between the populist Long-Coughlin uprising

---

121 FDR, 5 February 1935, in Lester G. Seligman and Elmer E. Cornwell, Jr., *New Deal Mosaic: Roosevelt Confers with His National Emergency Council* (Eugene: University of Oregon Books, 1965), p. 437; Morgenthau Diaries, 22 March 1935, book 4, p. 143.

122 *New York Times*, 5 March 1935, p. 10.

123 *New York Times*, 4 May 1935, p. 12; *New York Times*, 4 May 1935, p. 2; *New York Times*, 23 April 1935, p. 1.

124 Arthur M. Schlesinger, Jr., *The Age of Roosevelt*, vol. 3: *The Politics of Upheaval* (Boston: Houghton Mifflin, 1960), p. 20.

(with which it more closely identified) and the more intellectual middle-class Farmer-Labor wing (whose anticapitalist production-for-use slogan it endorsed), the April 1935 convention advocated a new national party.[125] Talk of such a challenge to Roosevelt was rife across the political spectrum; liberal journals such as *Common Sense* (the mouthpiece of the "cooperative commonwealth" production-for-use philosophy) and the *New Republic* saw a particular urgency, fearing that Roosevelt's tack toward the right might allow the Long-Coughlin cult (mistrusted as demagogic and potentially fascistic) to ensnare growing radical frustration. In late 1934 and mid-1935, the *Common Sense*–Farmer-Labor group organized conventions to consolidate the stream of Midwestern and Western insurgent successes into a national party.

National efforts could not paper over the splintered condition of the left, however. This was a fatal weakness, for no single group had a viable national political constituency. For example, even as the 1936 presidential campaign loomed, only 10 percent of polled Americans declared that an endorsement by Townsend would incline them to vote for a candidate; for Coughlin, the results were even worse.[126] Absent a broadly-based leader (say, Huey Long, or, to be fanciful, FDR himself), the dissident whole was less than the sum of its parts.

Nevertheless, the new popular upsurge had a clear impact, even in Congress. The radical Frazier-Lemke bill to refinance farm mortgages at 1½ percent interest, buoyed by endorsements from Father Coughlin and most state legislatures, would have reached the House floor by discharge petition were it not for the rule change and administration pressure (though discharge-petition signatures did not assure support for this inflationary measure, as indicated by its easy defeat the next year).[127] Congress felt its oats on the question of veterans' pensions, adopting a package that mandated financing by 2 billion dollars worth of new greenbacks. On 22 May 1935, Roosevelt personally delivered a ringing veto message that infuriated progressive agrarian forces. The House overrode his veto by 322–90, but the Senate came up several votes short.

Mounting dissatisfaction with Roosevelt activated the recently expanded House progressive ranks. Even before the session began, consideration

---

125 *Progressive* 4 (4 May 1935): 1–2; John L. Shover, *Cornbelt Rebellion: The Farmers' Holiday Association* (Urbana: University of Illinois Press, 1965), pp. 194–6.
126 Cantril, *Public Opinion*, p. 598.
127 Edward C. Blackorby, *Prairie Rebel: The Public Life of William Lemke* (Lincoln: University of Nebraska Press, 1963), pp. 208, 214; Charles J. Tull, *Father Coughlin and the New Deal* (Syracuse, N.Y.: Syracuse University Press, 1965), p. 107.

had been given to organizing this force.[128] As the veterans' bonus bill neared the House floor in late February, advocates found that "they had a community of interest in many bills too 'radical' for administration acceptance."[129] In March, third-party congressmen and others to the left of Roosevelt formed a Progressive Open Forum Discussion Group (dubbed the Mavericks after the liberal Democratic organizer who bore that convenient name). Thirty-four members signed an uncompromising policy statement, which demanded higher income and death taxes, social insurance, government ownership of natural resources and monopolies "invested with a public interest," higher (prevailing) wages on public-works projects, a shortened workweek, guaranteed farm profits beyond the cost of production, the Frazier-Lemke refinancing bill, banking reform, and avoidance of "foreign entanglements."[130] Members of this group soon flexed their muscles, successfully forcing inclusion of a 100 percent excess-profits tax in the House version of a military mobilization bill.

The Senate also made trouble for Roosevelt. In late January 1935, urged on by a mail campaign generated by Father Coughlin, it failed to approve Roosevelt's proposal to adhere to the World Court. Although efforts to increase the public-works–relief appropriation fell far short (owing to the solid opposition of senators from urban states), the agrarian insurgent bloc overcame administration opposition on a proposal to reduce the interest rates on Federal Land Bank loans.[131]

The Senate insurgent bloc was a focal point for protests against FDR's tax policy. It had become clear by 1934 that Roosevelt could only hope to garner strong insurgent support if he took on concentrated wealth.[132] Burton Wheeler (D–Mont.), arguing that the manifold evils of corporate size necessitated a breakup of giant businesses, offered a graduated tax plan (a variant of a pet idea of Felix Frankfurter's, drafted by Tom

128 Dennis N. Mihelich, "The Congressional Mavericks, 1935–1939" (Ph.D. diss., Case Western Reserve University, 1972), p. 50. Also see Alfred Bingham to Thomas Amlie, 15 January 1935, box 14, Thomas Amlie Papers (Wisconsin Historical Society, Madison).
129 *New York Times*, 24 February 1935, p. 1.
130 "Third Party Labor Pains," *Plain Talk* 11 (May 1935): 40; Mihelich, "Mavericks," pp. 52–9.
131 Hanlon, "Urban–Rural Cooperation," pp. 141–2, 147; E. Pendleton Herring,"First Session of the Seventy-fourth Congress, January 3, 1935, to August 26, 1935," *American Political Science Review* 29 (December 1935): 996.
132 Ronald A. Mulder, *The Insurgent Progressives in the United States Senate and the New Deal, 1933–1939* (New York: Garland Publishing, 1979), p. 79.

Corcoran and Benjamin Cohen) to penalize large companies.[133] James Couzens (R–Mich.) hoped to breathe life into the existing capital-stock/ excess-profits tax by expropriating as much as 40 percent of corporate profits in excess of 30 percent of the company's declared value.[134] George Norris (R–Neb.) crusaded against wealth concentration, advancing a stiff progressive tax on mammoth estates.

Though these proposals went even further than Congress was willing to go, they sprang from fertile soil. The Roosevelt administration's failure to redistribute income had become a focus of attack. Ironically, economic recovery worsened the situation. Because corporate profits had fallen through the floor between 1929 and 1932, their rise appeared astronomical once production revived. Robert Wagner (D–N.Y.) was only one of many to complain that "the realignment of profits and wages, which we contemplated so confidently in the spring of 1933, had not taken place."[135]

More justly, the New Deal was also widely indicted for the lack of a redistributive tax policy. Charging that the New Deal had made only the slightest of adjustments in the Republican tax system, liberals viewed taxes as "the weakest link in the Roosevelt program."[136] Declaring that "social taxation is by all odds the most important element of both reform and recovery," the *Nation* accused the administration of not trying to implement such a policy, and urged it to immediate action.[137] Support for tax reform was a litmus test of one's liberal credentials, and FDR had failed. In a national radio speech on 28 April 1935, Robert La Follette (Progressive–Wis.), the leader of the Senate insurgents on taxes, laid down the gauntlet: "The administration of President Roosevelt has thus far failed to meet the issue of taxation. . . . Progressives in Congress will make the best fight of which they are capable to meet the emergency by drastic increases in taxes levied upon wealth and income."[138]

133 Ellis W. Hawley, *The New Deal and the Problem of Monopoly* (Princeton, N.J.: Princeton University Press, 1966), p. 344.

134 *New York Times*, 14 March 1935, p. 8.

135 Joseph Huthmacher, *Senator Robert F. Wagner and the Rise of Urban Liberalism* (New York: Atheneum, 1968), p. 195.

136 Harry E. Barnes, "The Liberal Viewpoint," *New York World-Telegram*, 19 March 1934, in U.S., Congress, Senate, *Congressional Record*, 73d Cong., 2d sess., 1934, 78, pt. 5: 4993.

137 "Mr. President, Begin to Tax!," *Nation* 140 (6 March 1935): 264; "Gambling on a Boom," *Nation* 140 (8 May 1935): 525.

138 Robert La Follette, Jr., 28 April 1935, in U.S., Congress, Senate, *Congressional Record*, 74th Cong., 1st sess., 1935, 79, pt. 7: 7648.

Thus new political forces threatened Roosevelt's sluggish conservative drift in the spring of 1935. With some exaggeration – for even Roosevelt's liberal proposals met resistance, particularly in congressional committees – the *London Times* noted that "all the President's difficulties come from those who would move faster than he thinks safe and in directions which he does not approve."[139] Yet at the same time that the waxing of the left presented an electoral menace, it opened up new avenues of support. Now that business hostility was moving FDR toward a more liberal camp, he finally followed advice to confer with progressive leaders. Felix Frankfurter helped arrange a 14 May 1935 White House dinner with five of the Senate insurgents. They impressed upon Roosevelt the need for his leadership. Secretary of Interior Ickes chimed in that Roosevelt could capitalize on business opposition and left with the impression that Roosevelt would battle for progressive policies.[140] Earlier predictions that Roosevelt might need to embrace a "refined" version of the tax schemes of liberals and "extremists" finally neared realization.[141]

Political pressures, then, drove Roosevelt toward a shift in New Deal tax policy. Strong ideological influences pushed him in the same direction. Liberals in and out of the economics profession tended to embrace underconsumption or oversaving theories that had major tax implications. One cause of the Depression, they felt, was that the fruits of prosperity had been maldistributed. The rich, who were less likely than the masses to spend their incomes on consumer items, had gotten too big a piece of the pie. The mass of consumers were thus unable to buy back the mounting volume of the things they made. This created a downward spiral in which production was cut back, savings became a further drag on the economy as they piled up in rich men's bank accounts for lack of investment opportunities, workers were fired, purchasing power declined further, and so on. Roosevelt hit this "underconsumption" theme repeatedly in his 1932 presidential campaign, warning that the economic system was doomed if buying power continued to be stifled by wealth concentration at the top. The belief, one historian notes, was that "money was like manure, good only when spread around."[142]

---

139 *New York Times*, 29 March 1935, p. 4.
140 Ickes, *Secret Diary*, 1: 363–4.
141 Walter Lippmann, *Interpretations 1933–1935* (New York: Macmillan, 1936), p. 312; *Kiplinger Tax Letter*, 16 March 1935, p. 1.
142 Clarence H. Cramer, *American Enterprise* (Boston: Little, Brown, 1972), p. 223.

The only way out, therefore, was to expand consumer purchasing power by transferring currently stagnant savings of corporations and the rich to people who would spend it. Taxation was a natural way of tapping these savings. As Federal Reserve Board chairman Marriner Eccles explained to Congress in March 1935, "our problem now is one of distribution of income. The most effective way of achieving a better balance is through income taxes."[143] This emphasis on the failure of the wealthy to contribute to purchasing power, one that FDR would endorse by explaining that one objective of his 1935 Revenue Act was "to restrain the growth of unwholesome and sterile accumulations,"[144] gave the United States the most compelling theoretical underpinning for redistributive taxation in its history. For Americans who felt that the days of economic expansion were gone, this redistributive imperative was even more compelling. The investment capital of the rich, formerly a prime argument for the utility of income maldistribution, now became a menace in an economy whose growth was bounded; redistribution, on the other hand, would create buying power that could allow the revival of existing industrial capacity while permanently forging a more equitable, if less expansionary, society. Redistribution of income through taxation was a new key to maximizing stable economic growth. Many New Dealers considered such redistribution to be "the fundamental need of the country," practically a panacea.[145]

Did this underconsumption/oversavings theory lead inevitably to a fixation on taxing the super-rich? Judging from much contemporary political debate, it did. Yet even statistics available at the time, which exaggerated the concentration of savings at the top, showed that a greater total was saved annually by the so-called lower or middle $2,000–$20,000 income group than by Americans receiving above that amount.[146]

This does not negate the fact that savings were a luxury that millions of average Americans could not afford. Again, the point is that income-tax payers were *not* "average Americans"; they were a relatively affluent bunch. If the object was to convert private savings into government spending,

143 *Washington Post*, 7 March 1935, p. 2.
144 *Addresses of FDR*, 4: 355 (2 September 1935).
145 David C. Coyle, *Brass Tacks* (Washington, D.C.: National Home Library Foundation, 1935), pp. 35–6.
146 Maurice Levin et al., *America's Capacity to Consume* (Washington, D.C.: Brookings Institution, 1934), p. 93; U.S., National Resources Committee, *Consumer Expenditures in the United States* (Washington, D.C.: Government Printing Office, 1934), p. 77.

Why We Have Depressions

Source: *The Progressive* (11 April 1936): 1. Reprinted by permission of *The Progressive*; print courtesy of The Sterling Memorial Library, Yale University.

why weren't all income taxes, rather than only the top-bracket rates, raised in 1935?

Part of the answer to this question lies in another ideological influence on the Roosevelt tax package. Roosevelt's 1935 tax proposal would be very much in the philosophical mold of Supreme Court Justice Louis

Brandeis, the patron saint of those who sought to scale down big business and the bloated super-rich. Brandeis felt that industrialization had made possible an unmanageable concentration of power that threatened political democracy and economic opportunity; his solution was less to redistribute wealth than to redistribute power and to revive small-scale capitalism.[147] Taxation played a central regulatory role in his scheme of things. It could combat the "curse of Bigness" through draconian levies on giant corporations and extravagant bequests, without – and this should not be underplayed – requiring the kind of giantism in government that Brandeis had feared in private life. By leveling off the top, Brandeisian taxation would rejuvenate society through a process of what may be called deconcentration.

In the words of David Cushman Coyle, a popularizer of both Brandeisian philosophy and the New Deal:

> If the American people want to regain the economic liberties that are lost, and to avoid losing the rest, they cannot afford to be too gentle with elephants that tramp with heavy feet through the crowded market place. . . . The power to tax is the power to destroy and the power to save. . . . Taxes are the strong sword of democracy, by which it can protect itself against the tyranny of plutocrats.[148]

It was this philosophy – complete with its mystical idea that the lower orders would harvest the gains once special privilege and excessive power were curbed – that Louis Brandeis, largely through his disciple Felix Frankfurter, helped press on the New Deal. By the fall of 1934, Frankfurter was convinced that he had persuaded Roosevelt of the merits of a Brandeisian tax package. Thereafter, the president brought Frankfurter in on the tax-drafting process.[149]

The direct influence of Brandeis should not be overstated; he held no monopoly on anticoncentration feeling. Public-opinion polls revealed considerable resentment toward concentrated wealth, though there was less agreement about what to do about it. Although the public did not clamor for a government breakup of large businesses, it did feel that big business made excessive profits, that monopoly was harmful, and that there was "too much power in the hands of a few rich men and large corporations."[150] Roosevelt had occasionally tapped these resentments, as in his famous

---

147 For a perceptive discussion of this theme, see Nelson L. Dawson, "Louis Brandeis, Felix Frankfurter, and the New Deal" (Ph.D. diss., University of Kentucky, 1975), pp. 259, 367.
148 Coyle, *Why Pay Taxes*, pp. 79, 180.
149 Dawson, "Brandeis," p. 260.
150 Cantril, *Public Opinion*, pp. 345, 684, 480.

1932 campaign address in Columbus, in which his denunciation of "concentrated economic power in a few hands" included a warning that "a
few powerful interests" should not "be permitted to make industrial cannon
fodder of the lives of half of the population of the United States."[151] There
is also little doubt that Roosevelt himself harbored a special antagonism
toward holding companies, part of his distaste for corporate skulduggery
and intrigue. Thus when FDR was asked at a press conference in February
1935 if "bigness in business" – apart from holding companies – was in
itself undesirable, he at first misleadingly answered, "I should say yes,"
before moving back to more familiar ground by adding, "the question of
mere bigness is not as important as the control of bigness. If you center
in the hands of a very small number of people a great many interlocking
companies, you get a control of industry of the nation in too few hands."[152]
Roosevelt's special concern with the potential for financial and social
manipulation provided an important opening for the Brandeisian viewpoint.
    Within the Treasury, this viewpoint was furthered by General Counsel
Herman Oliphant, a legal wizard who became the Svengali of New Deal
tax reform. Oliphant was outside the Brandeis–Frankfurter axis, but he
shared some of the same ideological premises. "Large aggregations of
corporate and individual wealth," he reiterated to Secretary Morgenthau
in mid-1935, were a threat to "the safety of democratic institutions."[153]
    Thus, ideological and political factors were converging to propel Roosevelt
toward tax reform. Just as importantly, the main barrier to tax reform –
a fear of alienating the business community – had shattered, not because
that fear was ungrounded, but because it was belated. Earlier in the New
Deal, with economic survival and political stability hanging in the balance,
businessmen had good reason to go along with the New Deal's "concert
of interests" theme. But rising economic indicators quelled the sense of
desperation. No longer did businessmen need to view the New Deal as
a last line of defense against assaults on their property and reputation.
Overt discontent soon followed, with the bitter fight in 1934 over stock-
exchange regulation crystallizing earlier business malaise. After this, many
in the business world considered the New Deal beyond redemption. After
conciliatory gestures in the wake of the liberal sweep in the 1934 election,

---

151 *Addresses of FDR*, 1: 679–80 (20 August 1932).
152 Roosevelt, *Press Conferences*, 15 February 1935, 5: 116.
153 Herman Oliphant to Henry Morgenthau, 7 June 1935, "Oliphant, Herman May
    June 1935" folder, Henry Morgenthau, Jr., Papers (FDR Library).

conservative opposition again swelled. By the spring of 1935, the reactionary American Liberty League was in full swing, and business associations were trumpeting the call for the New Deal to shelve most major proposals and certain existing programs in order to clear the route to recovery. Business spokesmen had reverted to a familiar economic fundamentalism. Henry Harriman, a leading business moderate, explained that "the co-operation between government and business was forced by the emergency and should not imply the permanent intrusion of government in business."[154]

Roosevelt felt betrayed and a bit resentful. Raymond Moley complained that "hot-headed administration subordinates talked of the need for 'clipping business' wings'."[155] Roosevelt was quoted by Hugh Johnson as fuming that "industry had bucked him before, and when they saw him again they were going to come to him on their hands and knees."[156] By the beginning of May 1935, any pretense of cooperation disintegrated. For the first time, Roosevelt even refused to send a message of greeting to the annual convention of the U.S. Chamber of Commerce. He must have suspected what was coming. Amid tirades against administration efforts to "sovietize the country," fire-breathing conservatives took over that convention and easily pushed through stinging condemnations of the New Deal.[157] The stage was set for a dramatic clash.

FDR thus possessed powerful political and ideological motives to embrace a "soak-the-rich" initiative. And the Treasury Department had provided him with the means. In December 1934, after an intensive Treasury study of the tax system, Morgenthau presented a major tax-reform program to Roosevelt. That package clearly appealed to Roosevelt's distaste for holding companies; the Treasury, in fact, with Frankfurter's and Oliphant's support, undertook a parallel campaign to convince Roosevelt to use tax penalties rather than outright prohibitions in his upcoming public-utilities holding-company bill. Personal taxes received short shrift; income taxes were left alone (top-bracket increases would only be added late in the drafting process), though there was a visionary proposal to supplement the existing estate tax with a steeply progressive inheritance tax (on the recipient of the bequest, rather than on the estate itself) and higher gift taxes. The

---

154 *New York Times*, 10 May 1935, p. 1.

155 Raymond Moley, *After Seven Years* (New York: Harper & Brothers, 1959), p. 312.

156 Hugh Johnson, "Address," in American Iron and Steel Institute, *Year Book 1938* (New York: American Iron and Steel Institute, 1938), p. 269. See Lawrence Sullivan, "Reflections on Adjournment," *Forbes* 41 (15 June 1938): 31.

157 *New York Times*, 1 May 1935, p. 1.

other major proposals unabashedly sought to curb economic oligarchy. There was a tax on corporate surpluses to force companies to distribute dividends, a tax on intercorporate dividends (money paid by a subsidiary firm to the parent company that owned its stock) designed to break up "some of the larger business units that dominate our economic life," and a graduated corporate-profits tax, scaled according to size, to prevent holding companies and others from avoiding the intercorporate dividends tax through merger.[158]

Political circumstances, however, were not yet ripe for such a far-reaching program. FDR promptly shelved it, requesting no new taxes in his January budget address. Yet he by no means abandoned the idea. He broached it with White House visitors.[159] He instructed the Treasury Department to consider Felix Frankfurter's program to penalize interlocking companies and shady corporate practices.[160] In April 1935, he gave prior approval to Secretary Morgenthau's well-publicized suggestion to Congress that the passage of a veteran's bonus should be accompanied by an inheritance tax to cover its cost.[161]

Then, in May 1935, FDR began to take the whole tax package very seriously. This timing is not hard to explain. Motive and means had come together. Mounting threats from FDR's left, in Congress and in the hinterlands, argued for a more vigorous reform stance, especially because he could not have relished the prospect of defending his disappointing tax record in the 1936 campaign. The potent left wing, the barrage of decentralization arguments from the Treasury, and a dash of vindictiveness against ungrateful businessmen led FDR to adjust his political gyroscope to a new balance. By ostentatiously expelling businessmen from his political coalition, FDR could stem its threatened disintegration. Also, improving economic conditions had eased fears that tax hikes might break the economy's back; there was even some feeling that higher taxes on the upper brackets could prevent the recovery from getting out of control.

Felix Frankfurter was exuberant. He assured Justice Brandeis that Roosevelt was mobilizing behind "tax policies along your line of thought."[162] FDR had told Frankfurter that "Old Brandeis is undoubtedly right about

158 Morgenthau Diaries, 11 December 1934, book 2, p. 281.
159 Felix Frankfurter, "Memorandum on Tax Message," 24 June 1935, "Taxation: Federal, Miscellany" folder, box 185, Felix Frankfurter Papers (Library of Congress).
160 FDR to Henry Morgenthau, 16 January 1935, "January–December 1934" folder, Official File 137, FDR Papers.
161 Morgenthau Diaries, 22 April 1935, book 4, p. 252.
162 Frankfurter to Brandeis, 22 May 1935, in Dawson, "Brandeis," p. 265.

taxing bigness"[163] and had asked him to tell Brandeis of his tax plans. Frankfurter reported back in mid-May, with some literary license, that Brandeis's "eyes became glowing coals of fire, and shone with warm satisfaction."[164] Brandeis would continue to heap praise on these proposals and the philosophical approach they seemed to reflect.

By the end of May, the die was certainly cast. Roosevelt had assured Morgenthau that he intended to send Congress a tax message.[165] He already faced the desertion of the right and the disaffection of the left. The crowning blow came on 27 May, when the Supreme Court's Schechter decision overturned the National Industrial Recovery Act. The main institutional remnant of FDR's earlier policy of national unity through "partnership" with business interests was now dead. Backed into a corner, Roosevelt came out swinging. If big businessmen had been untrustworthy allies, they made highly reliable scapegoats. In a competitive environment typical of Roosevelt, Frankfurter (in collaboration with his protégés, the "little hot dogs" Tom Corcoran and Ben Cohen) and Treasury aides drafted his speech, with its added proposal for higher taxes on giant personal incomes. Also assisting was a resentful Raymond Moley, who came to regard the proposal as divisive and demagogic and who was permitted to torpedo the corporate-surplus tax and to limit the graduation of the corporate-income tax. In much of this effort, strangely, he was assisted by Felix Frankfurter, who felt that the Treasury proposals for a surplus-profits tax and an intercorporate-dividends tax were inadequately thought out and not tightly enough focused around the single central theme of "unhealthy and mischievous concentrations of wealth."[166] Endorsing this shift in emphasis from holding companies to antibigness, Roosevelt also expressed concern that excessive complication might confuse his pitch to the man on the street.[167] The intercorporate-dividends tax was retained, but as a subordinate proposal designed to discourage firms from evading the graduated-profits tax by partitioning themselves into smaller commonly owned firms.

163 Felix Frankfurter, "Memorandum on Tax Message," 24 June 1935, "Taxation: Federal, Miscellany" folder, box 185, Felix Frankfurter Papers.
164 Felix Frankfurter to FDR, 16 May 1935, "Roosevelt, Franklin D., April–June 1935" folder, box 98, Felix Frankfurter Papers.
165 Morgenthau Diaries, 27 May 1935, book 5, p. 182.
166 Felix Frankfurter, "Memorandum on Tax Message," 24 June 1935, "Taxation: Federal, Miscellany" folder, box 185, Felix Frankfurter Papers.
167 Morgenthau Diaries, 19 June 1935, book 7, p. 139.

Roosevelt was now armed to take on his political opposition, to recapture the initiative after a difficult spring. As he envisioned the effects of his radical-sounding message, his spirits rose. "Pat Harrison's going to be so surprised he'll have kittens on the spot," he said of the conservative Senate Finance Committee chairman.[168] On the day of the message, FDR boasted to one cabinet member that "it was the best thing he had done as President."[169]

As William Leuchtenburg points out, an eventual New Deal shift toward progressive tax legislation may have been inevitable.[170] But the tone and character of that shift was not. Although comparisons to World War I taxation could have been and occasionally were made, FDR's 19 June 1935 tax message contained no conciliatory "we're all in this together" elements. In response to the new political calculus, FDR unmistakably embarked on a "political strategy of division."[171] Rebutting the wealthy's Social Darwinist claim to their riches, he lectured that "wealth in the modern world does not come merely from individual effort; . . . without mass cooperation great accumulations of wealth would be impossible save by unhealthy speculation."[172] With government itself, contended Roosevelt, lay part of the blame: "Our revenue laws have operated in many ways to the unfair advantage of the few, and they have done little to prevent an unjust concentration of wealth and economic power." Thus he urged "the very sound public policy of encouraging a wider distribution of wealth." He decried the lack of tax graduation for incomes over 1 million dollars (creating an ambiguity over whether he favored increased taxation below this level; late drafts of the message suggest that he did indeed mean only to target incomes of a million dollars or more).[173] In a revealing passage that was frequently cited by his supporters, he warned that "social unrest and a deepening sense of unfairness are dangers to our national life which we must minimize by rigorous methods" – i.e., stiff taxes on large incomes. He singled out "vast fortunes" acquired by inheritance, which he found

168 Moley, *After Seven Years*, p. 310.
169 Ickes, *Secret Diary*, 1: 384.
170 Leuchtenburg, *Franklin D. Roosevelt and The New Deal*, p. 163.
171 Leon Keyserling to Arthur Schlesinger, 9 April 1958, in Schlesinger, *Politics of Upheaval*, p. 692. I have discussed the strong parallel between my analysis here and the so-called Two New Deals model in Leff, "New Deal and Taxation," pp. 209–26.
172 All quotations from the tax message may be found in *Addresses of FDR*, 4: 271–5 (19 June 1935).
173 Morgenthau Diaries, 17 June 1935, book 7, p. 1.

inconsistent with American values and attitudes. This "inherited economic power" rested upon "static wealth, not upon that dynamic wealth which makes for the healthy diffusion of economic good." Finally, he tackled big corporations. Tipping his hat to small businesses, he asserted that "the vast concentrations of capital should be ready to carry burdens commensurate with their powers and their advantages." Roosevelt had offered up the "gospel according to Brandeis":[174] deconcentration pure and simple. Brandeis gloated that Roosevelt now seemed "to appreciate fully the evils of bigness."[175]

Although it could be argued that it misses the point to venture further into the message, it should not be overlooked that Roosevelt interspersed actual tax proposals throughout this oratorical masterpiece. Hazy enough not to seem out of place, they provided for a corporate income tax graduated between $10\frac{3}{4}$ and $16\frac{3}{4}$ percent; an intercorporate-dividend tax; and an unprescribed level of inheritance, gift, and income taxes. In addition, Roosevelt made a fleeting reference to his advocacy of a constitutional amendment ending the tax exemption for government bonds. He also suggested that inheritance-tax revenues be applied to the national debt, an empty recommendation added (after some teasing) to please Secretary Morgenthau.

The combination of a nod toward the share-the-wealth groups, a slap in the face to the wealthy, and a recitation of the Brandeisian credo was destined to startle. Although the House cheered and applauded the message, the Senate listened in silence. Huey Long, however, effervesced. While the clerk read the message, Long pointed to his chest, grimaced, and sauntered around the chamber in what proved to be a premature victory march. At the speech's conclusion, only Long offered an instant appraisal for the *Record*: "I wish to make one comment. I just wish to say 'Amen!' "[176]

The speech delivered and the joy of battle restored, Roosevelt dashed off to New London for the Harvard–Yale boat races. But, as Senator Hastings (R–Del.) pointed out, the Congress he left behind was now "tired, sick and sore and in confusion."[177] The oppressive Washington summer heat and humidity had set in with a vengeance. Before 1938,

174 Schlesinger, *Politics of Upheaval*, p. 328.
175 Louis Brandeis, quoted in Norman Hapgood to FDR, 3 August 1935, "Norman Hapgood" folder, President's Personal File 2278, FDR Papers.
176 Huey Long, in U.S., Congress, Senate, *Congressional Record*, 74th Cong., 1st sess., 1935, 79, pt. 9: 9659.
177 Roy G. Blakey and Gladys C. Blakey, *The Federal Income Tax* (New York: Longmans, Green, 1940), p. 370.

only certain select havens (such as the legislative chambers and the Ways and Means Committee hearing room) were blessed with air conditioning. The health of many congressmen, not a sprightly youthful group under the best conditions, suffered in the steaming heat.[178] Though the consequent desperate quest for adjournment may have facilitated the rapid passage of the avalanche of legislation supported by Roosevelt, it also assured short tempers and protracted resentment.

Besides, Roosevelt's tax proposals took much of Congress by surprise. Although FDR had worked out the timing of his message with committee chairmen Harrison and Doughton,[179] most congressional leaders were not consulted. Never a great respecter of the legislative process anyway, Roosevelt may have hoped to present Congress with a fait accompli before pressure-group opposition could coalesce. This would not have been an irrational tactic, had he hoped to rush a prepared program through Congress, but under the circumstances, this surprise attack made little sense. Congressional leaders encountered a general speech, no draft of legislation, and a vacationing president who had given them little guidance. This was just the start of a legislative fiasco. It soon became clear that the 1935 revenue bill belonged not on a "must list" but on a "might list." Opponents, seeing the measure as a mere demagogic gesture, hopefully voiced their assurances that Roosevelt would not push the bill. They were closer to the truth than they knew. In the previous month, Herman Oliphant had repeatedly urged Secretary Morgenthau to block a presidential tax message, because in his overly pessimistic assessment, prospects for it in Congress seemed so bleak.[180] Morgenthau's response highlights, in the starkest terms, the political motives behind the Wealth Tax. This was one issue, Morgenthau explained, that Roosevelt "could well afford to be defeated on"; what the president simply had to do was "make his record clear."[181] The important thing, in other words, was to get on the record as a tax reformer who took no guff from carping businessmen. Morgenthau's appreciation of the politics of symbolic reform is also revealed in a later comment. "The tax message which the President is sending up," he pointed out, "is more or less of a campaign document laying down the principles as to where he stands. He does not expect any action on this

178 James T. Patterson, *Congressional Conservatism and the New Deal* (Lexington: University of Kentucky Press, 1967), p. 68.
179 Morgenthau Diaries, 19 June 1935, book 7, p. 140.
180 Morgenthau Diaries, 27 May 1935, book 5, p. 182.
181 Ibid., p. 182.

but gives the people a year to think it over."[182] In late June, Morgenthau received similar signals from Roosevelt. "Mr. President, just strictly between the two of us," he asked, "do you or do you not want your Inheritance Tax Program passed at this session?" FDR answered that he didn't know.[183] Less than a week later, FDR confided that he would not fight a congressional move to adjourn without a revenue act,[184] though, at other times, he did seem committed to his tax bill.

Given Roosevelt's attitude, and given the fact that this nebulous proposal had been thrust forward at the tail end of the congressional session, it is no surprise that rumors flew around the Capitol that the president didn't really mean it. Alarmed and dismayed, progressives, led by Senators La Follette, Borah, Norris, and Johnson, resolved to force the administration's hand. A resolution extending the expiration date of existing excise taxes (amounting to half a billion dollars) was sailing through Congress with Roosevelt's support. La Follette and his cohorts threatened an attempt to tack Roosevelt's 19 June program onto that excise-tax resolution and to block the needed taxes if they were unsuccessful.[185] Spurred by the langorous or hostile attitudes of most congressional leaders, progressives organized a round robin signed by twenty-two senators that demanded enactment of Roosevelt's tax scheme before the end of the session. Senator Nye even warned that if the proposal was simply a campaign trick, it might backfire: "What the President does on this question will in my opinion decide whether he can hope to have the Progressive Republicans with him next year."[186]

Nye was speaking Roosevelt's language. The progressive revolt could neutralize the political appeal of the tax message. Perhaps also hoping that quick passage would avert the coalescence of opposition, FDR returned to Washington and pressured congressional leaders, in a tough session lasting two hours and forty minutes, to accept the progressives' plan to amend the excise-tax resolution. It was a tall order, for that resolution had to be passed in five days or the excise taxes would expire. But Senate Finance Committee chairman Pat Harrison held his nose and immediately followed orders, caucusing in nighttime sessions with Treasury and other experts to draw up the tax schedules.[187] It was to no avail. The Senate

182 Morgenthau Diaries, 14 June 1935, book 6, p. 81.
183 Morgenthau Diaries, 26 June 1935, book 7, p. 156.
184 Blum, *Morgenthau Diaries: Years of Crisis*, p. 303.
185 Maney, *"Young Bob" La Follette*, p. 165.
186 *New York Times*, 22 June 1935, p. 2.
187 Martha H. Swain, *Pat Harrison* (Jackson: University Press of Mississippi, 1978), p. 110.

Finance Committee refused to ram through the chairman's tax schedule without hearings. Indignant that FDR expected them to rubber-stamp several complicated taxes by the end of the week, Congress revolted, and the press was in an uproar. Less than two days after setting this whole process in motion, FDR denied having given the marching orders. This left his congressional lieutenants stranded on the battlefield, hardly an endearing tactic. But, for Senate progressives, the fiasco did have one major positive effect, for they had secured a promise from Harrison that the tax proposals would be considered during the current session.[188]

The amendment that Harrison had presented at Roosevelt's behest gives some indication of how narrow were the president's objectives. The suggested inheritance tax exempted legacies under $300,000 and established progressive rates reaching 75 percent over $10 million (as was the practice, taxes on gifts were pegged at three-quarters of these rates).[189] Income-tax revisions began at $1 million, with a theoretical 84 percent rate for incomes in excess of $10 million. The proposed corporate-profits tax was scaled from 10 percent on the first $2,000 to 17½ percent on profits exceeding $20 million. This proposal is a revealing caricature of the eventual 1935 Revenue Act. Its maximum rates would have reached only a trivial number of individuals and corporations. What makes the proposal most significant is that Roosevelt himself, in conversation with Harrison, had signed off on the tax rates. His only suggestion, which Harrison adopted, was to boost the inheritance-tax exemption to $300,000 in order to "save the middleman."[190] In Roosevelt's mind, in other words, this tax proposal only targeted the super-rich. Senator La Follette complained that "it puts the Administration in a hell of a spot to have a swell message like that come up here and then these futile things proposed to implement it."[191] But La Follette apparently failed to recognize that his own objectives and Roosevelt's were different; unlike the president, La Follette was concerned with collecting enough money to truly redistribute income. Secretary Morgenthau discovered this himself when he protested to Roosevelt that Treasury experts felt that the high inheritance-tax exemption had obliterated that tax's revenue yield. FDR's response was simply: "We will have to step it up steeper on the bigger boys."[192] As one commentator noted, the Harrison rate schedules were "so trifling as to make the whole

188 Schlesinger, *Politics of Upheaval*, pp. 330–1.
189 *New York Times*, 26 June 1935, pp. 1–2.
190 Morgenthau Diaries, 26 June 1935, book 7, p. 161.
191 Ibid., p. 166.
192 Ibid., p. 161.

Table 2. *Annual revenue estimates for House, Senate, and final versions of the Revenue Act of 1935 (in millions of dollars)*

Source	House bill	Senate bill	Bill as agreed to in conference
Surtax increases	45	4	45
Graduated corporation tax	15	60	37
Capital-stock tax	0	55	44
Excess-profits tax	100	10	10
Inheritance tax	86	0	0
Estate tax	0	80	80
Gift tax	24	21	21
Intercorporate-dividends tax	0	39	28
Total	270	269	265
Corporation deduction for charitable gifts	15	15	15
Net total additional revenue	255	254	250

Source: U.S., House, *Congressional Record*, 74th Cong., 1st sess., 1935, 79, pt. 13: 14633.

program look ridiculous."[193] From what was perhaps the closest approximation of the direct intentions of FDR's tax message emerged Brandeisian decentralization *reductio ad absurdum*, rather than a realistic share-the-wealth scheme.

The bills that cleared the Senate and House marred the ideological purity of the Harrison suggestion but heightened its revenue potential. After the conference committee completed the grueling task of reconciling the highly divergent House and Senate versions (see Table 2), the resultant compromise showed somewhat greater concern for the revenue aspects of the program than the Brandeisian ones. Income-tax increases began at $50,000, reaching a maximum rate of 79 percent (the previous high had been 63 percent) at $5 million (a scheme estimated to net $45 million, eleven times the added collections of the one-million-and-up plan). The graduation of corporation taxes ranged from 12½ percent on

193 Ernest K. Lindley, *Half Way with Roosevelt* (New York: Viking Press, 1936), p. 254.

on profits below $2,000 to 15 percent over $40,000. This was less than Roosevelt's suggested tax, especially at upper levels, and it failed to even recover the ground that small corporations had lost when their $3,000 tax exemption had been removed by the 1932 Revenue Act. A new intercorporate-dividend tax survived, but in a diluted form that amounted to no more than a 1½ percent tax on dividends received. Counterbalancing these cutbacks, however, were hikes in two taxes not mentioned in the president's message: the capital-stock tax, and its companion, an ineffectual graduated-excess-profits tax. A heavier estate tax, with corollary gift taxes, replaced the proposed inheritance levy. The estate-tax exemption receded from $50,000 to $40,000 (FDR had proposed nothing of the sort), whereas rates along the scale advanced until reaching 70 percent (60 percent was the previous maximum) for $50 million estates – a package that recouped the revenue from Roosevelt's proposal without providing the desired incentive to distribute bequests more widely.[194]

In less than two and a half months, the Revenue Act of 1935 had moved from proposal to enactment. It had swept through the House and Senate by respectable margins: 282–96 and 57–22.[195] In the House, only 18 Democrats cast votes against the bill and 254 voted in favor. In the Senate, 48 Democrats voted for the bill and only 10 balloted against it, 7 of whom had previously shown little hesitancy to oppose the New Deal.[196] No strict geographical pattern emerged in the House and Senate Democratic opposition, but, of 25 Republican members of Congress voting for the revenue bill, only 3 held constituencies east of Iowa. This Republican distribution is perhaps a partial reflection of the income tax's long-term association with a sectional attack upon Eastern industrial and banking wealth.

The final tallies proved poor indices of the damage inflicted upon Democratic congressional solidarity by the handling of the 1935 Revenue

---

194 "Federal Taxes," *Washington Review* 3 (28 October 1935): 6.
195 U.S., Congress, House, *Congressional Record*, 74th Cong., 1st sess., 1935, 79, pt. 11: 12499; U.S., Congress, Senate, *Congressional Record*, 74th Cong., 1st sess., 1935, 79, pt. 12: 13254.
196 Senators Burke, Byrd, Copeland, Gerry, Glass, Moore, and Tydings had voted against at least two of the six other "key" New Deal enactments that session. The three remaining Senators (Adams, Lonergan, and McCarran) are on Patterson's list of "most conservative Democrats." Patterson, *Congressional Conservatism*, pp. 70, 348–9.

Act. Arthur Krock claimed that "except for Republican Progressives in the Senate, I have yet to hear from any member of Congress anything but resentment over the pressure for passage of this measure at this session."[197] According to one report, some Southern congressmen felt that the Revenue Act of 1935 signaled the necessity for party realignment along liberal–conservative lines.[198] Though this bitterness cooled somewhat with the weather, it lingered long. Raymond Moley contends that the Wealth Tax initiated a Democratic schism by inflicting "wounds on the party that would fester and corrupt."[199] On its surface, the Revenue Act of 1935 was an impressive victory. But, as James Patterson points out, it was also a "Pyrrhic" one, for the tax bill bred unprecedented controversy and FDR's handling of it antagonized conservatives and loyalists alike.[200]

What had this costly victory achieved? Although Congress altered Roosevelt's proposals, the common historical observation that it weakened them can only be justified if adherence to Brandeisianism is the main criterion. Yet antibigness remains the saving grace of the Revenue Act of 1935. Despite the congressional attempts to increase its revenue output, it only augmented tax collections by an estimated $250 million – 82 percent of which did *not* come from the income-tax increase (see Table 2). For 1935, this two-dollar-per-capita rise represented less than ½ percent of the national income, less than 10 percent of the federal deficit, and less than 4 percent of federal expenditures. Humbling a tiny fraction of 1 percent of the population, it was more successful at raising the salaries of astute tax lawyers than at lessening the power of "economic royalists." Even the new higher rates were deceptive. Study of the tax system reveals that loopholes are an integral part of it and that part of the reason that rates can be set so high is that almost no one will pay them. The political system seemed to be spinning its wheels.

Even more importantly, the whole concept of redistribution, if in any sense it is gauged by financial benefits to the bulk of the population (a principle generally associated with the New Deal ethos), was rather alien to New Deal taxation. The problem, as was noted at the time, was that "any real sharing of wealth" required that the administration "do more than skim the top."[201] But this is exactly what had been done. In the three

---

197 *New York Times*, 14 July 1935, sec. 4, p. 3.
198 Paul Mallon, "The Washington Notebook," *Chicago Daily News*, 3 July 1935, p. 9.
199 Moley, *After Seven Years*, pp. 312, 316.
200 Patterson, *Congressional Conservatism*, p. 69.
201 *New York Times*, 30 June 1935, sec. 4, p. 11.

years after the new top bracket for income tax was established, only John D. Rockefeller was subject to that top rate.[202] As economist Henry Simons incisively points out: "We have been so preoccupied with dramatic levies upon fabulous incomes and estates that we have almost forgotten to tax the large ones at all."[203] The Revenue Act of 1935 reaped a political whirlwind, but it generated only a financial breeze.

Pretend to Take the Money and Run: The Cooptation of the Left

Whatever the real effects of the Revenue Act of 1935, the electorate's response to it promised to be favorable. Members of Congress well recognized this. With some exaggeration, the Republican *Hartford Courant* noted that "virtually all agreed" that the Wealth Tax was "politically smart." "For once the members of the House had an opportunity to vote for taxes that would directly affect only a small proportion of their constituents. They grasped it eagerly."[204]

The probable political impact left Republicans distraught. Senator Hastings (R–Del.) charged that "this particular bill was conceived in political intrigue. . . . It has for its principal object the Presidential election of 1936. . . . It is a bid for the votes of those who have but little."[205] The fiscal insignificance of Roosevelt's tax proposal, the very fact that it nominally penalized wealth concentration without remotely threatening the "masses," was its political strength. Many were pleased and few were injured. Arthur Krock's observation on the negligible economic impact of the tax was most incisive: "Not enough people will be acutely aware of its existence . . . to elect a Sheriff if they gathered in one county."[206] FDR had again displayed his flair for the symbolic. He had chosen his enemy well, drafting a program that institutionalized his divisive rhetoric. Felix Frankfurter marveled at his "professional skill" in gaining "the momentum of an accomplished program with which to enter the [presidential] campaign."[207]

Besides, the Revenue Act of 1935 had undercut a potential anti–New Deal issue. As Roosevelt admitted in a well-publicized defense of his

202 John W. Hanes, in U.S., Congress, House, Committee on Ways and Means, *Tax-Exempt Securities, Hearings*, 76th Cong., 1st sess., 1939, p. 12; Morgenthau Diaries, 4 March 1943, book 613, p. 290.
203 Simons, *Personal Income Taxation*, p. 218.
204 *Hartford Courant*, in *Washington Post*, 12 August 1935, p. 7.
205 *New York Times*, 15 August 1935, p. 8.
206 *New York Times*, 28 July 1935, sec. 4, p. 3.
207 Felix Frankfurter to FDR, 27 June 1935, in Max Freedman, ed., *Roosevelt and Frankfurter* (Boston: Little, Brown, 1967), p. 280.

SO LONG AS HE DOESN'T KNOW WHAT HITS HIM
Copyright, 1935, by The Inquirer

Source: *Philadelphia Inquirer* (15 August 1935): 8. Reprinted by permission.

taxes, the share of consumers' taxes rose from roughly 30 to 60 percent of ordinary federal revenues from 1929 to 1934–5.[208] Vulnerable on taxation grounds to both Republican and share-the-wealth forces, he applied a progressive patina to the tax structure that rendered its actual composition immaterial. Conservative economist Friedrich Hayek was not far off the mark when he observed that "the illusion that by means of progressive taxation the burden can be shifted substantially onto the shoulders of the wealthy has been the chief reason why . . . the masses have come to accept a much heavier load than they would have done otherwise."[209] This effect did not escape the notice of Republicans, who charged unavailingly that the Wealth Tax proposal was a smokescreen for high processing and excise taxes needed to cover exploding New Deal deficits.[210]

Roosevelt's general political strategy can be reduced to a narrower political tactic. Almost all historical accounts have at least partly attributed the tax's introduction to the desire to undercut the left, particularly Huey Long and his popular Share Our Wealth movement. In light of this emphasis on the preemptive intent of the 1935 revenue bill, it is necessary to assess both FDR's political motivations and the actual response of the left to the tax program.

To contemporary commentators, there was little doubt that Roosevelt's tax bill was designed to propitiate and quiet the clamor on the left. Long's antics on the Senate floor during the reading of the message surely bolstered this impression. Hearst's *New York American* entitled its editorial on the revenue bill: "Kingfish Swallows Donkey" (Republicans were particularly quick to grasp this theme, because they felt it emphasized FDR's political irresponsibility).[211] The *New York Tribune* capsulized press comment on the tax message as an "attempt to steal Long's thunder," and the *Washington Daily News* cited the belief that the address had "burst Long's balloon."[212] Others appended additional names to the list of demagogues coddled by Roosevelt. The *Philadelphia Inquirer* depicted the tax plan as

---

208 *Addresses of FDR*, 4: 356 (2 September 1935).
209 F. A. Hayek, *The Constitution of Liberty* (Chicago: University of Chicago Press, 1960), p. 311.
210 John Robsion, in U.S., Congress, House, *Congressional Record*, 74th Cong., 1st sess., 1935, 79, pt. 11: 12340.
211 *New York American*, in U.S., Congress, Senate, *Congressional Record*, 74th Cong., 1st sess., 1935, 79, pt. 9: 10146.
212 U.S., Congress, Senate, *Congressional Record*, 74th Cong., 1st sess., 1935, 79, pt. 9: 9907.

designed "to lure hosannahs from the something-for-nothing followers of Huey Long, 'Doc' Townsend, Upton Sinclair and the whole tribe of false prophets."[213] The *Chicago Tribune* railed: "The stability of a great office has been lost while its holder scrambles for the support of the least stable element of our population in competition with men known as the leaders of the lunatic fringe."[214]

The fact that so many analysts credited Long with the Wealth Tax does not make it so. It is clear, though, that Roosevelt had increasing reason to worry. Long discussed plans to embark on a national tour in the summer, and his hints of interest in the presidency fueled press speculation on this prospect. Democratic leaders fretted that he might topple their political hegemony in parts of the South.[215] By mid-1935, it appears that Long planned to organize a Share Our Wealth candidacy in 1936 in hopes of capturing sufficient Democratic votes to elect a Republican.[216] A third-party challenge from Long, disclosed a secret Democratic National Committee poll that set party leaders back on their heels, might claim more than 3 million votes, perhaps enough to allow Republican pluralities to snatch electoral votes from Roosevelt outside the South.[217] We know that Roosevelt and other members of his administration took this threat seriously;[218] it was only to be expected that legislative proposals would be aligned with this concern.

Aside from the appeal in the tax message to minimize social unrest, however, little direct evidence substantiates this link (this also holds for any other explanation of Roosevelt's motives); most of the evidence comes from political opponents. Columnist Paul Mallon, not always entirely accurate, claimed that "from good New Deal sources, you can learn off the record that this phase was intended primarily as a little political sweetening for Huey Long, who has been sour on the New Deal lately."[219] Presidential adviser Raymond Moley, whose departure and ultimate break with the administration largely emanated from its tax policy, contends that the Wealth Tax was "pure Huey" and that Roosevelt had moved

213 *New York Times*, 21 June 1935, p. 3.
214 Ibid., p. 3.
215 Moley, *After Seven Years*, p. 305.
216 Williams, *Huey Long*, pp. 843–4.
217 James A. Farley, *Behind the Ballots* (New York: Harcourt, Brace, Co., 1938), pp. 249–50.
218 See the preceding section of this chapter at footnotes120–3.
219 Paul Mallon, "The Washington Notebook," *Chicago Daily News*, 24 June 1935, p. 11.

toward the Share Our Wealth plan in order to "counteract" Long's potential influence on the 1936 election.[220] He maintains that Roosevelt used the phrase "steal Long's thunder" when discussing political plans.[221] Moley feared that FDR had adopted Long's "demagogic tactics": "I began to wonder ... whether he [Roosevelt] wasn't beginning to feel that the proof of a measure's merit was the extent to which it offended the business community."[222]

The clearest corroboration of the influence of the left is an account of a discussion between Moley, Vincent Astor, and E. D. Coblentz.[223] As related by Coblentz, Hearst's emissary and supervising editor, Roosevelt's words were direct – remarkably direct:

> I am fighting Communism, Huey Longism, Coughlinism, Townsendism. I want to save our system, the capitalist system; to save it is to give some heed to world thought of today. I want to equalize the distribution of wealth. Huey Long says that 92 per cent of the wealth of this country is controlled by 8 per cent of the population. He would change this situation by giving a five-thousand-dollar home to each head of a family, twenty-five hundred dollars a year, etc. To combat this and similar crackpot ideas, it may be necessary to throw to the wolves the forty-six men who are reported to have incomes in excess of one million dollars a year. This can be accomplished through taxation.

This conference took place on 8 May 1935, just as Roosevelt's tax-reform plans were solidifying in his own mind. Perhaps he was using this group as a sounding board for a possible rationale for the Wealth Tax. Even more characteristically, he may have just been teasing them. Besides, although FDR undoubtedly broached the tax question, one gets the impression that the words were changed to condemn the innocent. Coblentz, fearing that Roosevelt would backtrack on his offhand remarks, called Hearst to vouch for his report of the meeting.[224] Yet Roosevelt comes off too much as the dangerous happy-go-lucky dilettante that conservatives swore he was. In a tragicomic scene in which multimillionaire Astor,

220 Raymond Moley, quoted in Frances Fox Piven and Richard A. Cloward, *Regulating the Poor* (New York: Random House, Vintage Books, 1971), p. 91.
221 Moley, *After Seven Years*, p. 305.
222 Moley, quoted in Piven and Cloward, *Regulating the Poor*, p. 91; Moley, *After Seven Years*, p. 313.
223 Edmond D. Coblentz, *William Randolph Hearst* (New York: Simon and Schuster, 1952), pp. 177–8.
224 Rodney P. Carlisle, *Hearst and the New Deal: The Progressive as Reactionary* (New York: Garland Publishing, 1979), pp. 98–9.

anticipating being thrown "to the wolves," despairs that his estate will be bankrupted, Coblentz describes Roosevelt's reaction: "The President laughed. His attitude seemed to be, 'Well, that's just too bad.'"

The basic theme of the passage, however, rings true. Out of conviction, rationalization, or as a response to charges of being a traitor to his class, Roosevelt often emphasized his service to the capitalist system. As Moley observed, "the President expressed amazement that capitalists did not understand that he was their savior, the only bulwark between them and revolution."[225] "All hands agreed" that FDR had moved "distinctly to the Left," but he sought more to moderate the demands of the left than to further them.[226] Roosevelt was certainly not alone in this tactic. Ways and Means Committee chairman Robert Doughton, for example, poured out warnings in his private correspondence that "there is a radical element in this country that is extremely dangerous, and we may be forced to go further in some matters than we like, in order to check the advancing radicalism."[227] Tax reform, then, was "necessary to prevent extremists like Huey Long and others from producing a situation in the Country that will result in National disaster."[228] Roosevelt's basic approach was to appeal to this "radical element" by appropriating its fulminating rhetoric, not by following through on any economic restructuring that this rhetoric portended. A discussant at the March 1936 meeting of the American Economic Association thus viewed the tax as "a shrewd political stroke for heading off a far more objectionable, if not positively dangerous, share-the-wealth movement which was assuming ominous proportions in the early part of the year."[229] He concluded that the bill's "very failure to effect significant changes" was practically a virtue. His analysis was a trenchant one. To disparage the economic impact of the Revenue Act of 1935 is to pay tribute to the political acumen of Franklin Roosevelt.

The precise impact of the Revenue Act of 1935 upon those on the left of the political spectrum is difficult to gauge. Did it, despite its limited scope, succeed in gaining their favor? There is no easy answer. Many

225 Moley, *After Seven Years*, p. 321.
226 J. F. Essary, quoted in "Topics of the Day," *Literary Digest* 119 (29 June 1935): 3.
227 Robert L. Doughton to C. A. Cannon, 6 July 1935, folder 496, Robert L. Doughton Papers (Southern Historical Collection, University of North Carolina Library, Chapel Hill).
228 Robert L. Doughton to Thurmond Chatham, 27 June 1935, folder 1494, Robert L. Doughton Papers.
229 Royal S. Van de Woestyne, "Discussion," *American Economic Review* 126 (March 1936, supplement): 193.

spokesmen, such as the progressive bloc in the Senate, were rather pleased, feeling that FDR was finally beginning to see things their way. They moved closer to the president's camp in the conviction that he had moved closer to theirs. Others were skeptical and resentful. Roosevelt, they said, had promised so much and provided so little. Now that empty promise threatened to deprive them of their following.

There was, in fact, good reason for protest leaders to fear that Roosevelt was cutting the ground out from under them. The Wealth Tax and the rhetoric accompanying it had considerable appeal, even to many voters who had been skeptical of Roosevelt's reform commitments.[230] Southern agrarian intellectuals, attracted to any attack on plutocratic power, "welcomed" the tax.[231] The American Federation of Labor supported the proposal, and the legislature of Wisconsin adopted a resolution endorsing it.[232] The tax bill even elicited a halfhearted endorsement from Upton Sinclair, who indicated that it at least was an improvement, and a fulsome commendation from Father Coughlin, who announced that "the President's new tax program is perfect."[233] Among the insurgent bloc in Congress, the response was overwhelmingly favorable. Although the possibility that Roosevelt had merely proposed the bill for rhetorical effect temporarily angered them, they were among its most enthusiastic proponents. They called Roosevelt's message "excellent" and "splendid," "the most notable, best balanced, fundamentally just and constructive tax program in our history."[234] The *Progressive*'s reaction was more complex. At first, it could barely contain its glee, declaring that implementation of FDR's proposal would allow him to chalk up "the outstanding achievement" of his administration.[235] The ultimate product was less satisfying, but even then the *Progressive* considered the 1935 revenue bill an important step "as a declaration of policy."[236]

230 McElvaine, *Great Depression*, pp. 260–1.
231 Edward S. Shapiro, "Decentralist Intellectuals and the New Deal," *Journal of American History* 58 (March 1972): 947.
232 "Taxing the Rich," *American Federation of Labor Weekly News Service* 25 (29 June 1935): 1; U.S., Congress, Senate, *Congressional Record*, 74th Cong., 1st sess., 1935, 79, pt. 12: 12533.
233 "Topics of the Day," *Literary Digest* 120 (6 July 1935): 4.
234 Senators Wheeler and La Follette, quoted in *Washington Post*, 20 June 1935, p. 2: Edward P. Costigan, "Taxes on Wealth," *Vital Speeches* 1 (15 July 1935): 674.
235 "Roosevelt Action Endorses Bob's Fight to Rush 'Wealth Distribution' Program," *Progressive* 4 (29 June 1935): 1; "Carrying on the Tax Fight," *Progressive* 4 (6 July 1935): 4.
236 "Not Very Impressive," *Progressive* 4 (10 August 1935): 4.

Many of the more radical political leaders and intellectuals, however, were not appeased. "It is a creampuff, milk-and-toast, innocuous, and meaningless gesture," reproved Representative Vito Marcantonio.[237] The *New Republic* considered it "of negligible importance," and the *Nation* dismissed the bill's Brandeisian objectives by stating that "social control of industry seems to us preferable to breaking up bigness into littleness."[238] Such criticisms sometimes paralleled those of Robert La Follette, who sought to extend tax increases beyond the wildly rich. But even more often, the complaint was that the super-rich themselves had gotten off too lightly; *Common Sense* castigated the legislation as "a sham attack on great wealth," and agrarian radical William Lemke called the tax proposal "an attempt to steal the words, but not the program of 'Share Our Wealth' from Sen. Huey Long," because it did not limit fortunes.[239]

Huey Long's reaction, in fact, was the most volatile. After his initial "Amen," he indicated that he would bring the Share Our Wealth clubs into the Roosevelt ranks if the ultimate tax legislation conformed to his interpretation of the 19 June message.[240] In a less than reverential letter to the president, he boldly conceded that "my elimination from politics would be the immediate and sure result of your enactment of the share-our-wealth legislation," magnanimously explaining that this would please him greatly, for it would be sure to further Roosevelt's political career. All the tax bill needed to do, he divulged, was to institute certain principles – which turned out to be the entire Share Our Wealth program. "Do not give us this voice of Jefferson and this hand of Mellon any more," he thundered in a speech on the Senate floor. "The Democratic party is on trial. The whole administration is on trial. Let us have your bill!"[241]

When Harrison released his first draft of the Wealth Tax, Long's reaction was predictable. "The bill proposed is not a third cousin, it is not a fourth cousin, it is not a hundredth cousin to the message sent to us by the President of the United States." Long considered it "preposterous and ridiculous" "to have a whole lot of hubbub and flurry that we are

237 U.S., Congress, House, *Congressional Record*, 74th Cong., 1st sess., 1935, 79, pt. 11:12317.
238 "The Week," *New Republic* 84 (4 September 1935): 85; *Nation*, quoted in Paul A. O'Rourke, Jr., "Liberal Journals and the New Deal" (Ph.D. diss., University of Notre Dame, 1969), p. 125.
239 "News Behind the News," *Common Sense* 4 (September 1935): 4; "Progressives in Congress Say," *Progressive* 4 (6 July 1935): 3.
240 Blakey and Blakey, *Federal Income Tax*, p. 369.
241 U.S., Congress, Senate, *Congressional Record*, 74th Cong., 1st sess., 1935, 79, pt. 9: 9906–7, 9912.

enacting a great redistribution-of-wealth bill," when the anticipated collections from that legislation were so small.[242]

Long made some telling points in his attack on the bill, conveniently sloughing over the fact that the low revenue yield was an indictment of his own soak-the-top-brackets approach. It seems evident, though, that he was running scared. The propaganda sheet of the Share Our Wealth movement carried such headlines as "Millionaires Laugh at FDR's 'Soak-Rich' Fake."[243] The Townsend movement had a different response to the same challenge: a retreat into confusion. Some comments labeled the program "feeble," others echoed conservative warnings that discrimination against large corporations and the rich could harm the economy, whereas others commended the effort to restore "to the community a modicum of the wealth that was filched from it."[244] Given this inconsistency, perhaps the best tactic was to pretend the whole thing was not happening. That, basically, was the approach of the house organ of the Farmers' Holiday Association. Only later did it pull its head far enough out of the sand to gripe that "the left-wingers did not make a real tax of it" and that FDR's "'share the wealth' bill hasn't amounted to anything anyhow."[245] The award for deviousness goes to *Plain Talk Magazine*, which slipped the Revenue Act of 1935 onto its list of important votes by labeling it the "La Follette tax bill."[246] Such tactics are indicative of the defensiveness that radical leaders must have felt.

How justified was this defensiveness? The answer to this question is permanently obscured by the fact that Long was assassinated in Baton Rouge little more than a week after the enactment of the 1935 Revenue Act. Roosevelt's blunting of the redistribution issue thus coincided with the loss of the single most powerful protest spokesman; it is difficult to

242 U.S., Congress, Senate, *Congressional Record*, 74th Cong., 1st sess., 1935, 79, pt. 9:10145-6.
243 "Millionaires Laugh at FDR's 'Soak-Rich' Fake," *American Progress* 2 (August 1935): 3.
244 Francis E. Townsend, "Founder Pleased by Progress Toward Social Justice," *Townsend Weekly* 1 (1 July 1935): 1; "President's Tax Plan," *Townsend Weekly* 1 (8 July 1935): 6; "Soaking the Succesful," *Townsend Weekly* 1 (26 August 1935): 8.
245 "There are Other Smirks on the Beach," *Farm Holiday News* (Marissa, Ill.), 10 September 1935, p. 4; "Roosevelt Makes Promise to Keep Taxes on Poor," *Farm Holiday News* (Marissa, Ill.), 10 October 1935, p. 1.
246 "Congress Improves," *Plain Talk* 13 (August 1936): 10–12. Paul A. O'Rourke, Jr., "Liberal Journals and the New Deal" (Ph.D. diss., University of Notre Dame, 1969), p. 125.

Coaxing Him Back!

Source: *Memphis Commercial Appeal* (22 June 1935): 6. © *The Commercial Appeal*; reprinted by permission.

disentangle the independent weakening impact that the Wealth Tax might have had on the protest movement. But we do know that the Wealth Tax controversy appealed to the same "deep hatred of massed wealth and privilege, of almost mythologized bankers and millionaires," that was at the core of mass agitation.[247] We also know that these radical groups were politically anemic at the national level in 1936. Norman Thomas argues that FDR "cut the ground out pretty completely from under us."[248] Even more disappointed were leaders of the new Union Party, which had been formed by the nation's surviving movement triumvirate: Coughlin, Townsend, and Gerald L. K. Smith (the inheritor of the mailing lists of the disintegrating Share Our Wealth clubs). Plagued by inner dissension, a lackluster candidate, unsuccessful attempts to appear on many state ballots, and the aura of progress surrounding the New Deal and its recent legislation, the Union Party mustered less than 2 percent of the vote in the 1936 election. It may be true that the hopes for a viable third-party alternative died in a corridor of the capitol building of Louisiana, but the 1935 Revenue Act and the New Deal's more combative reform approach had also been debilitating.

The non-Democratic Wealth Tax advocates, most of whom had toyed with the idea of opposing Roosevelt's reelection in early 1935, largely abandoned that idea in 1936. By the time of the 1936 campaign, nearly all progressives had joined Roosevelt's ranks, partially because they approved of the legislation enacted in the summer of 1935.[249] Progressive Republican Senators Nye, Borah, and Johnson failed to support Landon, and Couzens, Norbeck, Shipstead, LaGuardia, the EPIC-controlled California Democratic Party, and the Minnesota Farmer-Labor Party threw their support behind FDR. Senators Norris and La Follette chaired the Progressive National Committee, a left-wing pro-Roosevelt campaign group. One of its selling points was taxation, a striking transformation, because before 1935 this was the New Deal's Achilles heel.[250] The pitch zeroed in on the evils of the previous Republican administrations and the charge that the GOP candidate Landon would repeal the new Roosevelt taxes on the wealthy.

247 Paul K. Conkin and David Burner, *A History of Recent America* (New York: Crowell, 1974), p. 248.
248 Schlesinger, *Politics of Upheaval*, p. 180.
249 Leuchtenburg, *Franklin D. Roosevelt and the New Deal*, pp. 190–1.
250 Maurice P. Davidson, "Roosevelt Reality and Landon Legend," 15 October 1936, "Press Releases" folder, Progressive National Committee Papers (Library of Congress).

The Revenue Act of 1935 alone, of course, cannot account for Roosevelt's oft-noted success in knocking the props out from under his opposition. When it played a role, it was usually as part of the whole battery of rhetoric and reform measures of 1935. By itself, even this record would not have sufficed. The conversion to Roosevelt was often reluctant and belated. Other factors – organizational failures on the left, the inability to drum up a palatable candidate, the support of mass-production labor for the administration, Roosevelt's personal appeal – were more important. But the Revenue Act of 1935 had helped set the tone and define a political approach that succeeded in coopting the challenge from Roosevelt's left without buckling to the demands of the more radical leaders. To call this "cooptation" may seem harsh; to the extent that it encompasses any compromise short of capitulation, and to the extent that it fails to recognize that the limitations of the Revenue Act of 1935 were the limitations of the whole soak-the-rich approach to taxation, the term may be too elastic. But it is significant that Franklin Roosevelt had made a show of throwing several dozen rich Americans "to the wolves," fashioning this effort into a potent campaign symbol. He had pretended to take the money – and had run on this record in 1936. His success in tranquilizing opposition though tax reform of negligible impact offers a useful insight into the system-preserving functions of New Deal reform.

The Alienation of the Right

"This is a hell raiser, not a revenue raiser," one congressman said of FDR's 1935 tax proposal.[251] That, of course, was one of its functions. It takes two to tangle. The Revenue Act of 1935 evoked from businessmen a hysterical self-destructive opposition that only underlined Roosevelt's theme of "the people" versus the "special interests."

Although originality of political expression is an unreasonable standard, the shallow reservoir from which conservatives drew their arguments is conspicuous. In 1933, businessmen had "suspended" their ideology in accepting and seeking certain New Deal legislation.[252] But after the acrimonious divorce from Roosevelt, these signs of flexibility evaporated, as business spokesmen reverted to a 1920s rhetoric turned sour.[253] Their

---

251 "Hell Raiser," *Time* 26 (5 August 1935): 9.
252 Linda Keller Brown, "Challenge and Response: The American Business Community and the New Deal, 1932–1934" (Ph.D. diss., University of Pennsylvania, 1972), p. 174.

language fossilized, seeming more reactionary as the world changed around them. The president's rhetoric and his legislative proposals drove them to the ultimate rigidification of their ideology, imposing upon them a unity unsurpassed in the twentieth century.[254] A popular version of classical economics, laced with Social Darwinism, defensiveness over business's social contribution, distrust of government, and a mystical faith in the centrality of incentive and confidence, informed all business statements.

But now there was a special kind of desperation. Prior to mid-1935, businessmen saw themselves as defending their prerogative to define the government's proper role. Now their concern went deeper: that the government would take the lead in imposing an ideology that was decidedly hostile to business.

If businessmen had chosen to be optimistic, they could have seen a bright side to Roosevelt's new activism. FDR's capacity for outrage against excessive wealth concentration and business selfishness, Rexford Tugwell suggests, revealed his "underlying faith" that beneath the corporate finagling and surplus wealth lay a basically sound business system.[255] But, as Raymond Moley contends, even Roosevelt's delimited diatribes against the " 'small, bad' minority" among businessmen were a clear threat to the business community, inasmuch as he did not exercise himself over corrupt politicians, irresponsible labor unions, or unscrupulous lawyers.[256]

FDR's sharply etched battles with the overprivileged wealthy may have made great political copy, but these dramatic political crusades broke down any remaining rapport with business leaders.[257] By the summer reform push in 1935, Roosevelt could not speak to business assemblies for fear of embarrassment, and his name "was a profanity in the boardrooms and country clubs of the wealthy."[258] The Commerce Department's Business Advisory and Planning Council, mortified by a selective administration attempt to use it to exaggerate cracks in the business viewpoint, virtually

253 Thomas C. Longin, "The Search for Security: American Business Thought in the 1930s" (Ph.D. diss., University of Nebraska, 1970), p. 307.

254 Ibid., 316.

255 Rexford Tugwell, *In Search of Roosevelt* (Cambridge, Mass.: Harvard University Press, 1972), p. 146.

256 Moley, *After Seven Years*, p. 400.

257 Conkin and Burner, *Recent America*, pp. 237, 234.

258 Otis L. Graham, Jr., "The Democratic Party 1932–1945," in *History of U.S. Political Parties,* ed. Arthur Schlesinger, Jr., (New York: Chelsea House, 1973), 3: 1943.

dissolved in an acid bath of resignations.[259] "The cooperation between Mr. Roosevelt and business has largely been replaced by hostility," reported *Business Week* in July 1935.[260] And nothing did more to intensify that hostility than the tax fight.[261]

To conservatives, one of the most outrageous aspects of the Wealth Tax campaign was its denigration of the status of wealth. With the Depression, their reputations had suffered a severe blow anyway. Laid low by the crumbling of their economic miracle and by evidence of ineptitude and scandal, business leaders, as Walter Lippmann observed in 1934, had "fallen from one of the highest positions of influence and power that they have ever occupied in our history to one of the lowest."[262] They had become accustomed to the cries of Coughlin and Long that holders of fortunes were "wicked men" whose "harsh, cruel and grasping ways" abrogated any right to their holdings.[263] Roosevelt's 19 June 1935 message – the mere reading of which, one leading corporation lawyer confessed, practically left him "frothing at the mouth"[264] – had dignified these insolent utterances by stressing the role of mass cooperation and government beneficence in the accumulation of wealth. Even worse, Roosevelt held his conservative opponents up to ridicule. In response to their campaign to discredit his proposal as a "Soak the Thrifty" tax, Roosevelt used biting preplanned remarks in a press conference to characterize those with annual incomes over 1 million dollars as "the 58 thriftiest people in the United States . . . the thriftier you are the nearer you will come to being included among the 58." He then asserted that these people had been "so thrifty" that they had avoided paying taxes on large chunks of their incomes.[265] Businessmen would not easily forget that FDR had kicked

259 Longin, "Search for Security," p. 216. See resignation letters in "Business Advisory Council for Dept. of Commerce" May–August 1935 folders, box 35, Winthrop Aldrich Papers (Baker Library, Harvard University, Cambridge, Mass.).
260 "Business and the President," *Business Week*, 20 July 1935, p. 32.
261 Schlesinger, *Politics of Upheaval*, p. 337.
262 Walter Lippmann, "Big Business Men of America," *American Magazine* 117 (April 1934): 18.
263 Charles A. Beard, ed., *Current Problems of Public Policy* (New York: Macmillan, 1936), pp. 42, 49.
264 Ralph M. Shaw to Jouett Shouse, 21 June 1935, "The American Liberty League, 1935" folder, file 771, Pierre S. du Pont Papers (Eleutherian Mills Historical Library, Wilmington, Del.).
265 "Notes by FDR for a Speech on taxes and tax evasion," undated [31 July 1935?], "July 1935" folder, Official File 137, box 1, FDR Papers; Roosevelt, *Press Conferences*, 31 July 1935, 6: 67.

them when they were down, a tactic that they would not hesitate to turn against the president several years later.

Roosevelt's derisive remarks went to the heart of a philosophical system that united businessmen. Those historians who have helped to dispel the myth of business homogeneity receive little ammunition from the Wealth Tax clash. With the notable exception of reformer-merchant Edward Filene – who set himself off from his fellows by emphasizing consumer buying power and by urging higher income taxes ("Why shouldn't the American people take half my money from me? I took *all* of it from them") – businessmen created an almost solid wall of opposition to FDR's tax proposal.[266] The president, they felt, had "deliberately slapped them in the face."[267] If financial standing became a badge of obloquy rather than one of status, the very social position of the businessman was at stake. By nimbly severing the claimed link between business success and virtue, FDR helped establish businessmen as whipping boys.[268] "Success beyond the mediocre in these latter days appears almost a crime," complained the *Manufacturers Record*.[269]

To a group that apotheosized stability and reassurance, FDR's foray outside the "acceptable" realm of justification for taxation assumed a dangerous, demagogic cast. Talk of redistribution of wealth, the American Liberty League warned, only "opens the door to all sorts of wild ideas."[270] Roosevelt's break with that party line seemed a vindictive reprisal against the foremost protectors of conservative ideology: the Supreme Court and the businessman. Charles Hilles, an Old Guard Republican, echoed this battle cry when he wrote that the 19 June address put forward "a tax not only for revenue, but for revenge."[271] The conservative reaction had elements of both paranoia and prescience. Never in U.S. history would the wealthy be scapegoated as they were in the 1936 presidential campaign.

266 Edward Filene, 28 October 1936, in Sherman F. Mittell, ed., *Speaking of Change: A Selection of Speeches and Articles by Edward A. Filene* (Washington D.C.: National Home Library Foundation, 1939), p. 270.
267 B. C. Forbes, "Roosevelt More Politician Than Statesman?" *Forbes* 36 (1 July 1935): 23.
268 See James M. Burns, *Roosevelt: The Lion and the Fox* (New York: Harcourt, Brace & World, 1956), p. 240; and Herbert Stein, *The Fiscal Revolution in America* (Chicago: University of Chicago Press, 1969), p. 83.
269 "Destructive Taxation," *Manufacturers Record* 104 (July 1935): 16.
270 American Liberty League, *The President's Tax Program: An Analysis of a Transparent Political Gesture* (American Liberty League Document #47, July 1935), p. 9.
271 Charles D. Hilles to James Wadsworth, 24 June 1935, box 28, James W. Wadsworth Papers (Library of Congress).

To conservative critics, the Wealth Tax was not only unfair; it was economically foolhardy. Corporate investment, the magic beanstalk to economic prosperity, was at stake. It was the old confidence game: Meet business demands or lose that quicksilver quality, "confidence," without which "incentive" would vaporize and the economy would fall apart.[272] The correlation between low tax rates and high yield in the prosperous 1920s, conservatives claimed, showed them that the Revenue Act of 1935 would only decrease federal revenues by drying up incomes it intended to tax. In one of the more imaginative renderings, the income tax was already in the process of transforming "natural giants" into "artificial Lilliputians," palaces into hovels, and skyscrapers into shacks.[273] To modern ears, accustomed to Reaganomic tax-reduction crusades, such arguments may seem familiar – an indication of the durability of business fundamentalism.

It comes as no surprise that the business community could rally in opposition to higher income taxes. But when business lobbyists descended on Washington, the personal income tax was not first on their list of outrages. Instead, the proposal to introduce a graduation feature into the corporation income tax excited the most intense opposition. What makes this intriguing is that corporate-income-tax graduation was the one proposal that might have been assumed to drive a wedge into the business community. Smaller firms (or, rather, corporations making small profits) were getting a break. This was not an inconsiderable number. More than 85 percent of all profit-making corporations fell in the under-$25,000 bracket that stood to gain from the tax proposal. The remaining corporations, likely to be assessed more highly, captured over 90 percent of total net corporate income. However, businessmen were not inclined to break ranks, especially with the siege mentality induced by the Roosevelt administration. Even those corporations that would have had their taxes lowered by the new revenue bill kept silent, almost never so much as dispatching a private letter to their congressmen.[274]

272 See George Wolfskill and John A. Hudson, *All But the People: Franklin D. Roosevelt and His Critics 1933–1939* (New York: Macmillan, 1969), p. 234.

273 American Taxpayers League, *Bulletin* 142, 25 May 1935.

274 There was not total unanimity, however. A national U.S. Chamber of Commerce referendum, though biased toward ratification of the chamber's stands and unrepresentative of smaller companies whose purview did not extend to national business issues, revealed an undercurrent of dissent. The vote on a question relating to the graduated corporation tax found members ranged against such taxes by 1393 ½ to 226 ½. Chamber of Commerce of the U.S., "Referendum

The Big Stick—1935 Model

—Hutton in *the Philadelphia* Inquirer

Source: *Literary Digest* 120 (10 August 1935): 5. Reprinted by permission of *The Philadelphia Inquirer*.

Having so easily surmounted the administration's appeal to small corporations, the business community swung into action on a broad front. The National Association of Manufacturers, the National Industrial Conference Board, the New York and Philadelphia boards of trade, the Steel Institute, the Association of American Railroads, and Associated Business Papers were among the groups registering strong public antipathy – usually before congressional committees – toward the proposed tax provision. Even the Commerce Department's Business Advisory Council, which historians have identified as the core of a more flexible, forward-looking faction, lambasted the tax and encouraged congressional opposition.[275] Though "caught flatfooted by the president's sudden stroke," the Chamber of Commerce of the U.S. launched a vigorous campaign against FDR's proposals by mid-July.[276] Local affiliates also participated, calling special meetings to mobilize opposition. Numerous corporations sent letters to stockholders urging them to protest the tax to their congressmen and warning that the policies pursued by the New Deal "mean serious impairment, if not the ultimate destruction of your investment in this and other companies."[277]

Noncorporate big-money groups (often funded by the DuPonts) were also active. In early July, the Liberty League produced a comprehensive evaluation of the tax that was widely distributed to newspapers, congressmen, and the public through its sophisticated dissemination network.[278] The National Economy League warned New England senators of the evils of the Roosevelt proposal, and a representative of the Fair Tariff League got so carried away in his harangue against Roosevelt's demagogic espousal of the tax that the Ways and Means Committee struck his testimony from their record.[279] The just-organized "Minute Women," nattily attired in

Number Seventy: Federal Taxes and Expenditures," Special Bulletin, Washington, D.C., 28 February 1936, p. 2, in Library of Chamber of Commerce of the U.S., Washington, D.C.

275 Business Advisory Council, "Report on the Tax Bill," 13 August 1935, "1933–1935" folder, box 19, Official File 3Q, FDR Papers.

276 Paul Mallon, "The Washington Notebook," *Chicago Daily News*, 27 June 1935, p. 19; *New York Times*, 12 July 1935, p. 8.

277 James F. Bell to "The Stockholders of General Mills, Inc.," 26 July 1935, "August–December 1935" folder, box 2, Official File 137, FDR Papers. Also see W. B. Bell to "The Stockholders," 15 July 1935, p. 2 at Baker Library, Harvard University; Dan Moran to "Stockholders of Continental Oil Company," "August–December 1935" folder, box 2, Official File 137, FDR Papers.

278 *New York Times*, 5 July 1935, p. 2; American Liberty League, *President's Tax Program*.

279 *Washington Post*, 6 August 1935, pp. 1–2; *New York Times*, 11 July 1935, p. 6.

colonial dress, met in Boston's Old South Meeting House to protest the "proposed vicious and un-American tax bill" and then traveled by horse and buggy to present pertinent resolutions to the governor.[280] The Women Investors of America, the Crusaders, and the American Taxpayers' League also contested the tax bill.

The impact of this opposition is impossible to trace precisely but relatively easy to identify. Swept up in the antilobbying furor produced by Senator Black's special investigating committee on the utility lobby, Senator Schwellenbach (D–Wash.) called for a similar investigation of the mechanism through which anti-Wealth Tax "propaganda" surfaced in newspapers.[281] Representative Samuel Hill (D–Wash.) complained of receiving a number of individually signed attacks on the tax bill that repeated identical phrases and appeared to have been written on the same typewriter.[282] Even Senator Hastings (R–Del.), a stalwart opponent of the tax, erupted: "I hold in my hand exactly 100 typed letters . . . containing the exactly same language and signed by individuals living in New York City, New Jersey and the city of Baltimore. . . . the envelopes were exactly alike and clearly written on the same typewriter."[283]

This campaign produced some results. The 1935 Revenue Act carried a bevy of special provisions supported by tax lobbyists. Some businessmen, especially the U.S. Chamber of Commerce, prized their contribution to vitiating the antibigness component of Roosevelt's message. The message's Brandeisian bark, they felt, had been worse than its legislative bite. Even after the president's rhetoric took its less fearsome legislative form, the bill was molded to meet business objections. The inheritance tax was replaced, and business lobbyists achieved their main goal when the graduation feature of the corporation tax was narrowed and transformed from a penalty against bigness to a rebate for smallness (whereas the Harrison draft had proposed new brackets up to $20 million profits, the final legislation ceased graduation at $40,000). They viewed their role as diluting the anti-big-business tendency while protecting the revenue component. The result was that the final bill jacked up the revenue yield with excess-profits and capital-stock taxes, along with higher estate, gift, and income taxes on what was still a small wealthy portion of the population. That

280 *New York Times*, 4 August 1935, sec. 4, p. 6.
281 *New York Times*, 24 July 1935, p. 5.
282 U.S., Congress, House, *Congressional Record*, 74th Cong., 1st sess., 1935, 79, pt. 11:12299.
283 *New York Times*, 19 July 1935, p. 8.

fact concerned them less than might be expected. Theirs was something of an antiprogressive tradition. They reacted to Brandeisianism on its own terms, assessing a political strategy according to the extent to which they thwarted it. Thus Winthrop Aldrich found FDR's initial proposal "much worse . . . than the bill finally passed," and financier James Warburg concluded that Congress had "only loaded the gun with bird-shot and a very small charge of powder."[284] Businessmen were generally more upset with the Revenue Act of 1935 and the philosophy behind it than these statements indicate, but they were pleased that the implicit program in Roosevelt's address had not been translated into legislation.

Nevertheless, New Deal opposition clearly burgeoned in the tax campaign. The *Nation* declared that "no measure proposed by the Roosevelt Administration has been subjected to a more bitter attack from the right than the tax bill."[285] The Wealth Tax, Raymond Moley maintains, "had thrown the business community into paroxysms of fright."[286]

Business antagonism to the New Deal was not merely a product of the Wealth Tax. But the tax proposal and the accompanying reform surge had widened the split between Roosevelt and business leaders into an unbridgeable gulf. The voices of reason and compromise had been routed. They repented their earlier misguided complicity; now businessmen jointly had "come to our senses."[287] This break between Roosevelt and business, concluded *Business Week*, "seems complete and permanent."[288] The Revenue Act of 1935 had not created this distrust and alienation, but it had irremediably aggravated and reinforced it.

Conclusion

Even European Marxists have been accused of promoting worker acclimatization to industrialization by attacking the industrial elite rather than the industrial process.[289] This critique might better apply to Franklin Roosevelt, whose pillorying of evil capitalists deflected blame from the

---

284 Winthrop W. Aldrich, "Business Revival and Government Policy," *Vital Speeches* 2 (30 December 1935): 92; James P. Warburg, *Still Hell Bent* (Garden City, N.Y.: Doubleday, Doran, 1936), p. 61.

285 "The Tax Bill and the Tories," *Nation* 141 (21 August 1935): 200.

286 Moley, *After Seven Years*, p. 316.

287 Editorial, *Commercial and Financial Chronicle* 140 (22 June 1935): 4114.

288 "Business and the President," *Business Week*, 20 July 1935, p. 32.

289 Michael P. Rogin, *The Intellectuals and McCarthy* (Cambridge, Mass.; MIT Press, 1967), p. 169.

capitalist system itself. The circumstances that spawned the Revenue Act of 1935 transformed Roosevelt's inevitable alienation of the right into a staged performance designed to bolster his popularity and coopt the challenge from forces whose approach he deemed unrealistic and radical.

The administration had not drifted into the politics of ostracism. This was a conscious choice. The rhetorical wrapping with which Roosevelt packaged his legislative program is of paramount importance. The president was sensitive to the benefits of polarization. To "the liberals of the Nation," the *Progressive* declared in August 1935, "one of the most encouraging aspects of the New Deal" was "the current bitter attack being directed at the Roosevelt administration by the forces of wealth and privilege."[290] One of the common themes of Roosevelt's 1936 presidential campaign was "we judge him by those who hate him." [291] In 1936, more enamored of Andrew Jackson than ever, FDR recalled the "relentless hatred" directed against Old Hickory by "material power," "sterile intellectualism," the "great media," and "outworn traditionalism." "It seemed sometimes that all were against him – all but the people of the United States." For they were not deceived: "They loved him," Roosevelt noted, "for the enemies he had made."[292]

The screams of powerful opponents thus had become the New Deal's theme song. In his January 1935 State of the Union message, Roosevelt had proclaimed "that Americans must forswear that conception of the acquisition of wealth which, through excessive profits, creates undue private power over private affairs and, to our misfortune, over public affairs as well." In early 1935, these words were still bathed in the glow of FDR's hopes for "a genuine period of good feeling."[293] But later in 1935, and in 1936, recriminations flowed more freely. Earlier conciliatory assurances faded out. Assailing "entrenched greed," "resplendent economic autocracy," "an unjust concentration of wealth and economic power," and "static wealth," FDR embarked on a class-conscious rhetorical tack that culminated in his 1936 presidential campaign against "economic royalists." Roosevelt, argues Rexford Tugwell, needed a "foil, some group to pillory as anti-social, dangerous to the economy and to the nation." This exploited public discontent more effectively than could mere legislation. "Up and

290 "New Deal Reforms," *Progressive* 4 (31 August 1935): 4.
291 Emma Guffey Miller, in Democratic Party, *Official Proceedings of the Democratic National Convention 1936* (n.p., n.d.), p. 269.
292 *Addresses of FDR*, 5: 40 (8 January 1936).
293 *Addresses of FDR*, 4: 17 and 25 (4 January 1935).

down the land, he beat the 'economic royalists' until the dust obscured all other issues."[294]

This colorful oratory cloaked policies with only limited impact. Garbed in rhetorical abrasiveness, the Revenue Act of 1935 was institutionalized oratory, with political teeth but without an economic bite. The Revenue Act of 1935 became the forum for a debate over shibboleths and ideology rather than over income redistribution or economic interests. Congress was awash in bombast. "It looks like we have a sham battle fixed up here," sighed Senator Long. "The Senator from Kentucky is going to accuse the Senator from Michigan of being reactionary, and then the Senator from Michigan is going to get up and charge the Senator from Kentucky with being a Socialist."[295]

But even sham battles have victors and victims. Though the Revenue Act of 1935 was probably a boon to Franklin Roosevelt, few others received more than psychic satisfaction. The same rhetoric that undermined the confidence of those business leaders who might have initiated a recovery within the existing system also undermined the compensating structural changes advocated by the left. The double-edged sword of Roosevelt's programs cut throats on either side, while perhaps impaling industrial expansion. As presidential adviser Adolf Berle observed in 1938, attacks on business had "shattered morale" without providing a substitute economic motor. "We have not, in the absence of a large Government ownership program, any class or group to whom we may turn for economic leadership," he warned.[296] The problem was that FDR's corporate villains still sat at the economy's instrument panel. Businessmen, John Maynard Keynes later pointed out in a letter to Roosevelt, needed special handling: "If you work them into the surly, obstinate, terrified mood, of which domestic animals, wrongly handled, are so capable, the nation's burdens will not get carried to market."[297] Roosevelt's cherished strategy of ostracism gained political points at the expense of demoralizing businessmen, thus making them even less likely to invest in new facilities or to expand production.[298] This placed even more responsibility for economic recovery on the public

---

294 Tugwell, *Democratic Roosevelt*, p. 426.
295 U.S., Congress, Senate, *Congressional Record*, 74th Cong., 1st sess., 1935, 79, pt. 9:10147.
296 Beatrice Berle and Travis Jacobs, eds., *Navigating the Rapids 1918–1971: From the Papers of Adolf A. Berle* (New York: Harcourt Brace Jovanovich, 1973), p. 171.
297 John M. Blum, *From the Morgenthau Diaries*, vol. 1: *Years of Crisis, 1928–1938* (Boston: Houghton Mifflin, 1959), p. 404.
298 See Conkin and Burner, *Recent America*, pp. 237, 243–4.

sector in the form of major countercyclical spending or enhanced government direction of the economy, burdens it was not organized to bear.

Talk, in other words, was not cheap. It expended political and economic capital by embittering the economic elite. Most important of all, it short-changed reform forces. It attracted support from the dispossessed without significantly bettering their lot. The economic status quo may have been the winner. Businessmen howled that Roosevelt had added insult to injury. They were wrong. It was a mere substitution.

The Revenue Act of 1935 was a test of Franklin Roosevelt's commitment to redistribution of income. Before 1935, the income-tax system was virtually immobilized. To decrease taxes was politically infeasible, but to raise them on the rich threatened dire economic consequences. Now the fears had lifted. When Roosevelt failed to rise to the challenge, the *Nation* had this to say:

> In its "share-the-wealth" tax program the Administration has followed what has become an established pattern. First the President makes a pronouncement setting forth the fundamental principles behind a needed reform in terms so sweeping and courageous that he fires the imagination of the country. This creates a demand for immediate action. Then concrete proposals are brought forth which fall far short of the bold concepts contained in the pronouncement. Thereupon public interest subsides, and the final action is little more than a travesty of the principles originally set forth. . . . So it is with social taxation. No action could be more consistent with the philosophy of the New Deal as it is understood by the great majority of people than a redistribution of wealth through a socially conceived tax program. From time to time, the President has held out promises that this would ultimately be done, though it was difficult to see why he should allow more than two years to elapse before initiating the most-needed reform of the day. His message of June 19 appeared to open the way for specific action. . . . Probably that large section of the public which reads only headlines still believes that the President's program will place a large share of the cost of government on the shoulders of the wealthy.[299]

To put it simply, the *Nation* viewed the Revenue Act of 1935 as a hoax. It pointed out that FDR could only achieve his professed aims through a plan similar to La Follette's: hiking levies on "wealthy" groups earning over $5,000 annually and broadening the tax base. Yet one can question whether Roosevelt could realistically have been expected to discard the "other people's money" philosophy that had molded U.S. income taxation

299 "The Tax Fiasco," *Nation* 141 (10 July 1935): 33.

throughout its history and that apparently enjoyed wide popular support. The real hoax, it turned out, was on the future. Still assessing the 1935 Revenue Act within the rhetorical framework of the 1930s, we have too often failed to examine the role of that rhetoric and the politico-economic relationships that established that framework. As a redistributive measure, the Wealth Tax can be overrated; as a historical tool, it is underemployed.

4. Before the Fall: New Deal Tax Reform, 1936–1937

The Revenue Act of 1936

The year 1936 was another contentious one for tax legislation. Yet it was not scheduled to be. When the fight over the 1935 Revenue Act came to a close, the publisher of the Scripps-Howard newspaper chain, Roy Howard, had dispatched a stern letter to the president. Many businessmen, he pointed out, had become alienated from Roosevelt. They were "not merely hostile" to the administration, they were "frightened," feeling that "you fathered a tax bill that aims at revenge rather than revenue – revenge on business." They had come to believe that recovery was only achievable by allaying the "fears of business," by granting industry "a breathing spell" from "further experimentation."[1]

This routine plea could easily have been filed away and forgotten. Instead, it offered Roosevelt a timely opportunity. His tack toward the left may have been politically effective in coopting his radical opposition, and the consensus of political wisdom was that his tax bill was a sure vote getter, but parts of the public seemed uneasy. It seemed time to consolidate gains, lowering the level of public acrimony. To draft a reply to Howard, FDR not only solicited advice from the Treasury Department; he also brought in Raymond Moley, the speechwriter most inclined toward a conciliatory posture. The president himself inserted a few reassuring words.[2]

At Howard's instigation and with his cooperation, the original letter and the response were then publicized. Roosevelt defended the New Deal in general and his tax policy in particular, declaring that its intent was "to create broader range of opportunity, to restrain the growth of unwholesome and sterile accumulations and to lay the burdens of Government where they can best be carried." But he also included a riveting phrase

1 Roy Howard to Franklin D. Roosevelt, 26 August 1935, in Samuel I. Rosenman, comp., *The Public Papers and Addresses of Franklin D. Roosevelt*, 4 (New York: Random House, 1938): 353 (hereafter cited as *Addresses of FDR*).
2 Raymond Moley, *After Seven Years* (New York: Harper & Brothers, 1939), p. 318.

169

that moved straight to the headlines: "The 'breathing spell' of which you speak is here – very decidedly so."[3]

Roosevelt seemed committed to fulfilling this pledge. According to Arthur Schlesinger, even FDR's rip-snorting 1936 State of the Union address was a smokescreen of militant words, designed to excite the left, while allowing a continued "lack of deeds" to win over the right.[4] Whether Roosevelt really clung to this thin reed – for his chances were slim of broadening his limited support from businessmen, particularly if he persisted in rhetorically diabolizing them for political effect – is immaterial. It *is* clear that Roosevelt was not in search of new reform crusades; he was prepared to run on his past record and his present and future rhetoric. In particular, he ruled out tax hikes for this election year, which would have made 1936 the first year since 1931 without a major tax increase. In his State of the Union speech, Roosevelt stressed that "based on existing laws," new taxes were neither "advisable" nor "necessary."[5] The prospect was for a calm spring.

The joker in the deck was the phrase "based on existing laws." FDR had carefully balanced the budget except for what were considered "emergency" expenditures on relief for the unemployed. If Congress mandated some new expenditure, however (here, Roosevelt referred to the Veteran's Bonus), it would also have to come up with the money to cover that outlay, for Roosevelt declared it "important as we emerge from the depression that no new activities be added to the Government unless provision is made for additional revenue to meet their cost."[6] He further warned that "some form of new taxes" would be needed to finance the agricultural program if the courts knocked out existing processing taxes.[7]

Hopes for an uneventful session were shattered three days after these guarded declarations were made. The Supreme Court invalidated the processing tax. Then, at the end of the month, the other shoe dropped; over FDR's pro forma veto, Congress provided that almost $2 billion in bonuses should be distributed to World War I veterans in 1936 instead of in 1945. A $120 million carrying charge would have to be added to the budget in each of the next nine years to borrow money to fund the

---

3 FDR to Roy Howard, 2 September 1935, in *Addresses of FDR*, 4: 355, 357.
4 Arthur M. Schlesinger, Jr., *The Age of Roosevelt*, vol 3: *The Politics of Upheaval* (Boston: Houghton Mifflin, 1960), pp. 502–3.
5 *Addresses of FDR*, 5: 17 (3 January 1936).
6 Ibid., 5: 24 (3 January 1936).
7 Ibid., 5: 28 (3 January 1936).

accelerated payment of this bonus. This cost, in conjunction with the roughly $500 million annually that the invalidated processing tax would have brought in, amounted to an estimated $620 million annual revenue shortfall for the administration.

The Treasury was galvanized into action to repair this hole in the budget. The product of their efforts was the extraordinary undistributed-profits tax (also known as the "surplus-profits" tax). Basically, this was a levy on any profits – whether hoarded or invested in new machinery for internal expansion – that were not distributed as dividends to stockholders.

The undistributed-profits tax was not as unprecedented as opponents would make it out to be. In fact, it had a not-undistinguished lineage. The income taxes of the Civil War had backhandedly imposed a tax on undistributed profits. At the end of World War I, the Treasury and many businessmen favored this tax as a replacement for the stiff war levy on corporate excess profits. Although most of them soon turned against the tax, it remained a lively issue in the 1920s, even passing the Senate in 1924. Moreover, a few European countries imposed the tax, and a great many economists felt that this method of taxing profits at the level of the individual stockholder brought corporate taxes closer to the ideal of taxation according to the individual's ability to pay.

In the thirties, the undistributed-profits tax did not owe its consideration to a groundswell of popular sentiment. The issues involved were far too esoteric to have resonance in the public arena. Internal influences, rather than direct pressure from below, would inevitably be determinant in the development of an undistributed-profits tax. For that reason, it is important to examine the ideological dynamics within the Roosevelt administration that fostered the tax.

A tax on undivided corporate profits was susceptible to many rationales, and it never lacked proponents in the New Deal. Evaluations of the value of the tax, however, varied both over time and from group to group. Many on the left saw undistributed profits as a cause of economic imbalance, urging that these surpluses be taxed out of existence. In Roosevelt's inner circle, the tax had considerable support. At the outset, it was a mainstay of the planning mentality that is associated with FDR's Brain Trusters. Rexford Tugwell's *The Industrial Discipline,* along with an important May 1932 memorandum to FDR from his advisers, argued that corporate managers, freed from the constraints of the market by tremendous retained profits, often unwisely kept this money from the stockholders and channeled it into redundant expansion. This created a "disastrous" imbalance between productive capacity and consumer buying power, one that had precipitated the Depression. By taxing away undistributed profits, the government could right this balance. Shorn of their profit reserves, firms would then be forced into an open investment market for expansion funds. There, any wild-eyed schemes would meet with greater skepticism.[8]

The undistributed-profits tax, then, was initially viewed as an important economic tool. It could well be argued that it was a prescription for averting the 1929 Crash, equivalent to locking the barn door after the horse had been stolen. Given existing depressed expectations, corporations were unlikely to enlarge operations without eminent justification. Still, the emphasis on transforming "surpluses" into needed consumer buying power was a pervasive one all through the 1930s.

Aside from any inferences one might draw from Roosevelt's July 1932 acceptance speech, which partly ascribed the Depression to the fat "corporate surpluses" that had been squandered during the 1920s on "unnecessary plants" and stock-market speculation, such plans rarely surfaced in the public forum.[9] Yet Tugwell had aroused Roosevelt's interest in the idea. In 1933, the two of them had discussed Tugwell's plan for a "Bank for Corporate Surpluses," which would have impounded all undistributed profits, lending out the money for expansion projects deemed in the national interest, but only returning it to the depositing industry after payment of a substantial tax.[10] This proposal to put government at the center of the investment market had some appeal in the more ambitious days of the early New Deal, but Roosevelt never pursued it. Revealingly, although the idea of the tax survived, the initial rationale behind it faded along with the rest of the economic-planning ethos of the early New Deal.

8 Rexford G. Tugwell, *The Industrial Discipline and the Governmental Arts* (New York: Columbia University Press, 1933), pp. 206–7. Bernard Sternsher provides an excellent discussion of Tugwell's ideas and influence in Bernard Sternsher, *Rexford Tugwell and the New Deal* (New Brunswick, N.J.: Rutgers University Press, 1964), pp. 316–19; "Memorandum of May 19, 1932," box 1/ safe, Raymond Moley Papers (Hoover Institution, Stanford University). Raymond Moley, the author of this memorandum, recalls that he demonstrated to FDR after his 1932 nomination that such a corporate-surplus tax was "unsound." That is unlikely. As late as 1934, Moley still favored the tax. Moley, *After Seven Years*, p. 310; "King Log and King Stork," *Today* 1 (10 March 1934): 13. Also see Elliot A. Rosen, *Hoover, Roosevelt, and the Brains Trust* (New York: Columbia University Press, 1977), pp. 142–3.

9 *Addresses of FDR*, 1: 651 (2 July 1932).

10 Rexford G. Tugwell, "Addendum to Diary for the Hundred Days," pp. 2–3, box 19, Rexford G. Tugwell Papers (Franklin D. Roosevelt Library, Hyde Park, N.Y.; hereafter cited as FDR Library).

By the time the tax received approval at the top levels of the Treasury, Tugwell's notion of government supervision of the investment process seems to have played a smaller role. Although opponents sought to slander the tax by speaking of its "Tugwellian philosophy," this was simply not the case.

Underlying the tax instead was a related desire to disperse economic control, placing more of it in the hands of shareholders rather than in the grasp of large corporations, financial experts, or the government. When the Treasury first thrust forward the undistributed-profits tax in its December 1934 tax package, this rising Brandeisian concern with decentralization played a role. The tax, the Treasury explained, was "designed in part to reduce the existing concentration of economic control in few hands."[11]

In 1936, this rationale was still important. Within the Treasury, Morgenthau and Oliphant viewed the tax as an antitrust weapon that could force large corporations to loosen their hold on their profits, thereby freeing funds that stockholders could invest in small, innovative firms.[12] Democratization of corporate finance, therefore, could democratize the whole corporate structure. Robert Jackson, then head of the Tax Division of the Justice Department, defended the tax in a major radio speech by depicting it as the savior of small enterprise and the small stockholder. Large firms, he argued, could use their mammoth retained earnings to buy out competitors, to strengthen their own positions, and thus to promote monopoly – all the while allowing rich stockholders to circumvent taxes on dividends at the expense of the small stockholder who would have preferred to receive his share of the profits.[13] When Roosevelt later mentioned the undistributed-profits tax in his 1936 election campaign, he too adopted this antitrust stance, which was shared by his speechwriters Tom Corcoran and Ben Cohen. Roosevelt boasted that the tax "made it harder for big corporations to retain the huge undistributed profits with which they gobble up small business."[14]

Although the theme of dispersing power to the stockholders cropped up frequently, the allied antimonopoly thrust was secondary. Well it should

11 Morgenthau Diaries, 11 December 1934, book 2, p. 277, Henry A. Morgenthau, Jr., Papers (FDR Library).
12 John M. Blum, *From the Morgenthau Diaries*, vol. 1: *Years of Crisis, 1928–38* (Boston: Houghton Mifflin, 1959), p. 307.
13 Robert Jackson, "The Proposed Revision of Corporation Taxes," *Vital Speeches* 2 (6 April 1936): 431–4.
14 *Addresses of FDR*, 5: 521 (21 October 1936).

have been, for this argument was built on quicksand. Small and medium-sized enterprises, with less access to capital markets, were far more likely than big corporations to plow their own profits back into the firm. A tax on these undistributed profits could therefore weaken smaller firms vis-à-vis their larger competitors by drying up their investment funds. Thus only the most carefully drafted law would not have *promoted* monopoly. The monopoly question, in fact, was the primary argument against the tax. Louis Brandeis himself was skeptical of the undistributed-profits tax, preferring a more straightforward approach to deconcentration in the form of a graduated corporate income tax.[15]

Forming a bridge between the old-style Tugwellian economic-management idea and the fashionable decentralization ethos was the fiscal theory of Federal Reserve Board Chairman Marriner Eccles. As early as 1933, before Eccles even entered the government, he had called for a heavy tax on corporate surplus as part of a program to convert idle resources into mass purchasing power.[16] In his later arguments, Eccles touched all the bases. By preventing corporations from becoming a tax haven for the income of rich stockholders, and by discouraging corporations from piling up big cash reserves for a "rainy day," he argued, the tax would serve as a check on "the creation of great fortunes" and the "growth of huge aggregations of idle capital." It was necessary to reach these undistributed profits by taxation because they were largely immune to the monetary manipulations of the Federal Reserve Board; to leave such profits untouched clashed with the objective of pumping money "back into the expenditure stream."[17] Thus Eccles envisioned an undistributed-profits tax that would simultaneously undermine corporate oligarchy (an almost Brandeisian rationale) while moving toward his own version of the Tugwellian goal of more government control of corporate investment. In lobbying within the administration for an undistributed-profits tax in early 1936, Eccles put forward an even broader range of arguments, highlighting the economy's need to "discourage bigness" and to put stagnant funds into circulation, the government's need to prevent tax evasion and to collect more revenue, and the stockholder's need to have more control over what corporate boards were doing with his profits.[18]

15 Brandeis to Frankfurter, 5 April 1936, box 28, Felix Frankfurter Papers (Library of Congress, Washington, D.C.).

16 Marriner S. Eccles, *Beckoning Frontiers* (New York: Knopf, 1951), p. 130.

17 Ibid., pp. 258–61.

18 Untitled memorandum, 4 February 1936, and "Telephone Conversation with Chairman Eccles," 8 January 1936, "Personal and Confidential Notes, 1932–

Thus diverse ideological strands, all converging on the same cure, became mutually reinforcing. Yet ideology should not be overemphasized. The economic-management ideas of Tugwell and Eccles, for example, seemed to have little influence on the two most important actors in the 1936 selection of the undistributed-profits tax: Morgenthau and Roosevelt. What does appear quite important is the narrower perspective of Treasury Department officials. These officials adhered to the view, then common in the economics profession, that corporate income should be treated like other income accruing to the individual stockholders; it should neither be doubly taxed (as were corporate dividends, which were first taxed as corporate profits and then as individual income) nor should it escape personal taxation (at the time, retained profits were only subject to the corporate income tax). The proper course would be to encourage the distribution of profits to shareholders through tax policy. Although it is not surprising that the Treasury, with its complement of economic experts, should be receptive to such reasoning from economist confreres, it had additional motivations. The natural concern of a revenue-collecting agency with the prevention of tax evasion piggybacked on broader complaints that the rich and powerful were not paying their fair share of taxes. In this context, undistributed profits were viewed as a deliberate tax shelter for high incomes. Of all the arguments underpinning the undistributed-profits tax, this was the most popular. The Treasury's Division of Research and Statistics had a simple answer to the question of what was "the primary purpose of the undistributed profits tax." In addition to raising revenue, the tax would "increase the fairness and effectiveness of the present individual income tax."[19] In the process, the division explained, the tax "would be paid principally by recipients of large direct and indirect incomes who, under the present law, are able to avoid part of their just burden of income taxation."[20]

This was the kind of argument that appealed to Franklin Roosevelt, for it combined superficially uncontroversial statements on tax equity with a stab at the upper incomes. In characteristic fashion, he simplified this argument into a self-evident moral question. In his speech proposing the tax, he talked of the "fundamental equity" of treating distributed and undistributed income equally for tax purposes. Otherwise, he argued, corporate taxes would continue to "dip too deeply into the shares of

42" folder, box 7, Emanuel A. Goldenweiser Papers (Library of Congress).

19 Morgenthau Diaries, 25 February 1936, book 18, p. 63.

20 Morgenthau Diaries, 25 February 1936, book 18, p. 61.

corporate earnings going to stockholders who need the disbursements of dividends; while the shares of stockholders who can afford to leave earnings undistributed escape current surtaxes altogether."[21]

This argument involved a sleight of hand, for it treated disbursement of dividends as a way of allowing rich stockholders to escape income taxes at the expense of their needy brethren, rather than as a decision based on the financial needs of the firm. With the emphasis now shifted to "corporations controlled by taxpayers with large incomes," it was easy to highlight the question of tax evasion, which FDR called a growing "evil."[22] Treasury witnesses extended this logic to note that lower- and middle-income stockholders, whose dividends were taxed at rates lower than the 12½–15 percent rates currently assessed on corporate profits, would in effect be paying less tax if their share of the corporate profits were converted into dividends. The profit share of a rich stockholder, on the other hand, would be subjected to his much higher personal tax rate.

Exploiting suspicions that the wealthy were not carrying their weight, this argument was quite influential. In conjunction with another, hallowed, equity argument – that unincorporated businesses (whose profits had always been allocated to the owners for tax purposes) would now be treated similarly to corporations – it carried the brunt of the case for the undistributed-profits tax. In the press conference that succeeded the tax message, Roosevelt concocted an illustrative corporation for himself and the press. He and a partner owned 51 percent of the hypothetical stock, while the members of the press owned the rest. He and his partner, already living high on "outside sources of income," would decide to put all the profits into an addition to the plant, while the poor members of the press, who "really need the dividends," would be left out in the cold. This affront to fairness, Roosevelt said, could not "be emphasized too strongly."[23] In his major 1936 campaign defense of his tax policy, FDR continued to depict the undistributed-profits tax as "merely an extension of the individual income tax law and a plugging-up of the loopholes in it, loopholes which could be used only by men of very large incomes."[24]

21 *Addresses of FDR*, 5: 105 (3 March 1936).
22 Ibid., 5: 105 (3 March 1936).
23 Franklin D. Roosevelt, *Complete Presidential Press Conferences* (New York: Da Capo Press, 1972), 3 March 1936, 7: 170–2.
24 *Addresses of FDR*, 5: 527 (21 October 1936).

This emphasis on equity and morality was of course typical of Franklin Roosevelt's approach toward tax policy.[25] Yet even a cynical recognition of the fact that Roosevelt reserved this fine moral sense for politically visible situations and directed it at particularly vulnerable groups can leave one gaping at Roosevelt's depiction of the undistributed-profits tax. Here was a dazzlingly innovative proposal, one which required sweeping revisions in corporate finance and revolutionized existing corporate taxation. Yet in justifying this tax, Roosevelt spotlighted a problem of tax evasion that paled beside such loopholes as tax-exempt bonds or favorable capital-gains rates, the abolition of which had somehow not been accomplished despite the president's vaunted sense of fairness. When opponents charged Roosevelt with a willingness to slaughter hundreds of innocent corporations to penalize a few who stretched the law, they had a point. The murky bathwater was not the best excuse for throwing out the baby.

Still, decision makers in the Treasury were particularly taken with the idea of achieving equity by integrating the corporate and individual income taxes. In what can best be seen as a case of economic theory gone wild, the proposal that the president approved made the undistributed-profits tax the *only* corporate profits tax, abolishing over $1.1 billion worth of corporate-income and capital stock/excess-profits taxes. For the moment, the limitations of this untried proposal (including its uncertain revenue prospects and the recognized fact that it would disrupt investment markets) were shunted aside.

The response from conservatives and business representatives was pre-dictable. They were "aghast"[26] at this new and rather substantial tax increase on corporations and their stockholders. An already suspect administration had placed a "condemned" sign on a practice of corporate savings that was integral to current business practices. These factors inspired vigorous opposition. When ruffled, conservatives and businessmen responded with the customary apocalyptic flourishes. It is unnecessary to cover that familiar ground in any detail here, especially because Chapter 6 surveys it in the context of the campaign to repeal the undistributed-profits tax. Suffice it to say that it would have been a true sign of admin-istration failure in promoting its program had the tax proposal not been

25 See Walter K. Lambert, "New Deal Revenue Acts: The Politics of Taxation" (Ph.D. diss., University of Texas at Austin, 1970).
26 Alfred G. Buehler, *The Undistributed Profits Tax* (McGraw-Hill, 1937), p. 23.

branded "the most dangerous and revolutionary tax principle that this country has ever seen," and "a climax in the unsound, wishful, disruptive economics which have become the national curse."[27] One important new element, aside from a more insistent claim that a tax on corporate thrift would promote economic instability, did characterize this debate, however. More than ever, the tax was branded as the scourge of small corporations.

The administration was vulnerable to this charge. A substantial number of giant enterprises, with large accumulated reserves (surpluses that the new law could not touch) to pay debts and to protect against setbacks, and with easier access to capital markets, were in a position to slash their tax bills by distributing a large share of their profits in dividends. The administration position, in fact, was crippled by evidence that such blue-chip corporations as the Great Atlantic and Pacific Tea Company and General Electric would get away scot free. Despite the Treasury's argument that such cases were irrelevant to the purpose of reaching corporate income through the taxes on individual stockholders, the situation was embarrassing for an administration engaged in exploiting the rancor against bigness. Opponents of the tax extended their symbolic advantage by using the threat to small corporations as a battering ram against the tax on undistributed profits. It became the opposition party line to say that such a tax would only accentuate the advantages of large corporations.

This challenge was more than a strategem of hiding under the skirts of small enterprise, the business community's most appealing symbol. Many giant corporations really would receive favorable tax treatment. It is interesting that, just as smaller corporations opposed a graduated corporate income tax that might have benefited them in 1935, large corporations joined a united business front against the undistributed-profits tax in 1936, despite the fact that many would save tax dollars under this new levy.[28] An element of self-interest was still involved; business men felt menaced by a tax program that involved government regimentation of

27 Thurmond Chatham to Robert Doughton, 6 March 1936, folder 535, Robert L. Doughton Papers (Southern Historical Collection, University of North Carolina Library, Chapel Hill); Arthur Vandenberg, "Vampires on the Blood Stream of the Public Credit," *Vital Speeches* 2 (15 July 1936): 643.

28 Roosevelt supporter Thomas Watson is something of an exception. Though he kept a low profile during the congressional debate, he later wrote the administration that he favored the replacement of existing corporate taxes by an undistributed-profits tax. Watson's growing International Business Machines Corporation, interestingly, was *not* one of the firms that would automatically have escaped most of its taxes through such a change. Blum, *Morgenthau Diaries: Years of Crisis*, p. 321.

their investment decisions. Equally important, however, were the centripetal forces at work within the business world; to desert the business coalition on one tax issue might prompt disunity on others, thus vitiating the political influence that a unified coalition could command.

Considering this solid and vociferous business opposition to the tax, it fared surprisingly well in the House of Representatives. Ways and Means Committee Democrats, who had barred Republicans from drafting sessions, were content merely to remove a temporary processing tax proposed by Roosevelt. Otherwise, the bill followed administration specifications, including a 4–42.5 percent tax rate on undistributed profits. Despite the fact that few in the House understood this complex and technical bill, they trooped in on 29 April 1936 to pass it on a party-line vote (with only 4 Republicans and 11 Democrats crossing over).

In the Senate Finance Committee, however, the administration began to run into trouble. The committee's dominant and rebellious conservative bloc was determined to quash the undistributed-profits tax. The resolve of the Treasury Department was also weakened, as it proved inept in responding to opposition charges. The history of the undistributed-profits tax from this point on has charitably been called "inglorious" by its own supporters.[29] The Treasury simply had not done its homework on this tax question and soon had to back away from the House bill. Treasury witnesses were uninformed about the experience with the undistributed-profits tax in other countries. Statistical knowledge of patterns of corporate savings was so rudimentary that department officials persisted in claiming that their bill aided small business and that there was "no general rule" relating retained profits to corporate size (one and a half years later, the Treasury itself would find that smaller corporations retained several times the share of profits that large corporations did).[30] Likewise, Treasury witnesses were not aware of the average relationship between the size of a corporation and the income of its stockholders. These were not minor gaps in the Treasury's knowledge; they were the key questions in determining what effect the tax would have on the income-tax burdens of the wealthy and on the corporate structure. One could scarcely have manufactured better evidence to cast doubt on the government's capacity to administer

29 Eccles, *Beckoning Frontiers*, p. 260.
30 U.S., Congress, Senate, Committee on Finance, *Revenue Act of 1936, Hearings* on H.R. 12395, 74th Cong., 2d sess., 1936, p. 25; U.S., Congress, House, Committee on Ways and Means, *Revision of Revenue Laws, 1938, Hearings*, 75th Cong., 3d sess., 1938, p. 126.

major structural reform. Yet this was no idle experiment; it involved a wholesale renovation of the corporate tax structure.

The coup de grace was administered when the revenue estimates of the Treasury also came under challenge. At this point, the administration position began to crumble. In desperation, Secretary Morgenthau told Oliphant in early May 1936 that "I place my reputation in your hands. . . . We are gambling . . . and you fellows must be triply sure that you are right."[31] At the same time, it was becoming clear that the tax's effect might be pernicious. Roosevelt was upset when he learned that the House bill would slash the taxes on American Telephone and Telegraph from $30 million to nothing.[32] Morgenthau had also come to fear that the bill would handicap new, small, and medium-sized businesses. He was ready to cut his losses on the administration's bill. "The pride of authorship," he proclaimed, "is not important if it is going to hurt small business."[33] Most importantly, Morgenthau was committed to safeguarding revenue yield, and given the uncertain quality of the Treasury's estimate, and the threat that the new tax measure could become embroiled in litigation, he got cold feet about sacrificing more than 1 billion dollars in current corporate taxes. "I cannot take the risk," he concluded, "of giving up something I have in hand, namely: $1,132,000,000. . . . I would rather be sorry now than be desperate a year from now."[34]

As this chaotic situation was coming to a head in the Treasury, Roosevelt was reaching a conclusion similar to Morgenthau's. Much to Morgenthau's jealous displeasure, it was Marriner Eccles's call for the retention of the existing corporate taxes and the exemption of smaller corporations from the undistributed-profits tax that guided Roosevelt's thoughts.[35] Yet even as FDR and Morgenthau were deciding to give ground on the House bill, the Senate Finance Committee was showing a strong inclination to go much further and tear it to shreds. The Treasury had lost much of its influence in this process; the head of its Division of Research and Statistics was virtually in tears at the prospect of defending his estimates and the administration's waffling position before the Finance Committee.[36] The administration was in an unenviable position, reneging on a bill that

31 Blum, *Morgenthau Diaries: Years of Crisis*, p. 311.
32 Ibid., p. 312.
33 Ibid., p. 310.
34 Morgenthau Diaries, 11 May 1936, book 24, p. 13.
35 Ibid., pp. 55, 63–5.
36 Ibid., p. 102.

it had rammed through the House. Ways and Means Chairman Doughton, fearing that he would look like a stooge, appealed to FDR: "You can't let us down. We have gone through this thing and we wanted to change it and [the Treasury representatives] wouldn't let us. We are sick and tired of giving in to the Senate."[37]

The administration eventually had to make a considerable compromise. Even after a month of wrangling and the threat of a veto, the tax bill reported out by the conservative Senate Finance Committee was deemed unacceptable, although it did shift a considerable tax burden to corporations. It retained only a token 7 percent undistributed-profits tax, retrieving the foregone revenue mainly by hiking the rates of the existing graduated corporate income tax. Senators Black and La Follette initially planned to go to the Senate floor with a substitute undistributed-profits tax plan backed by the administration, but they refrained when it became clear that such a proposal would garner negligible support. After the Finance Committee bill passed the Senate by a vote of 38–24, the Treasury lobbied the conference committee for a more substantial undistributed-profits tax. The result was a compromise that set the undistributed-profits tax rate at 7–27 percent, with special allowances for smaller corporations. With Congress eager to adjourn for the party nominating conventions, this compromise bill was adopted with 18 Senate and 22 House Democrats in opposition.

The administration's undistributed-profits tax program had been humbled, but it had brought much of the humiliation on itself. Its limited achievements were partly a product of even more limited administration understanding of the all-important technical questions underpinning the tax plan.

Marriner Eccles termed the law "better than nothing, but not very much better."[38] This judgment is too harsh. It is true that, in terms of the administration's flawed original scenario, the new revenue bill was both a disappointment and a legislative defeat. It is also true that the conference bill lessened the safeguards for hardship cases, a decision that would return to haunt the administration. Nevertheless, there was reason to be pleased. The final bill made visible and politically discreet concessions to small business. Most importantly, it was a money-maker. According to the generous official forecast, it would increase revenue yield by $800

37 Ibid., p. 55.
38 Eccles, *Beckoning Frontiers*, p. 264.

million in its first full year of operation.[39] In addition, Roosevelt had succeeded in introducing a new form of taxation and had kept the sexy political issue of tax evasion in the public eye. He had also shifted the tax burden toward the wealthy, extracting unexpected revenues from the politically vulnerable corporate sector and from the affluent stockholders who would receive the accelerated distribution of taxable dividends that the law would bring about. The administration had hoped for more, but it had often previously settled for considerably less.

Political resistance and haphazard technical preparation may go a long way toward explaining the limits of tax policy in 1936. But it is still necessary to account for a more complex and tantalizing circumstance: the New Deal's willingness to attempt so much in the first place. The undistributed-profits tax was an uncharacteristically bold innovation, designed to bring about a fundamental reorientation of the government's relationship to corporations. It is worth considering what could have impelled Roosevelt to embark on such substantive tax reform.

The catalyst, at least, is easy to identify. Facing a $620 million annual revenue shortfall produced by the hatcheting of the processing tax and by the passage of the soldier's bonus, the president felt compelled to act. This is not to say that he *was* compelled. Congress was not chomping at the bit to pass any new taxes in an election year. But to protect both the government's credit and his own credibility with the voters, Roosevelt was determined to project an image of fiscal integrity. Although he repeatedly explained that to balance the federal budget immediately would take an unpardonable human toll, a balanced budget was still one of his major intermediate term goals. He would prove this – with disastrous consequences – when he slashed spending to climb out of the red only a year later. In light of this commitment, the revenue lost in 1936 could not be ignored. So both for the Treasury Department and for Roosevelt, a desire to fill the sudden revenue gap paved the way for the undistributed-profits tax proposal. In fact, before the opposition coalesced in agreement that Roosevelt's tax program was a nefarious outrage, some allowed that it was

---

39 Randolph E. Paul, *Taxation in the United States* (Boston: Little, Brown, 1954), p. 199. This estimate takes into account not only the undistributed-profits tax, but also certain technical changes plus a penalty tax assessed on the "unjust enrichment" of agricultural processors who had received a processing-tax refund as a result of the recent Supreme Court decision.

because it revealed an inclination toward "retrenchment" and reduction of the national debt.[40]

Given this revenue imperative, FDR was ultimately forced to do something drastic. The old recourses would no longer suffice, not when one was playing for real money instead of for political stakes. Six hundred and twenty million dollars was a substantial sum, fourteen times as much as had been raised by the 1935 Revenue Act hike on personal income taxes.

Where, then, could Roosevelt turn? Additional sales, excise, and other indirect taxes could collect enough money, but they clashed with the administration's image as a champion of the people. Treasury Department memoranda, using statistics that FDR himself had quoted, pointed out that government relied on consumer taxes for an embarrassing 61 percent of its revenue, a burden that was even more onerous to lower-income groups because of new state sales taxes and the upcoming social security payroll taxes.[41] Worst of all, there was nowhere to hide new consumer taxes. Roosevelt had been able to bring in earlier nonprogressive taxes as an adjunct to broad popular programs (liquor taxes for repeal of Prohibition, processing taxes for the AAA, payroll taxes for social security), but he had run out of Trojan Horses. The other tactic, merely renewing existing regressive taxes, was not applicable here. Or was it? To the horror of his advisers, Roosevelt's first inclination was to impose a new processing tax, presumably to be presented as a refined continuation of the previous unconstitutional one. Perhaps convinced by protests that this tax burdened the poor and drained mass purchasing power, or perhaps simply deterred by the threat that the reinstitution of the tax would revive bitter opposition and again be found unconstitutional, Roosevelt finally relented, after considering the tax for over a month.[42]

One logical alternative to the processing tax was an increase in the personal income tax. This, naturally, was Senator La Follette's suggestion for meeting the budget shortfall; it was also Secretary Morgenthau's. But Roosevelt had already milked the top brackets for much of their revenue potential, and he was disinclined to increase taxes further down the income scale. In fact, he refused to endorse the objective of a tax system that scaled down regressive taxes on the poor in favor of an income-tax schedule that tapped middle incomes more adequately. His September 1935 letter

---

40 *New York Times*, 4 March 1936, p. 20.

41 Morgenthau Diaries, 30 January 1936, pp. 143–4.

42 See Morgenthau Diaries, 18 January 1936 and 27 January 1936, pp. 47, 56.

to publisher Roy Howard interestingly omitted the following sentence in Moley's draft: "I am heartily in favor of broadening the tax base, but it should be done at the same time that we repeal a great many so-called nuisance taxes, which, as everybody knows, are paid in far greater proportion by poor people than by rich people."[43] But the final letter did use the argument that indirect taxes were far too high to justify such an income-tax increase. To argue this was to fall into the popular trap of treating the over 99 percent of Americans below the super-rich brackets as a uniform mass. Two of the more conservative Treasury advisers, Viner and Magill, avoided this trap, favoring lower exemptions and an increase in tax rates on incomes below $50,000, in the belief that while "the rich and the poor are overtaxed, the middle class is getting off easy."[44] Despite this viewpoint, the Treasury officially opposed a proposal in Senate committee that would have reached the still relatively affluent lower brackets of the income-tax schedule. The Treasury focused instead on the problem of tax evasion, using the fallacious argument that the income-tax increase "would be greatest on the great mass of the population, which falls in the small income groups."[45] Symbolic reform would not yield enough revenue, and substantive reform was politically unacceptable. The income tax would not transcend its role as a check on surplus wealth rather than as a significant redistributive tool.

With so many avenues closed, and with intense pressure to come up with new money rapidly, the selection of the undistributed-profits tax becomes understandable. Bureaucratic analysts have noted that, at any given time, "the menu of alternatives defined by organizations in sufficient detail to be live options is severely limited in both number and character." In a crisis, the time available for the development and refinement of new alternatives may be even more restricted; hence a bureaucracy may virtually be forced to fall back on policy prescriptions already in its "repertory" of proposals.[46] The selection of the undistributed-profits tax appears to conform to this analysis. It had been circulating in administration circles for some time and was available for "emergency" circumstances. Susceptible to many rationales, its appeal cut across the divisions within the New Deal itself. It was therefore not surprising that the Treasury would remove

---

43 Draft of letter from FDR to Roy Howard, 3 September 1935, box 2/ safe, Raymond Moley Papers.
44 Jacob Viner, in Morgenthau Diaries, 26 February 1936, book 18, p. 116.
45 Morgenthau Diaries, 18 May 1936, book 24, p. 168.
46 Graham T. Allison, *Essence of Decision* (Boston: Little, Brown, 1971), p. 90.

it from the shelf, dust it off, and present this inadequately thought-out program to the president. Finally, the undistributed-profits tax fit neatly into Roosevelt's political strategy. Herman Oliphant had touched a resonant chord when he told his Treasury colleagues that "if we have to fight we might as well fight the people who are our enemies anyway."[47] Thus, the undistributed-profits tax could spotlight the New Deal's fight for the people. It also attracted support from Roosevelt's left; despite charges from some quarters that the tax was a sham, it met with a favorable response from many liberals and radicals, including endorsements by the *Nation*, the *New Republic*, and the *Progressive*. At the same time, a tax on undistributed profits was so complex that it seemed to tax no one in particular (even most stockholders would only feel the bite through the rather painless mechanism of paying taxes on increased dividends). Historians have upheld the notion, popular at the time, that it was the "political innocuousness" of this revenue-raising innovation that disposed Roosevelt to accept it.[48] Roosevelt's experiment with substantive tax reform was an artifact of an unusual budgetary, bureaucratic, and political situation. New Deal tax policy would soon return to its more familiar role as an extension of Roosevelt's rhetorical symbolic politics.

Taxation, the 1936 Campaign, and the Politics of Ostracism

If pressing revenue needs had introduced a meaningful substantive component into the undistributed-profits tax of 1936, the presidential race of that year soon restored the issue of taxation to prominence as symbolic politics. This political role for taxation meshed neatly with Roosevelt's rhetorical strategy. His reelection campaign forged the politics of polarization into a weapon for ostracizing business from the New Deal coalition. This ceremonial banishment of the "overprivileged" provides the context within which Roosevelt as candidate could interpret his tax policy and neutralize partisan criticisms of the impact of New Deal taxation.

The combative style of the 1936 presidential campaign was established in advance. Previewing his tactics, Roosevelt informed the cabinet in late 1935: "We will win easily next year but we are going to make it a crusade."[49]

---

47 Morgenthau Diaries, 26 February 1936, book 18, p. 115.
48 Schlesinger, *Politics of Upheaval*, p. 507.
49 Harold L. Ickes, *The Secret Diary of Harold L. Ickes*, vol. 1: *The First Thousand Days 1933–1936* (New York: Simon and Schuster, 1954), p. 465.

The character of that crusade had been augured in the president's presentation of the Wealth Tax in the summer of 1935. Then, in January 1936, FDR amplified his rhetorical campaign approach. His State of the Union address was vintage Rooseveltian politics: vague and measured in content, but strident in tone. Delivered to an evening session of Congress to maximize his radio audience, it was designed to launch the presidential campaign. FDR instructed his speechwriters to draft "a fighting speech," one that would accommodate left-wing sentiment.[50] The speech pilloried the "minority in business and industry," what he called a "resplendent economic autocracy," who prated of individualism while conspiring to "'gang up' against the people's liberties" and restore their former power. The legitimate power that Roosevelt had brought to the "people's government" could enslave the public if placed in the hands of the political puppets of this autocracy. The New Deal, by regulating and ending the political domination of these selfish financial and industrial groups, had "earned the hatred of entrenched greed."[51] Roosevelt whipped congressional Democrats into a lather of rebel yells, whooping and footstomping, as all "thundered defiance at unnamed and unseen forces of darkness."[52]

As Roosevelt had projected, this abrasive style set the tone for the presidential campaign. At the convention and in subsequent rallies, Democratic speakers emulated the president's approach. The dominant theme of both the Democratic convention and the campaign – the contrast between the Republican Depression and the better times brought by the relief and reform initiatives of Franklin Roosevelt's New Deal – translated easily into the platform's attack on "12 years of Republican surrender to the dictatorship of a privileged few."[53] There was thus ample opportunity for withering reprimands of greedy business villains. The nominating speech for Roosevelt rejoiced that "the new tax laws" and "a score of other measures" had shorn the privileged financial and business interests of their former influence on government.[54] The president's draft of the Democratic platform promised a continuation of the struggle to "rid our

50 Moley, *After Seven Years*, p. 331.
51 *Addresses of FDR*, 5: 13–16 (3 January 1936).
52 Paul W. Ward, "Klieg Lights and Crisis," *Nation* 142 (15 January 1936): 65–6.
53 Donald B. Johnson and Kirk H. Porter, *National Party Platforms 1840–1972* (Urbana: University of Illinois Press, 1973), p. 360.
54 Democratic Party, *Official Proceedings of the Democratic National Convention 1936* (n.p, n.d.), pp. 213, 249.

land of kidnappers, bandits, and malefactors of great wealth," although moderates succeeded in extricating the wealthy malefactors from their exalted company and placing them in the succeeding sentence on their own.[55]

Roosevelt put the finishing touches on this portrait of his opposition with his extraordinary, marvelously crafted speech accepting the nomination. Anxious to pack the address with maximum emotional appeal, Roosevelt compared the current battle against "economic tyranny" with the revolutionary struggle of 1776 against the "royalists who held special privileges from the crown"; hence speechwriter Stanley High's ringing phrase "economic royalists," a small group of "privileged princes" who had sought to protect their control over "other people's lives."[56]

Thus President Roosevelt's rhetorical politics of ostracism reached its fruition in the 1936 campaign. Taking the cue from the convention, Roosevelt and his supporters continued, throughout the election contest, to sound these symbolic divisive chords. Speakers warmed up the crowd for FDR's speeches by spitting out the names and sins of the nation's financial titans, allowing listeners to greet each one with a frenzied chorus of boos, "like the whine of the hurricane before it strikes."[57] The message was straightforward. "We love him," said Senator Norris of the president, "for the enemies he has made."[58] Roosevelt hammered this theme home with repeated warnings of the dangers to democracy and economic life from monopolistic power and concentrated wealth. This crusade culminated in Madison Square Garden, where Roosevelt used his oratorical skills to stunning effect. Bravely, he took on "business and financial monopoly" and other "forces of selfishness and of lust for power." These forces, he said, "are unanimous in their hate for me – and I welcome their hatred."[59] In response, "a raucous, almost animal-like roar burst from the crowd, died away, and then rose again in wave after wave."[60]

55 William E. Leuchtenburg, "Election of 1936," in *History of American Presidential Elections, 1789–1968*, ed. by Arthur M. Schlesinger, Jr., vol. 3 (New York: Chelsea House in association with McGraw-Hill Co., 1971), p. 2828.
56 *Addresses of FDR*, 5: 231–4 (27 June 1936).
57 Thomas L. Stokes, *Chip Off My Shoulder* (Princeton, N.J.: Princeton University Press, 1946), p. 459.
58 George Norris, 11 September 1936, in Donald R. McCoy, "The Progressive National Committee of 1936," *Western Political Quarterly* 9 (December 1956): 460.
59 *Addresses of FDR* 5: 568 (31 October 1936).
60 James M. Burns, *Roosevelt: The Lion and the Fox* (New York: Harcourt, Brace and World, 1956), p. 283.

Roosevelt had seemingly embarked on a form of class politics. The irresponsible few had always been grist for his mill, but never had he so persistently struck this chord, or so vehemently asserted that this group sought to wrest away the reins of power. Yet if this was class politics, it was a special, sterile strain. The villain's portrait was often drawn in such deliberately fuzzy moral terms that it was virtually unidentifiable. At most, one can say that Roosevelt diverted pressure from the capitalist system by attacking capitalists themselves. But Roosevelt himself shied away from going even this far. The president rejected the implication that his was a vendetta against *all* capitalists. He assured businessmen that he merely sought to rescue them from the grip of a "handful" of monopolistic masters.[61] To accusations that FDR had incited class hatreds, the response was that his only demons were "criminal businessmen and evil business conditions" – the "rascals" and not the "honest fellows."[62]

Such comments do not absolve Roosevelt of the charge of antibusiness rhetoric. His attacks on "economic inequality"[63] and concentrated wealth, even if confined to a small group at the top, failed to make the moral distinctions Roosevelt had claimed for his position and undermined the business argument of the contribution of capital to society. Moreover, FDR was too perceptive a politician to ignore the provocative implications of the fact that, in a time of business defensiveness and public intolerance of wealth amid poverty, it was financiers and industrialists whose excesses he chose to condemn and ridicule. Still, the distinction between class politics and Roosevelt's symbolic politics of ostracism can be clarified if one notes that FDR retained considerable (though minority) business support, that he made no specific threat against corporate profits, and that his voting support, though markedly class-stratified, was no more so than in succeeding elections. The hallowed dichotomy of "the people" versus "the interests" may have intensified the enmity of organized business groups, but the division was amorphous enough so that its appeal could still transcend class lines.

Given Roosevelt's tax-reform thrust, his campaign assault on concentrated wealth and power seems ideally suited to the manipulation of the tax issue. This, however, is somewhat deceptive. As recently as early 1935, taxation had been the weak link in the New Deal's claims of concern for

61 *Addresses of FDR*, 5: 536 (23 October 1936).
62 George Creel, "Roosevelt's Plans and Purposes," *Colliers* 98 (26 December 1936): 8–9.
63 *Addresses of FDR*, 5: 233 (17 June 1936).

the forgotten man. As Roosevelt and other members of his administration admitted both in public and private, the tax burden had swung sharply toward poorer Americans since the onset of the Depression.

Thus, if opponents were vulnerable to Roosevelt's recent forays against wealthy individuals and corporations, Roosevelt himself was vulnerable to attacks on the actual composition of the tax structure. In the campaign, he was hit from both sides of the political street. On the left, Roosevelt was castigated for not going far enough in his reform efforts. The Socialist and Communist platforms both urged stepped-up income, inheritance, and corporate-profits taxes.[64] The Coughlin-dominated Union Party, dismissed by many liberals as fascist, and rather confused on the notion of redistributing income, still zeroed in on "concentrated wealth"; *Social Justice*, now the party's propaganda organ, took the New Deal to task for subjecting the "little fellow" to a heavier diet of "consumer taxes."[65] Socialist candidate Norman Thomas took a similar tack. Far from soaking the rich, he said, the new tax system relied on "various forms of sales tax" that meant "an enormous increase of burden borne by the poor."[66] The Communist Party went further, calling for the repeal of all sales taxes.[67]

Understandably, it was the Republican Party that really sought to take the initiative on the tax issue. Republican arguments fell into two main categories. The first was sincere alarm over the direction of New Deal soak-the-rich tax reform. Unlike the Democratic platform, which virtually ignored FDR's tax record, the Republican platform pledged to "use the taxing power for raising revenue and not for punitive or political purposes," an unmistakable reference to the 1935 and 1936 revenue acts. Indeed, presidential candidate Alf Landon reserved special venom for the Revenue Act of 1936, which he pledged to repeal immediately if elected. The "vicious" undistributed-profits tax, he charged, shrank job opportunities and penalized the small, growing firms that were needed as a check on monopoly – in all, "the most cock-eyed piece of legislation ever imposed in a modern country."[68] More generally, Landon echoed the standard Republican line on soak-the-rich New Deal taxes: that lower individual

---

64 Johnson and Porter, *Platforms*, pp. 372, 358.
65 "Actual Performance Since 1932," *Social Justice*, 2 November 1936, p. 9.
66 Norman Thomas, *After the New Deal, What?* (New York: Macmillan, 1936), p. 39.
67 Johnson and Porter, *Platforms*, p. 358.
68 Alf M. Landon, "Federal and Family Finances," *Vital Speeches* 2 (15 September 1936): 763–4.

tax rates would bring in more revenue; that higher taxes stifle investment, economic growth, and charitable contributions; and that the corporate tax structure discriminated against small investors in large corporations.

This set of arguments, understandably, had special appeal to businessmen, the group most intensely hostile to Roosevelt. Taxes on top brackets and corporate surpluses convinced many wealthy people that the New Deal threatened future tax increases; this specter was at the core of their extreme alienation from an administration that they considered "inimical to business." Commenting on this attitude, Harold Ickes concluded that "the fundamental political issue today is taxation."[69]

Though attacks on New Deal tax reforms tapped deep emotions, it was the assault on the New Deal tax burden on the masses that showed greater electoral promise. If the New Deal's "invisible" taxes could be made visible, Roosevelt would obviously be more open to attack. Thus, in speech after speech, the GOP harped on the fact that the tax share of indirect taxes had ballooned since 1932. John Hamilton, the Republican National Chairman, pointed out that "61.3 percent of the federal revenues are made up from taxes based on consumption, and are thus a burden on the great mass of the people of whom he [Roosevelt] pretends to be so solicitous."[70] *Chicago Daily News* publisher Frank Knox, the Republican vice-presidential candidate, cited FDR's tax figures showing a rise in the proportion of indirect taxes from 30 to 60 percent between the Hoover and Roosevelt administrations.[71]

It was left to Landon to sharpen this argument to a fine edge. Professing a lifelong preference for direct over indirect "hidden" taxes, Landon claimed that people earning less than twenty-five dollars a week shouldered a disproportionate and growing share of the tax burden under the Roosevelt administration. He reminded his audience of the taxes they paid on tobacco and admissions to movies or baseball games and took Roosevelt to task for "the fourteen laws levying hidden taxes" during his tenure as president.[72]

Others seized the opportunity to tabulate the damning statistics. One Republican campaigner charged that "through new Federal taxes on the necessities of life, more than 20,000,000 new taxpayers have been added

69 Ickes, *Secret Diary*, 1: 652.
70 John D. C. Hamilton, "The Rebirth of the Republican Party," *Vital Speeches* 2 (1 July 1936): 612.
71 Frank Knox, "The Most Expensive Amateur Hour in History," *Vital Speeches* 2 (1 September 1936): 748.
72 *New York Times*, 23 October 1936, p. 17.

to the Federal tribute lists under the New Deal."[73] The primary devices used to bring these daunting numbers home were fallacious or exaggerated claims that some specified portion of the rent bill or a pair of shoes was paid in taxes, or that the average citizen paid some outrageous number of taxes every day (922, according to one estimate). Most popular of all was the assertion that fifty-three or fifty-eight taxes – the number varied as readily as the number of communists on a celebrated list fourteen years later – were paid on a loaf of bread.

Even leaving aside the fact that such calculations cumulated all conceivable taxes (even those that had been repealed or that were only applicable in certain states) on every individual and product involved in producing the item, the central deception was that these statistics incorporated a bevy of state and local taxes that were not conceivably the New Deal's re-sponsibility.[74] Moreover, the Republican assault on federal indirect taxes could be sustained only in highly general terms. As one columnist pointed out, "There are but few people, and they do not include the anti–New Deal campaigners, who would seriously recommend abolition of the tobacco and liquor taxes";[75] not incidentally, these were the two weightiest hidden federal taxes. With the processing taxes already terminated, this only left the selected manufacturers' excise taxes on such items as automobiles, admissions to amusements, and phone calls. All such excises combined accounted for only a tenth of federal revenues; moreover, the Roosevelt administration had renewed but not originated them. A more exact rendering of differences between the Democratic and Republican approaches to indirect taxation, therefore, might well have left Republicans floundering for an alternative revenue source and unable to disavow the specific indirect taxes then in effect.

Yet the Democrats' acute sensitivity to Republican "tax misinformation" reveals an awareness of the political weakness of the New Deal tax system.[76] After all, the New Deal had just introduced an upcoming social security payroll tax (in fact, a major campaign by administration opponents, complete with dire warnings inserted in pay envelopes, warned workers that they would be forced to throw their money away on an empty promise of future benefits). Moreover, the tax system as a whole *was* heavily dependent on

---

73 Robert Bacon in *New York Times*, 23 October 1936, p. 14.

74 Tax Policy League, *Tax Bits* (New York) 3 (September 1936): 1, 2, 4.

75 *New York Times*, 13 September 1936, sec. 4, p. 6.

76 *Addresses of FDR*, 5: 528 (21 October 1936).

"consumer taxes," even though the GOP may have exaggerated the extent of this dependence.

Defenders of the New Deal tried to wriggle out from under this fact by changing the baseline for tax comparison from 1929 or 1932 to 1933, *after* the enactment of excise taxes in the Revenue Act of 1932, and *after* the bottom had dropped out of the economy and thus out of the progressive components of the tax system as well.[77] Roosevelt and his supporters also took it for granted that the liquor tax – declared by Landon to be "a hidden tax imposed by his [FDR's] administration"[78] – was an inevitable result of the end of Prohibition that should be excluded from any calculation of the tax burden. Finally, Secretary of the Treasury Morgenthau added that the major impact of New Deal tax reform was not yet reflected in revenue collections. He further tried to assuage concern about the tax burden by declaring that the administration would not raise taxes in 1937, although it might close some loopholes and eliminate some minor consumer taxes.[79]

Roosevelt's backers, however, did not confine themselves to defensive gestures in the campaign. In the revenue acts of 1935 and 1936, FDR had staked out a distinct tax-reform position, underlined by the protests of corporations, millionaires, and his Republican opponents, that washed adverse realities away. Thus the keynote address at the Democratic convention blithely contrasted the rise in consumer taxes under Hoover with the New Deal's form of taxation according to ability to pay.[80] The New Deal tax system was a matter of pride, for it had placed the burden "upon the great corporations and the recipients of huge private incomes."[81] "It would have been popular among certain groups of our population," noted Secretary Morgenthau, "to have raised additional revenues by new excise and sales taxes – taxes that would have fallen most heavily on those least able to pay." But, as Morgenthau told it, this was unthinkable (to a regime that had merely enacted processing taxes, revitalized liquor taxes, and

---

77 See Democratic National Campaign Committee, *Democratic Blackboard, Republican Blackmail* (1936 handout), p. 1.
78 *New York Times*, 24 October 1936, p. 8.
79 *New York Times*, 14 August 1936, p. 1; *New York Times*, 24 October 1936, p. 10.
80 Alben W. Barkley, "Rededication of the New Deal," *Vital Speeches* 2 (23 June 1936): 608.
81 "Excerpts from a Speech by Senator Lewis B. Schwellenbach at Columbus, Nebraska, September 4, 1936," p. 5, box 1, Lewis B. Schwellenbach Papers (Library of Congress).

extended manufacturers' excise taxes), so the administration instead relied on "primarily income and estate taxes."[82]

Thus the New Deal tax system became a weapon of attack, a cherished progressive instrument under siege by Republican reactionaries. Franklin Roosevelt cast it as part of his "fight against monopolies," arguing that it boosted taxes on intercorporate dividends, "big corporations," "big incomes," and "big fortunes."[83] Two weeks before election day, Roosevelt devoted a major nationally broadcast address to the subject of taxation. Again invoking the spirit of 1776, FDR noted the persistence of the revolutionary struggle against dominance by a privileged minority. As if to demonstrate how snugly his tax rhetoric fit into the populist-progressive tradition, Roosevelt offered voters a simple choice: "democracy in taxation" (implemented by the "American principle" of fair play: taxation "according to ability to pay") or "special privilege in taxation." He contrasted the Republican favoritism toward the wealthy in the 1920s with his "American" tax plan: the earned-income credit, decreased taxes for smaller corporations, higher levies on personal incomes over $50,000 (FDR counted this one twice, because he also boasted of "still further" hikes on incomes over $1 million), heavier exactions on "very large estates," and an undistributed-profits tax to close loopholes used "only by men of very large incomes." "Wasn't that the American thing to do?" he queried. As Roosevelt was careful to note, "the answer to this talk about high taxes under this Administration" was that less than 1 percent of American families paid higher income taxes, leaving taxes lower for the "average American," the more than 99 percent "who can afford to pay less."[84] (Roosevelt was stretching the truth a bit here, for the scanty tax relief provided to lower brackets by Congress's Revenue Act of 1934 was of no value to the over 96 percent of Americans who paid no income tax.)

Throughout the 1936 campaign, Roosevelt's supporters were able to exploit such themes. The tax initiatives of 1935 and 1936 weakened Republican efforts to link New Deal expenditures to broad popular financial sacrifices. It is doubtful whether Republicans achieved better than a standoff on this issue, although they started with the better debating points. Symbolic politics had neutralized the realities of the tax system.

82 *New York Times*, 24 October 1936, p. 10.
83 *Addresses of FDR*, 5: 521 (21 October 1936).
84 *Addresses of FDR*, 5: 525–9 (21 October 1936).

The Revenue Act of 1937

> "I should lay the heaviest kind of odds that your tax message of Tuesday will find a place fifty years, and a hundred years after that, in even the slenderest volume of American state papers."[85]

So wrote the reverential Felix Frankfurter to FDR on the occasion of the speech that set in motion the Revenue Act of 1937. Alas, that message has not proved one of Roosevelt's more timeless efforts. Even more revealingly, its legislative product received only scanty treatment in the "slim volume" of the daily newspaper. Clamping down on tax dodges is not inherently a trivial exercise, but the Revenue Act of 1937 was decidedly minor legislation.

This tax bill is still worth examining, however, for it highlights the moralistic and political role of New Deal taxation. Given the Roosevelt administration's focus on making the super-rich pay their "fair share," and given the fact that loopholes used by the wealthy could cripple an income-tax structure that relied on incomes exceeding $50,000 for over half its revenue yield, it was logical to expect some tightening of income-tax provisions. Treasury Secretary Morgenthau suggested as much in the 1936 campaign, and joint studies by Treasury and congressional experts in late 1936 moved along that road. But Franklin Roosevelt's interests were elsewhere (primarily with the Supreme Court fight), and the president instead promised no immediate changes in the tax structure.

By April 1937, however, the situation was changing. On both revenue and political grounds, some shift in tactics was called for. Roosevelt was shocked to learn that income-tax revenues had fallen more than a quarter of a billion dollars short of Treasury estimates, and other taxes of even greater value were being held up by various lawsuits. To New Deal opponents, the reason for this catastrophe was obvious: Treasury incompetence. After all, this was the same Treasury that had so bungled the revenue estimates in its presentation of the Revenue Act of 1936. The first collections under the two untried New Deal reform bills – the Revenue Act of 1935 and the undistributed-profits tax (which would swell the yield of the personal income tax by spurring dividends distribution) – were now coming due, and many conservatives were glad to see that soaking the rich was something of a bust. But Roosevelt and Treasury aides, in an analysis supported by later departmental study, pointed to tax avoidance

---

85 Felix Frankfurter to FDR, 3 June 1937, in Max Freedman, ed., *Roosevelt and Frankfurter* (Boston: Little, Brown, 1967), p. 424.

as the primary cause of the shortfall. Furious over mounting evidence that millionaires were slipping out from under the new high rates, Roosevelt announced on 20 April 1937 that the Treasury would, by the following November, suggest to Congress substitute taxes and tighter provisions to remedy loopholes.[86] In itself, this was more a technical than a political suggestion; it was, after all, the Treasury's responsibility to safeguard revenue, especially in cases in which sharp tax lawyers were helping to circumvent the clear intent of the law.

Roosevelt, however, was not content to let the issue remain purely technical. On 26 April, he decided that he did "not want to wait until next Fall," and he directed the Treasury to speed its report on tax evasion.[87] He presented the resulting Treasury findings to Congress on 1 June. It was a bristling message. Quoting Oliver Wendell Holmes's dictum that "taxes are what we pay for civilized society," Roosevelt declared that "too many individuals, however, want the civilization at a discount." FDR characterized tax-evasion schemes as nothing less than an assault on the fabric of government and society; such tax dodging also mulcted the Treasury of its "just due" and shifted the tax load to "others less able to pay." Sloughing over the distinction between tax "avoidance" (actions taken within the boundaries of the law to minimize taxes) and tax "evasion" (actual violation of statutes), he denounced the "widespread" efforts to escape "the spirit" of the tax law. Further Treasury investigation and congressional legislation would be needed in the current session, he concluded.[88] Why was Roosevelt overcome by this sudden feeling of urgency? Three major motivations converged to bring about this decision: the reality of enhanced tax evasion, Roosevelt's moralistic outrage against these "clever little schemes," and the seductive political potentialities of a renewed assault on "economic royalists."

Tax evasion, obviously, was not uniquely a New Deal affliction, but the nature of the problem had changed. Applicable tax rates for income above 1 million dollars had tripled, from 25 percent in 1925–31 to 77–79 percent in 1936. The incentive for tax avoidance had thus increased immensely. Intensifying this incentive was the animus felt by millionaires toward Roosevelt. The corporate community mobilized to counteract new government exactions, with tax lawyers and accountants taking the lead. The *Journal of Accountancy* justified tax avoidance with this observation:

86 *Addresses of FDR*, 6: 167 (20 April 1937).
87 Blum, *Morgenthau Diaries: Years of Crisis*, p. 326.
88 *Addresses of FDR*, 6: 238–9, 245–7 (1 June 1937).

"When taxes are oppressive and unscientific, the instinct of self-preservation asserts itself strongly."[89] The president of the American Institute of Accountants, calling income-tax legislation "a major menace" that fostered "resentment" and thus "evasion," went on to develop his major theme before the American Management Association: that refined accounting methods were necessary to allow businessmen to take "every legal means" to avoid overstating their taxable profits.[90] In 1937, the financial weekly *Barron's* carried a long series of articles on minimizing tax bills, justifying its advice in terms of the current "era of unparalleled expenditure of public funds resulting in tremendous increases in taxation."[91] This theme of tax avoidance as a kind of "pocket veto" of government trends was a common one. One of the president's cousins wrote him to characterize the "true patriot" as one who, recognizing the evils of government boondoggling and patronage, claims "every exemption the law allows," leaving himself more income for "enduring contributions to the betterment of mankind."[92] Tax avoiders had thus, perversely, joined the ranks of principled resisters to unjust government.

The uprising against Roosevelt and his policies, perhaps only to be expected from a group that smarted from FDR's recent campaign against "entrenched privilege," became a major part of the sales pitch of tax-avoidance propaganda. Roosevelt's arguments of equity and fairness were turned on their heads. Various tax provisions, such as those taxing profits while limiting the deductions for losses, were featured as manifest affronts to the "sense of fair play" that was necessary to gain taxpayer cooperation.[93] "When you outrage a citizen's sense of equity," the Ford Motor Company's radio spokesman warned ominously, "you school him in evasion."[94] To a large extent, such arguments were rationalizations for the growing financial gains to be enjoyed from manipulating the tax laws; the so-called inequitable provisions were far down the list of tax revisions demanded by the wealthy.

89 "Editorial: Tax 'Avoidance' and Tax 'Evasion'," *Journal of Accountancy* 64 (July 1937): 4.
90 Robert H. Montgomery, "Report of the President," *Journal of Accountancy* 62 (November 1936): 330; Robert H. Montgomery, "Accounting Methods Must Be Revised to Meet the Increasing Burden of Taxation," *Journal of Accountancy* 62 (August 1936): 92, 95.
91 J. Blake Lowe and John D. Wright, "Tax Avoidance Versus Tax Evasion," *Barron's* 17 (2 August 1937): 20.
92 Alexander Forbes to FDR, in Elliott Roosevelt, ed., *FDR: His Personal Letters 1928–1945* (New York: Duell, Sloan and Pearce, 1950), 1: 692.
93 *New York Times*, 6 July 1937, p. 18.
94 W. J. Cameron, "Tax Blunders," *Vital Speeches* 3 (1 July 1937): 570.

Yet Roosevelt did have a bona fide tax revolt on his hands. A New York financier was quoted as pledging to keep his fortune in its tax haven "as long as that bastard is in the White House."[95] The *Commercial and Financial Chronicle* attested that "no way is likely to be found to compel large individuals and corporations to pay outrageously heavy levies to serve political ends."[96] There was a bitter reality behind Roosevelt's concern over tax evasion; as they say, even paranoids have real enemies.

Roosevelt's sudden awakening to the need for immediate loophole-closing legislation also has an elusive moralistic component, one that is difficult to assess. Studies of such diverse figures as Roosevelt, Secretary of the Treasury Morgenthau, and Senator Pat Harrison depict all of them in various states of indignation over tax fraud; moralistic statements about this bill, in other words, are a poor index of broader tax philosophy. It is enlightening, for example, to attempt to square Roosevelt's distaste for tax avoidance with his own tax forms, which included perennial losses on his gentleman farms and persistent, legally dubious, efforts to escape higher tax rates by invoking the constitutional provision against altering a president's compensation during his term of office.[97]

The tax bill of 1937 transported all participants into a realm of sleazy tax chiseling that engendered broad feelings of disgust. From Cornelius Vanderbilt himself, FDR received offhanded word of the artful procedure for incorporating a personal yacht. In this sensational tax dodge, a taxpayer would turn over securities to his new yacht corporation, rent the yacht at nominal cost when he wanted it, and then wipe out all taxes on the securities by deducting the maintenance and operating expenses of the yacht (including wages for the crew) as a business expense. Only slightly less farcical were the hundreds of schemes to transfer income-earning assets to dummy corporations in countries, such as Panama or the Bahamas, where taxes were low.

---

95 Paul, *Taxation in the United States*, p. 201.
96 "The Tax Inquiry," *Commercial and Financial Chronicle* 144 (19 June 1937): 4061.
97 "Schedule of Farm Income and Expenses for 1929" and other material, "Income Tax Returns – Federal" folder, box 140, "Papers Pertaining to Family, Business, and Personal Affairs, 1882–1945," FDR Papers; FDR memorandum for the Commissioner of Internal Revenue, 7 March 1942, and others. "FDR Income Tax folder 1942," box 181, President's Secretary's File, "Roosevelt, Franklin D., Finances," FDR Papers. This is not to suggest that Roosevelt's tax forms, filled out in his own hand, were not more scrupulous than those of most taxpayers in his bracket.

Even more common than these so-called foreign personal holding companies was the domestic variant. Tax rates on corporations were so much lower than the rates on high incomes that this device was increasingly popular. Wealthy taxpayers formed personal holding companies as a repository for their income from investments, personal-service contracts (a neat scheme, known as "incorporated talents," in which movie stars and the like worked at low salaries for their holding company while allowing it to accrue huge profits by contracting out their services at going rates), and rents. It seemed that anyone who was anyone – the Lamonts, the duPonts, the Alfred Sloans, and both Scripps and Howard of newspaper fame – had one or several. These "incorporated pocketbooks," which reportedly saved one family $791,000, became especially appealing when a little-noticed provision in the Revenue Act of 1936 eased the penalty on corporations formed for personal use. Multiple personal holding companies were also ideal ways to avoid the upper brackets of the penalty tax while confusing tax authorities, with the result that one man owned ninety-six such companies.[98]

This brazen form of tax avoidance left Roosevelt "all steamed up."[99] Stories of such chicanery were what, in another context, was referred to as "red meat for the President." Roosevelt thrived on indignation over the stunted sense of social responsibility among the wealthy. The identification of a new, if familiar, scapegoat lifted his spirits; according to Morgenthau, FDR was "having a grand time" feeding the press information on the techniques of tax avoidance.[100] He regaled visitors with repeated accounts of the especially seamy evasion schemes used by the Schick razor tycoon.[101] When the Attorney-General came to him with a proposal for an out-of-court settlement in a clear tax-evasion case, Roosevelt became incensed. Pounding his desk, he declared that this was a moral issue, and that the evader ("Why don't you call him a son of a bitch?" FDR raged) should be put behind bars (he was).[102] Bedeviled by the Supreme Court fight, Roosevelt became so addicted to this tax dirt that, when he left for vacation, he instructed the Treasury to cable him "any good stories on how people evade taxes."[103]

98 Blum, *Morgenthau Diaries: Years of Crisis*, p. 331.
99 Morgenthau Diaries, 26 April 1937, book 66, p. 73.
100 Blum, *Morgenthau Diaries: Years of Crisis* p. 332.
101 Morgenthau Diaries, 26 April 1937, book 66, p. 72.
102 Blum, *Morgenthau Diaries: Years of Crisis*, p. 328.
103 Morgenthau Diaries, 26 April 1937, book 66, p. 72.

Roosevelt was prepared to go on the radio to "name names" (he was dissuaded from stirring up "class hatred" in this questionably legal way, though the special joint congressional investigating committee's release of special cases served the same purpose of exposure).[104] His case against immoral tax evasion was clinched when financier J. P. Morgan returned from London unprepared for the recent tax-evasion tempest that FDR had stirred up. The *New York Times* quoted Morgan as declaring that "Congress should know how to levy taxes, and if it doesn't know how to collect them, then a man is a fool to pay the taxes." A slightly different report in *Time* had Morgan denying that tax evasion was a "moral issue," for "anyone has the right to do anything as long as the law does not say it is wrong."[105] Morgan's was the very attitude that Roosevelt sought to dispel through new legislation and through publicity of tax-avoidance devices. The contemptuous Morgan comments were a perfect showcase for illustrating Roosevelt's point. FDR humored reporters with the story that one of his political associates had bribed Morgan to make the statement.[106]

Roosevelt, then, was good and mad over unethical tax avoidance. This helps explain the urgency of his call for new legislation, but it is essential to recognize that there was political method to his madness. Some of the evidence for this political strategy is inferential. When Roosevelt urged reporters to make clear that "this kind of tax evasion pays only for people in the very, very high brackets and does not apply to the great majority of income tax payers," he was plainly trying to replicate the campaign against "economic royalists" that had previously served him so well.[107] Political opponents made much of this tactic, accusing Roosevelt of an "obsession against the rich" that impelled him to scapegoat "his old enemies, the 'economic royalists.'"[108] A leading Republican compared Roosevelt's tax-evasion message to the Wealth Tax message of 1935, because "that, also, was a political gesture."[109] Even a liberal reporter, who was inclined toward the perceptive explanation that the Treasury was using the tax-evasion campaign to develop a more critical public attitude toward tax dodging, noted that FDR "has always been able to tighten up his loose

104 Blum, *Morgenthau Diaries: Years of Crisis*, pp. 328–9.
105 Paul, *Taxation in the United States*, p. 203.
106 Roosevelt, *Press Conferences*, 8 June 1937, 9: 422.
107 Ibid., 28 May 1937, 9: 406.
108 *Boston Herald*, in *New York Times*, 2 June 1937, p. 16.
109 Allen Treadway, in U.S., Congress, House, *Congressional Record*, 75th Cong., 1st sess., 1937, 81, pt. 5: 5447.

coalition of supporters when he has been successful in focusing attention on the iniquities of the rich."[110]

Roosevelt did not need others to educate him about the political potentialities of a campaign against tax avoidance. When Congress in 1934 had made its first cut at penalizing personal holding companies, Roosevelt had commented that "getting after corporate holding companies is awfully popular, believe me."[111] In selling his prospective tax message to Robert Doughton and Pat Harrison in 1937, Roosevelt came down hard on this theme. When his stories about "these terrible people" failed to sufficiently agitate the congressional leaders, he finally told Harrison that 10 million votes were involved in this sortie against tax dodgers. When asked by Morgenthau how he arrived at that figure, he airily conceded, "I don't know, but it sounded good!"[112]

In this case, the political argument was merely one of Roosevelt's tools of persuasion, but the evidence is clear and direct that political strategy was very much on the president's mind. By April of 1937, the Supreme Court fight was tearing Roosevelt's seemingly invincible coalition apart at the seams. Upon receiving the embarrassing news of the revenue deficiency (a deficiency that would be thrown in his face by opponents), he instructed the Treasury that he wanted "to say flatly that our estimates and our method of estimating were correct," placing the blame on Americans who had discovered "a trick way of finding loopholes."[113] This was war. "The time has come," FDR told Morgenthau on May 7, "when we have to fight back." And "the only way to fight back," he went on, was "to begin to name names of these very wealthy individuals who have found means of avoiding their taxes both at home and abroad."[114]

From a narrow attempt to defend the Treasury, Roosevelt broadened his objectives. Throwing himself back in his chair, he denounced the conservative Democrats who refused to go along with "any reform measures." Morgenthau, relaying the White House message, told his staff, "There has got to be a fight and there has got to be a purge. We have to go out and get the support of the men who are really on our side."[115] Taxation,

---

110 Ernest K. Lindley, "Tax-Dodgers on Parade," *Nation* 144 (12 June 1937): 667.
111 Morgenthau Diaries, 1 May 1934, book 1, p. 41.
112 Morgenthau Diaries, 26 May 1937, book 70, p. 92.
113 Morgenthau Diaries, 26 April 1937, book 66, p. 72.
114 Blum, *Morgenthau Diaries: Years of Crisis*, p. 327.
115 Morgenthau Diaries, book 69, p. 11, in Lambert, "New Deal Revenue Acts," p. 369.

and the rhetorical attacks on the abuses of the rich which accompanied it, was an integral part of Roosevelt's political strategy.

Yet, in extracting political significance from the Revenue Act of 1937, its overall insignificance should be kept in mind. It was difficult even to get a good debate going. Many newspapers, in particular, condemned the tax-evasion campaign. They saw it as a vindictive exercise in politics, designed to cover up Treasury ineptitude and the unbalanced budget, eclipse the Supreme Court–packing fiasco, and stir up class antagonisms by making whipping boys of the wealthy. The accusatory spirit of the congressional tax investigation had resulted, according to a few accounts, in unfairly besmirched reputations and legislation that would create hardships for honest taxpayers in certain situations. (This critique, incidentally, reflects a classic Catch 22 situation for the Treasury: When tax laws were loosely drawn, tax evaders asserted the right to take advantage of the letter of the law at the expense of its spirit; and when the government responded by tightening the loopholes, opponents dredged up extremely atypical victims of the new legislation, victims whose tax practices were in consonance with the spirit of the law but not its letter.)

The dominant response in the business world, however, was startlingly restrained. Early on, the *Commercial and Financial Chronicle* reported that "the financial community seems to have arrived at the conclusion that no legislation of real importance is likely to result from this investigation."[116] The tax-evasion campaign was considered an adverse development, but it was generally expected to have "only indirect and minor influence on the business situation as a whole."[117] In Congress, there was some criticism of Roosevelt's tactics and motives and some sour feeling over the fact that this was technical legislation – part of the eternal battle between the Treasury and ingenious tax attorneys – that would better have been considered without all the ballyhoo. But, at base, the Revenue Act of 1937 was an apple-pie issue. Even two of the least enthusiastic congressmen conceded that no one would vote against it, for "no one wants to be put in the position of defending tax dodgers."[118] Thus before the half-empty

116 "The Financial Situation," *Commercial and Financial Chronicle* 144 (12 June 1937): 3881.
117 "Factors in the Business Outlook," Standard Statistics Company, *Outlook for the Security Markets* 2 (7 June 1937): 147.
118 Roy Woodruff, in U.S., Congress, House, Committee on Ways and Means, *Tax Evasion and Avoidance, Hearings*, 75th Cong., 1st sess., 1937, p. 44; Allen Treadway, in U.S., Congress, House, *Congressional Record*, 75th Cong., 3d sess., 1938, pt. 10: 1273.

galleries and chamber, and after almost no discussion of the substance
of the bill, the House passed the 1937 Revenue Act by 173–0. In the
Senate, the bill received the classic railroad treatment for minor legislation
at the end of a session, logging no more than fifteen minutes of total floor
discussion. The entire legislative processs – presidential message,
congressional-Treasury investigation, hearings, debate, and enactment –
had taken less than three months.

The Revenue Act of 1937 was as notable for what it did not contain
as for what it did. The new bill closed down incorporated yachts (for
which the Treasury provided only two documented cases of malfeasance),
while leaving untouched oil-depletion allowances, favorable treatment of
capital gains, and tax-exempt government bonds (three of the biggest
leaks in the tax system). Its only important advance was to tighten the
definition of personal holding companies and to impose severe penalties
upon them. The administration was not oblivious to the major loopholes
remaining; it had even suggested methods of shrinking them. On the
whole, however, Roosevelt had framed the tax-evasion issue in such a
way that legislation was geared to the flagrancy of the abuse rather than
to its significance in undermining tax collections. This approach reduced
the Revenue Act of 1937 to a moral victory. The projected additional
yield from the act was only $50–100 million, whereas the embarrassing
income-tax revenue gap that had given the original impetus to the war
on tax dodgers had been $267 million. It is peculiarly appropriate that
this exercise in tax morality was the last gasp for New Deal tax reform.
It was emblematic of a policy that had pinpointed the villainous few while
carrying a minimal social impact. Meaningful fiscal and social reform had
been subordinated to symbolic politics.

Part III

New Deal Taxation under Siege, 1937–1939

TRYING TO MAKE THE BABY LAUGH!

Source: *Washington Evening Star* (12 November 1937): 1.

A political cartoon summed it up best. On the front page of the 12 November 1937 *Washington Evening Star*, a smiling Roosevelt bounced a screaming, bandaged baby, labeled "business," on his knee. Poorly hidden behind a door was Roosevelt's arsenal of rhetorical clubs – "economic royalists," "princes of privilege" – that had battered the child. Secretary of the Treasury Morgenthau anxiously brought in more amusements "to make the baby laugh," including a clown tagged "promised tax adjustment." The recession had dawned, and the baby was now in command.

Exaggeration is the essence of the cartoonist's skill. In fact, the erosion of reform in the late 1930s by no means represented a complete capitulation to business demands. Until World War II, opponents only repulsed the New Deal without dismantling it. However, this caricature more aptly described the disintegration of the New Deal tax position.

Clearly, special forces molded tax disputes. Chief among them was the political fallout generated by the recession of 1937. Columnist David Lawrence's prediction that "the last panic was blamed on Wall Street – the next one may be blamed on the tax policy of the Government" proved prophetic.[1] The unprecedentedly rapid collapse, which erased half the economic gains of the New Deal years, turned the political tables and permitted the business community to set the political agenda. The "economic royalists," ceremonially banished from the New Deal coalition in 1935–6, now returned to exact tribute for the symbolic punishments they had endured. Taxation disproportionately suffered the conservative renaissance. Once the pinnacle of New Deal symbolic reform, tax policy now became its lightning rod.

Tax legislation in the late 1930s is too insubstantial to merit much attention from a historical community interested in chronicling the advance of reform. Yet only the balance of power had shifted since taxation was a front-line symbolic issue in 1935. Even the buffeting of a feather indicates which way the wind is blowing. Tax issues mattered deeply to businessmen and to Franklin Roosevelt. To ask why taxes changed as they did in 1938 and 1939 is to reveal much about the forces contesting the decline of the New Deal.

This part approaches that task from three different directions. Chapter 5 traces the coincidence of mounting congressional conservative opposition to the New Deal and accumulating grievances against the undistributed-profits tax of the 1936 Revenue Act. The 1937 recession unleashed new administration policy approaches that modified relations with this opposition and led FDR to a spirited proprietorial defense of his tax system. The stage is thus set for the legislative controversies over taxation.

The business community played the most important role in setting the terms of the debate. The content of business ideology, the choice of taxation to plant the colors for that ideology, and the process by which that tax stance gained hegemony are the subject of Chapter 6. Finally, Chapter 7 examines the interaction of these forces in the tax legislation of 1938 and 1939. Taxation appeared as a safety valve for the political system. It allowed businessmen to let off steam. But when the smoke cleared little had really changed.

1 David Lawrence, *Washington Star*, 3 April 1936, quoted in U.S., Congress, House, Committee and Means, *Revenue Act, 1936, Hearings*, 74th Cong., 2d sess., 1936, p. 434.

5. The Recession Cometh

The decline of the New Deal, following so closely on the heels of the crushing 1936 electoral victory, has intrigued and confounded historians. Paradoxically, the very magnitude of that victory was a seedbed for later discontent. Amid predictions of "no opposition worth mentioning" in the next Congress, long-standing fears of executive dictatorship intensified.[1] Hiram Johnson (R–Calif.) embarked on a career as New Deal Jeremiah, echoing the concerns of the Senate insurgent bloc: "All sorts of experiments we may see, some of which will give us cold shivers."[2] Conservatives feared the combination of Roosevelt's electoral mandate and a lopsided, compliant Congress. "The trouble about it all is," Senator Josiah Bailey (D–N.C.) admonished, that "when democracy gets free to do what it pleases, it usually does the wrong thing."[3]

The 1936 landslide, however, although a ringing ratification of Roosevelt, was hardly a mandate for further change; few Roosevelt supporters either anticipated or sought a leftward turn by the administration.[4] Recovery even led the Roosevelt administration to counsel budget cuts out of fear of inflation and an incipient boom–bust cycle. The conviction grew among businessmen and conservative congressmen that the return of social and economic stability permitted a reversion to orthodox governmental tenets. In a May 1937 radio address, South Carolina's James Byrnes eagerly justified the postponement of reform by declaring: "The emergency has passed."[5] Americans polled in April 1937 apparently agreed, with only

1 Paul Mallon, "The Washington Notebook," *Chicago Daily News*, 5 January 1937, p. 13.
2 Hiram Johnson to Hiram Johnson, Jr., 15 November 1936, in Fred Greenbaum, "Hiram Johnson and the New Deal," *Pacific Historian* 18 (Fall 1974): 26.
3 Josiah Bailey to Earl Godbey, 20 November 1936, in John R. Moore, *Senator Josiah Bailey of North Carolina* (Durham, N.C.: Duke University Press, 1966), p. 127.
4 Bernard Sternsher, "Reflections on Politics, Policy and Ideology," in Robert Bremner and Gary W. Reichard, eds., *Reshaping America* (Columbus: Ohio State University Press, 1982), pp. 379–80.
5 *New York Times*, 4 May 1937, p. 13. James Patterson [in *Congressional Conservatism and the New Deal* (Lexington: University of Kentucky Press, 1967), p. 141] cites

one-fifth denying that the Depression was even partly over and over a quarter affirming its end.[6] For the public and its representatives, the crisis *was* over. For Roosevelt, it had only begun.

The reduced threat of economic collapse weakened the sanction for wide-ranging executive initiative. The rise of Hitler, Mussolini, and Stalin heightened sensitivity to presidential power. Roosevelt's proposal to "pack" the Supreme Court uncorked this specter of dictatorship, succeeding as could few other issues in welding the vague concerns about executive domination that lurked below the uneasy response to the New Deal. As the decade wore on, then, the New Deal found the ranks of its reliable congressional allies thinning on questions of economic policy. Most notable among the defectors were Southern Democrats, Senate leaders Byrnes and Harrison (the latter following FDR's support for a rival as Senate majority leader), Senate urban Democrats, and the predominantly Republican Senate insurgents. These groupings, fortified after 1938 by a Republican revival, were instrumental in the coalescence of a conservative coalition that inflicted a series of rebuffs to the New Deal, of which taxation was only the capstone. Fed by a popular consensus that FDR had lost some of his magical popularity, and invigorated by a recession that sent Congress scurrying to placate business, the conservative coalition took charge on tax legislation.

The Challenge to the 1936 Revenue Act

Even before the recession enthroned the conservative coalition, business spokesmen had marked the 1936 Revenue Act's undistributed-profits tax for extinction. First, they claimed, the tax discouraged investment. *Business Week* reported Horace Stoneham's lament for the decline of free enterprise: that tax barriers to the amassing of surplus profits would prevent his New York Giants from cementing their hold on the pennant by purchasing Triple Crown winner Joe "Ducky" Medwick.[7] Second, the 1936 Revenue Act penalized financial conservatism and burdened corporations fulfilling commitments to pay debts. Third, it encouraged monopoly while eating

Byrnes's statement and develops the "emergency is over" theme at length. Even in supporting New Deal measures, Byrnes had long made the point that such regulation would be temporary.

6 Hadley Cantril, ed., *Public Opinion 1935–1946* (Princeton, N.J.: Princeton University Press, 1951), p. 755.

7 "What Taxes Are Doing to Business," *Business Week*, 11 December 1937, p. 44.

away the main source of funds for small and growing enterprises. Finally, lower reserves and resultant lessened confidence would accentuate the business cycle, remove the cushion against economic downturn, and lead to another crash. This argument, held in abeyance during the year of accelerated recovery following the law's enactment, was the most portentous. Republicans would soon revel in their 1936 minority report's warning of instability and dislocation; "accurately prophetic," they would call it.[8]

It has always been a tactic of tax opponents to parade hypothetical hardships, even if there are few or no actual cases, to discredit revenue laws – while at the same time ridiculing excessive complication. This maneuver aided the assault on the undistributed-profits tax. A technical litany of hardships soon emerged. Opponents of the undistributed-profits tax highlighted the oppressive treatment of debt-ridden corporations. To prevent corporations from drawing down their taxed undistributed profits by prematurely clearing their debts, the 1936 Revenue Act confined its debt credit to corporations with prior written debt-repayment contracts that expressly restricted dividends. This was not an insubstantial category.[9] However, less formalized agreements, along with certain generally avoidable state restrictions on dividends, failed to qualify for this credit. Other complaints included lack of provision for dividend readjustment after the final year's-end computation of undistributed profits. Most importantly, corporations flooded Congress with declarations that the tax hindered their expansion of facilities and employment. House Ways and Means Committee chairman Doughton would later claim, with understandable pique and exaggeration, that not a single corporation had established the fact of undue hardship in the course of committee hearings.[10] After further corporate objections to his committee's proposed revisions in early 1938, Doughton responded to corporation executives: "I can see no justification for your shedding any more tears or losing any further sleep over any imaginary hardship that may be imposed upon your Company."[11]

---

8 U.S., Congress, House, Committee on Ways and Means, *The Revenue Bill of 1938: Views of the Minority*, H. Rept. 1860 to Accompany H.R. 9682, 75th Cong., 3d sess., 1938, p. 77.

9 George E. Lent, *The Impact of the Undistributed Profits Tax 1936–1937* (New York: Columbia University Press, 1948), pp. 178, 87–8.

10 U.S., Congress, House, *Congressional Record*, 75th Cong., 3d sess., 1938, 83, pt. 3: 2762.

11 Robert L. Doughton to E. H. Lane, 1 March 1938, folder 696, Robert L. Doughton Papers (Southern Historical Collection, University of North Carolina Library, Chapel Hill).

The primary remedy for the perceived deficiencies of the 1936 Revenue Act was a credit for profits invested or set aside for debts. This might have opened huge loopholes and created a revenue debacle, encouraging a bonanza of debt retirement. It would have rewarded repayment of short-term loans and routine replacement of facilities and would have allowed corporations to retain profits tax-free by funneling their retained earnings into the retirement of new loans. Yet the virtually unanimous business community was not alone in its support for such measures. Even Federal Reserve Board chairman Eccles, obsessed with the danger of idle funds, counseled an investment tax credit – a position with which Secretary of Agriculture Wallace concurred.[12] The more conservative and business-oriented allies of the administration joined the protest. Chairman Jesse Jones of the Reconstruction Finance Corporation began espousing both investment and debt credits while the 1936 revenue bill was still being considered, and Joseph Kennedy demanded more severe revision.[13] The Interstate Commerce Commission, without clearing its position through proper administrative channels, used its annual report for 1936 to censure the law's curb on vital railroad modernization.[14] Robert Wood, a progressive businessman whose displeasure with the undistributed-profits tax later helped bring his departure from the administration, urged an allowance for modernization and debt, as did Senate Finance Committee chairman Harrison in his transition from benign neglect to all-out opposition.[15]

The 1936 Revenue Act challenged business's most sacred prerogative, the employment of its own profits, the perceived engine of economic growth. It constricted the authority of the politically potent corporate managerial class. Each decision to obtain new equipment, redeem a debt, or restore backup funds as insurance against future slumps imposed a tax penalty. The insinuation of a government partner into such decisions

12 U.S., Congress, House, *Congressional Record*, 75th Cong., 2d sess., 1937, 82, pt. 3: 56.
13 U.S., Congress, Senate, Committee on Finance, *Revenue Act, 1936, Hearings* on H.R. 12395, 74th Cong., 2d sess., 1936, p. 887; Joseph P. Kennedy, *I'm for Roosevelt* (New York: Reynal & Hitchcock, 1936), pp. 75–6.
14 Henry Morgenthau to Franklin D. Roosevelt, 12 January 1937, "January–October 1937" folder, box 3, Official File, 137, Franklin D. Roosevelt Papers (FDR Library, Hyde Park, N.Y.; hereafter cited as FDR Library); U.S., Interstate Commerce Commission, *Fiftieth Annual Report* (Washington, D.C.: Government Printing Office, 1936), pp. 17–19.
15 *New York Times*, 11 May 1939, p. 1; Robert E. Wood to FDR, 13 October 1937, President's Personal File 1365, FDR Papers; Pat Harrison, "Our Tax Problems," *Vital Speeches* 4 (15 December 1937): 139.

seemed more onerous and disruptive than the previous simple assurance that higher profits would bring standard higher levies. The individual firm might well incur a lower total levy than before (an outcome usually masked by improving industrial conditions) but it still confronted a clear disincentive to bolster its financial soundness or to expand rather than to distribute dividends. This defied the whole business success formula. "That villainously unsound thing will be changed, must be changed; it will be changed, or this nation will be changed," bristled Montgomery Ward president Sewell Avery.[16] But for all the unity and alienation of the business community, it was not yet in the position to dictate legislation.

The Recession of 1937

The economy had already begun to sputter in the spring and summer of 1937. Then, in the midst of world recovery, the United States suffered the steepest nose dive in its history. The administration euphemistically dubbed it a "recession," continuing the tradition of assuaging public fears and outrage through a debasement of labels. Before the economy picked up in the late spring of 1938, industrial production fell by a third, durable-goods production and stock prices slipped by half, and profits skidded to one-fifth their 1937 highs. Unemployment, always a tragic embarrassment to the New Deal, shot up by nearly 4 million.[17]

The crippling of the economy, a timely counterpart to earlier political setbacks, stripped away the veneer of success that had restrained disaffection and sustained popular faith in the New Deal. Buffeted from within and spurned from without, the administration stumbled through six months of vacillation, inconsistency, and failure. A ferocious business lobbying effort greeted the ill-starred congressional session summoned by FDR in November 1937. Political leaders provided an enthusiastic reception. The four Democratic and two Republican New England governors joined in lambasting the undistributed-profits and capital-gains taxes as fonts of the economic downturn and counseled their repeal. Sixty Republican congressmen adopted a caucus resolution demanding undistributed-profits tax repeal to restore business confidence.[18] Alarm over recession had

16 *New York Times*, 24 April 1937, p. 23.
17 Kenneth D. Roose, *The Economics of Recession and Revival: An Interpretation of 1937–38* (New Haven, Conn.: Yale University Press, 1954), p. 237; Paul K. Conkin and David Burner, *A History of Recent America* (New York: Crowell, 1974), p. 278.
18 *Commercial and Financial Chronicle* 145 (27 November 1937): 3432, 3428.

precipitated a stampede into the business camp. As one business observer assessed the situation:

> Both Houses of congress have veered sharply to the Right since the last session ended. If the lull in business has accomplished no other beneficial end, it has put the Fear of Depression in the heart of every member who must face the voters next year. For wholly selfish reasons, if for none other, congress now craves to do something *for* business instead of something more *to* business.[19]

In earlier times, business would have appeared the villain rather than the beneficiary of an economic crack-up. But the New Deal's assumption of credit for recovery, reflected in Roosevelt's October 1935 boast that "we are coming back soundly because we planned it that way," condemned government policy to a share of responsibility for what was tagged the "Franklin D. Roosevelt Depression."[20] The Gallup Poll reported that most Americans traced the recession partly to the administration, though they pointed the finger of primary responsibility about as often at business and somewhat more frequently at economic forces.[21] A more important aspect of public reaction was that the atmosphere of stolidity generated by the recovery years served to stave off visions of total breakdown. Paradoxically, the New Deal now faced ebbing political fortune in both recovery and adversity. Assistant Attorney General Jackson's depiction of big business as "saved from ruin and restored to arrogance" applied more generally to the reemergence of a more conservative orientation, as better times restored psychic equilibrium.[22] This orientation laid the groundwork for intensified attentiveness to business's claim that New Deal capital-gains and undistributed-profits taxes precipitated the downturn. With the discrediting of New Deal economic policies, Congress unabashedly endeavored to woo business away from stagnation. The House Ways and Means Republicans reported in early 1938:

> We are of the firm conviction that the greatest need of the hour, and the only thing which will turn our footsteps toward the road to recovery, is continuous, unwavering encouragement to business. The most important

19 William P. Helm memorandum, [1937], "General Tax Folder 1937–38," box 254, U.S., Congress, Senate, Special Committee to Investigate Lobbying Activities, 75th Cong., Record Group 46 (National Archives, Washington, D.C.).

20 William E. Leuchtenburg, *Franklin D. Roosevelt and the New Deal 1932–1940* (New York: Harper & Row, 1963), p. 250.

21 Cantril, *Public Opinion*, pp. 62–3.

22 Robert H. Jackson, "The Philosophy of Big Business," *Vital Speeches* 4 (15 January 1938): 210.

and far-reaching way in which such encouragement can be given is by relieving business of the restrictions and impediments which this administration has placed in its way, foremost among which is the present policy of repressive taxation.[23]

Franklin Roosevelt's first public response to the recession was similar to the Congress's: to placate the business community and not to further rock the boat. By 1937, this readiness to step back from reform to secure business support for recovery had considerable precedent; Roosevelt had assumed an accommodating posture in 1933, the winter and spring of 1934–5, the autumn of 1935, and the postelection months of 1936. Secretary of the Treasury Morgenthau, seconded by Cabinet members Farley and Roper, counseled this approach to recession. This budget-balancing group, which also included Jacob Viner, Jesse Jones, Bernard Baruch, and Joseph Kennedy, keyed on "business confidence" and led Roosevelt to his initial reliance on restored private investment to bring recovery. Morgenthau urged Roosevelt to "do something to reassure business," a sentiment that even the First Lady came to share, upholding concessions that appealed to her chiefly for their "psychological effect." Roosevelt agreed to replay "the old record" of assurances to business, though urgings from deficit-spending advocates and swelling social needs had cooled his ardor for fiscal restraint.[24] He conferred approval on Morgenthau's 10 November 1937 speech, which championed "determined movement toward a balanced budget" so that "private capital funds" could take up the economic slack.[25] Although reiterating this budget-balancing position, Roosevelt reluctantly ratified the substantial tax concessions worked out in the Ways and Means subcommittee. In January, he expressed interest in reviving a voluntary cartel version of the NRA and entered into well-publicized conferences with prominent businessmen.

These efforts to appease business, combined with a lull in New Deal proposals, met with little success. Businessmen had long ago shed their trust for FDR. "Washington 'conciliation,'" Forbes intoned, "consists chiefly of the first three letters."[26] Roosevelt had played an active role in the

23 U.S., Congress, House, Committee on Ways and Means, *Revenue Bill of 1938: Views*, pp. 83–4.
24 John M. Blum, *From the Morgenthau Diaries*, vol. 1: *Years of Crisis 1928–1938* (Boston: Houghton Mifflin, 1959), p. 392; Eleanor Roosevelt to Bernard Baruch, 15 March 1939, "Baruch 1939" folder, box 1485, Eleanor Roosevelt Papers (FDR Library).
25 Blum, *Morgenthau Diaries: Years of Crisis*, p. 396.
26 "Two-Line Editorials," *Forbes* 41 (1 June 1938): 4.

alienation of business leaders. Now, with political success in their grasp, their position hardened. Eager to inflict a psychic defeat upon the New Deal, they targeted Roosevelt's prized undistributed-profits tax.

The business community's refusal to be wooed only confirmed FDR's natural instincts. Though the president had stationed himself in the camp of his most orthodox advisers, he expressed doubts all along the way. FDR was most at ease when he could isolate a scapegoat, preferably a greedy and unscrupulous industrial magnate or financier. As early as October 1937, Roosevelt is quoted as telling his cabinet:

> I know that the present situation is the result of a concerted effort by big business and concentrated wealth to drive the market down just to create a situation unfavorable to me. . . . I have been around the country and know conditions are good. . . . The whole situation is being man-ufactured in Wall Street.[27]

About two thousand men, he felt, were sabotaging the economy by engaging in an "unconscious conspiracy" of "organized wealth" against government to force a rollback of reform.[28] Charles Michelson, the Democratic National Committee's hatchet man, chimed in with the pronouncement that "today the process is for the ganged super-capitalists to withhold investment from the economic stream and so make business languish, with the same idea of forcing the Government at Washington into subservience to the big interests."[29] Although Senator Robert La Follette and others derided this view that businessmen would "cut their economic throats just for the fun of seeing their own blood bespatter a political enemy,"[30] the idea played some role in FDR's sometimes simplistic conception of economic operations.

In addition to reinforcing Roosevelt's suspicions of business motivations, the apparent failure of benign inaction gave freer rein to alternative theoretical approaches to recovery, particularly trust-busting and countercyclical spending. Roosevelt's rancor toward business provided a ready opening

---

27 Franklin Roosevelt, 8 October 1938, quoted in James A. Farley, *Jim Farley's Story: The Roosevelt Years* (New York: McGraw-Hill, 1948), p. 101.

28 Franklin Roosevelt, 6 November 1937, quoted in Harold L. Ickes, *The Secret Diary of Harold L. Ickes*, vol. 2, *The Inside Struggle 1936–1939* (New York: Simon and Schuster, 1954): 241, 243; Blum, *Morgenthau Diaries: Years of Crisis*, pp. 390, 393.

29 Charles Michelson, "Dispelling the Fog," 9 January 1938, "Michelson, Charles: 1938–39" folder, Official File 300, FDR Papers.

30 Robert La Follette, quoted in "The Week in the Nation: National Progressives," *Social Justice*, 23 May 1938, p. 7.

for Brandeisian antimonopolist administration stalwarts like Assistant Attorney General and Antitrust Division head Robert Jackson, Secretary of Interior Ickes, Tom Corcoran, Benjamin Cohen, Herman Oliphant, and Leon Henderson. The antimonopoly forces built on the analysis, though not the prescription, of economist Gardiner Means, who traced the Depression and assorted other economic maladies to the cartelized "new" economy's tendency to cut production rather than to permit its administered prices to fall to an equilibrating and competitively determined level. Adherents of this school of thought were quick to attribute the 1937 recession to damaging price rises and a capital sitdown strike.[31]

Spurred by Roosevelt's sympathy for this position, the trust-busters group mobilized in December 1937 to provide a counterforce to his policy of inaction. After Robert Jackson's first speeches failed to arouse public interest, Corcoran and Cohen drafted him a couple of bombshells that harked back to the spirit of the 1936 campaign. They placed the recession on the doorstep of "monopolists" whose administered prices and profiteering "priced themselves into a slump."[32] Jackson blasted corporate concentration and exorbitant corporate salaries and defended the fiscal wisdom of taxing the savings of the super-rich while using relief to remedy faltering purchasing power.[33] In a 30 December radio speech, Ickes added his own touches to another Corcoran-Cohen production, depicting a fight "to a finish" pitting "democracy" and the "people" against the "Sixty Families," who controlled the 200 corporations dominating the U.S. economy and who posed the danger of a "big-business Fascist America."[34]

This antitrust attack served a number of functions for FDR. If, as historian Ellis Hawley so compellingly argues, Franklin Roosevelt internalized the ambiguities in the popular fear of concentration and need for planning, the Jackson-Ickes tirades accorded perfectly with the primarily rhetorical position to which Roosevelt consigned his distaste for abuses of corporate power. Jackson and Ickes made the same arguments and

31 Ellis W. Hawley, *The New Deal and the Problem of Monopoly* (Princeton, N.J.: Princeton University Press, 1966), pp. 293–5, 383–4; Leon Henderson, "Boom and Bust," 29 March 1937, "Industrial Recovery, 1937–1938" folder, President's Secretary's File, FDR Papers; "Economic Dissertation," *Time* 12 April 1937, p. 15; Leon Henderson, untitled memorandum, 31 August 1937, "Leon Henderson Memoranda 1937–38" folder, box 54, Harry Hopkins Papers (FDR Library).

32 Robert Jackson, 26 December 1937, quoted in the *New York Times*, 27 December 1937, p. 1.

33 Robert H. Jackson, "The Philosophy of Big Business," *Vital Speeches* 4 (15 January 1938): 208–11.

34 *New York Times*, 31 December 1937, p. 6.

cited the same statistics that FDR fumed about privately, adding personal attacks that might have seemed beneath the dignity of the presidency. Not only did these speeches pose an alternate explanation of the recession that absolved the administration of all responsibility, but they offered a psychic release by waging a counterattack without circumscribing Roosevelt's own policy options. As Jackson had assured the president in September, "great political possibilities" attached to a dramatization of administered monopoly price swindles, for "people can be made to understand this issue. I think you can seize this subject in a way that neither your economic nor political enemies can withstand."[35] Though Roosevelt softened the Jackson-Ickes position by accenting the increasingly employed escape clause that it applied to only a socially irresponsible minority, its very fury allowed his subsequent action to appear more moderate. As *Kiplinger's Washington Letter* informed its business readership: "The best way to get business to accept reform is to frighten it first. This is an old Roosevelt artifice, being used again now. An interesting point is that it usually works, probably will work now."[36] Roosevelt himself noticed that the Jackson-Ickes blasts brought people to his January spate of business conferences who would formerly have stayed home.[37]

Although politically expedient, it is hard to assess the broader intent of the Jackson-Ickes rhetoric. Did these speeches signal a substantive shift in the objectives and policies of the New Deal? "The theory," Ickes said, "was that Jackson and I were to lay down a heavy barrage under which the president would advance."[38] Yet for the next several months, FDR's actions went little beyond pledging to submit a monopoly message, commissioning studies of monopolistic practices, and claiming in press conferences that the distorting effects of monopoly prices retarded recovery.[39] Roosevelt finally went public in a slam-bang 29 April address that assembled the arguments of the antitrusters. He proclaimed that "a concealed cartel system" was putting an end to free enterprise. He loosed a volley of statistics to depict a "concentration of private power without equal in

35 Robert H. Jackson to FDR, 23 September 1937, Morgenthau Diaries, book 89, p. 271, Henry A. Morgenthau, Jr., Papers (FDR Library).

36 *Kiplinger Washington Letter*, 8 January 1938, p. 1.

37 Ickes, *Secret Diary*, 2: 295.

38 Ickes, *Secret Diary*, 2: 287.

39 Samuel I. Rosenman, comp., *The Public Papers and Addresses of Franklin D. Roosevelt*, 7 (New York: Macmillan, 1941): 12 (3 January 1938) (hereafter cited as *Addresses of FDR*); Hawley, *New Deal and the Problem of Monopoly*, p. 400; Blum, *Morgenthau Diaries: Years of Crisis*, pp. 411–12.

history." He then noted that rigid monopoly prices muddied the road to recovery, complained that government "repeatedly" received identical bids for contracts, and suggested that a heavier intercorporate-dividend tax and further graduation in the corporate income tax might foster competition.[40]

This speech's interpretative schema dwarfed its main proposal: a "thorough study of the concentration of economic power," soon to become the Temporary National Economic Committee (TNEC). Although many of the monographs commissioned by the committee provided a forum for liberal-radical economic analysts, the investigation as a whole had a negligible impact. TNEC has thus come to be viewed as what Raymond Moley called "the final expression of Roosevelt's personal indecision,"[41] or even as an attempt to preempt more wide-ranging legislation, such as the Borah-O'Mahoney federal incorporation bill. Despite the public's retreat from destabilizing reform and reconciliation with corporate culture, the antimonopoly symbol still had a considerable following in Congress and out. Roosevelt may well have wished to combat the dissatisfaction among liberals that led to Philip La Follette's formation of the National Progressives of America, announced one day prior to the TNEC address. But facing a burgeoning conservative coalition, any imagined threat to moderation from La Follette or the Borah-O'Mahoney bill was the least of Roosevelt's problems. Granted that the administration's willingness to entice big business toward recovery in 1933–4 and into military production in World War II indicated that the antimonopoly issue did not head FDR's priority list, the fact remains that he sanctioned the operation between 1938 and 1941 of the most vigorous Antitrust Division in American history.[42]

The most that can be said of Roosevelt's commitment, however, is that he was in but not of the antibigness crusade. At no point in his presidency did it figure strongly in his overall economic policy. The fostering of small business, though a useful counterpoint to attack concentrated power, had little appeal to Roosevelt. He was more at home with the often interrelated themes of financial chicanery, abused power, and denial of social responsibility. Thus gestures like the 1935 Revenue Act, stepped-up antitrust

---

40 *Addresses of FDR*, 7: 306–30 (29 April 1938).
41 Raymond Moley, *After Seven Years* (New York: Harper & Brothers, 1939), p. 376.
42 Hawley, *New Deal and the Problem of Monopoly*, p. 421.

prosecution, and salary limitation defined the limits of his restricted and primarily rhetorical brand of Brandeisianism.

The countercyclical-spending approach met with greater ultimate success. By the mid-1930s, Keynesian and Brandeisian concepts, which usually mixed poorly outside the administration, comingled in the philosophies of Frankfurter, Corcoran, Cohen, Henderson, and the unofficial New Deal economic popularizer and theoretician, David Cushman Coyle. Antimonopoly efforts, many administration liberals concluded by 1937–8, were a vital supplement to a compensatory fiscal policy, assuring that higher prices would not choke off the multiplier effects of higher government spending on consumer purchasing power.[43]

Attempts to account for the recession immediately brought such ideas to the fore. In early November 1937, Leon Henderson and Lauchlin Currie (economic advisers to Harry Hopkins and Marriner Eccles respectively), along with Commissioner of Labor Statistics Isador Lubin, brought together a "BrandeKeynesian" diagnosis of the recession's incubation.[44] FDR seemed receptive to their depiction of purchasing power as locked in a vise between shrinking deficits and unwarranted, soaring prices. Marriner Eccles carried the ball for a purely Keynesian solution, tracing the recesssion to idle capacity and savings. Depressed demand would continue to throw the economy out of kilter unless the government soaked up savings with progressive taxes and created investment markets by boosting consumption through deficits.

FDR initially rejected this advice, hoping that a balanced budget could help achieve business cooperation in recovery. It soon became clear that business was in no mood for reconciliation. Inaction and Morgenthau's orthodox advice had brought neither economic nor political respite. In March 1938, the House pruned the administration's appeasement tax bill of its main face-saving reform, the Senate Finance Committee responded to business demands to decimate the bill, and the stock market took another tumble. Monetary manipulation and government-business planning had already failed in the early New Deal. As FDR desperately groped for a plausible path to recovery, he warmed to Harry Hopkins's prospending arguments, leading to the pump-priming program of 14 April 1938. In

43 Blum, *Morgenthau Diaries: Years of Crisis*, p. 414; William E. Borah to E. E. Allen, 22 April 1938; "Monopoly" folder, box 644, William E. Borah Papers (Library of Congress, Washington, D.C.); Donald Winch, *Economics and Policy: A Historical Study* (New York: Walker, 1969), p. 249.

44 Isador Lubin, Leon Henderson, and Lauchlin Currie, "Causes of the Recession," "Recession" folder, "General Correspondence, 1933–1940," Harry Hopkins Papers.

a decision that brought resignation from conservative Treasury economist Jacob Viner and the threat of it from Morgenthau, Roosevelt requested a $3 billion package (a billion of it in loans) to increase relief and revive the public-works program, and he announced strong measures to expand the money supply.[45] With a little help from the election-conscious Congress, this program annexed an administration-opposed farm-parity payment scheme and totaled $3.75 billion – a hefty if halfhearted concession to Keynesianism, especially because some of it would have been appropriated anyway.

This deficit-spending approach touched key chords in New Dealers' understanding of chronic weaknesses in the modern economic structure. The fact that budget cutbacks immediately preceded the economic downturn substantiated the widespread prior belief of liberal administration supporters that the economy tended toward oversavings and underconsumption, necessitating government deficits and some form of income redistribution to restore economic balance. A similar perception of economic imbalance had underlaid the economic-planning movement in the early 1930s. This belief in "secular stagnation" now flourished in the wake of the failure of private investment to fill the void left by the disappearing government deficit that precipitated the recession. The old oversavings theory seemed particularly apt to New Deal adherents like Senator Robert La Follette, who had long believed that mass purchasing power should replace investment as the motor of the economic system. "In an economic period when the closing of the physical frontier ... and other factors, are diminishing investment opportunities, it may well be necessary to apply taxes against savings in order to maintain economic stability, and to prevent the economic collapse which results when capital funds are not invested," explained La Follette in his lonely defense of the undistributed-profits tax. "Our problem is a lack of effective buying power on the part of the people; and until that situation is remedied, we could repeal all taxes without producing business recovery."[46]

With economist Alvin Hansen in the vanguard, this analysis extended to the claim that the outlets for private investment were so puny that only the steady stimulus of deficit-financed public investment could productively

45 Hawley, *New Deal and the Problem of Monopoly*, pp. 408–410; Patterson, *Congressional Conservatism*, pp. 234–41.
46 U.S., Congress, Senate, *Congressional Record*, 75th Cong., 3d sess., 1938, 83, pt. 5: 4931, 4933.

employ national savings.[47] At its height in 1939, variants of this theory buttressed the stillborn spend-lend bill and began to drown out administered-price explanations. Roosevelt's 1939 and 1940 budget messages rigorously defended the desirability of running deficits in depression and surpluses in prosperity.[48] On Eccles's advice, he directed his cabinet in January 1939 to publicly second his advocacy of a "compensatory fiscal policy."[49] Although an establishment consensus of congressional and press opinion had assembled around a business-appeasement approach to recovery, the Keynesian alternative had achieved a miniconsensus among New Dealers.

Keynesianism represented a subtle change in emphasis from the over-savings theories that preceded it, for it placed greater emphasis on the role of investment and the deficit itself in bringing recovery. *An Economic Program for American Democracy,* a Keynesian primer by seven Harvard and Tufts economists that has been called "a bible of the New Dealers,"[50] combined a neo-Turnerian observation of paralyzed private initiative due to "insufficient promise of profitable investment and expanded markets" with a plea for a speedup in public investment.[51] To some, this cast a more favorable light on an economic program geared toward encouraging capital expenditures by corporations and the rich – a disposition that fostered support for shifting part of the income-tax burden to the less investment-prone lower and middle brackets.

How much influence did the compensatory budget framework have on tax policy? Surprisingly, very little. The potential was there; even Hansen's secular-stagnation school looked with favor upon a program of encouraging demand and soaking up idle funds by lifting taxes on consumption and substituting certain progressive and corporate levies. But taxes took a back seat to the emphasis upon the innate importance of government spending in meeting the shortfall in private investment.

Conceivably, tax cuts might have played a greater role. Keynes himself had previously countenanced them as a legitimate supplementary tool to prop up purchasing power. With the onset of the recession, Beardsley Ruml, whose ties to the business community fostered a disposition toward

47 Winch, *Economics and Policy,* p. 248.
48 *Addresses of FDR,* 8: 37 (5 January 1939); Idem., 9: 12–13 (3 January 1940).
49 FDR memorandum to the Secretary of the Treasury, et al., 21 January 1939, 1939 folder, box 2, Official File 962, FDR Papers.
50 Elliott Roosevelt, ed., *FDR: His Personal Letters 1928–1945* (New York: Duell, Sloan and Pearce, 1950), 2: 858.
51 Richard V. Gilbert and others, *An Economic Program for American Democracy* (New York: Vanguard Press, 1938), pp. 89, 46.

tax reduction not matched by other advocates of countercyclical budgets, suggested that the fourth-quarter 1937 installment of income taxes be canceled to boost the economy.[52] By 1939, the business campaign to lower taxes showed its pervasive influence. Certain Keynesian advisers occasionally allowed that lower business taxes might inflate national income in a parallel way to deficit spending, and others carried a social security tax freeze through the administration and counseled tax deductions to encourage private investment.[53] But this tax-reduction advice had little effect on the New Deal. Before the recession, deficit finance could only be justified in terms of expenditures to meet the peculiar hardships of the Depression; the game was to cover the "ordinary" operating budget with taxes, while placing the Depression-related costs in a separate "emergency budget" category. The utilization of the tax system to direct idle funds into consumers' pocketbooks took a back seat to the image of fiscal responsibility.

Even in the late 1930s, susceptibility to Keynesianism was often rooted in opportunism; at the same time that FDR acclaimed the economic benefit of deficits, he argued that congressional additions to agricultural subsidies should be financed by taxation and demanded that any corporate tax breaks be retrieved from other corporate levies. Keynesianism's primary appeal derived from the sturdy economic rationale it proffered liberals for their social inclination toward expanded government reform; advocacy of tax cuts might instead encourage conservative demands to slash levies on corporations and the wealthy. Thus the adherents of deficit spending doomed taxation to a non-Keynesian limbo.

The recession, then, transformed the political atmosphere of the New Deal. Within the executive branch, it unleashed a pack of solutions. The cooperative-appeasement approach favored by Morgenthau and business-oriented advisers left room for tax concessions. The periodic antimonopoly outbursts sanctioned tax breaks for small corporations but rebuffed attempts to secure tax advantages for wealthy individuals and corporations. The Keynesian stand had ambiguous implications for tax reform and ultimately had little bearing on the administration's revenue position.

52 Leon Henderson to Beardsley Ruml, quoting notes from 18 October 1937, folder 4, box 3, series 1, Beardsley Ruml Papers (University of Chicago, Chicago); Beardsley Ruml memorandum, 26 September 1938, Morgenthau Diaries, book 142, p. 233; Herbert Stein, *The Fiscal Revolution in America* (Chicago: University of Chicago Press, 1969), pp. 101–02, 180.

53 Albert Lepawsky, "The New Deal at Midpassage," *University of Chicago Magazine* 67 (Summer 1975): 32; Harry White, 23 February 1939, Morgenthau Diaries, book 165, p. 186. Also see Lubin, Henderson, and Currie, "Causes of Recession."

Instead, the New Deal revenue strategy was shaped defensively as a response to the embryonic conservative coalition. As the economic collapse tarnished the administration's reputation as an economic manager, Southern congressional delegations and urban Senators proved especially eager to permit business to resume a place at the helm of the recovery program. Congress stood ready to pass virtually any placatory administration suggestion. Confronted by firm business assertions that tax concessions were a prerequisite for recovery, and challenged by an often unsure and vacillating administration, Congress moved beyond the administration on tax revision.

FDR's Tax Philosophy

The forces released by the recession served to trivialize FDR's tax position. As opponents of the New Deal tarred the 1936 Revenue Act as the major specific program precipitating the economic disaster, Roosevelt moved to simplify his defense of the tax; he spotlighted administration resistance to "special privilege," the least common denominator for which public support could be assured.

FDR had always found denunciation of tax evasion a congenial fallback point. The president personalized most national problems in a down-to-earth manner that made it difficult to interrelate or systematize solutions. In 1938, he took his moralistic antimalefactor approach to an extreme. After keeping a safe distance from the 1934 amendments for income-tax and corporate-salary publicity, and then countenancing the 1935 repeal of income-tax publicity, FDR now labeled corporate-salary publicity "a question of simple morality. . . . a question of morals, public morals." That a million-dollar income should incur a greater proportionate tax than a ten-thousand-dollar one was "a moral principle," not a "theory of taxation." He depicted both the 1936 and 1937 revenue acts as "intended to end certain forms of special privilege," noting the country's sympathy with that point of view. By emphasizing the ethics of taxation, FDR could dismiss conservative contentions with this comment: "Now, what do I do? Do I say again, 'Oh, well, let us encourage business, to Hell with principle.'?" For Roosevelt, tax battles were morality plays.[54]

Equity, evasion, ethics, and the ubiquitous phrase "ability to pay" probably represented the most effective short-term method of popularizing com-

54 Franklin D. Roosevelt, *Complete Presidential Press Conferences* (New York: Da Capo Press, 1972), 4 March 1938, 11: 202, 204, 212; idem., 21 April 1938, 11: 355, 354; *Addresses of FDR*, 7: 299 (25 April 1938).

plicated tax bills. Had New Deal tax initiatives relied primarily on more ambitious rationales, such as boosting the economy by using taxes to funnel "surpluses" into consumer purchasing power, deteriorating economic conditions in 1937–8 might have marked those taxes as failures. The 1936 Revenue Act proved more vulnerable than other New Deal tax reforms precisely because it was more tenuously linked to the homilies of special privilege.

However, the substitution of vague moral principles for a coherent tax philosophy had clear limitations. During and after the recession, it left a vacuum that enhanced popular susceptibility to the timeworn solutions of the business community. The issues of equity and tax evasion were most popular when presented in a growing economy, but they necessarily lost some of their luster with the return to dependence upon investments by the rich for recovery. As a direct disincentive to investment, the un-distributed-profits tax looked especially bad. Senate Finance Committee chairman Harrison claimed that the tax had battered one hundred corporations for every one that had previously abused undistributed profits to minimize personal income taxes, and Senator Key Pittman admonished that "when you shoot at a bandit, you don't shoot into the crowd."[55] These attacks typified a wider conviction that Roosevelt's crusade against tax evasion was a dispensable priority in a crumbling economy.

The business community's programmatic emphasis on promoting investment, by contrast, appeared eminently sensible under recession conditions. If shallow and self-interested, this program nevertheless had the virtues of comprehensiveness, defined objectives, and a symbiotic relationship with "experts" who conferred credibility upon it.

Whatever Roosevelt's own policy preferences, therefore, he found himself in the position of having to place a great deal of political capital on the line just to prevent the dismantlement of past New Deal initiatives. On this most conspicuous reversal of the New Deal, explanations of presidential inertia, such as claims of executive preoccupation with foreign affairs or a lack of new ideas, do not wash. In each congressional session from autumn 1937 to summer 1939, Roosevelt was the bulwark against the growing sense of Congress that a more conservative tax philosophy had much to offer. Much of the administration, particularly those quarters

---

55 Pat Harrison, "Our Tax Problems," *Vital Speeches* 4 (15 December 1937): 139; Key Pittman, November 1937, quoted in Martha H. Swain, *Pat Harrison* (Jackson: University Press of Mississippi, 1978), p. 174.

most responsive to business (such as the Department of Commerce, Jesse Jones, and the Business Advisory Council), deserted FDR on the issue of the undistributed-profits tax.

Most telling was the Treasury's equivocal position. As tax expert Stanley Surrey points out, tax bills encounter intense interest-group pressure for loopholes and reductions, whereas they generally fail to mobilize lobbying groups with a substantial stake in tax hikes.[56] In the absence of a successful presidential effort to foment public indignation over tax questions, the responsibility devolves upon the Treasury to represent a wider public interest. In almost all cases, the Treasury is the only counterforce with the technical expertise to combat loopholes. When the Treasury draws back from the struggle because of sympathy with the perspective of tax-reduction advocates, their objectives may confront little resistance. Such was the case in 1938 and 1939. As the balance of congressional power tilted against New Deal taxes, there was a corresponding shift in the Treasury to business conciliation.

Before the recession, the Treasury had embarked on intensive efforts to rework the tax structure.[57] It considered discarding certain regressive excise taxes, narrowing loopholes, and raising rates in the substratospheric brackets of the income tax – efforts that promised a more rigorously redistributive tax system. But congressional hesitancy to tax the influential middle brackets combined with doubts as to the economic wisdom of any tax increase in a recession to doom such ambitious schemes. Still, some efforts continued. In November 1937, Morgenthau asserted that "we would be applying the principle of capacity to pay more justly if we were to reduce the number of consumer taxes and at the same time to increase the number of income tax payers.[58] With growing Treasury profession-alization and use of economist tax staffs, such a redistributive shift in the tax system gained favor. This combined with resumed accentuation of private investment to lend credence to Jacob Viner's depiction of the tax system: "I think it is sufficiently stiff on the poor, it is deadening to investment and enterprise on the very rich, and that it's the $2,500 to $10,000 income people who are so well off in this country, as compared to almost anywhere in the world."[59] Late 1938 and 1939 preparation for

56 Stanley S. Surrey, "The Congress and the Tax Lobbyist: How Special Tax Provisions Get Enacted," *Harvard Law Review* 70 (May 1957): 1164.
57 Blum, *Morgenthau Diaries: Years of Crisis*, p. 440.
58 Henry Morgenthau, Jr., "Federal Spending and the Federal Budget," *Proceedings of the Academy of Political Science* 17 (January 1938): 541.
59 Jacob Viner, 9 December 1938, in Morgenthau Diaries, book 155, p. 168, FDR Library.

an ultimately suppressed tax increase zeroed in on taxpayers in the $10,000 to $50,000 range. In conference, Morgenthau argued: "We have never begun to tax the people in this country the way they should be. . . . I don't pay what I should. People of my class don't. People who have it should pay."[60] Though leery of its political implications, FDR apparently came to recognize this, for on a couple of occasions in mid-1939 he seemed to sanction higher levies on sub-$50,000 incomes and lower income tax exemptions.[61] Yet such proposals failed to receive official administration endorsement. FDR was inclined to suspect suggestions that paralleled the business approach toward taxation and recovery. In any case, Roosevelt would have had legitimate grounds to fear that business would withdraw from the certain political uproar, forcing the administration to face the storm alone, an untenable position until war-revenue needs dramatized the necessity for such tax sacrifice.

Despite an organizational commitment to maximizing revenue collection, high Treasury Department officials set a tone of responsiveness to the business perspective that suffused the agency and rendered it a prime conservative force within the administration. Many Treasury employees, already influenced by an economics or legal education that celebrated the status quo and praised the wealthy as the linchpins of national prosperity, had in earlier pre-Depression years used the department as a way station to a more lucrative private practice. Thus, in a pattern common for regulatory agencies, there was a conspicuous tendency for the department to fall under the sway of its most powerful clients, corporations and the wealthy. Yet a potent countervailing influence intervened. The overriding criterion for departmental effectiveness was revenue intake, a measure that led to overzealous implementation in certain cases and that created some resentment within the agency over loopholes that got in their way. The Board of Tax Appeals, which overruled a large proportion of IRS assessments appealed to it, testified to what business spokesmen deemed a "tough" Treasury attitude.[62]

Because of changes in the tax base, the tax laws, and collection procedures, no clear pattern of superior effectiveness presents itself in comparing the enforcement record of the Treasury Department during the New Deal with the Coolidge-Hoover record that came under so much fire. Representatives of the populist left railed against the considerable carryover of tax officials from Andrew Mellon's Treasury Department into the New

60 Morgenthau Diaries, 9 May 1939, book 189, pp. 41–2, FDR Library.
61 *New York Times*, 17 June 1939, pp. 1, 6.
62 "U.S. is Tough on Taxpayers," *Business Week*, 10 July 1937, p. 36.

Deal. "A whole book could be written on the ideas which Andy left behind," proclaimed Representative McFarlane (D–Tex.) "There is no department in our Government, other than the courts, which has as many ideas of our Republican predecessors as the Internal Revenue Bureau."[63] Noting Washington's inclination to overrule deficiency assessments made in field audits, McFarlane accused the Treasury of "sleeping sickness" and chided it for selling FDR's antiloophole drive "down the river" by displaying too much solicitude for the legality of "ridiculous tricks."[64]

It is a revealing commentary on the tax lawyers who manned the Treasury Department that the ceaseless conservative tirades against muddleheaded bureaucrats usually exempted all Treasury officials except Herman Oliphant. Treasury Undersecretary Roswell Magill, a Republican law professor with Treasury experience under Mellon, faithfully presented the Roosevelt case in 1937–8 for loophole closing and the undistributed-profits tax. He won frequent plaudits from Republicans and business representatives for his understanding and responsiveness, though FDR deemed him "too conservative."[65] The appointment of Magill's successor was hailed with even greater enthusiasm. John Hanes was the fulfillment of a conservative dream: a practical businessman in charge of the impractical, visionary, and punitive New Deal tax system that so inflamed the business community. Armed with credentials as an investment banker and a director of more than a score of corporations, Hanes was a prominent reminder that Morgenthau and even Roosevelt had not jettisoned the business-appeasement option. During his short tenure in government service, Hanes was cast as the prime protector of Wall Street interests within the administration. He conspired against administration tax policies from within, maintained close ties to the Republican Party after his December 1939 resignation, and by 1947–8 was lambasting the New Deal's steps toward socialism. At least, Randolph Paul has observed, "Hanes was always consistent; in and out of office he was for business appeasement first, last, and all the time."[66] Morgenthau's decision to turn over the administration's tax program

63 U.S., Congress, House, *Congressional Record*, 75th Cong., 1st sess., 1937, 81, pt. 10: 2284–5.
64 U.S., Congress, House, *Congressional Record*, 75th Cong., 1st sess., 1937, 81, pt. 8: 9057, 9052, 9051.
65 Blum, *Morgenthau Diaries: Years of Crisis*, p. 440.
66 Randolph E. Paul, *Taxation in the United States* (Boston: Little, Brown, 1954), p. 255.

to such a man poses intriguing questions as to whether parts of that program were considered expendable.[67]

Morgenthau bore responsibility for the Treasury's transformation into a mouthpiece for the conservative position. The Treasury Secretary gloried in his new departmental slogan, which picked up on the prevalent theme that recovery and reform were somehow counterposed, prompting FDR to snap, "I think that sign you have on your desk, 'Does it contribute to recovery' is very stupid."[68] The recession stripped Morgenthau's position of much of its redeeming compassion and indignation over tax evasion. His case to the president for achieving a higher national income through concessions fostering confidence, lower risk, higher profits, and private investment was a mere recital of the standard business line. In 1939, at Hanes's instigation, the Treasury began a formal solicitation of business tax views, a policy of continued importance into World War II. Although one might rather emphasize the lack of such consultation in the past, the voluminous correspondence and 83 conferences with businessmen betokened a decided shift in the derivation of Treasury tax proposals.[69] This shift led Roosevelt to supplement or bypass the Treasury on a number of tax issues in 1939.[70] Roosevelt needed Treasury support to carry his enervated postrecession tax policy, but it would not be forthcoming.

The Waning of Progressive Tax Forces

FDR arrayed only a meager support force against the growing disenchantment with New Deal tax policies. Antagonism to the concessions granted the "New Mellonism" was largely confined to a shrinking liberal group encompassing administration countercyclical spending advocates, journals such as the *Nation* or *New Republic*, and a subdued congressional force led by Maverick in the House and extending little beyond La Follette in the Senate. Even House Ways and Means Committee chairman Robert Doughton abandoned the sinking New Deal ship. In 1938, he had criticized the tax-reduction movement as "so selfish" that its version of a tax law

67 Joseph Alsop and Robert Kintner, "Business Viewpoint Seen in Treasury Under Hanes Guidance," *New York Times*, 30 November 1938, p. 6; *New York Times*, 2 July 1938, p. 17.

68 "March 8, 1939 Meeting at the White House at 11 a.m. on Taxes," p. 3, box 178, "Chronology – Tax Bill – 1939." Record Group 56, General Records of the Department of the Treasury (National Archives, Washington, D.C.).

69 Roy Blough, *The Federal Taxing Process* (New York: Prentice-Hall, 1952), p. 25.

70 Paul, *Taxation in the United States*, p. 255; Elliott Roosevelt, *FDR: His Personal Letters*, 2: 889–90.

wouldn't collect "enough to run this Government for 1 year, 1 month, or 1 day,"[71] and characterized the undistributed-profits tax campaign as "an excuse" to "shift as much of the tax burden as possible from those who are most able to pay to the backs of the consumer."[72] But by 1939 he pressured Roosevelt to sanction the Treasury's conciliatory gestures.

FDR's basic problem was the virtual disappearance of the radical push that had eased past initiatives. Unstated assumptions that the radical left presented a monolithic front have obscured the determinants of this eclipse. The most notable collapse of leftward pressure arose from ideological vagaries of the populist anti–Wall Street circle. Indicative of this collapse is the changing stance of *Plain Talk*, a peripheral journal whose editor Morris Bealle skated the lunatic fringe from Huey Long to William Lemke to initial World War II opposition to an intensified virulent anti-communism that helped draw him to Joe McCarthy, Barry Goldwater, and George Wallace.[73] Concerned over the "unhealthy, top-heavy majority of Democrats" elected in 1936, stung by the dictatorial aura surrounding the Supreme Court–packing plan, and enraged over the rise of the CIO and the administration's tolerance for sit-down strikes,[74] *Plain Talk* moved from the left to the right in opposition to FDR's noninflationist, prolabor, interventionist, expanded-government stance. After berating FDR in 1936 for belatedly proposing the undistributed-profits tax "two and a half years behind *Plain Talk*," it moved repeal of the tax to the top of its 1938 platform, charging it with "stifling commerce, preventing business expansion, and KEEPING MILLIONS out of work."[75]

Plain Talk had seemingly come a long way from its 1935 claim that the super-rich use "the old deck of Wall-Street marked cards and call it a new deal,"[76] but it followed a common path. Even Western progressive

---

71 U.S., Congress, House, Committee on Ways and Means, *Revision of Revenue Laws 1938, Hearings*, 75th Cong., 3d sess., 1938, p. 431.
72 Robert L. Doughton to W. L. Dowell, 16 March 1938, folder 700, Robert L. Doughton Papers (Southern Historical Collection, University of North Carolina Library, Chapel Hill).
73 Information on Bealle's later years was received from Mrs. Morris Bealle, telephone interview, Washington, D.C., 3 April 1974.
74 Napoleon Jones, "Majority Leader," *Plain Talk* 14 (January 1937): 1; editorial introduction to Colent, "Plain Talk about the Supreme Court," *Plain Talk* 14 (April 1937): 2; "Editorials," *Plain Talk* 14 (May 1937): 74.
75 "Editorials," *Plain Talk* 12 (May 1936): 3; "Politicians Vs. the People," *Plain Talk* 16 (September 1938): 1.
76 "The Wisdom of the Rockefellers, Morgans and Baruchs," *Plain Talk* 11 (January 1935): inside cover.

Senators Joseph O'Mahoney and William Borah, who continued to defend liberal positions, declared that "taxation is the great incubus upon the back of enterprise" and that "before we can hope for permanent business prosperity, we must reduce government expenses and cut down taxes."[77]

The recession also brought support for the business tax position from an unexpected quarter: the American Federation of Labor. The AFL had toiled diligently against state and federal sales taxes, but had traditionally steered clear of other tax controversies. It did endorse FDR's 1935 Wealth Tax plan in its press releases, but its congressional lobbying effort was unimpressive.[78] Even this nonchalant support gave way by early 1938. Sapped by the recession and threatened by National Labor Relations Board decisions that furthered the CIO surge, the AFL expelled recalcitrant industrial unions from its ranks and showed little hesitation in opposing the New Deal's reorganization and wages-and-hours proposals. Taxation of business, an issue that had always been peripheral to the narrow goals of the AFL chieftains, proved a convenient aid to the formation of a corporate–AFL alliance against the CIO. On 8 February 1938, the AFL executive council advocated repeal or modification of the federal taxes on undistributed profits and capital gains, citing the business pledge that such government action would rectify the lack of confidence that had torpedoed employment.[79] Even after the concessions of the 1938 Revenue Act, the AFL executive council continued to press this position, urging that "a political and economic state of mind should be created which would enable all financiers and the owners and management of industry to face the future with confidence."[80]

Industrial unions occasionally derided this position but usually confined their efforts to the social security payroll tax and more exigent issues until

77 Joseph O'Mahoney, quoted in U.S., Congress, House, *Congressional Record*, 76th Cong., 1st sess., 1939, 84, pt. 11: 1003; William E. Borah to Dan Harrington, 28 February 1938, "Monopoly" folder, box 644, William E. Borah Papers (Library of Congress).

78 "Taxing the Rich," *American Federation of Labor Weekly News Service* 25 (10 August 1935): 1. See American Federation of Labor, *Report of Proceedings of the Fifty-fifth Annual Convention, 1935* (Washington, D.C.: Judd & Detweiler, n.d.), p. 856, for John L. Lewis's claim that the AFL did little to further the tax bill.

79 Philip Taft, *The A. F. of L. from the Death of Gompers to the Merger* (New York: Harper & Brothers, 1959), p. 291.

80 "Statement upon the Business and Economic Conditions of the Nation Issued by the Executive Council of the American Federation of Labor, Miami, Fla., February 14, 1939" in U.S., Congress, House, Committee on Ways and Means, *Social Security, Hearings* Relative to the Social Security Act Amendments of 1939, 76th Cong., 1st sess., 1939, 2: 1358.

late 1939, when the CIO complained that labor and consumers shouldered an inordinate share of the tax burden and outlined a program for corporate excess-profits taxes and higher upper-bracket income and inheritance levies.[81]

This assertiveness on taxation was too little and too late to save the undistributed-profits tax or to counteract the AFL. In 1938 and 1939, organized labor fueled conservative tax efforts to a greater extent than they had ever furthered New Deal tax proposals.

Although the AFL and populist, isolationist anti–Wall Streeters had peeled off from the New Deal coalition, a hard core of what had previously constituted a leftward threat took shelter in Roosevelt's camp. This shift was neither immediate nor total. With the gutting of the public-works and relief programs, the tendency toward internationalism betrayed in the Quarantine speech, and the absence of FDR's magic in dealing with the economy or with Congress, a base existed for dissatisfaction on the left. As FDR floundered in indecision in early 1938, thirty-three left-leaning congressmen presented him with a liberal program encompassing a more progressive tax structure through heavier exactions on inheritances, higher intercorporate-dividend taxes, and revisions of the capital-gains and un-distributed-profits taxes to ease burdens on small incomes. Even this friendly nudge – so different in tone from the demands of 1934–6 – vanished with the 1938 election. Most of the "Mavericks" failed to retain their seats, and the decimated liberal bloc disintegrated soon after.[82]

When Philip La Follette also tried to press a liberal resurgence upon FDR without undermining the president's influence, he met a fate similar to the Mavericks. His formation of the National Progressives of America in late April 1938 as a reform alternative to the Democrats spurred FDR's purge efforts to secure a more liberal Democratic Party, but fizzled after the Wisconsin electorate buried Governor La Follette and five of the seven progressive congressmen. *Common Sense*, the leading organ for past liberal third-party efforts, captured the basis for the movement's failure in the observation that "the new political alignment must coalesce around and with the New Deal."[83]

Much of the remaining political left adopted this perspective. Before 1937, they had faced a political-economic system that was off-balance

81 *New York Times*, 18 December 1939, pp. 1, 5.
82 Dennis N. Mihelich, "The Congressional Mavericks, 1935–1939" (Ph.D. diss., Case Western Reserve University, 1972), pp. 237–8, 279, 284.
83 "Progressives, What Now," *Common Sense* 7 (June 1938): 3 quoted in ibid., p. 276.

and in flux; a reform program far more comprehensive than Roosevelt's seemed capable of capturing the public imagination. By the 1937–8 recession, a more pessimistic assessment prevailed. The fluidity of the system had evaporated, and the public seemed willing to sanction a freeze on the limited progress that had occurred. The *Nation* portrayed a conspiracy of "doctored public opinion": "The press, using the Goebbels technique of reiteration, has repeated so often that business needs to be free of its tax burden before it will invest and create employment that the man in the street has come to believe it."[84]

If there was one thing worse for the political fortunes of the radical left than Roosevelt in the ascendancy, it was Roosevelt on the decline, for the alternative power centers were far worse. In such a hostile atmosphere, FDR's rhetoric and program, much of which they earlier would have dismissed as empty or palliative, seemed more appealing. The Supreme Court–packing plan, which sent many old progressives scurrying in defense against centralization and dictatorship, enlisted the aid of liberal journals and younger progressives against the institution they had depicted as the most dangerous nemesis of progress. Perhaps most significantly, the success of the CIO assumed central importance to this progressive faction. FDR's refusal to call out the troops against sit-down strikes, along with his advocacy of a narrow-gauged wages-and-hours bill, thus carried considerable weight with them. They also solidly supported the undistributed-profits tax and defended Roosevelt against onslaughts from the Treasury and Congress, warning that "a psychological sop to the business men . . . won't work,"[85] while urging a more progressive tax framework to buck up consumer purchasing power.

The political tides had ceased to run their way. Liberals thus hesitated to attribute the recession to the breakdown of capitalism, and they advocated countercyclical spending, which they had earlier castigated for its waste and planlessness. Their jaundiced eye now accustomed itself to a narrowed vista.[86] Liberals thus assumed a position that they would maintain throughout Roosevelt's presidency: They hung onto him like a life preserver. FDR had gained a clique of press agents and true believers, but this was a sign

---

84 "Government by Deadlock," *Nation* 146 (23 April 1938): 457.
85 "Mr. Morgenthau Proposes," *New Republic* 99 (7 June 1939): 117.
86 Paul A. O'Rourke Jr.'s doctoral dissertation ["Liberal Journals and the New Deal" (Ph.D. diss., University of Notre Dame, 1969), p. 185 and passim] brings together much of the evidence for this theme.

of weakness, not strength. With labor reeling from internecine strife, progressive ranks thinned by defections to the right, and Congress and the electorate on a conservative tack, Roosevelt found the cards stacked against him when combatting business demands. In an unaccustomed deviation from his role as an interest-group broker, FDR had to take the lead in defense of the New Deal tax program.

6. New Deal Taxation and the Business Community, 1937–1939

The Business Tax Program and Ideology

From the vantage point of 1984, one is scarcely in a position to smugly dismiss the tax-revision campaign of the late 1930s as a business conspiracy. For a historian of the Depression, the sense of déjà vu is overwhelming. The recent gutting of the corporate income tax, along with the Reagan administration's three-year 25 percent tax cut, rest largely on the same logic that New Deal opponents had used. Lower taxes, we are told, will enhance private incentives and release capital for investment, thus producing a healthy economic expansion that will in the long run overwhelm the temporary drain on federal revenues.

Susceptibility to this fundamentalist business message is deeply ingrained in our political culture. Only in times of reform or antibusiness feeling is this message submerged. The early New Deal was such a period. Until 1937, the Roosevelt administration set the terms of debate on taxation. But the recession changed that, allowing the business community to take charge. With astonishing ease, business opinion coalesced around a rigorous tax ideology, producing a consensus that guided the tax roll-back in 1938–9.

Where had the business community set its sights? What economic assumptions lay behind its solutions? To the extent that this postrecession period deserves to be salvaged from historical neglect, the network of business thought is basic to its understanding. To put my inquiry more formally, what "ideological filter" operated to forge business attitudes into a "set of principles, programs and goals" that would "give coherence to their hopes and fears, and prepare themselves mentally for social or political action"?[1]

The business tax program incorporated a simplistic model of the inhibitory impact of taxes. Central to this approach was the apotheosis of investment. Noting that the recession slashed employment and profits in capital- and

---

1 George M. Fredrickson, "The Uses of Antislavery," *New York Review of Books* 29 (16 October 1975): 38.

durable-goods industries, business spokesmen often averred that recovery efforts should be geared to this group.[2] Pump priming was "low powered" because it benefited consumer-goods firms, whereas savings used for investment were "high powered" because of the boost given capital-goods industries.[3]

Taxes on upper income brackets and corporations froze these high-powered investment funds, sending investors "into a cyclone cellar," or at least into tax-exempt bonds or foreign markets.[4] The ensuing dearth of private expenditures brought unemployment. New York Democratic congressman Emanuel Celler, the congressional coordinator of business tax pressure, placed what he called the "investment brackets" at the core of the formula for renewed economic growth.[5] "We may as well recognize the fact that it is only men with large incomes who are the sparkplugs of industry and prosperity, and if you cripple them the machine won't operate satisfactorily," said Celler.[6] Thus, business spokesmen, in the name of minimizing investment risk, justified a suspension of the soak-the-rich philosophy toward which they had always been so hostile. Desired business initiative, according to *Business Week*, could only be "obtained when investors and speculators alike can put head and soul in their market decisions free from the intrusion of their personal tax problems" – an objective hard to envisage without repeal of the corporate and personal income taxes.[7]

The tax-reduction effort embodied a recognition of the politically circumscribed revenue alternatives. For the sake of fiscal credibility, a plan for more lenient corporate taxation had to recoup lost revenue elsewhere. A long-standing business alternative was the imposition of a federal sales tax. This goal received a setback when the federal sales-tax movement, despite its popularity among nonretailing firms, was forced into hibernation in the mid-1930s. The congressional rebellion against the 1932 revenue bill had dealt the sales tax a near-fatal blow, tainting it as a symbol of

2 George H. Houston, "The Economic Situation," *Vital Speeches* 4 (1 June 1938): 503.
3 Emanuel Celler, in U.S., Congress, House, *Congressional Record*, 76th Cong., 3d sess., 1940, 86, pt. 13: 464.
4 Emanuel Celler, quoted in *Commercial and Financial Chronicle* 148 (4 March 1939): 1252.
5 *New York Times*, 1 July 1938, p. 5.
6 U.S., Congress, House, *Congressional Record*, 76th Cong., 1st sess., 1939, 84, pt. 12: 1830.
7 "What Taxes Are Doing to Business," *Business Week*, 11 December 1937, p. 43.

selfish business insensitivity to the woes of the rest of society. William Randolph Hearst, sporadically joined by the NAM and a legion of never-say-die businessmen, kept the flame burning until World War II, when the distention of the revenue system again made the sales tax a viable alternative to bucking up exactions on the wealthy.

Roosevelt asserted that his tax opponents represented the same crowd of self-interested income tax payers who tended "to attack all taxes based on the principle of ability to pay," the "same complainants" who favored a sales tax.[8] Ironically, the federal sales tax's closest brush with success in the late 1930s occurred in the Treasury Department. In late 1938, Secretary Morgenthau recommended a sales tax to the president, receiving a go-ahead for top-level consideration of that tax as a budget-balancing and military-preparedness measure, an idea that was soon rejected.[9]

Given the political infelicity of the sales tax and the opposition of selected industrial groups to excise taxes, a widened application for the income tax leapt into the breach. The remedy, endorsed by conservatives since the inception of the income tax, casts some light on the relationship between the business community's concern with minimizing its taxes and the economics profession's concern with the redistributive effects of taxation. The proposal to raise tax rates on middle-bracket incomes – a popular reform among economists – received support from many newspapers, accountants, tax lawyers, and revenue-oriented Senate conservatives. Yet business platforms rarely included it. Businessmen commonly favored a severe cut in exemptions, with perhaps some increase in the lower brackets of the income tax. Most of them disregarded the economists' arguments

8 Samuel I. Rosenman, comp., *The Public Papers and Addresses of Franklin D. Roosevelt* 7 (New York: Macmillan, 1941): 9 (3 January 1938) (hereafter cited as *Addresses of FDR*).

9 FDR's main contribution to this sales-tax discussion appears to have been a suggestion that consideration be given to an exemption for raw foodstuffs, which he said would "have the effect of increasing the consumption of fresh vegetables which would be a good thing for the American people." "Conference with the President on November 16, 1938," "White House Conference November 16th, 1938" folder, box 179, Record Group 56, General Records of the Department of the Treasury (National Archives, Washington, D.C.). Also see Morgenthau Diaries, 9–10 December 1938, book 155, pp. 162–5, 281–2, Henry Morgenthau Jr., Papers (Franklin D. Roosevelt Library, Hyde Park, N.Y.; hereafter cited as FDR Library). John Blum seems to have mistakenly transferred the sales-tax rap from Morgenthau to Jacob Viner. Viner actually leveled a wide-ranging attack on the proposal. John M. Blum, *From the Morgenthau Diaries*, vol. 2: *Years of Urgency* (Boston: Houghton Mifflin, 1965), p. 17; Jacob Viner, in Morgenthau Diaries, 9 December 1938, book 155, pp. 165–6, 168–9, 174.

that this new tax should be counterbalanced by lower excise taxes; they often spoke as if the poor currently paid no taxes at all. At best, business representatives only envisaged the repeal of the less regressive minor nuisance taxes, rather than the major federal levies on the poor: tobacco and liquor excises. In fact, lower rates for the upper income brackets were the most frequent supplement to a broadened tax base. Business spokesmen lost no sleep over the possibility that a universal income tax superimposed on the excise system would merely raise the tax burden on the new income tax payers; such was usually their precise intention. If the budget was to move into balance, it would be with other people's money. Conservatives also hoped to reap political benefits from a broadened tax base. They anticipated that the new taxpayers, once conscious of the government burden, would join the effort to clamp down on New Deal expenditures.

The proposal to beef up the lower ranges of the income tax had extraordinary popularity among newspapers, bankers, and corporate executives. The *New York Herald Tribune* and the *Chicago Daily News*, columnists Arthur Krock and Frank Kent, the *Commercial and Financial Chronicle* and the Investment Bankers Association, the New York Board of Trade and the National Millers Federation, the Small Business Conference and the Business Advisory Council – the list of conservative advocates of lower exemptions is almost endless. In February 1941 (a time, it should be noted, when the obvious need for further taxes tended to deepen support for hikes on lower and middle incomes), a *Fortune* poll of the business elite found that 94.2 percent favored "broadening the base for the income tax," whereas only 3.2 percent opposed this suggestion.[10]

The business consensus on tax broadening had little immediate impact. When an immovable object (the long-standing public opposition to taxing "the people") meets a resistible force (business tax lobbyists were usually more intent on reducing taxes than on introducing new ones; the U.S. Chamber of Commerce and the NAM did not even include tax broadening in their legislative programs), the result is no paradox. The business consensus on the need for tax breaks, however, was more imposing. Virtually every tax program put forward by businessmen called for an end to the undistributed-profits tax, the repeal or modification of the tax on capital gains, markedly reduced personal income taxes on wealthier Amer-

10 "Fourth *Fortune* Forum of Executive Opinion," *Fortune* 23 (February 1941): 172.

icans, and the revision of many "inequitable" provisions – usually of recent vintage – that had been designed to close loopholes.

This almost catechismic tax program, with its focus on turning back New Deal tax revisions, makes the business community seem deceptively rigid and reactionary. It is well known, for example, that a significant portion of the corporate elite by the late 1930s endorsed many New Deal reforms that had contributed to industrial stability. Why did the business position on taxation lack this flexibility? The answer lies partly in the symbolic function of politics on the New Deal/business battlefront. Businessmen invested tax disputes with their own status anxieties. Even a minor tax adjustment could vindicate their reputation.

Business spokesmen demanded a return to a larger business contribution to political outputs, vowing to "return corporate policies to corporation directors."[11] The quest for a symbolic victory, however, extended beyond the injection of more business representatives into the policy process. Government would have to refurbish the business image to purchase recovery. The president of Studebaker pledged that government cooperation in adopting a base program of capital gains and undistributed-profits tax liberalization and a "rebuilding of confidence in the soundness and fairness of business leadership" would soon render the recession "a thing of the past."[12]

Though many analyses asserted a mystical connection between the politically cultivated public cynicism toward business and the failure of economic recovery, a more common plaint linked administration rhetoric to industrial stagnation through its direct effects on business decision makers themselves. "Fear of Rooseveltian business-baiting" had built "the fatal barrier to optimism, enterprise, expansion."[13] Denunciation of greedy business crooks by members of the administration, interpreted as part of an inclination to foment divisive class hatreds, hit a raw nerve among numerous businessmen. The business community, Thomas Lamont lectured, "cannot be spanked into prosperity."[14] A Senate minority report joined the fray:

11 "New Law Gives Real Tax Relief," *Business Week*, 30 April 1938, p. 15.
12 Paul Hoffman, quoted in Randolph E. Paul, *Taxation in the United States* (Boston: Little, Brown, 1954), p. 209.
13 B. C. Forbes, "America Definitely Turns the Corner," *Forbes* 43 (1 March 1939): 20.
14 Thomas W. Lamont to Adolf A. Berle, Jr., 28 December 1937, box 84-7, "Berle, Adolf A., Jr., 1933–1938," Thomas W. Lamont Papers (Baker Library, Harvard University, Cambridge, Mass.).

Extravagant utterances, in which whole classes of people are insulted and nameless individuals are lambasted over the radio ... tend to frighten the businessman ... It is clear, therefore, that this kind of talk tends to discourage new business ventures. ... In the interest of creating new jobs, such talk should stop.[15]

Condemnation of Roosevelt's rhetoric was a standard part of businessmen's own rhetorical repertoire. The vital precondition for escape from the economic doldrums was "confidence": public confidence in businessmen and businessmen's confidence in both themselves and their profit prospects.

Businessmen pursued this search for "confidence" relentlessly in the wake of their divorce from FDR in the mid-1930s, tailoring their arguments rather selectively to fit current circumstance. Allegations of the incompatibility of administration vituperation and business advance, for example, easily glossed over their simultaneous peak in 1935–7. Almost by definition, poor economic reports were the wages of New Deal sins, whereas good times derived from natural economic forces and probusiness legislation. When an economic upturn (probably goaded by the best cure for "fear" and "uncertainty": the promise of future profits from deficit spending) coincided with the enactment of the 1938 Revenue Act, warnings that FDR had vitiated the act's impact by threatening future tax initiatives faded into assertions that tax reduction had prompted recovery. With equal facility, conservatives turned the "sit-down strike" explanation of the recession on its head; the administration, said Thomas Lamont, had "locked out" capital through such measures as the undistributed-profits tax.[16] To entice capital back to work would entail substantial concessions – and with a smile. It was a common conservative rebuke that the 1938 and 1939 tax bills came " 'too late and too grudgingly' to have the beneficial psychological effect that might otherwise have resulted."[17]

The New Deal's polarization of business had erected a wall of skepticism that mere words could not penetrate. Businessmen, fearing future taxes, sought a predictable, secure, and accommodating political and economic environment. Yet their own rhetoric damned their cause. While talking

---

15 U.S., Congress, Senate, Special Committee to Investigate Unemployment and Relief, *Unemployment and Relief, Preliminary Minority Views*, pt. 2, Preliminary S. Rept. 1625 pursuant to S. Res. 36, 75th Cong., 3d sess., 1938, included in U.S., Congress, Senate, Special Committee to Investigate Unemployment and Relief, *Unemployment and Relief, Hearings* pursuant to S. Res. 36, 75th Cong., 3d sess., 1938, 2: 1394.

16 *Commercial and Financial Chronicle* 146 (22 January 1938): 534.

17 *New York Times*, 2 June 1939, p. 9.

of the need to unleash business on the one hand, opponents of New Deal taxation painted a picture of business paralysis on the other. It seemed as if only huge prospective profits and wholesale government capitulation could return "confidence" to requisite levels. This the political system neither could nor would deliver. Government spending might be the only solution.

Businessmen as Deficit Taxers

In business circles, "deficit" was a dirty word. But there were worse sins than profanity. Particularly in the period succeeding the 1937 recession, the business community registered a profound ambivalence toward deficits. The deficit problem can be defined, after all, either in terms of a revenue deficiency – a tax problem – or as an expenditure excess – a spending problem. The two alternative solutions, budget cuts and tax increases, need not be viewed with equal fervor or alarm by a given economic sector. Businessmen, it appears, were less wedded to the ideal of the balanced budget than might have been presumed from their rhetoric of fiscal responsibility. This partially disguised truth was a function of budget-balancing sensibilities more closely attuned to rectifying the spending side of the equation than to adjusting the revenue side.

Even federal deficit spending did not always appear as an unmitigated evil. Whereas businessmen were still urging a budget-balancing push as part of their business-appeasement package in the dawn of the recession, they had second thoughts as the economy continued its plunge. The New Deal countercyclical-spending contingent bolstered its position by reporting underground business rumblings desirous of a federal spending fix, though the *New Republic* pointed out that those same wealthy conservatives would ambush Roosevelt "if he acceded to their desires."[18] Both economists and business leaders had belatedly realized that the ruthless shutdown of the deficit, acting upon the huge fiscal stimulus from the 1936 soldier's bonus, could, in the National Conference Board's guarded assessment, "hardly fail to produce an unsettling effect on the national economy."[19] Moreover, the often skittish stock market refused to panic at word of FDR's recovery-relief package; the Standard Statistics Company's *Outlook for the Security*

18 "The President and the New Depression," *New Republic* 93 (15 December 1937): 159.
19 National Industrial Conference Board, *Conference Board Business Survey* 12 (21 June 1938): 1.

Markets even counseled subscribers to buy on the strength of it.[20] Granted, business commentators tended to distinguish between "temporary" and "real" recovery; conservatives had long argued that pump priming could only impart a temporary spurt that would cease the moment impending bankruptcy forced an end to government profligacy.

Despite this widely accepted theoretical objection to deficit spending, it seems likely that countercyclical fiscal policy was judged most harshly for the company it kept. When business spokesmen sang the praises of balanced budgets in the late 1930s, their primary object was to reduce New Deal spending, particularly "extravagant" relief programs directed toward nonproductive groups deemed unworthy of federal aid.

On the revenue side of the deficit-producing equation, however, conservatives played another tune, one somewhat at variance with their pre–New Deal approach. In the late 1930s, the curtailment of taxes clearly assumed a higher priority than the minimization of federal debt. Although many businessmen had similarly worked to minimize corporate taxes in World War I and the 1920s, the monumental fiscal crisis of 1931–2 put a different complexion on fiscal policy. Incipient chaos in the international monetary system, bank failures, and the specter of hyperinflationary deficits forged business acceptance of the budget-balancing premises of the mammoth 1932 Revenue Act, the reigning tax statute for the 1930s and the largest peacetime tax increase in U.S. history. Though each proposed excise tax mobilized the opposition of the affected industry, business leaders flocked to the standard of a broad program of excise or sales taxation and a beefing up of the lower ranges of the income tax. The priorities involved in this support were clarified in a U.S. Chamber of Commerce referendum completed in early 1932. Almost all member organizations favored immediate steps to balance the budget by 1934, plunking for federal expenditure cuts as the top priority. But, significantly, "new-debt borrowings" as far "as may be consonant with the maintenance of the credit of the government" received second billing in order "to keep tax increases moderate." Only then, the chamber agreed by a vote of 2615½ to 94½, should a temporary tax increase come into play. Lower exemptions and a moderate increase in the income tax, along with a broad-

20 "Outlook for the Security Markets," Standard Statistics Company, *Outlook for the Security Markets* 5 (18 April 1938): 259; "Continued Government Spending Promises Business Upturn," Standard Statistics Company, *Outlook for the Security Markets* 7 (29 May 1939): 668; "Backlog of Sound Income-producing Stocks Advisable," Standard Statistics Company, *Outlook for the Security Markets* 7 (27 February 1939): 870.

based excise tax, were endorsed as part of this program. However, the recommendation for a moderate corporate-tax increase reaped unusual dissent for a chamber referendum, only passing by 1952½ to 723½, whereas a freeze in the estate tax and a reduction in the capital-gains tax proved popular suggestions.[21] Businessmen staked out a narrow interest-group preference for balancing the budget out of someone else's pocket, but they did support limited sacrifice to avert immediate collapse.

It is a mark of the economic progress attending the New Deal that businessmen soon jettisoned this limited sanction for tax hikes. Within a few months of Roosevelt's accession, the economy reversed its downward slide, the banking system was back on its feet, and the act of severing the dollar from the gold standard freed the United States from international monetary destabilization. The fear that deficits would magically create inflation in the deflated U.S. economy dissipated somewhat with the relative price stability that accompanied the rising national debt. Similarly, the extraordinarily low interest rates on government borrowing dissolved concern over the strength of national credit. Not knowing when or if the economy would fully recover, businessmen still worried that deficits would culminate in higher future taxes, but they proved eager to trade away present levies against the prospect of future ones. Most business leaders would never abandon the hallowed ideological position of the balanced budget, but never again would they opt for a corporate-tax increase when they could settle for a larger deficit.

If New Dealers can be better described as deficit spenders than as Keynesians, businessmen can best be viewed as deficit taxers. Neither group shared the faith of Keynesian theorists in the expansionary powers of the deficit itself, but each perceived independent economic benefits from spending programs or tax reductions that swelled deficits. In its attack on the 1935 revenue bill, the Business Advisory Council put forward a popular view in its argument that "the price of a balanced budget may be too high . . . for the country to pay at this time" because "the collection of drastic taxes could literally paralyze business."[22] Many spokesmen parried

21 Chamber of Commerce of the U.S., "Referendum Number Sixty: Federal Taxation 1932," Special Bulletin, Washington, D.C., 22 April 1932, pp. 1–2; Chamber of Commerce of the U.S., "Referendum No. 60 on the Report of the Special Committee on Federal Taxation," Washington, D.C., 19 February 1932, p. 12. Both of these pamphlets are available at the library of the Chamber of Commerce of the U.S., Washington, D.C.
22 U.S., Department of Commerce, Business Advisory Council, "Report on the Tax Bill," 13 August 1935, p. 1, 1933–35 folder, box 19, Official File 3Q, Franklin D. Roosevelt Papers (FDR Library).

New Deal wealth-taxing plans with compensatory-revenue proposals, but they often cheerfully declined to offer revenue alternatives at all. As Chamber of Commerce tax lobbyist Fred Clausen boasted in the 1936 meeting of that organization:

> We are always confronted with the query, what substitute tax proposal have you to offer in its place? To this question our answer invariably has been, we have no plan to offer until Congress demonstrates the purpose to curtail substantially the expenditures of our National Government. (Applause)[23]

Business leaders and their allies pressed this point of view with more persistence after the recession strengthened their cause. A slew of Republicans, including the Ways and Means Committee contingent, announced that they would oppose all tax increases or extensions until the administration seriously pared expenditures. Everett Dirksen – asking "How much difference would it make if the Budget were unbalanced a little further for a period of 1 or 2 years?" – echoed Sears Roebuck president Robert Wood in asserting that Congress should "take a chance" and respond to business's insistence "that tax reduction must precede recovery."[24] When Treasury Secretary Morgenthau allowed the deficit to mushroom by refusing in 1939 to cover defense-spending hikes with new taxes, all commentators recognized that this decision would placate business rather than affront any budget-balancing sensibilities. Regarding taxes, business spokesmen affected a long-range view that excused slight initial expansion of New Deal deficits in terms of the resultant tax stimulus to business confidence and profits.[25] They felt this was the only path to long-range recovery, which in turn was the only sort of economy that could furnish sufficient tax receipts to cover federal expenditures.

---

23 Chamber of Commerce of the U.S., "Minutes of Twenty-Fourth Annual Meeting April 28, 29, 30, 1936, and Thirty-First Meeting of National Council, April 27, 1936," p. 72, Washington, D.C., Library of the Chamber of Commerce of the U.S., Washington, D.C.

24 Robert E. Wood to FDR, 12 May 1939, President's Personal File 1365, FDR Papers; U.S., Congress, House, *Congressional Record*, 76th Cong., 1st sess., 1939, 84, pt. 7: 7476.

25 Only the inflation-sensitive banking community held off from this deficit-taxation position, as reflected in *Commercial and Financial Chronicle* editorials noting that "to reduce tax revenues at this time, or even to fail to increase them, is but to add to the ever present danger of drastic inflation" – and even they fell in line for tax reduction when specific levies came under attack. Editorial, *Commercial and Financial Chronicle* 146 (12 March 1938): 1602; Editorial, *Commercial and Financial Chronicle* 148 (25 February 1939): 1062.

Although businessmen had little or no faith in the restoratory power of the deficit itself, they assembled an array of other contentions to legitimize their position as deficit taxers. Most important was the theory that underpinned 1920s Republican tax policy: Lower tax rates promoted the capital investment that would fuel economic growth and thus garnered more revenue than would higher rates. Theory here of course coincided with self-interest, but there was no less coherence in this business position than in the New Dealers' hope that deficit spending would permit consumer demand to induce recovery.

A corollary to this Mellonist approach was that the economy could not support the tax burden it was forced to bear. Ellsworth Alvord, a former Mellon aide then serving as a tax lobbyist for the Chamber of Commerce, testified, "My honest personal opinion is you cannot devise a revenue system which over the next 10 years will average in excess of $6,500,000,000 per year. It just is not there."[26] (Actually, the unanticipated World War II boom, combined with unprecedentedly severe tax rates, permitted federal revenues to quintuple this estimate – though the chamber would fight tooth and nail to prevent this result). Thus conservatives were not satisfied with the Treasury Department's stress on eliminating minor tax deterrents, for they sought a reduction in the total tax burden. Businessmen had always located the incidence of a tax wherever it best suited their argument; emphasis on the total load simply meant that any incidence pattern fitted their attack. The social security payroll tax, in spite of the fact that it contributed so mightily to narrowing the budget deficit, drew intense fire for the double sin of sidetracking investment-bound profits and tamping down needed purchasing power. Though certain business spokesmen allowed that they would accept a higher normal corporate tax rate in exchange for the repeal of deterrents like the undistributed-profits tax, ranking Ways and Means minority member Allen Treadway proclaimed it "beyond my comprehension how business can be relieved by the bill when the majority admits they are not going to collect any less revenue under the bill." Fellow Republican Harold Knutson also dismissed tax reshuffling with the comment, "As I understand it, they are going to discontinue the use of chloroform and try ether."[27]

Conservatives demanded a substantial reduction in tax rates, not as a cyclical tool, but as a permanent policy to maximize investment and,

26 U.S., Congress, House, Committee on Ways and Means, *Revenue Revision – 1939, Hearings*, 76th Cong., 1st sess., 1939, pp. 78, 82.
27 U.S., Congress, House, *Congressional Record*, 75th Cong., 3d sess., 1938, 83, pt. 3: 2772, 2865.

incidentally, to encourage immediate cuts in federal spending. Many congressmen represented this perspective, though with a twist of their own. In 1938, Congress responded to the exigencies of the forthcoming election by approving a spending program that went far beyond any sanction granted by the ambivalent business position on deficits. Despite Roosevelt's hectoring, Congress thrilled the processors who bombarded them with requests to squelch a processing tax, refusing to provide new revenues to fund the expanded farm-subsidy program they created. Congressional leaders also played major roles in implementing business demands for a freeze in the social security payroll tax and for modification of corporate and capital-gains taxes. In 1939, Congress exercised its postelection freedom to reject spending hikes and the expanded New Deal role they encompassed, bringing it more closely in line with a business antispending position that had also hardened over the past year. Congress was perhaps more traditionally conservative in the hesitancy of many members to endorse the full-scale tax-reduction plans put forward by business organizations, but by 1939 it had planted itself firmly in the camp of the deficit taxers.

The Coalescence of Business Pressure

The basic business tax objective, the minimization of burdens upon and interference with corporations, had changed little since 1933. But after the recession, business leaders pressed this position with less ambivalence and greater confidence, knowing that they had the ear of Congress and the public. A burst of speeches, advertisements, and summary articles on tax philosophy swept business circles in the late 1930s, combining the functions of indoctrination and ideological formalization.

The platitudinous din of this rhetoric was less indicative of any intellectual shallowness of business spokesmen than of the depth and breadth of the business consensus. The ability to identify key dividing lines in the "pluralistic" world of American business may be a mark of historical sophistication, but students of the business community of the 1930s tend to instead be struck by the broad-based common belief structure of business spokesmen and by the system of business leadership and communication that fostered this community solidarity. The shock of the Depression brought a brief period of consideration of alternatives to the old fundamentalist business ideology in 1932–4, but after this moment of panic, the experiments with modernist solutions arguably gave way "to a position of ideological and organizational unity unsurpassed before or after in the twentieth century."[28] Businessmen, Herbert Stein notes, are always leery of public disagreement, and this was doubly so as they felt themselves under siege from the New Deal and the popular forces it represented.[29]

The pervasiveness and intensity of this ideological rigidity gave business leaders a base for resurgence after the 1937 recession and during World War II. Industrialists had traditionally underpinned economic progress and overseen economic understanding. By countermanding their clearly delineated advice, and then suffering a recession, the administration skated onto thin ice. When the public in 1938 meted out the customary election penalty upon the "ins" for bad times, they also lent legitimacy to business shibboleths, allowing them to move into the vacuum left by discredited New Deal economic theories.

The coalescence of business pressure against New Deal taxation thus is partly attributable to characteristics of the business community itself. But the special properties of tax controversies amplified the tendency toward conformity. More is involved here than the symbolic freight that taxation came to bear in New Deal political strategy. Theodore Lowi's model of public-policy decisions contrasts the politics of "redistribution" (which pits broad social and economic groups against one another) with "distribution" issues like excise-tax exemptions (in which individual industrialists or firms can independently acquire benefits through logrolling that do no direct harm to other firms) and with "regulation" issues like discriminatory taxes on chain stores (in which Congress mediates the demands of competing interest groups).[30] New Deal income- and profits-tax proposals, which fit snugly in Lowi's "redistribution" category, faced the response that Lowi's model predicts: coherent and vehement business opposition, spearheaded and reinforced by leading business associations like the Chamber of Commerce.

Some indication of the tightness of this business alliance is given in the galaxy of questionnaires from trade associations and other business organizations on the undistributed-profits tax. Each survey found much corporate clamoring that the undistributed-profits tax had forced them

28 Thomas C. Longin, "The Search for Security: American Business Thought in the 1930s" (Ph.D. diss., University of Nebraska, 1970), p. 219.

29 Herbert Stein, *The Fiscal Revolution in America* (Chicago: University of Chicago Press, 1969), p. 458.

30 Theodore J. Lowi, "American Business, Public Policy, Case-Studies, and Political Theories," *World Politics* 16 (July 1964): 677–715.

to curtail expansion plans, as corporate observers proved eager to excoriate the tax rather than to examine their own hesitancy to invest. Less than 1 percent of the companies in a National Industrial Conference Board survey felt that the advantages of the undistributed-profits tax outweighed its disadvantages. Another typical questionnaire result, tainted by a covering letter expressing the fear that "the ultimate effect of the present law will be disastrous," registered such votes as 1226–4 and 1212–13 in support of certain revisions in the tax or in opposition to the undistributed-profits tax itself.[31] Even after Congress had practically capitulated to business demands by reducing the undistributed-profits tax to insignificance in 1938, a *Fortune* poll reported that only 8.1 percent of businessmen wanted the eviscerated tax "kept," with 66.2 percent advocating its repeal and 22.5 percent its modification. No other New Deal measure found most polled businessmen unwilling to salvage it even in modified form.[32] The undistributed-profits tax thus represents the height of business homogeneity. "Certainly, with respect to no other legislative action of the last several years," noted one contemporary observer, "has business presented such a strong and united front."[33]

To some extent, this unity reflected the dominance of giant corporations in industrial associations. A number of studies have ascertained that "big business" (roughly defined as companies with over two thousand employees and annual sales over $10 million) reached the peak of its influence in the NAM during the Roosevelt presidency, holding strong majorities on both the board of directors and the executive committee – in marked contrast to the command of smaller concerns in the 1950s and pre-1930s.[34] Despite this shift, the small-business symbol endured, for the largest firms found it a politically useful link with American individualist values.

Championship of small business also reinforced the internal unity of the business community. As J. P. Morgan partner Thomas Lamont expressed

31 M. Slade Kendrick, *The Undistributed Profits Tax*, Brookings Institution pamphlet no. 20 (Washington, D.C.: Brookings Institution, 1937), pp. 96–9.
32 "What Business Thinks," *Fortune* 20 (October 1939): 52, 90.
33 Willard L. Thorp, "The Undistributed Profits Tax," American Management Association, *Financial Management Series* no. 53 (1938): 11, in Kenneth D. Roose, *The Economics of Recession and Revival: An Interpretation of 1937–38* (New Haven, Conn.: Yale University Press, 1954), pp. 213–14.
34 Philip H. Burch, Jr., "The NAM as an Interest Group," *Politics and Society* 4 (Fall 1973): 101–7; Richard W. Gable, "A Political Analysis of an Employers' Association: The National Association of Manufacturers" (Ph.D. diss., University of Chicago, 1950), pp. 242–3, 465.

it: "Little businesses grow into medium-sized and then into big businesses. . . . In other words, they are one."[35] To a pronounced degree, smaller businessmen bought this ideological rationalization. "Large oaks from little acorns grow," one sapling enthused. "I ask you, 'Shall we cut down or curb the growth of our oaks?' "[36]

The New Deal's rhetorical attempt to widen the cracks in this solid front met with much resentment but little success. FDR should perhaps have realized that he had more control over the small-business image than over small businessmen themselves. Instead, he sanctioned a Commerce Department–sponsored conference of small businesses (those firms with less than a million dollars in assets) for 2 February 1938. Hoping to exploit a presumed rift in corporate ranks, Roosevelt only succeeded in providing a forum for the very force he intended to restrain.

Because tax complaints anchored the anti-New Deal feelings of small businessmen, the administration stage-managed a discussion schedule that bypassed taxation. But the delegates shouted down this intended program and formed a taxation committee. The conference was something of a national joke, a three-ring circus centered on efforts to capture the rostrum to denounce the New Deal and each other. But for all the "farcical" and "tragic" aspects of the proceedings, business opinion leaders gratefully embraced the recommendations that the conference generals had railroaded through the chaos. Conservatives widely rejoiced that, excepting bouquets thrown to fair-trade laws, special loans, and antitrust enforcement, "it would be difficult without identification to know whether the suggestions came from little or big business."[37] Failing to bite at FDR's studied distinction between the specially privileged "power-seeking minority" and "the less articulate but more important elements that constitute real American business,"[38] the resolutions scored the "malicious attacks on business by administration spokesmen." The conference considered the substitution of a sales tax for the unemployment-insurance payroll tax and demanded the repeal of the undistributed-profits tax, revision of the capital-gains and -loss tax, and lower income-tax exemptions.[39] Even the *Nation*, in mourning that the conference signaled an intensified assault

35 Thomas W. Lamont to Adolf A. Berle, 14 December 1937, box 84-7, "Berle, Adolf A., Jr., 1933–1938," Thomas W. Lamont Papers.
36 Henry G. Tremmel, quoted in "Stop Big Business and You'll Stop Me," *Forbes* 41 (1 February 1938): 14.
37 "Little Business has Big Ideas," *Minneapolis Journal*, 5 February 1938, p. 4.
38 *Addresses of FDR*, 5: 12–13 (3 January 1936).
39 *New York Times*, 4 February 1938, p. 1.

upon the tax structure, conceded that small businessmen "still feel . . . that their interests lie with big business, even though each of them knows that in his everyday economic life big business is his great enemy."[40]

Things were not quite as bad for the New Deal as they seemed. A Gallup Poll uncovering "no marked difference between the attitude of little business men and big business men toward the President" reported that small businessmen only declared themselves "against" Roosevelt by a ratio of three to two.[41] Also, some issues did elicit differences according to business size. After the 1938 undistributed-profits tax exemption was granted to small corporations, a *Fortune* poll found that 20.4 percent of small retailers wanted the tax kept, whereas less than 2 percent of large retailers and manufacturers favored retention.[42] Nevertheless, in trying to woo small business, New Dealers had fallen victim to their own rhetoric.

Taxation Spearheads the Business Attack

In the public arena, and particularly on broad tax questions, the New Deal faced assertive, unified opposition from the business community. When the recession hit, conservatives readily transformed earlier vague prognostications of adverse tax effects into a full-blown explanation of the collapse. The spokesman for the NAM deemed taxes "the principal reason for the present unemployment situation."[43] "This is a tax depression," maintained Chamber of Commerce advertisements.[44]

Taxation, then, spearheaded the campaign to dramatize government responsibility for the recession. Given past rhetoric and contemporary business economic understanding, it was a natural choice for this role, though it would soon transcend this stalking-horse position to dominate the entire probusiness campaign. Tax reform served as what sociologists term a "condensation symbol,"[45] condensing the gamut of attitudes, hopes, resentments, and status insecurities into a single set of demands. The *New York Times* editorialized that the repeal of the undistributed-profits

40 "Little Business Revolts," *Nation* 146 (12 February 1938): 173.

41 *New York Times*, 2 February 1938, p. 8.

42 "What Business Thinks," *Fortune* 20 (October 1939): 90.

43 Walter D. Fuller, in U.S., Congress, Senate, Committee on Finance, *Social Security Act Amendments, Hearings* on H.R. 6635, 76th Cong., 1st sess., 1939, p. 205.

44 "We Ought to Cut Government Spending But," advertisement, *Nation's Business* 27 (April 1939): 84.

45 Murray Edelman, *The Symbolic Uses of Politics* (Urbana: University of Illinois Press, 1964), p. 6.

tax was "psychologically so important" because the tax "has become for the business community a symbol for Government 'persecution' of business."[46] Repeal of the tax would not only establish business hegemony; it would block the application of a tax technique that could pose a considerable threat. The combined influence of symbolism, the centripetal requirement of business unity, and dread of future tax extension helps untangle the vexing question of why giant corporations, whose coffers often received a decided boost from the 1936 Revenue Act, joined the antagonists of the undistributed-profits tax. They feared government intervention into a politically vulnerable, faltering investment process.

Thus tax reform often headed the list of corporate demands upon government and was a universal business prescription for recovery. "The loudest noise in the land today," observed George Creel, "is the anguished outcry of finance and industry against the Administration's tax policy."[47] The repeal of the undistributed-profits tax in particular, asserted the representative of the New York Board of Trade, had "become something of an obsession in business circles."[48]

Business tax suggestions, though often conjoined with protests over New Deal labor and public-utility policy, proffered Congress only the sparsest of legislative menus. Testimony by industrial executives before the Senate's Special Committee to Investigate Unemployment and Relief contributed the usual business themes of confidence, government and labor excesses, and budget balancing. Yet the committee's majority report, although itself a challenge to the administration, found that their "only specific recommendation" for remedying the recession "was that Congress either repeal or modify the tax on undistributed profits and modify the tax on capital gains."[49]

Even in 1939, after higher incomes, the shriveling of the undistributed-profits tax in the 1938 Revenue Act, and the poor outlook for wholesale tax reduction had taken the edge off the business tax campaign, a *Fortune* poll found that the undistributed-profits tax ranked second to the Wagner Labor Relations Act in business enumerations of the "worst" New Deal

46 "The Profits Tax," *New York Times*, 3 March 1938, p. 20.
47 George Creel, "The Battle Cry of Business," *Collier's* 101 (8 January 1938): 16.
48 M. L. Seidman, in U.S., Congress, House, Committee on Ways and Means, *Revision of Revenue Laws 1938, Hearings*, 75th Cong., 3d sess., 1938, p. 154.
49 U.S., Congress, Senate, Special Committee to Investigate Unemployment and Relief, *Unemployment and Relief*, Preliminary S. Rept. 1625, 75th Cong., 3d sess., 1938, included in U.S., Congress, Senate, Special Committee to Investigate Unemployment and Relief, *Unemployment and Relief, Hearings*, 75th Cong., 3d sess., 1938, 2: 1379.

statutes.[50] *Forbes* proclaimed that "excessive taxation" had replaced the New Deal itself as "the greatest menace to American prosperity."[51] Tax reform carried a symbolic, ideological, and social burden wholly disproportionate to its prospective economic impact. It would fundamentally warp the use that the business community made of its mounting political influence.

Business Sells Itself: The Anti-Tax Public Relations Campaign

The success of the business tax campaign hinged on the degree to which the public embraced the corporate cause as its own. "The hazard facing industrialists is the newly realized political power of the masses," proclaimed an NAM sales pitch in 1937. "Unless their thinking is directed toward sane and established measures we are definitely headed for adversity."[52] Businessmen imagined themselves pelted by a "constant black rain of vilification and abuse." They faced attacks "so many and so vicious that no single unit or branch of industry could cope with the 'smearings' single-handed." The response was counterattack through a "nation-wide educational movement."[53] In search of electoral weight they moved to meet "the great and pressing need to do a real sales job with the American public."[54]

Business leaders thus confronted the political challenge of the Second Hundred Days with a political "defense"; they would operate "as a *political* unit, attempting to direct and to control public opinion just as political partisans always have done" – with the ironic objective of depoliticizing

---

50 "What Business Thinks," *Fortune* 20 (October 1939): 90.

51 B. C. Forbes, "Taxes, Not New Deal, U.S. Menace," *Forbes* 43 (1 April 1939): 10.

52 H. O. Patton to Horace Hayden, Jr., 24 September 1937, in U.S., Congress, Senate, Committee on Education and Labor, *Violations of Free Speech and Rights of Labor, Hearings*, before a subcommittee of the Committee on Education and Labor, pursuant to S. Res. 266, 75th Cong., 3d sess., 1938, pt. 17: 7693.

53 H. A. Batten, "Public Relations," *Vital Speeches* 3 (1 June 1937): 496; National Industrial Information Committee, *Re-Selling the American Way to America*, (n.p.: 1939), p. 2.

54 Lewis H. Brown, "What Industry Can Do – and Should Do – About Public Relations," *Sales Management* 41 (15 November 1937): 20; Ray Bill, "Comment," *Sales Management* 42 (15 July 1937): 76.

their ideology back into the popular culture.[55] The vituperative 1936 presidential campaign deepened the publicity effort. And when labor assertiveness in 1937 and late 1936 demonstrated the menace of the Wagner Labor Relations Act, the business public-relations effort accelerated (NAM expenditures on "public information," for example, increased twentyfold between 1934 and 1937, rising to a majority of the NAM budget).[56] By 1938–9, "selling itself" had become a business craze, heralded in letters, speeches, and conventions. In early 1939, reflecting the key role of taxes in business legislative objectives, the U.S. Chamber of Commerce emblazoned its theme "Less Taxes – More Jobs" on 25,000 billboards passed daily by an estimated 72 million people.[57] In its newspaper and magazine advertisements, it resurrected the assertion that "there are 154 taxes wrapped up in a cake of soap" and featured overalled workers reaching such insights as: "Suppose they do break business down with all this sniping and regulating and taxing – who's ahead?"[58] "It seems a sad thing," one advertising periodical lamented, "that such obvious truths have to be told to the mob in paid space."[59]

Appeals to stockholders supplied an important supplementary tool of corporate influence, particularly on tax questions. The first major steps in this direction came with the spate of letters to stockholders in the summer of 1935, urging them to blitz their congressmen with complaints over the destruction that the 1935 revenue bill would wreak upon large companies. Though the NAM sponsored shareholder letters in 1936,[60] this method had already given way to a more propagandistic use of corporate reports. These reports now tended to carry separate sections on taxation, complaining that the outrageous industrial tax burden snuffed out recovery.

55 Lawrence W. Nolte, *Fundamentals of Public Relations* (New York: Pergamon Press, 1974), p. 41; S. H. Walker and Paul Sklar, "Business Finds Its Voice, Part 2," *Harper's* 176 (February 1938): 317.

56 Richard S. Tedlow, "The National Association of Manufacturers and Public Relations during the New Deal," *Business History Review* 50 (Spring 1976): 33.

57 "25,000 Billboards All Over America," *Nation's Business* 27 (February 1939): 78.

58 "$120,000 a Minute," advertisement, *Nation's Business* 26 (December 1938): 76; "That Makes Sense to Me!" advertisement, *Nation's Business* 26 (February 1938): 73.

59 *Sales Management*, quoted in "52,000,000 Daily," *Nation's Business* 26 (February 1938): 11.

60 U.S., Congress, Senate, Committee on Education and Labor, *Violations of Free Speech and Rights of Labor, Hearings*, 75th Cong., 3d sess., 1938, pt. 18: 8051.

Perhaps most importantly, the industrial public-relations campaign represented an effort to buck up business dignity. Businessmen complained that their public image was of "a grasping, heinously selfish, public enemy" or "a portly and self-satisfied oldster in a silk hat and tails sitting on a pile of money bags."[61] Several analysts highlight this psychological component of New Deal opposition, one that is crucial to understanding the disparity between the New Deal's actual impact on corporations and the vigorous corporate reaction against it. To businessmen, the New Deal served as a symbol of the frustration and displacements brought by economic failure, of the erosion of their political and moral authority that compromised their place in the body politic.[62] As Roosevelt's program and his upstart intellectual bureaucrats threatened to change the ground rules through regulations that inherently "challenged the businessman's belief system, profaned his idols, and depreciated his myths," and as Roosevelt's taunts of "tories" and "economic royalists" underlined this fall from popular esteem and economic trust, business leaders resolved that "the world would once more look to business for its economic salvation."[63]

This obsession with reputation drained much of the public-relations effort into a headlong self-proselytizing quest for reassurance – one of the many reasons why one should not overrate the public-relations impact. Business periodicals carried the most concentrated advertising campaigns, and businessmen were the most avid consumers of public-relations speeches. Yet by the end of the 1930s, the well-oiled publicity machine could point to much progress. Most importantly, publicity efforts seem to have reinforced a more sympathetic public attitude. Advising expanded measures to take advantage of public receptivity, business promoters gloated that "thanks to educational effort," Americans were "becoming tax-conscious" and supportive of the industrial way of life.[64]

61 Edgar M. Queeny, *The Spirit of Enterprise* (New York: Scribner, 1943), p. 71; Howard Wood, "Business Must 'Sell' Itself," *Nation's Business* 26 (January 1938): 27.

62 Linda Keller Brown, "Challenge and Response: The American Business Community and the New Deal, 1932–1934" (Ph.D. diss., University of Pennsylvania, 1972), pp. 159, 161; Everett Ladd, Jr., *American Political Parties* (New York: Norton, 1970), p. 190.

63 Robert E. Lane, *The Regulation of Businessmen* (New Haven, Conn.: Yale University Press, 1954), p. 19; "Business Takes Its Own Part," *Nation's Business* 26 (March 1938): 72.

64 National Industrial Information Committee, *Re-Selling the American Way*, inside pages; "2-Line Editorials," *Forbes* 43 (1 March 1939): 5.

Of course, the commanding influence of the business tax position was not achieved by industry singlehandedly. Mainstream economists in the late 1930s placed a stress on corporate investment that bolstered the case for corporate tax revision. Even the corporate liberalism of *Fortune*'s Round Table adapted itself to the developing consensus, and the Brookings Institution, by 1939 deemed "the 'research' staff of the tories," gave no quarter in its wide-ranging assault on the New Deal tax philosophy.[65]

The common ground established by the experts and the business community was occupied in turn by the press and politicians as well. News articles analyzed the recession from this perspective, judged prospects for employment according to business standards for proper government action, and diligently covered the shower of business tax protests. Congressmen fell over each other to voice their support for business demands, leading business periodicals to exult that "Congress has become an alert defender of business and is anxious to provide constructive aid to business expansion."[66] Just as conservatives began to fear that "taxation with representation" could be quite as tyrannous and confiscatory as taxation without it, they found that they had regained some influence over the American political process.[67] Hindered only by calls in the wilderness from an enfeebled political left and a discredited administration, business ideology framed the understanding of the recession and directed the consideration of its solutions. A broad segment of national opinion leaders had mandated a far-reaching business-and-investment-oriented renovation of the tax structure. At no time in the New Deal had the public received such undifferentiated counsel from its opinion leaders to turn back administration policy. It would not be unmoved.

The Public Sanctions Business Leadership

The recession, then, allowed a previously discredited economic philosophy to breach the barrier of public contempt. By April of 1938, an editor of a business periodical confessed himself "more encouraged over the evolution

---

65 "The Second *Fortune* Round Table," *Fortune* 19 (May 1939): 67–8, 113–14, 116–18; Roger Bacon, "Tory Tax Revision," *National Issues* 1 (July 1939): 19.
66 "Congress Sympathetic Toward Business," Standard Statistics Company, *Outlook for the Security Markets* 7 (20 March 1939): 823.
67 R. J. C. Dorsey, quoted in U.S., Congress, House, *Congressional Record*, 76th Cong., 1st sess., 1939, 84, pt. 11: 998.

in the public attitude than discouraged over the contraction in trade and industry."[68]

Public-opinion polls, although in their infancy and hence not especially reliable, reflected the resurgent hegemony of the business community over the economic and political world views of the populace. The most commonly proffered remedy for the recession, embraced by roughly one-third of those polled, was to "remove restrictions on business initiative." Between October 1937 and March 1939, the percentage declaring the Roosevelt administration "not friendly enough" to "big business" climbed from 34 to 52 percent, and the share judging the administration too friendly had halved to 9 percent. One of the two reasons most frequently advanced for deserting Roosevelt's standard was his hostility to business. Two-thirds of the people wanted the administration to abandon its present course for a more conservative one, and believed that the administration's attitude toward business hindered recovery. In a startling indication of the limited attitudinal changes brought by the New Deal, a majority in 1939 deemed the ideas and leadership of "big business" preferable to those of the administration in bringing about lower unemployment and improved business conditions, though the public did not fancy the suggestion that business leaders should take charge of governnment.[69]

Although most Americans had reverted to advocacy of economic renovation through appeasement of business, they had not become unalloyed boosters of wealth and bigness. More people considered big business too unfriendly toward the administration than vice versa. Imputation of inhibitory economic effects to business leaders and their antagonism toward the administration matched similar allegations against the New Deal. By substantial margins, the survey sample contended that "large corporations should pay special taxes not levied on small corporations," that taxes on the rich should not be reduced, and that too much power accrued to a

---

68 B. C. Forbes, "Encouragement in the Change in Public Views; Rise By-and-By," *Forbes* 41 (1 April 1938): 24.

69 Hadley Cantril, ed., *Public Opinion 1935–1946* (Princeton, N.J.: Princeton University Press, 1951), pp. 63, 345, 64; *New York Times*, 24 July 1939, p. 2. George Gallup, "Public Opinion," *Banking* 31 (November 1938): 33; "American Institute of Public Opinion – Surveys, 1938–1939," *Public Opinion Quarterly* 3 (October 1939): 586–7; George H. Gallup, *The Gallup Poll: Public Opinion 1935–1971*, vol. 1 (New York: Random House, 1972), pp. 145–6; "The *Fortune* Survey: 18," *Fortune* 19 (February 1939): 69.

very small number of families and large corporations.[70] Businessmen had not recovered their position as national heroes. Yet on economic questions, their prescriptions offered the primary alternative to FDR. Economic leadership thus fell back into their laps by default when economic failure discredited their only competitor, the New Deal.

It has always been hazardous to use poll results to ascertain the range of politically acceptable economic policies. Popular economic conceptions are usually inchoate and ill-informed. Through the 1930s and since, hefty majorities have assembled in favor of balancing the budget through governmental economies; yet a 1946 poll found only half its sample able to correctly describe what "balancing the federal budget" meant.[71] Just as significantly, survey experts point to a long-standing incongruity between "ideological" and "operational" dispositions. Americans have tended to ritually embrace broad, laissez-faire, conservative abstractions on such shibboleths as individual initiative, negative welfare stereotypes, free enterprise, balanced budgets, and limited government, whereas at the same time they have advocated the advance of the welfare state into such areas as minimum wages, guaranteed jobs, and free medical care for the poor.[72] Something of this tendency is also evident in the late 1930s. Mixed poll results seemed to show a majority favoring a cutback in total relief expenditures, even though most people denied that relief expenditures in their own communities were excessive. Public-works cuts also met mixed reviews, but questions suggesting 10 percent cuts in expenditures for armaments, slum clearance, farm benefits, or old-age pensions were rejected by ratios ranging from two to six to one.[73]

On the question of tax reduction, however, there was less ambiguity. One-sided tallies considered diminished business taxes a more potent

70 "American Institute of Public Opinion – Surveys, 1938–1939," *Public Opinion Quarterly* 3 (October 1939): 586; Cantril, *Public Opinion*, pp. 64, 136, 852, 317, 481.

71 Cantril, *Public Opinion*, pp. 58–9.

72 Lloyd A. Free and Hadley Cantril, *The Political Beliefs of Americans* (New York: Simon and Schuster, 1968), pp. 10, 30–1. The distinction between conservative attitudes and liberal actions requires refinement. It fails to account for negative images of the super-rich, and only a sophisticated definition of liberalism and conservatism – one that probably could not apply to the balance of forces in the 1930s – could permit this division to apply to the simultaneous popular condemnation of big business and sanction for ineffectual antitrust activities.

73 Cantril, *Public Opinion*, pp. 920–1, 697, 941, 6, 545; Rudolph Weissman, ed., *Economic Balance and a Balanced Budget: Public Papers of Marriner S. Eccles* (New York: Harper & Brothers, 1940), p. 260.

recovery measure than the administration's proposed countercyclical spending; one survey even found most relief recipients and 69 percent of Democrats championing business tax cuts over pump priming.[74] The boast of one corporate president that "on no subject have the people been more awakened than on the subject of taxation and its vital relation to business" was not an idle one.[75] By a ratio of three to one in a 1939 Gallup Poll, Americans agreed that "this country would be more prosperous if taxes on business were reduced." Yet though business had received a passive sanction to seek lower taxes, it could not capture the public imagination on such a forbidding and abstruse subject. Concerns like unemployment and neutrality crowded tax reduction out of the picture; at no point did tax cuts surpass the 1 percent level in public selection of America's most vital issue. Although 69 percent of those familiar with the arguments on the despised undistributed-profits tax advocated repeal or reduction, 70 percent of the sample had to be excluded for lack of that knowledge.[76]

The business community had not won a detailed mandate for political and fiscal retrenchment. Nevertheless, the public had given its go-ahead for businessmen to call the economic shots. Congress could accommodate business demands without fear of electoral backlash. Businessmen must have found this prospect inviting. At a time when other business demands were diffuse or politically infeasible, the business community had pulled together a common tax package. Succored by a limited popular endorsement and by support from a broad range of opinion leaders, it focused its symbolic and economic future on that package. It would now transform these recommendations into political pressure.

74 George Gallup, "Help Business by Reducing Taxes, 79% Advocate as Depression Cure," *Washington Post*, 17 April 1938, sec. 3, p. 1; Cantril, *Public Opinion*, p. 920.

75 W. B. Holton, Jr., "Let's Go to Work," *Vital Speeches* 4 (15 May 1938): 474.

76 Cantril, *Public Opinion*, pp. 136, 678; Gallup, *Gallup Poll*, 1: 154; George Gallup, "Many Voters Oppose Undistributed Profits Tax; Most Have Not Followed The Arguments," *Washington Post*, 25 March 1938, p. 2.

7. The Unkindest Cuts of All: Tax Legislation in 1938 and 1939

The Revenue Act of 1938

A lightning-paced mumble rose from the front of the Senate chamber. Urged on by Vice-President Garner's slurred one-word refrain, "Withoutobjectionamendment'sagreedto," the clerk seemed intent on setting a new record. Adept at skipping through committee drafts, his current challenge was the Finance Committee's version of the 1938 revenue bill. Occasional senators vainly challenged the torrent to interpose objections, only to find that they were too late by a page or two, though four amendments were held over for later consideration. "We passed 224 pages of the Tax Bill in 20 minutes," Garner gloated as he handed the gavel to his reliever.[1]

Thus the most generous capital-gains tax since Andrew Mellon moved toward the statute book, without so much as a separate vote. The undistributed-profits tax fell by a voice vote on which only five senators seemed to dissent. The final bill, despite intense administration distaste, casually passed on another voice vote, without an audible "nay."

How had the New Deal's vaunted tax program been so humbled? The recession, the coalescence of the business position, the public sanction for business economic leadership, and the disintegrating administration political position provide much of the explanation.

From the start, Roosevelt faced a difficult fight, if he chose to make it. Finance Committee chairman Harrison, from early 1937, lobbied for a sweeping liberalization of the undistributed-profits tax, though the administration's budget-balancing campaign and a revenue shortfall temporarily held him back. On 20 August, coincident with the enactment of FDR's politically face-saving Revenue Act of 1937, the House gave unanimous consent to Ways and Means Committee chairman Doughton's resolution for an intersession study of comprehensive revenue revision. Simultaneous rumblings emitted from the Senate Finance Committee and business protests against the undistributed-profits tax approached a fever pitch. Yet it still seemed likely that the Treasury investigation announced

1 *New York Times*, 8 April 1938, p. 3; *Chicago Tribune*, 8 April 1938, p. 8.

by FDR on 20 April 1937 would direct the tax agenda. In fact, tax increases seemed very much in the cards.[2]

The recession transformed the situation. As it deepened, Roosevelt beat a strategic retreat. In his 15 November address to Congress, he coupled a defense of the capital-gains tax with an implicit concession that small corporations needed relief from the undistributed-profits tax.[3] The only bright spot for the New Deal in the string of defeats inflicted upon it by the special congressional session was its escape with its undistributed-profits-tax shirt. Over the next half year, the administration would scramble to retain a tattered shirttail.

The special session had laid the foundation for a New Deal tax defeat. The Ways and Means tax-revision subcommittee delayed hearings until the November completion of the Treasury's data package and then proceeded to ignore its main proposals. Treasury Undersecretary Magill worked closely with the subcommittee, overseeing the first installment of concessions to business that the 1938 Revenue Act would force upon the administration. Roosevelt made it clear that he would block tax reductions in the special session. Perceiving far less merit in revision than either Morgenthau or Magill, he also demurred at the sizable cut in the undistributed-profits tax being considered. In late November, however, the subcommittee endorsed it anyway. The president's steadfast opposition threatened Magill's tenuous control of the proceedings. But subcommittee chairman Vinson, a respected tax authority and a firm FDR loyalist, drafted a tax on the retained profits of closely held corporations (those with so few owners that they tended to alter their profit distribution to provide maximum individual tax benefits) to conform to FDR's preoccupation with the role of undistributed profits in personal income-tax evasion.

With the backing of the Treasury and the reluctant sanction of the president, the subcommittee then reported out its package of sixty-three recommendations. Expressing the objective of encouraging business, it

2 The main secondary sources from which I have culled the legislative development of the Revenue Act of 1938 are John M. Blum, *From the Morgenthau Diaries*, vol. 1, *Years of Crisis 1928–1938* (Boston: Houghton Mifflin, 1959), pp. 439–51; and Roy Blakey and Gladys Blakey, *The Federal Income Tax* (New York: Longmans, Green, 1940), pp. 436–53. More detailed coverage may be found in Walter K. Lambert, "New Deal Revenue Acts: The Politics of Taxation" (Ph.D. diss., University of Texas at Austin, 1970), pp. 409–98.

3 Samuel I. Rosenman, comp., *The Public Papers and Addresses of Franklin D. Roosevelt* 6 (New York: Macmillan, 1941): 492–3 (15 November 1937) (hereafter cited as *Addresses of FDR*).

proposed numerous tax reductions. Most importantly, it reworked the tax schedule on capital gains and sheared the maximum undistributed-profits tax rate from 27 to 4 percent (levied in the form of a "20–16" plan, which credited dividends against the suggested 20 percent corporate income-tax rate to allow a 16 percent rate for corporations that distributed all profits to their stockholders). It completely lifted the undistributed-profits tax from corporations with net income of $25,000 or less, a category accounting for only 8 percent of reported profits but 88 percent of the corporations making them.[4] Though some would grumble that a revival of economic activity and employment hinged on the boost given the more economically consequential larger firms, they could scarcely protest legislative obeisance to the small-business symbol that had spearheaded the undistributed-profits-tax repeal drive.

The cause of tax revision received another fillip from Senate testimony by Bernard Baruch. In an extremely well-publicized statement, Wall Street's financial angel moved into the forefront of opposition to New Deal taxation.[5] He pinned the primary onus for unemployment on government policy, claiming that "the combined influence of high and unreasonable capital gains and unwise undistributed taxes has almost stopped the development of new enterprises."[6] On the next day, after over a thousand pages of testimony in which the Treasury (with the active backing of FDR) held the fort against over a hundred witnesses favoring additional tax relief, the Ways and Means Committee report left the subcommittee plan basically intact. Republicans filed a just complaint against their continued exclusion from markup sessions and the perfunctory Democratic rejection of their proposed repeal of the undistributed-profits tax.[7] Business representatives were not happy either, especially about the new tax on closely held corporations. Though many witnesses praised the subcommittee for the direction in which it had moved, they wanted more. Others were more vehement. *Forbes*'s Washington correspondent deemed the Ways and Means bill "primarily a measure of further economic destruction," and the New

4 U.S., Treasury Department, Bureau of Internal Revenue, *Statistics of Income for 1939*, pt. 2 (Washington, D.C.: Government Printing Office, 1942), p. 47.
5 Jordan A. Schwarz, *The Speculator* (Chapel Hill: University of North Carolina Press, 1981), p. 322.
6 U.S., Congress, Senate, Special Committee to Investigate Unemployment and Relief, *Unemployment and Relief, Hearings*, pursuant to S. Res. 36, 75th Cong., 3d sess., 1938, pt. 2: 847.
7 John F. Manley, *The Politics of Finance: The House Committee on Ways and Means* (Boston: Little, Brown, 1970), p. 169.

York Chamber of Commerce considered it "of no real help in restoring confidence to business or in stemming the tide of depression."[8] Chairman Doughton protested at one point that "there are so many deductions that there is little left,"[9] but the committee still fell short of its professed intent to placate business into recovery.

This business perspective was vital to the 1938 Revenue Act. Congressional mail registered almost no sentiment for the undistributed-profits tax; it was appropriately tagged the "tax without a friend."[10] A mountain of letters, many cast in the repetitive phrases of organized campaigns, castigated the tax. James Patterson has observed that the New Deal could usually carry the day when the issue in question mobilized significant parts of its coalition;[11] this pinpoints the fatal weaknesses of the undistributed-profits tax: It was arcane, and its benefits were disaggregatable. It is true that these same weaknesses prevented the channeling of repeal pressure from business to the public to Congress. Instead, repeal depended on Congress's perception of public acquiescence in the business community's intense concerns.

The psychological objection to the undistributed-profits tax proved the most penetrating one. Given the economic and political expectations that the business community invested in repeal, and given a corporate fetish for stability that had frozen out industrial expansion, even those who rejected the business analysis saw the need for concessions. "The immediate importance," wrote George Creel in *Collier's*, is "to bring business out of its tailspin, and since finance and industry refuse to budge until the changes have been made, then the intelligent course is to make them."[12] Robert Doughton concurred, concluding erroneously, "when our tax bill is finally written, if business does not go ahead, it will have to find some reason or excuse other than the tax laws."[13]

---

8 Lawrence Sullivan, "Why Washington is Wavering," *Forbes* 41 (1 February 1938): 42; *Commercial and Financial Chronicle* 146 (12 February 1938): 1013.

9 Robert L. Doughton to John C. Bernhardt, 4 March 1938, folder 697, Robert L. Doughton Papers (Southern Historical Collection, University of North Carolina Library, Chapel Hill).

10 "Bill to Revise Tax Levies Debated in Congress," *Scholastic* 22 (19 March 1938): 14-S.

11 James Patterson, *Congressional Conservatism and the New Deal* (Lexington: University of Kentucky Press, 1967), p. 249.

12 George Creel, "The Battle Cry of Business," *Collier's* 101 (8 January 1938): 30.

13 Robert Doughton to Thurmond Chatham, 21 April 1938, folder 710, Robert L. Doughton Papers.

The die-hard administration supporters of the undistributed-profits tax trotted out the tired arguments of 1936. The defense of the tax can be broken down into three major categories: rebuttal of claimed adverse effects, maintenance of revenue, and tax evasion by economic royalists. The revenue twist was of most recent vintage. It rang false in an administration that justified deficits that dwarfed proposed revenue cuts. Yet Roosevelt reiterated in 1938 and 1939 that he would not mandate reduced tax collections while a deficit continued, and he encouraged rumors that disregard of this symbolic show of fiscal responsibility might result in a veto. Some Democrats also baited business witnesses with the contention that the removal of the undistributed-profits tax from the subcommittee "20–16" plan would require a 22 percent corporate income tax to amass equivalent revenues.

The tax-evasion argument, upon which FDR relied so heavily, was logically the most compelling. Corporations responsive to their wealthy stockholders had a strong incentive to hoard profits because dividends were taxed at personal-income rates as high as 50 percent or more, whereas capital gains were taxed at a fraction of that level. The tax-code provision designed to block this form of evasion, Section 102, had never been terribly effective. Thus after the Ways and Means Committee stunted the undistributed-profits tax, the administration focused its tax-evasion crusade on the levy on closely held corporations. This provision, confusingly labeled the "third-basket tax" (because it added a third category to the division at $25,000 in the applicability of the undistributed-profits tax), marked a turning point in the fortunes of New Deal tax policy, rending the Democratic Party. On the House roll-call vote, a slight plurality of Democrats joined with the Republicans to buck the administration and sink the tax.[14]

Treasury Secretary Morgenthau branded this unanticipated drubbing "the worst slap" suffered by Roosevelt during his administration.[15] But the result should not have been surprising. Even House passage of the third-basket tax would only have thrown it into a Senate in which – in Pat Harrison's assessment – it didn't have "a tinker's chance in hell."[16] Business representatives had targeted their biggest guns on this proposal, and the recession-shocked Congress was inclined to surrender. The press

14 *New York Times*, 12 March 1938, p. 9.
15 Blum, *Morgenthau Diaries: Years of Crisis*, pp. 443–4.
16 Pat Harrison, March 1938, quoted in Martha H. Swain, *Pat Harrison* (Jackson: University Press of Mississippi, 1978), p. 177.

attack, fueled by the often-noted fact that newspapers and periodicals tended to be closely held operations, was ferocious. Also, for one of the few times during the New Deal, Roosevelt found himself on the wrong side of the symbolic fence. Opponents easily depicted their defense of family-held corporations in terms of the corner store, individual initiative, the "little fellow," and the American way of life. Contrary to images summoned by this opposition, Ma and Pa had no worries from the tax, even granted the possibility that exemption levels could later drop somewhat. Nevertheless, the conception was too strong of family corporations as the "backbone of the country," pioneers and innovators who built businesses up from nothing, insurers of competition and mobility, and bulwarks against monopoly and "the jaws of the Wall Street wolves."[17] It went against the waves of grain to place American gumption at a seeming tax disadvantage against corporate giants, especially at a time when the objective was to encourage all business. Roosevelt's tunnel vision on tax evasion marred his usual political acuity.

New Dealers also found that the recession had replaced their sure-fire economic symbols with blanks. New Deal tax defenders endlessly proclaimed that capital-gains revision would foster speculation while only marginally accelerating investment, since 80–85 percent of these gains came from the stock market. FDR, zeroing in on the speculative intent of a securities purchase, quoted H. G. Wells's conclusion that capital-gains tax revision would only help "the big fellows who have inside information."[18] "How in the world," asked Representative Dingell (D–Mich.), "can a man argue for a tax exemption on profits which he made without working?"[19]

Tax-revision forces parried by celebrating the extent to which "business depends on the psychology which is created in the stock market."[20] The previous capital-gains tax structure came under fire because the discontinuous drops in rates (ranging from 100 percent of the individual's tax rate if the asset were held a year or less to 30 percent if held for more

---

17 Arthur Lamneck, in U.S., Congress, House, *Congressional Record*, 75th Cong., 3d sess., 1938, 83, pt. 9: 750; Thomas O'Malley, in House, *Congressional Record*, 75th Cong., 3d sess., 1938, 83, pt. 3: 3129.

18 FDR to John W. McCormack, 22 October 1937, in Elliot Roosevelt, *FDR: His Personal Letters 1928–1945* (New York: Duell, Sloan and Pearce, 1950), 1: 722.

19 U.S., Congress, House, *Congressional Record*, 75th Cong., 3d sess., 1938, 83, pt. 3: 2882.

20 M. L. Seidman, in U.S., Congress, House, Committee on Ways and Means, *Revenue Revision – 1939, Hearings*, 76th Cong., 1st sess., 1939, p. 186.

than ten years) froze securities while owners awaited lower rate periods. The emphasis on investment by the rich led the Senate Finance Committee to clamp a 15 percent maximum capital-gains tax rate on assets held over one and a half years, regardless of the owner's tax bracket. The speculator image had given way to a new political mood condoning the hard-boiled argument that the economy demanded such subsidies to the rich.

The Senate Finance Committee made other important changes in the Ways and Means version passed by the House. Senate Finance Committee chairman Harrison, released from administration loyalism by Roosevelt's successful effort in July 1937 to deny him the majority leadership, immediately announced over nationwide radio that the remaining "skeleton of the undistributed profits tax" would still "haunt business."[21] His Finance Committee eagerly dropped the tax by a vote of 17–4. It substituted a straight 18 percent levy on corporate earnings, with an abatement for smaller enterprises. In all, the Senate Finance Committee had well lived up to the promise in its report to go "even further than the House bill in an effort to stimulate and encourage business."[22] Roosevelt, the only bulwark against such substantial revision, never made the countervailing public appeal hoped for by his supporters; indeed, he failed to bestir himself on any issue in March. In April, his new-found exuberance was siphoned off by his new spending proposal, and perhaps by recognition of the odds against his tax program in the Senate. After little substantive debate, the Senate Finance Committee draft sailed through the Senate on a voice vote on 9 April 1938.

Upon Senate passage, FDR exerted pressure for the House bill. He combined veto threats with flexible instructions to Doughton, Vinson, and the Treasury to drive the best bargain they could.[23] In a Treasury-drafted public letter to Doughton and Harrison on 13 April, he ripped into the Senate plan, bristling that a capital-gains ceiling favored "the capital of the speculator" over the progressively and more heavily taxed income of "the salaried man and the merchant," while the repeal of the undistributed-profits tax discriminated against partnerships and gave a green light to tax avoidance.[24]

21 *Commercial and Financial Chronicle* 146 (19 March 1938): 1808.
22 U.S., Congress, Senate, Committee on Finance, *Revenue Bill of 1938*, S. Rept. 1567 to Accompany H.R. 9682, 75th Cong., 3d sess., 1938, p. 1.
23 Morgenthau Diaries, 18 April 1938, book 119, p. 278, Henry A. Morgenthau, Jr., Papers (Franklin D. Roosevelt Library, Hyde Park, N.Y.).
24 *Addresses of FDR*, 7: 215–16 (13 April 1938).

A rancorous conference deadlock dragged on for almost a month, with Senate conferees temporarily banishing Treasury experts for overzealousness on the undistributed-profits tax.[25] In the end, Roosevelt's fixation on the principle of the undistributed-profits tax salvaged a token two-year levy. The capital-gains formula, however, left the administration little to cheer about. It was basically the Senate's: a top rate of 15 percent on sales of stock owned for more than two years, along with the most generous allowance since 1924 – and forever after – for losses on stock sales.

Roosevelt received mixed counsel on how to handle the 1938 revenue bill, with Treasury Secretary Morgenthau urging him to sign it without an accompanying attack, and Herman Oliphant (the wounded parent in the infanticide of the undistributed-profits tax) favoring a veto that would face a sure override in the Senate and a spirited fight in the House. Roosevelt, for the first time in his political life and in twentieth-century tax history, chose to allow the bill to become law without his signature. On 27 May 1938, in a nationally broadcast high school commencement address in Arthurdale, West Virginia (his wife's cherished subsistence-homestead project), Roosevelt made a belated stand, presenting his case that the bill repudiated principles of progressive taxation and instituted a capital-gains tax structure that "helps the very few ... at the expense of the many."[26]

"He slapped you in the face," one Republican later reminded the Democrats. "He pouted and refused to play the game."[27] In rebuttal, Pat Harrison icily took to the Senate floor as the first congressional Democratic leader to challenge the accuracy of a Roosevelt speech.[28] Before a packed chamber, he defended the revenue act's contribution to recovery, chastised the third-basket tax proposal, and pointed out that Roosevelt had overstated his case by claiming that "you and I" would have to pay the same 15 percent capital-gains rates on a $5,000 profit on stocks held for a few years as a man making a $500,000 stock-market profit. As Roosevelt had bellowed, "That, my friends, is not right."[29] The 15 percent rate was a ceiling; any individual with an income below $40,000 would be in a low enough tax bracket to fall beneath the long-term capital-gains maximum on a $5,000 profit. Perhaps Roosevelt's eagerness to let off steam and

25 *New York Times*, 23 April 1938, p. 2.
26 *Addresses of FDR*, 7: 364 (27 May 1938).
27 Thomas Jenkins, in U.S., Congress, House, *Congressional Record*, 76th Cong., 1st sess., 1939, 84, pt. 7: 7474.
28 Swain, *Pat Harrison*, p. 182.
29 *Addresses of FDR*, 7: 362 (27 May 1938).

make telling political points led him to neglect Treasury comments on the capital-gains distinction.[30]

Particularly after this exchange, business commentators – although noting that tax concessions still had a long way to go – joined Harrison in a defense of the law and its potential contribution to recovery.[31] The actual effects of the revenue act, however, are problematic. Economically, the tax package had only marginally reduced exactions on the corporate sector; even granted a psychological boost that was well disguised by continuing business tax protests, the distributive effects of tax revision within the business community outweighed the macroeconomic impact. The business tax issue was also not electorally significant in 1938. The revenue act may have staved off some criticism, though some Republican speakers still pilloried the New Deal tax burden. Perhaps the most notable change flowed from the reduction in the capital-gains and -loss tax. The extraordinarily generous provision for capital losses, following upon the harsh treatment in 1934–7, led many traders to dump their capital losses, thereby considerably reducing their taxable incomes. The capital-gains ceiling also proved a considerable boon, causing the effective rate of taxation to plummet for reported net incomes over $300,000. Capital gains accounted for most of the net income reported in the fifty returns in 1938 of over $1 million, a level not even approached in other years. Because regular income in this bracket would be taxed at marginal rates of 77–9 percent, it was scarcely surprising that a 15 percent capital-gains ceiling induced the super-rich to cash in some of their blue chips.[32]

30 Morgenthau Diaries, 31 May 1938, book 126, pp. 339, 341, 347–8.
31 See Mark H. Leff, "The New Deal and Taxation, 1933–1939: The Limits of Symbolic Reform" (Ph.D. diss., University of Chicago, 1978), pp. 530–1.
32 Gabriel Kolko, in a sideswipe at New Deal tax policy, makes the following observation: "Under Roosevelt, up to 1941, the actual, as opposed to the theoretical, tax rates on very high incomes were not very different from those under Herbert Hoover. . . . In 1932, the highest possible tax rate on incomes of $1 million and up was 54 percent, but only 47 percent was actually collected. In 1938, the maximum theoretical tax rate had increased to 72 percent, but only 44 percent was collected." Kolko's figures for maximum statutory rates are wrong (mainly because he neglected to add the 8% normal tax to the 1932 surtax rates and the 4% normal tax to the 1938 surtax rates), and the effective rate figures (what Kolko calls "actual" tax rates) were only chosen for aberrant years (effective tax rates for 1925–31 and 1933 were 16–17% and 32% respectively, and those for 1937 and 1939 were 72% and 65%). Most importantly, Kolko apparently failed to understand how little we learn from effective-rate figures. Effective rates only measure the percentage of net income paid in taxes, where net income equals gross income *minus all deductions*. Hence effective rates factor out expense accounts, most capital gains and losses, charitable donations, business losses, interest, tax-

From the vantage point of power relationships within American society, the 1938 Revenue Act is revealingly inconsequential. At a time when labor and government challenged corporate prerogatives, this symbolic tax victory failed to significantly lighten burdens on businessmen or to enhance their institutional leverage. Conservatives derived some benefits from their tax hegemony, by easing taxes on stock profits and by heading off general tax increases. But, on the whole, they squandered their influence on a superficial humiliation of the New Deal.

The Revenue Act of 1939

The symbolic functions of taxation also provide a backdrop for the Revenue Act of 1939. This conflict isolated Roosevelt as had no other. The much-

exempt government securities, and all the other items used to assess the effectiveness of a tax system. Usually, effective rates only demonstrate the extent to which the personal exemption and the gradual step-up in rates scale down the top rate applicable to an individual's income.

The 1938 Revenue Act made things more complicated. In 1934–7, preferential capital-gains treatment was achieved by removing certain percentages of the gains from net income, rather than by cutting the nominal tax rate applied to the taxable capital gains. Thus, the percentage of *gross* income taxed was reduced by the capital gains preference, but the "effective rate" on *net* income was unchanged. The 1938 Revenue Act, on the other hand, imposed a special ceiling on the actual tax *rates* applied to capital gains. This method thus shows up with a vengeance in the effective-rate statistic whenever a large share of someone's income was taxed at the special low capital-gains rate. Thus, when the million-dollar-plus incomes took the profits from their backlog of frozen capital gains, the effective rate plunged, only to revive in 1939 when the dissipation of the backlog reduced the share of capital gains in the reported incomes of the super-rich. Kolko's 1938 effective-rate figure, then, is a definitional artifact, exacerbated by the decision of fewer than fifty people to use the low rates of a New Deal–opposed law to unload the capital gains that they had held in abeyance to avoid the higher rates of a New Deal–sanctioned law. Sources: Gabriel Kolko, *Wealth and Power in America* (New York: Praeger, 1962), p. 32. Kolko returns to the scene of the crime in *Main Currents in American History* (New York: Harper & Row, 1976), p. 145. An effective-rate table is included in U.S., Treasury Department, Bureau of Internal Revenue, *Statistics of Income for 1940*, pt. 1 (Washington, D.C.: Government Printing Office, 1943), pp. 53–4. The net-income, capital-gains, and tax figures comprising the effective-rate statistic for 1938 may be found in U.S., Treasury Department, Bureau of Internal Revenue, *Statistics of Income for 1938*, pt. 1 (Washington, D.C.: Government Printing Office, 1941), pp. 92–3, 96–100. The acceleration of capital-loss claims in 1938–9 is evident in Treasury, *Statistics of Income for 1940*, pt. 1: 64–5. Stock-market analysts prescribed such manipulation of capital gains and losses. See "Tax Law Changes Important," Standard Statistics Company, *Outlook for the Security Markets* 5 (16 May 1938): 198; and "Highlights of the 1938 Tax Act from the Investor's Standpoint," Standard Statistics Company, *Outlook for the Security Markets* 6 (31 October 1938, supplement); 205–6.

touted prospect of a New Deal campaign to reinvigorate the capital-gains and undistributed-profits taxes evaporated with the debacle of the 1938 election. The recession-fueled conservatism that had carried the 1938 Revenue Act now locked itself into a position of political dominance. Not a single Republican congressman met defeat. Republicans picked up eighty-one seats in the House, eight in the Senate, and thirteen gover-norships.[33]

It is difficult to disentangle the causes of this Democratic setback. The Supreme Court–packing bill, popular weariness with reform, labor turmoil, local issues, FDR's attempted purge in the primaries, a dip in agricultural prices, and isolationist fears of an imperial presidency all played some part. But, of greatest importance, the New Deal had failed where it counted most: in economic management.

The historical tendency to assess a president's political party for the vagaries of the economy has cut deeply since the New Deal, when the federal government assumed inescapable economic responsibility. Political scientist Edward Tufte has constructed a statistical model of midterm elections for this modern period.[34] He portrays these elections as referenda on the performance of the president and the economy. These two factors alone permit adequate predictions of the degree to which midterm elections will diverge from the usual drop in the national congressional vote percentage by the president's party. In the case of the 1938 election, the severity of the decline rests with the recession, for FDR's personal popularity was still relatively high. Though this model is suggestive at best, Tufte's calculation for the 1938 election does provide confirmation for the centrality of the recession in the politics of the late 1930s.

The ideological repercussions of the electoral defeat were ambiguous. The Maverick bloc of third-party and Democratic liberals suffered the severest losses. It was wiped out as a significant leftward force, decimating the liberal influence in the upper Midwest.[35] Yet the still-substantial Democratic congressional majority hindered the conservative coalition from transcending a spoiler role. Moreover, a new Republican breed, those willing to condone basic New Deal reforms and Townsend old-age pensions, had been particularly successful. Thus one old-guard Re-

33 Richard Polenberg, "The Decline of the New Deal, 1937–1940," in *The New Deal: The National Level*, ed. John Braeman, Robert H. Bremner, and David Brody, vol. 1 (Columbus: Ohio State University Press, 1975), p. 259.

34 Edward R. Tufte, "Determinants of the Outcomes of Midterm Congressional Elections," *American Political Science Review* 69 (September 1975): 812–26.

35 Dennis N. Mihelich, "The Congressional Mavericks, 1933–1939" (Ph.D. diss., Case Western Reserve University, 1972), p. 279.

publican concluded that the election "was not an expression of confidence in the Republican party or an approval of its 57 varieties of platforms."[36]

The moderation of the Republican position, in itself a threat to Roosevelt by focusing opposition on the most vulnerable aspects of the New Deal, had some parallel in a growing corporate flexibility on labor questions but had no impact on the business tax position. Buoyed by the 1938 election results, business spokesmen now tended to dismiss the New Deal philosophy as an aberration and looked to the 1940 election for their salvation. Foreseeing a legislative stalemate and failing Democratic prospects without an economic resurgence, liberals moved toward conciliation. Even the *Nation* concluded in March of 1939 that recovery was "so important, not merely for its own sake but for the maintenance of the New Deal as a whole, that sacrifices in the field of taxation . . . might be justified if a large-scale expansion of private investment followed."[37] But conservatives were after bigger game. They had attained their psychological victory with the 1938 Revenue Act and were increasingly loath to compromise over their long-range goal of "substantial relief." The smiting of minor tax irritants seemed "tantamount to removing a cinder from a man's eye as he goes down into the water for the third time."[38]

On the political level, then, FDR faced continuing pressure for tax reform. Not enamored of futile political battles with little hope of electoral benefits, he assumed what was termed an "appeasement" stance. The year 1939 was not to be one of legislative advancement, and Roosevelt knew it. Moreover, it was widely recognized that Democratic prospects in 1940 hinged on the pace of economic progress. The administration depended on private investment to take up the slack, but the economy had again turned sluggish after a marked upturn in the latter half of 1938. In his annual message to Congress, FDR proclaimed:

> We have now passed the period of internal conflict in the launching of our program of social reform. Our full energies may now be released to invigorate the processes of recovery in order to preserve our reforms, and to give every man and woman who wants to work a real job at a living wage.[39]

36 Charles D. Hilles to Col. John O'Loughlin, 21 November 1938, "Nov. 21– 25, 1938" folder, box 205, Charles D. Hilles Papers (Yale University Archives, New Haven, Conn.).
37 "Appeasing Business," *Nation* 148 (4 March 1939): 252.
38 Everett Dirksen, in U.S., Congress, House, *Congressional Record*, 76th Cong., 1st sess., 1939, 84, pt. 7: 7475.
39 *Addresses of FDR*, 4 January 1939, 8: 7.

By counterposing recovery to the reform that many New Dealers considered its precondition, Roosevelt made a major symbolic concession. FDR also sought peace with Congress by denying intentions of executive dictation, toned down his rhetoric to replace denunciation of special interests with talk of preservation and unity, and paved the way for Harry Hopkins, his new Secretary of Commerce, to enlist business cooperation in recovery. Although somewhat embarrassed by the torpid private demand for credit that accompanied the new "appeasement of business," many business commentators took heart at the positive implications of change in "the tone, the spirit, and the official intention."[40] FDR's stubborn nominations of controversial liberals to high political positions, along with his support for the Works Progress Administration and deficit spending, indicated that this retreat was tactical and halfhearted, but he would not lack encouragement to maintain a conciliatory course.

In a fascinating conflict that primarily took place outside the halls of Congress, the Treasury Department coordinated a campaign of tax opposition to FDR that removed the face-saving remnants of the undistributed-profits tax. Amid a running battle with FDR, Senate Finance Committee chairman Harrison talked of the "splendid harmony" between congressional committees and the Treasury on the 1939 revenue bill.[41] As the Chamber of Commerce's E. C. Alvord expressed it in a top-level Treasury powwow with business tax lobbyists, "We naturally are very much interested in attempting to assist the Treasury in proving that tax revision doesn't necessarily mean decreasing revenues."[42] The 1939 Revenue Act was enforced appeasement, the product of a Harrison–Treasury–business alliance.

As late as January 1939, Roosevelt still talked of a tax boost to cover new armament spending and past congressional additions to farm-parity payments. The Treasury, upon Roosevelt's instructions, was putting the finishing touches on a comprehensive revenue-raising plan. But, at a 17 February press conference en route to a two-week vacation to inspect the fleet, FDR hit the front pages with a surprising comment that he did not expect to raise taxes. Less than a week later, Treasury Secretary Morgenthau, now a convert to the business community's tax position, put forward his

---

40 *Kiplinger Washington Letter*, 14 January 1939, p. 1; *Kiplinger Washington Letter*, 15 February 1939, p. 2.

41 U.S., Congress, House, *Congressional Record*, 76th Cong., 1st sess., 1939, 84, pt. 7: 7686.

42 Morgenthau Diaries, 23 March 1939, book 170, p. 249.

own view. "I sincerely hope," he announced in a prepared statement, "Congress will take a careful look at the tax law and see if there are any deterrents holding back businessmen from making future commitments."[43] In the context of the political debate of the time, this remark – especially the term "deterrents," a code word Roosevelt would never have used – framed the tax issue in terms of business complaints and scuttled the undistributed-profits tax. Anxious to thicken the ice under the advanced outpost he had established for an administration appeasement position, he immediately phoned Harrison, Doughton, and Speaker Bankhead, urging them to "back me up."[44]

Although Bankhead would later complain that the concept of tax deterrents could be used as a "pretext" for bigger things,[45] Doughton and Harrison were more responsive. The day after Morgenthau's press conference, Doughton chimed in that he was "very much pleased" with Morgenthau's statement, for it "states my own position exactly."[46] On 3 March, Doughton and Harrison released a letter to Morgenthau soliciting Treasury recommendations so as to further the effort to remove deterrents.[47] Morgenthau gracefully promised compliance. In the meantime, Secretary of Commerce Hopkins, urged on by a standard business tax proposal from his Business Advisory Council, had picked up on the Morgenthau and Roosevelt announcements. Noting the shift "from reform to recovery," Hopkins opposed a general tax increase and urged the replacement of taxes with the "deterring effect" of freezing necessary capital flows.[48]

When Roosevelt returned from the Caribbean and proved unwilling to carry through on his lieutenants' promises, he had a full-scale revolt on his hands. Businessmen thought they had the administration on the run, he told Morgenthau on 6 March, and "if they got adjustments in the taxes they would want adjustments in other fields."[49] Through the month of March, Roosevelt seemed to oppose any alteration in corporate taxes, chastising the Treasury for "falling into Senator Harrison's trap." In the process, he offended Morgenthau by asserting that the proposed changes

43 *Washington Post*, 24 February 1939, p. 1.
44 Morgenthau Diaries, 23 February 1939, book 165, pp. 165, 167, 172.
45 *New York Times*, 15 March 1939, p. 1.
46 *Commercial and Financial Chronicle* 148 (4 March 1939): 1252; John M. Blum, *From the Morgenthau Diaries*, vol. 2: *Years of Urgency 1938–41* (Boston: Houghton Mifflin, 1965), p. 18.
47 R. L. Doughton and Pat Harrison to Henry Morgenthau, 3 March 1939, "1939 folder," box 2, Official File 962, FDR Papers.
48 *New York Times*, 25 February 1939, p. 2.
49 Blum, *Morgenthau Diaries: Years of Urgency*, p. 19.

came from Harrison – an inaccurate if benign assumption, for Morgenthau and Hanes cribbed their suggestions from the same standard business tax plan used by Harrison.[50]

Roosevelt was especially perturbed by that Hanes-Treasury business-appeasement plan. It sliced the top surtax on personal income to 60 percent, and reworked corporate tax schedules to allow a carryover of operating losses, to drop the $2,000 limit on corporate capital losses, and to eliminate the undistributed-profits and capital-stock/excess-profits levies. Voicing his opposition to any cuts in total individual or corporate income taxes, FDR denounced this "Mellon plan of taxation" and warned the Treasury not to leak this reincarnation to Congress.[51]

In conferences with Morgenthau, Undersecretary Hanes, Harrison, and Ways and Means subcommittee chairman Jere Cooper (Doughton was ill), FDR pressed this position, even though it was becoming clear that Congress would neither authorize higher taxes nor prevent the lapsing of the undistributed-profits tax. Upon Roosevelt's instigation, Senate Majority Leader Barkley and House Speaker Bankhead deprecated tax revision, claiming that it would only subsidize giant corporations at the expense of small ones.[52] Roosevelt rang the same theme in his press conferences and announced that he would not abide any reduction in the corporate tax share. Although conceding to Morgenthau that neither of them had "any particular objection" to dropping the capital-stock/excess-profits tax in favor of a stiffer corporate income tax, he staunchly defended the role of the undistributed-profits tax in deterring income-tax evasion by the very rich[53] and argued that Harrison should be jockeyed into sponsoring his own revamping of corporate taxation. Actually, FDR had won much of the battle when he obtained leadership agreement that short-run corporate revenue yields should not decline. That gave conservatives little maneuvering room, placing them in the unpopular position of raising certain corporate taxes. A reluctance to exchange one tax for another

50 FDR to Henry Morgenthau, Jr., 25 March 1939, in Roosevelt, ed., *FDR: His Personal Letters*, vol. 2, pp. 866–7.
51 "March 8, 1939 Meeting at the White House at 11 a.m. on Taxes," pp. 2 and 5, box 178, "Chronology – Tax Bill – 1939," Record Group 56, General Records of the Department of the Treasury (National Archives, Washington, D.C.).
52 Barkley, in *New York Times*, 14 March 1939, p. 12; Bankhead, in *Washington Post*, 15 March 1939, p. 10.
53 FDR to Henry Morgenthau, Jr., 25 March 1939, in Elliott Roosevelt, ed., *FDR: His Personal Letters*, 2: 866.

helps explain the relative apathy of many businessmen over legislative removal of tax "irritants."

Although impeding the drive for corporate tax revision, FDR also sidetracked it by acquiescing in a freeze on social security taxes. This concession was certain to please the business community and carried the added benefit of tying up the Ways and Means Committee. In addition, Roosevelt secured Doughton's temporary agreement to drop plans for corporate tax revision. Such legislation, FDR wrote Morgenthau on 29 March, would "seriously jeopardize early adjournment and create a general mess."[54]

Roosevelt's efforts to control the tax agenda, however, were doomed to futility. In the wake of Morgenthau's vain efforts to obtain presidential approval for a promised Treasury statement before the Ways annd Means Committee,[55] the Treasury tax plan that FDR had flatly rejected was leaked to the *New York Times*, apparently through Harrison, Doughton, and the Chamber of Commerce. This only heated up the rebellion.[56] Once set in motion, the tax-revision process went beyond administration control. Within a week, it became clear that the undistributed-profits tax was doomed and that the Congress would pass a business-appeasement tax plan with or without FDR's support. Compromise was necessary to avoid a major confrontation and a "runaway" Senate bill.[57] The administration would eventually have to come to Harrison, for a half a billion dollars in excise taxes would expire on 30 June, and the $1.3 billion in corporate taxes had to be renewed before 1 January 1940. For months, Harrison had made no secret of the intention of his Senate Finance Committee to tack corporate tax revision onto any joint resolution to extend current taxes, and he now sharpened his threats. But even Harrison wondered if Hanes's Treasury proposals were not too blatant a concession to business. He backed Morgenthau's compromise position to the hilt.

Spurred on by the Henderson-Eccles-Corcoran-Cohen New Dealer wing, Roosevelt waged a spirited (and, thanks to continual leaks, very public) battle against virtually the entire political establishment. Even by early May, his position was manifestly on the decline. In late April, the Brookings Institution hastily released a fiscal analysis that endorsed the business community's program – and thus the Treasury-Harrison position

54 Blum, *Morgenthau Diaries: Years of Urgency*, p. 22.
55 Ibid., p. 24.
56 Morgenthau Diaries, 11 May 1939, book 189, p. 184.
57 *New York Times*, 17 May 1939, p. 1.

– from top to bottom. In early May, the Chamber of Commerce joined the National Association of Manufacturers and the American Federation of Little Business in a business blitz of support for thorough tax revision, entertaining an estimated three hundred senators and representatives at a string of dinners that symbolized its growing reliance on congressional initiative.[58] Roosevelt confronted plain evidence that his appeasement gestures had failed.

An early product of FDR's appeasement campaign, Undersecretary Hanes, may have sealed the president's defeat. While Roosevelt battled to stave off the Treasury plan, Hanes diligently curried conservative support for it. By May, he and Roosevelt were not on speaking terms, and Roosevelt temporarily barred him from tax conferences. Hanes, in a touching display of administration loyalty, sputtered: "Don't think that I have not been busy nights and I have got about 24 friends in the House and about the same number in the Senate that will stand with me on a fight on the tax program. . . . I do not like Mr. Roosevelt."[59]

Though Roosevelt had forsaken the appeasement route, and though he preferred a tax package combining the social security tax freeze, the extension of all existing taxes, and the formation of a joint congressional-Treasury study of tax revision, he acknowledged persistent Treasury-congressional pressure by relenting on the undistributed-profits tax. Noting that undistributed-profits tax collections would only total 2 percent of corporate taxes, he acccused corporations of "making a mountain out of a mole hill,"[60] but on several occasions in the month of May he allowed that he would accept repeal if other measures were taken to prevent income-tax avoidance and to retrieve the revenue from corporations with net incomes over $25,000.

With Harrison at his heels, FDR finally bowed to the inevitable. Eleanor Roosevelt may have provided the catalyst. Morgenthau had come to her on 18 May with a draft of his tax statement, justly complaining that FDR had humiliated him and given him the runaround. The next day, Morgenthau received word that FDR now supported a tax program for the current session. Roosevelt commented that he and his wife had discussed economics, flashing Morgenthau "a searching look." Before the end of the month, Morgenthau joined FDR in hammering out a package acceptable to the Finance and Ways and Means committees (it was basically Harrison's

58 "The Key to Recovery," *Nation's Business* 27 (June 1939): 59.
59 Morgenthau Diaries, 11 May 1939, p. 190.
60 *Addresses of FDR*, 8: 349 (22 May 1939).

compromise – considered by Hanes to be only "a small bite of the cherry"), and, at long last, Morgenthau secured FDR's endorsement of his tax statement.[61]

Rather than laying down a precise program to the Ways and Means Committee, Morgenthau presented areas worthy of their "special attention" or reexamination, but when John Hanes later observed that Morgenthau's recommendations were "fairly definite," he wasn't letting the cat out of the bag. Somewhat surprisingly, the Treasury secretary covered the gamut of the Hanes tax revamping, even including a suggestion that surtaxes on very large personal incomes might be reduced after lifting tax-exemption from government securities – an income-tax revision outside the prior compromise and anathema to FDR. The undistributed-profits tax, the capital-stock/excess-profits tax, the limit on corporate capital-loss deductions and the absence of a carry-over for operating losses – all came under fire as "irritants" or deterrents that "have been characterized as likely to hinder business expansion and investment."[62]

The legislative proceedings were merely a formality. Despite some partisan wrangling on peripheral issues, even Republicans deemed this tax-revision bill a definite advance. It whisked through the House by a tally of 357–1, after only four hours of debate, most of it for the record. The main Republican debating point was capsulized in a subtitle of the Ways and Means minority report: "TAX REVISION A REPUBLICAN VICTORY."[63]

Senate consideration was even more of a rubber-stamping process. The Finance Committee, a prototype of conservative bipartisanship, unanimously reported out the House bill. The ensuing four-hour Senate consideration (it could scarcely be called a debate; the subject of corporate taxation barely received substantive attention) was capped by a unanimous roll-call vote. The following day, the House accepted all Senate amendments to ward off the bother of a conference. FDR, who had declared the House bill "very good,"[64] quietly signed the 1939 Revenue Act on 29 June.

---

61 Blum, *Morgenthau Diaries: Years of Urgency*, p. 28.
62 U.S., Congress, House, Committee on Ways and Means, *Revenue Revision – 1939, Hearings*, 76th Cong., 1st. sess., pp. 2–6.
63 U.S., Congress, House, Committee on Ways and Means, *The Revenue Bill of 1939: Supplemental Views of the Republican Minority*, H. Rept. 855 to accompany H.R. 6851, 76th Cong., 1st sess., 1939, p. 51.
64 Franklin D. Roosevelt, *Complete Presidential Press Conferences* (New York: Da Capo Press, 1972), 20 June 1939, 13: 428.

As a fiscal measure, the 1939 Revenue Act deserves all the inattention it has historically received. Its paramount achievement was negative. By failing to extend the undistributed-profits tax beyond 1939, Congress cut short one of the New Deal's few significant tax innovations.[65] By slapping down a tax symbol cherished by FDR and his deficit-spending New Deal advisers, Congress also hoped to speed recovery through the easy and cheap step of handing the trivial remnant of the undistributed-profits tax to business on a platter.

A hike in the corporate income tax recouped most of the revenue escaping through this and other revisions. The statute also revived the two-year net operating loss carry-forward of the 1920s (allowing negative profits to be written off against positive ones for the next two years). Another section of the statute allowed corporations to submit higher (not lower, which might have helped smaller, stagnating businesses) declarations of capital stock in 1939 and 1940, thereby removing the capital-stock/ excess-profits tax as an immediate threat to a profit boom from war contracts. Congress also granted corporations the same generous treatment of capital losses (losses from the sale of assets – such as stocks – not part of the day-to-day transactions of the firm) given individuals the year before. Deductible corporate capital losses, primarily the province of financial institutions, jumped from $75 million in 1938 and $65 million in 1939 to $703 million in 1940 (8 percent of corporate net income) and $1 billion in 1941 (6 percent of income).[66]

Just as important is what the 1939 Revenue Act did not include. Though introducing several business-backed provisions that would ultimately save some firms millions,[67] it did not implement other business demands: a lower individual capital-gains rate, consolidated returns for affiliated corporations, or an easing of the tax on intercorporate dividends. Most importantly, it did not accede to demands that the corporate tax burden

65 The others were the graduated levy on corporate incomes (whose confinement to the sub-$40,000 brackets left little to recommend it as a deconcentrator over the $2,000–$3,000 corporate exemption employed in the 1920s), the intercorporate-dividends tax, the excess-profits tax as a guarantor of a proper capital-stock valuation, regressive taxes to support such programs as the AAA and social security, and a number of technical adjustments – some of them not sponsored by the administration – that alternately penalized or benefited special interests.

66 U.S., Treasury Department, Bureau of Internal Revenue, *Statistics of Income for 1940*, pt. 2 (Washington, D.C.: Government Printing Office, 1944), pp. 54, 64; U.S., Treasury Department, Bureau of Internal Revenue, *Statistics of Income for 1941*, pt. 2 (Washington, D.C.: Government Printing Office, 1945), pp. 60, 70, 273.

67 Leff, "The New Deal and Taxation," pp. 551–3.

be substantially reduced (Treasury estimates put the immediate cumulative revenue loss from the 1939 changes at only $5 million).

Interestingly, the 1939 Revenue Act failed to slice individual income tax rates on the super-rich. Support for this revision had spanned the conservative political spectrum, from the Treasury Department, to Pat Harrison, to the organized business community. Although its actual effects would have been paltry, its symbolic resonance for businessmen was large, despite their emphasis in 1937–9 on the undistributed-profits tax. The salience of this issue became especially apparent in late 1939. High surtaxes, keynoting the conservative tax attack, were adjudged "probably the greatest" deterrent to business expansion.[68] Yet despite a recession psychology according widespread elite acceptance to the theory that lower taxes would boost the confidence and thus the investment inclinations of the rich, FDR's opposition prevailed. Although the battle was rejoined immediately upon the enactment of the 1939 revenue bill, the cause never prospered. The public had never bought it, Roosevelt despised it as an affront to his anti-special-privilege view of income taxation, and it had suffered by being paired with a tax-exemption proposal that had little chance. As the economy heated up and demand for defense revenues loomed, tax reduction became a concept whose time had gone.

Despite the limited accomplishments of the 1939 Revenue Act, it had taken its political toll. FDR and the crippled New Deal left plainly had lost. FDR acquiesced *after* his appeasement stratagem foundered. He made what some consider his most important concession to the business community in 1939 without any hope that it would foster cooperation from business, Congress, or the Treasury.[69] Business responses paralleled those to the 1938 Revenue Act. They met Morgenthau's 27 May testimony to the Ways and Means Committee with some glee and took heart at the shift in congressional attitudes and influence over the administration. No one denied that the statute was an improvement. *Nation's Business*, the Chamber of Commerce journal, offered a typical response. It first argued: "From a united effort of outstanding congressional and administration leaders, business received recently the largest measure of tax relief in seven years – and the promise of more." However, it lambasted the rise in the corporate income tax, complained that the revenue act "removed

68 John McCormack, in U.S., Congress, House, *Congressional Record*, 76th Cong., 3d sess., 1939, 85, pt. 2: 156.
69 Lee R. Tilman, "The American Business Community and the Death of the New Deal" (Ph.D. diss., University of Arizona, 1966), p. 110.

only a few of the tax obstacles to business expansion," and urged Congress to spur business by lifting "the remaining impediments" to recovery.[70] The 1939 Revenue Act seemed only to have inflated business demands. It was what they called a "psychological stimulant," which can be loosely defined as an indication that government was inclined to heed their future protests.

Tax revision was what one business editor called a "symbol-issue."[71] Operating within the constraints of commitments to past positions, fears of endangering either revenue yields or social and economic stability, and a populist-progressive heritage that shielded the relatively affluent, tax revision was preeminently a measure of political intentions, a barometer that forecast more trouble for the New Deal.

This is not to suggest that certain business sectors failed to take advantage of heightened Treasury and congressional receptivity in 1938–9. The Treasury fostered "rationalizations" of the tax structure that favored special business interests, behavior markedly in contrast with the department's tougher stand during World War II and the Truman administration. The U.S. Chamber of Commerce, overseeing the details of tax legislation, served as a prime information source for many congressmen, even drafting major Republican amendments.[72]

But, in the big picture, the tax revisions made were insignificant. They had a lesser impact than the modest loophole closing of the 1937 Revenue Act. They were more an indication of the temper of the times. In former years, FDR exalted in slaying a few loophole dragons. In 1938 and 1939, they slew him. These skirmishes on the flanks left the battlefield itself unscathed.

The Social Security Tax Freeze

The year 1939 was a bumper year for tax revision. By February, Congress had passed an uncontroversial codification of the internal-revenue laws, a joint effort with the Treasury and Justice departments to streamline and reconcile conflicting and redundant tax laws. In early April, the long-standing conflict over reciprocal state and federal tax exemption of government salaries was resolved in the Public Salary Tax Act. The admin-

---

70 Lawrence Stafford, "Taxpayers Get a Break," *Nation's Business* 27 (September 1939): 15, 76.
71 *Kiplinger Washington Letter*, 13 May 1939, p. 2.
72 *New York Times*, 8 March 1938, p. 2.

istration also made one of its repeated efforts to close the loophole that granted tax-exempt status to government bonds and was repulsed by an effective state and local government lobby. But dwarfing all these tax revisions, both in immediate concern and long-term impact, was the social security revision of 1939. Between 1935 and 1939, an irresistible consensus had built up to topple from its pedestal the 1935 act's contractual private-insurance model. Paradoxically, the very fiscal conservatism of the 1935 plan may have undermined the long-term fiscal soundness of social security. The prospect of accumulating a mammoth reserve was a standing invitation to postpone politically unwelcome payroll-tax increases without seriously considering alternative ways of financing future pensions. The 1939 revisions, by simultaneously accelerating and raising benefits while freezing the old-age insurance tax on employees and employers, parried pressure from the left and appeased business complaints. But, more important, it helped set in motion a process that would lead to today's social security crisis.

As in the 1939 Revenue Act, with which it was contemporaneous, the legislative progress of the Social Security Act Amendments of 1939 is less interesting than the controversies that nurtured it. With little concern for ideological consistency, Republicans had exploited every potential chink in the armor of the social security system. The attack reached its pinnacle in the 1936 presidential campaign. The Republican platform sought to cast doubt on whether current contributors would even receive social security benefits, predicting that "the taxes collected in the guise of premiums will be wasted by the Government in reckless and extravagant political schemes." Its alternative was a noncontributory pension system, paid on the basis of need and financed by some undefined "direct tax widely distributed."[73] Republican candidate Landon elaborated on this attack in considerable detail, supplementing it with many of the themes developed by leftist critics of the New Deal. He zeroed in on the incidence of payroll taxes, noting that the poorest workers could not afford the tax, that they would only receive paltry benefits anyway, and that both the worker's and the employer's share would "be borne either by the employee or by the consumer through higher prices." This "wastefully financed" system, he charged, constituted the "largest tax bill in history," and the projected accumulation of a huge social security reserve fund was a "cruel

73 Donald B. Johnson and Kirk H. Porter, *National Party Platforms 1840–1972* (Urbana: University of Illinois Press, 1973), p. 367.

hoax," encouraging excessive government spending and paying off the national debt "out of the pay envelopes of our workers" "without any assurance that the workers will get back what they put in." Landon's alternative financing recommendations were as unclear as those in the platform (he too called for a specially earmarked "direct tax, widely distributed," which liberal Senator Wagner (D–N.Y.) speculated was merely a euphemism for "a good old-fashioned sales tax, loaded upon the backs of the poor"). But it was clear that he strongly objected both to the payroll tax and to the reserve fund, preferring a system of noncontributory, need-based pensions that would be funded "as we go along" by current taxes.[74]

Though there was every indication that responses from Roosevelt and other leading Democrats neutralized Landon's social security critique, these campaign themes continued to be important ones for the Republicans. Soon after Congress convened after the election, Republican Senator Vandenberg (R–Mich.), who had already introduced a resolution urging the depletion of the reserve fund through lower payroll taxes or higher benefits, cornered Social Security chairman Arthur Altmeyer into agreeing to establish a new advisory council to consider revisions to the social security system.[75] The chairman of the Republican National Committee paraded this incident as a major Republican victory, auguring a triumph for Republican social security demands.[76] The charge to the council included consideration of slower payroll tax increases, alteration of the reserve system, and accelerated and higher benefits. Thus, the founding fathers of Social Security faced an uncomfortable mix of challenge and opportunity. They suspected that a "temporary" payroll tax freeze would only be a first step to removing the discipline inherent in a contributory insurance plan. On the one hand, it might force the social security system to contract and *im*plode; a payroll tax freeze might eventually starve the program for funds, encourage cuts in benefits, and weaken an individual's claim to anything more than a minimum means-tested pension – the very result that contributory social insurance had been designed to avoid. On the other hand, the system might overexpand and *ex*plode; the combination of a hike in benefits and a freeze in taxes could encourage the feeling

74 *St. Louis Post-Dispatch*, 27 September 1936, p. 13A; *New York Times*, 1 Nov. 1936, p. 45; Robert F. Wagner, "Social Security is in Danger," 5 October 1936, box 120, Robert F. Wagner Papers (Georgetown University Library, Washington, D.C.).
75 Arthur J. Altmeyer, *The Formative Years of Social Security* (Madison: University of Wisconsin Press, 1966), pp. 89–92.
76 *New York Times*, 23 August 1937, p. 1.

that benefits could be increased as long as the reserve existed. This, they feared, was an "après nous le déluge" formula for disaster.[77] Edwin Witte constructed a disturbingly prescient scenario. He predicted that once the increasing ratio of new retirees to contributors began to exhaust the reserve fund, Congress would shy away from a general tax increase, instead choosing to "increase the payroll taxes, reduce benefits, or continue to incur deficits."[78] Eventually, the crisis would reach the point at which younger workers would be confronted with both higher payroll taxes and a cut in expected annuities. This could threaten the social security program itself.

Yet the social security entourage recognized in the Republican challenge a chance to improve the system – not only to revert to the more progressive financing system of government subsidies to the reserve fund that had been proposed to FDR in 1934–5, but also to allow social security to meet a greater share of the needs of the elderly.

Not coincidentally, the reports of the new Advisory Council on Social Security and the Social Security Board reflected these considerations. They adopted a number of recommendations that highlighted the attenuated connection between contributions and benefits: reducing the mandated trust fund to a smaller "contingency reserve," offering certain annuity benefits to the family of the contributor, and hastening and raising retirement payments in the first years of the program. Most importantly, the 1935 Roosevelt-Morgenthau decision to implement social insurance without any planned government subsidy came under fire. The advisory council argued that the profit to the nation from social insurance, combined with the flawed incidence of payroll taxes, justified a shift to a contributory system divided roughly equally between government, employees, and employers.[79] The Social Security Board agreed in principle to funding part of the old-age insurance from more progressive income and estate taxes, though it stressed that a federal contribution should not come into play until the payroll taxes already in the works failed to cover disbursements – a similar position to that taken by the cabinet Committee on Economic

---

77 Edwin E. Witte, "Thoughts Relating to the Old-Age Insurance Titles of the Social Security Act and Proposed Changes Therein," 1938, p. 29, box 13, Record Group 47, Records of the Committee on Economic Security (National Archives, Washington, D.C.)

78 Ibid., p. 24.

79 U.S., Advisory Council on Social Security, *Final Report*, S. Doc. 4, 76th Cong., 1st sess. (Washington, D.C.: Government Printing Office, 1939), p. 24.

Security in 1934–5.[80] However, despite this attenuation of the insurance model, the Social Security Board and a divided advisory council did not recommend any reduction in payroll taxes. They instead suggested that the slated tax increase be allowed to stand pending a study of financial arrangements to be completed by 1942, before the next scheduled increase.

Aside from the question of a tax freeze, these recommendations met general acclamation, for they included something for everyone. Most important to conservatives was the prescription for a much smaller reserve fund. Liberals exalted in the folding-in of a vast group (later much reduced by Congress) of new annuitants and a leap in retirement payments to everyone receiving them in the near future. To Roosevelt too, these recommendations – which he endorsed and sent to Congress in January 1939 – had much to recommend them. Politicians were naturally drawn toward distributing and raising pensions prior to the 1940 election. Amid widespread misunderstanding of the distinction between the social security system's noncontributory old-age assistance program and its insurance scheme to guarantee contributors retirement pensions, repeated polls demonstrated overwhelming support (of 89 percent and more after mid-1938) for government old-age pensions.[81] The social security payroll tax itself had wide (if shallow) acceptance, but much of the public felt that social security pensions should be increased and extended to new groups.[82] The noncontributory Townsend plan, which covered all retirees over the age of 60 and provided immediate and more generous pensions, made a comeback by capitalizing upon this dissatisfaction.[83] A Townsend-Republican alliance in the 1938 election had achieved considerable success; a majority of the Republican House delegates had made enough of a commitment to the Townsend plan to receive that organization's endorsement.[84] Finally, social security revision could mesh with FDR's effort to appease business and enlist its cooperation in recovery and perhaps in defense efforts.

80 Social Security Board, "Proposed Changes in the Social Security Act," *Social Security Bulletin* 2 (January 1939): 10.
81 U.S., Department of Health, Education, and Welfare, Social Security Administration, Office of Research and Statistics, *Public Attitudes Toward Social Security 1935–1965*, by Michael E. Schiltz, Research Report no. 33 (Washington, D.C.: Government Printing Office, 1970), pp. 83, 86, 36.
82 Ibid., pp. 63, 89–90, 46–7, 57.
83 Ibid., pp. 42–3.
84 Abraham Holtzman, *The Townsend Movement* (New York: Bookman Associates, 1963), pp. 104, 144.

Roosevelt found himself in an intriguing position. Full appeasement of business required the major concession that he, along with the advisory council and the Social Security Board, had been unwilling to make: a postponement of the slated payroll tax increase from 1 to 1½ percent. It seemed unlikely that even the rising conservative tide could carry this revision over his objections. On the other hand, by March of 1939, Treasury Secretary Morgenthau, the point man for the appeasement position, cast his lot with the opposition to the tax hike. Drawn into the business position, Morgenthau even embraced the suspicion that "somebody" would "raid" the social security trust fund.[85] A payroll-tax freeze could further Morgenthau's appeasement campaign while diverting pressure from New Deal corporate taxes. Moreover, most New Deal economic advisers favored a payroll-tax ceiling.

Though at loggerheads with Morgenthau for joining the conservative opposition to the undistributed-profits tax, Roosevelt reluctantly assented to the tax freeze. In rapid-fire succession between 20 March and 24 March 1939, he turned Morgenthau "down cold," Morgenthau retreated to the Treasury to sulk that he would testify for a tax freeze or he wouldn't testify at all, FDR relented, and Morgenthau presented his social security tax package to the Ways and Means Committee. In this statement, Morgenthau went through the formality of presenting the committee with several alternatives ("in view of the fact," he privately noted, "that everybody in the Treasury has wobbled all over the lot"). He also justified his 1935 animus against dipping into general revenues for social security by making ex post facto use of the Social Security Board's argument that the prospective wider coverage of old-age insurance now rendered it a broad national asset deserving of general tax support.[86]

Jubilation greeted the administration's proposal to stimulate business through tax reduction. The Washington headquarters of business orga-

---

85 Morgenthau Diaries, 22 March 1939, book 186, p. 44.
86 Morgenthau Diaries, 20 March 1939, book 185, pp. 248, 263; Morgenthau Diaries, 22 March 1939, book 186, pp. 34, 39. This was a terribly lame excuse, one that received its finishing touches in a Nixonesque scenario-building discussion just prior to Morgenthau's testimony (Morgenthau Diaries, 23 March 1939, book 186, pp. 63–4). Morgenthau's 1935 recommendation to the committee had made no reference to such logic. I have no evidence, in fact, that such an argument had occurred to him by that point. It would have been especially unfitting considering that the initial administration proposal had been quite comprehensive in its coverage until Morgenthau himself branded it administratively infeasible in his 1935 testimony.

nizations hailed the tax freeze "as a greater contributor to ultimate recovery than all the tax revisions they had been urging recently upon the Administration and Congress."[87] Here was a true tax cut, unmarred by accompanying revenue retrievers. *Business Week* deemed it "genuine business appeasement."[88] Republicans toasted their victory; Senator Vandenberg proclaimed: "This is the healthiest thing that has happened in a long time."[89] This was appeasement business-style, the pinnacle of that movement in 1939.

The 1939 Social Security Act Amendments were more controverted than controversial. As with the 1939 Revenue Act, this bill (which included the administration's new plan to freeze the old-age payroll tax on employers and employees at 1 percent, thus skipping the scheduled jump for 1940–2) had bipartisan support in committee and on the floor (it passed 364–2 in the House and 57–8 in the Senate). Republicans, still reeling from a Democratic maneuver that had forced the Townsend bill to the House floor to expose Republicans as hypocrites and wild spenders (the bill had failed by a vote of 302–97 on 1 June, with 55 Republicans – including only half of those who had received Townsend endorsement in the 1938 election – sticking with the plan), endeavored to assume credit for this social security revision, which in itself furnished a compelling political excuse to resist Townsendism.[90]

Though the business community had splintered over the extent and direction of social security revisions, its overall response to the 1939 amendments was quite favorable.[91] The administration's concessions represented a giant step for the business legislative program – a billion dollar

---

87 Turner Catledge, "Administration Yields on Social Security Tax," *New York Times*, 26 March 1939, sec. 4, p. 6.
88 "A $3,000,000 Reprieve," *Business Week*, 1 April 1939, p. 48.
89 *New York Times*, 25 March 1939, p. 3.
90 Holtzman, *Townsend Movement*, pp. 144–7.
91 A few die-hard, reactionary, inflation-obsessed budget balancers from the financial community opposed any cut in the social security reserve by either higher benefits or lower payroll taxes. For example, after the enactment of the 1939 Social Security Act Amendments a column in *Barron's* protested that popularity among conservatives neglected the inevitable "Day of Reckoning," which would slap rocketing taxes on business. Such protests went against the tide, but they stand out in comparison to the more monolithic business position on the revenue acts. Moreover, they presage a later split within the conservative bloc, when many newspapers championed payroll-tax increases to preserve the system's fiscal integrity, to tamp down inflation, and to head off future tax increases. Edson Blair, "Payroll Taxes and the Day of Reckoning," *Barron's*, 19 June 1939, p. 4.

tax cut over the next three years. *Business Week* celebrated this "boost to business" as "far more extensive than business men dared dream."[92]

This stance seems at odds with the standard portrayal of business opposition to government deficits. It is. The deficit-taxation stance described earlier is essential to understanding this position. The wide recognition that the surplus tied up in the social security system had contributed to the 1937 recession caused many businessmen to join in the chant from the left that payroll taxes had robbed the economy of needed purchasing power. The campaign to lower social security taxes and to dismantle the reserve fund also embodied intense hostility to federal spending. The reserve fund, which was invested in interest-bearing government bonds, eased the financing of New Deal expenditures. This fact, to most business thinking, more than counterbalanced the substantial chunk it cut from the overall deficit. From its inception, business leaders pilloried the social security reserve fund as an incitement to government profligacy. Even the Committee on Taxation of the Twentieth Century Fund, a bastion of corporate liberalism, joined other experts in backing up this position, favoring a shift to a current cost basis to avoid " 'raids' upon the fund" that would result in expenditures "that would not otherwise have been incurred."[93] To many businessmen and most Republicans, this expenditure argument, somewhat paradoxically, helped justify the accelerated and increased payment of early annuities, for this shrank the reserve fund.

Most importantly, businessmen wanted to reduce their taxes. The demand for at least a deferral of social security tax increases was almost universal among business representatives. A poll of business executives, published in February 1941, found that only 1.6 percent – a smaller percentage than for any other federal tax – favored higher social security tax rates.[94] They maintained this pressure through World War II. The public seemed ambivalent over a payroll tax freeze,[95] though both the AFL and the CIO opposed it. A hesitancy to further burden the new income tax payers in the lower brackets, combined with the bloated trust fund (well in excess of most past definitions of a "contingency reserve") resulting from the war boom, helped bring repeated congressional rejections

92 "Changes in 'SS' Help Business," *Business Week*, 19 August 1939, p. 22.
93 Twentieth Century Fund, Committee on Taxation, *Facing the Tax Problem* (New York: Twentieth Century Fund, 1937), pp. 496–7.
94 "Fourth *Fortune* Forum of Executive Opinion," *Fortune* 23 (February 1941): 66.
95 See Hadley Cantril, ed., *Public Opinion 1935–1946* (Princeton, N.J.: Princeton University Press, 1951), p. 362.

of administration proposals to implement the scheduled social security tax increases and to expand coverage and benefits. Despite the fact that payroll-tax increases squared well with the goal of curbing private consumption demands to smother inflation, the payroll-tax freeze brought out the same potent conservative coalition that worked in the House against FDR's other New Deal and tax initiatives, pitting Republicans and Southern Democrats against Democrats from new-stock districts.[96] In addition, in 1944 Congress offhandedly accepted a liberal senator's amendment to counteract the impression of irresponsibly sacrificing social security on the altar of tax minimization.[97] It authorized the use of general revenues when the trust fund could no longer cover promised benefits. This underlined the congressional rejection of the private-insurance model, a policy revised in 1950 when Congress jacked up payroll taxes to make the program self-sustaining.

By the late 1930s, conservatives had generally come to recognize that the concept of social security was sacrosanct. Scattered corporate liberals such as General Electric president Gerard Swope (who favored the scheduled tax jump for 1940) honestly hoped to expand and entrench the system. However, the suspicion among some New Dealers that conservatives were engaged in a conspiracy to cripple or curtail the social security system was not unfounded. Advocacy of general-revenue financing or universal flat pensions not related to past contributions, revisions that today might seem progressive, often subsumed the goal of clamping down on future pensions. The 1939 resolutions of the Chamber of Commerce favored a payroll-tax freeze, a conversion from the reserve system to pay-as-you-go, and hastened benefit disbursement, while also arguing that the eventual cost of the system should be forced below current estmates.[98] M. Albert Linton, the president of the Provident Mutual Life Insurance Company and probably the leading Republican theoretician on social security, was a prime proponent of this viewpoint. His bugbear was the huge intended reserve accumulation. To him, it symbolized the government's intemperate commitments to future pensions (because the trust fund's government bond holdings earmarked future government expenditures

96 Julius Turner. *Party and Constituency: Pressures on Congress*, Johns Hopkins University Studies in Historical and Political Science, vol. 69 (1951) no. 1 (Baltimore: Johns Hopkins University Press, 1952), pp. 113, 121, 139–41.
97 U.S., Congress, Senate, *Congressional Record*, 78th Cong., 2d sess., 1944, 90, pt. 1: 374.
98 *New York Times*, 5 May 1939, p. 6.

for this purpose), it threatened to encourage further annuity demands, it transformed what should have been a social obligation for retirement sufficiency into an individualist insurance policy, and it allowed wasteful deficits to be financed without "the appraisal of the financial community."[99] He thus favored both a payroll-tax freeze and a major jump in benefits for early annuitants, which would both deplete the reserve and mollify advocates of higher pensions.

Arguments of conservatives cast a somewhat distorted perspective on the Social Security Act Amendments of 1939. Vital to understanding this legislation is the confluence of the predominant positions of business and Republicans on the one hand and labor and the deficit-spending left on the other. Before the left found it necessary to fight inflation and scurry to the defense of social security in World War II, it presented a full bill of particulars against the Social Security Act. The *New Republic*, the *Nation*, the CIO, the AFL, the American Association for Social Security (which, revealingly, garnered financial support from Linton's Mutual Life Insurance Company),[100] the Workers' Alliance, the People's Lobby, and numerous other pressure groups on the left portrayed the reserve system and the payroll tax as arch-villains and blasted the incomplete coverage and paltry annuities of the act.[101] To them, social security was a botched opportunity for income redistribution.

The regressivity of the payroll tax particularly galled them. Imbued with the progressive ethos that divided society between the worker-consumer and the super-rich, they advocated a funding program based on progressive income taxes or substantial subsidies from general revenues – usually

99 Theron F. Schlabach, *Edwin E. Witte: Cautious Reformer* (Madison: State Historical Society of Wisconsin, 1969), pp. 164–5, 169.

100 Ibid., p. 171.

101 "Shoring Up Security," *New Republic* 97 (28 December 1938): 217–18; "The Shape of Things," *Nation* 148 (1 April 1939): 362; U.S., Congress, House, Committee on Ways and Means, *Social Security, Hearings*, 76th Cong., 1st sess., 1939, 2: 1037, 1480–1, 1194, 1404. The American Federation of Labor's position is confusing. As soon as FDR was safely reelected in 1936, AFL leaders began arguing that "employee contributions should be eliminated" because "labor believes that the burdens of insecurity should be lifted from its shoulders and that the costs should be a social responsibility." But despite this call for the replacement of payroll taxes by more progressive ones, the labor representatives on the Advisory Council on Social Security in 1938 opposed any freeze on old-age insurance taxes, preferring to raise an unsavory tax rather than to threaten the fiscal stability and desired expansion of the system. American Federation of Labor, *Report of Proceedings of the Fifty-Sixth Annual Convention 1936* (Washington, D.C.: Judd & Detweiler, n.d.), p. 151.

without grappling with the fact that general revenues were no model of progressivity themselves, and the income tax was so narrowly based that it lacked the flexibility to meet vast new revenue demands.

A macroeconomic argument also underlay the attack on social security. Many on the left had castigated the Social Security Act in 1935 for undermining economic stability by funneling consumer funds into a stagnant reserve. With the 1937 recession and the waxing influence of countercyclical economic theory, this argument cut more deeply. Benjamin Cohen and Lauchlin Currie coauthored a "Baby Townsend" plan, involving no increase in taxes, that would boost purchasing power by offering flat noncontributory pensions to everyone over 65.[102] Marriner Eccles was sympathetic with this idea and joined economists Harry White and Alvin Hansen in contending that the reserve fund "imposed a serious drag on recovery" that should be rectified through government subsidies, broadened coverage, and higher benefits. Otherwise, Eccles warned, "there is a danger of a repetition of the 1937 experience."[103]

Given its perception of basic flaws in the social security system, the left found much to recommend the Social Security Act Amendments of 1939. True, the legislation failed to significantly extend coverage or to raise annuities for the long term, proposals with which conservatives were ill at ease. But the primary goals of both the left and right to limit the payroll tax, bring an infusion of early benefits, and deplete the stifling reserve system had meshed perfectly. The founding fathers and head administrator of social security (Edwin Witte, J. Douglas Brown, and Arthur Altmeyer), opponents of the tax freeze, were crushed in the middle. Witte, a last-ditch defender of the reserve system and the individualist insurance principles it protected, greeted the administration's tax-freeze concession with "a sinking feeling about the future of old age insurance."[104]

The confluence of the liberal and conservative positions left an ambiguous legacy. The Social Security Act Amendments of 1939, by coupling early benefits with a decline in planned taxes, had seriously eroded the contractual insurance principle. Congress refused to face up to the consequences. It took the expedient route of blocking tax increases without establishing a clear framework for later generations to meet the benefit claims that had

---

102 Morgenthau Diaries, 19 March 1939, book 185, pp. 284–6.
103 Marriner S. Eccles to FDR, 20 March 1939, in Morgenthau Diaries, book 185, p. 274; Marriner Eccles, in Morgenthau Diaries, 10 January 1939, book 184, p. 134.
104 Edwin E. Witte, 30 March 1939, in Schlabach, *Witte*, p. 177.

accumulated. Never abandoning the insurance model sufficiently to provide open government contributions to old-age insurance, and never applying it rigorously enough to make the requisite increases in payroll taxes, the United States staggered into the recent social security crisis. Unlike most of the celebrated victories and defeats for New Deal taxation in the 1930s, the social security revision of 1939 really mattered. Taxation, when it is something more than a symbol, can be a very serious thing.

Conclusion

The social security tax freeze was a throwback to the earlier New Deal. In the early 1930s, tax laws with critical redistributive implications prevailed with little debate, for they built upon the common ground of major political forces. The payroll-tax freeze confirmed this pattern, but other tax bills in the middle and late 1930s did not. The 1938 and 1939 revenue acts were significant for the divisions they embodied and exacerbated. All sides invested them with a symbolic importance that transcended their minor impact on the future incidence of the tax structure. As one business observer noted early in the tax-revision controversy, the undistributed-profits tax had been "singled out – somewhat unfortunately – for general criticism." It had been "advertised so widely," he complained, "that it has crowded other obnoxious provisions from the picture."[105]

Looked at more broadly, the tax-revision campaign directed a newly potent business bloc into innocuous channels. Tax controversies were as much a constructive diversion for the New Deal in 1935–6, when the mock assault on economic royalists muffled the thunder on the left, as in 1938–9, when the eviscerated undistributed-profits tax so dominated opposition attention.

105 William P. Helm memorandum [Autumn 1937]. "General Tax Folder 1937–38," box 254, Record Group 46, Records of the United States Senate, Special Committee to Investigate Lobbying Activities, 75th Cong. (National Archives, Washington, D.C.).

8 Taxation, Symbolic Politics, and the New Deal Legacy

By the end of the 1930s, New Deal taxation, more even than the New Deal itself, had reached an impasse. Its opponents had captured the initiative. How ironic, then, that the income tax was on the threshold of a fundamental reorientation that would bring about a recognizably modern tax system. In World War II, the personal income tax ceased to be an indicator of affluence and became a mere token of citizenship. In 1943, the Current Tax Payment Act introduced the now-familiar withholding system in which estimated tax was deducted from paychecks (before World War II, tax bills only came due in quarterly installments in the year after the income was earned – an unsustainable system once the tax applied to most Americans, for it demanded too much of both the Internal Revenue Service and popular patterns of savings and accounting). No more than 5 percent of the population had been covered by taxable income-tax returns in any year in the 1930s; in World War II, the ranks of income-tax payers swelled to 74 percent.[1] No longer was the income tax reliant on the $50,000+ brackets for most of its revenue; in fact, by the end of the war, these opulent Americans, though several times as numerous as in the Depression, accounted for only 13 percent of income-tax collections. Treasury Secretary Morgenthau observed that "for the first time in our history, the income tax is becoming a people's tax."[2]

The conditions for this shift could scarcely have been more auspicious. Annual government spending would multiply tenfold over the course of the war. Many recognized that the wartime hike in taxes on the upper brackets "would not yield great revenue" because of already-high rates and because "the total of income in these brackets is not a large percentage of the national income."[3] To cap strong wartime inflationary pressures,

---

1 Lawrence H. Seltzer, *The Personal Exemptions in the Income Tax* (New York: Columbia University Press for the National Bureau of Economic Research, 1968), p. 62.
2 U.S., Congress, Senate, Committee on Finance, *Hearings* on H.R. 7378, vol. 1, 77th Cong., 2d sess., 1942, p. 3.
3 "Taxes Going Up," *New Republic* 104 (28 April 1941): 589.

287

the income tax needed to rein in mass purchasing power and to significantly narrow the budget deficit, and that required a revamped income tax. Revenue exigencies had thus forced a lifting of earlier tax immunities. Lower tax exemptions and higher tax rates were also sanctified by the ethos of universal wartime participation and sacrifice, in which it became an asset "that the greatest possible number of persons may contribute directly to the costs of the defense program."[4] Wartime economic advances facilitated this process, for it was far easier to raise taxes when paychecks, even after tax deductions, were substantially higher than those before the war. Even these combined factors did not bring a wholehearted endorsement of low exemptions from either the administration, Congress, or the public, and not until 1944 did exemptions reach their lowest level of the war. Still, by the war's end, these factors led to severe reductions in income-tax exemptions (most conspicuously in a supplemental "Victory Tax" that applied to anyone receiving over $624 a year), marked tax hikes even on the previously sheltered middle brackets, and income-tax withholding. By the end of the 1940s, Congress had partly restored exemptions and slightly pruned tax rates, but not nearly back to prewar levels. The mass income tax was here to stay.

As in the New Deal, however, the financial and economic context of taxation affords an incomplete understanding of its role. Though the relatively affluent middle brackets faced vastly increased tax bills over those of the New Deal years (a family with two children, for example, owed less than $50 tax on a $5,000 salary in the late 1930s, but theoretically could pay more than $700 by 1943), the tax hammer did not come down as hard as it might have on this group.[5] Despite this tax increase, a respected study of World War II government economic policy finds the greatest slack in the tax system to be on the middle incomes between $1,500 and $20,000 (especially when compared to foreign tax systems, which in the war and before had imposed much higher income taxes on those "middle brackets"), and correctly traces this to Congress's inertia in departing from the prewar income tax, which was still a "rich man's tax."[6] Congressmen, of course, still sought to defend the middle class

4 U.S., Congress, Senate, Committee on Finance, *The Revenue Bill of 1941*, S. Rept. 673 to Accompany H.R. 5417, 77th Cong., 1st sess., 1941, p. 5.

5 U.S., Department of Commerce, Bureau of the Census, *Historical Statistics of the United States, Colonial Times to 1970* (Washington, D.C.: Government Printing Office, 1975), p. 1112.

6 Lester V. Chandler, *Inflation in the United States 1940–1948* (New York: Harper & Brothers, 1951), pp. 90–91, 97.

from excessive tax increases. This group, after all, made up "the most articulate part of the voting public," and congressmen were quick to assert that this "good solid element of society upon which we have to depend" deserved protection as "the backbone of the country."[7] Though demands to tax the rich had slackened (particularly with the refurbished wartime reputation of industrialists), the previously discussed 1930s tendency to focus on taxing "them" (the surplus incomes of the specially privileged) carried over into the World War II conceptualization of income taxes. Thus, middle brackets were shielded from higher burdens by being included in the category of the presumptively overburdened common man.[8]

Taxation also continued to play an important symbolic function. President Roosevelt was acutely aware that "a fair distribution of the war burden," or at least the semblance of it, was "necessary for national unity" at a time when the government needed to "impose sacrifices on all of us."[9] Thus even before Pearl Harbor, FDR had responded to suspicions of war profiteering with repeated warnings that there should be "no new war millionaires" and that it was essential to assure "that a few do not gain from the sacrifices of the many."[10] Taxation and the rhetoric that accompanied it naturally were crucial to communicating this commitment. FDR thus spotlighted the corporate excess-profits tax as early as the summer of 1940, though at that point his reported priority was less on securing legislation than on publicly staking out an advantageous position for the 1940 campaign.[11] In conferences with financial aides in mid-1941, FDR cautioned that at a time in which the administration demanded broader sacrifices, wealthy corporations would have to be adequately taxed to avert "the political consequences."[12] This became increasingly important

7 "Tax Proposals," *Current History* 53 (June 1941): 29; U.S., Congress, House, Committee on Ways and Means, *Revenue Revision of 1941, Hearings*, vol. 1, 77th Cong., 1st sess., 1941, p. 668; *New York Times*, 20 October 1943, p. 15.

8 See Chandler, *Inflation*, p. 94.

9 Franklin D. Roosevelt, *Complete Presidential Press Conferences* (New York: Da Capo Press, 1972), 6 January 1942, 19: 34, 39.

10 Ibid., 23 May 1940, 15: 370; Samuel I. Rosenman, comp., *The Public Papers and Addresses of Franklin D. Roosevelt*, 9 (New York: Macmillan, 1941): 276 (1 July 1940). Public anti-profiteering attitudes are examined in Opinion Research Corporation, "Profit as a Public Relations Problem in Wartime," 1942, file 100Q, National Association of Manufacturers Papers (Eleutherian Mills Historical Library, Wilmington, Del.).

11 John M. Blum, *From the Morgenthau Diaries*, vol. 2: *Years of Urgency, 1938–41* (Boston: Houghton Mifflin, 1965), p. 289.

12 John Sullivan to Henry Morgenthau, Jr. [July 1941], "Sullivan, Daily Record July 1, 1941 – Aug. 30, 1941," box 200, Record Group 56, Records of the U.S. Department of the Treasury (National Archives, Washington, D.C.).

290 New Deal Taxation under Siege

as revenue exigencies forced the administration to impose an income tax on the majority of wage earners for the first time. Not to "cut the superfluities of the few" would "have a shattering effect on morale," for wage earners' sacrifice seemed contingent on the assurance that "their bosses are making at least faintly equivalent sacrifices."[13] This concern with the impression being made on the work force was intense, all the more so as the lower classes included vitally needed war workers rather than the mere unemployed. As the chairman of the National War Labor Board put it when talking about overtime pay: "If you say to the boys, 'Why don't you make a sacrifice for your country,' they are going to say, 'That is fine. I am making a sacrifice for my country, but I am not going to make it to increase the profits of General Motors.' "[14] This was not simple alarmism; the politics of sacrifice cut very deeply, as evidenced in AFL taunts: "What sacrifices are these fat cats making? Will someone tell us please?"[15] The United Auto Workers also not so subtly highlighted this theme with an "Equality of Sacrifice" program calling for a $25,000 wartime ceiling on executive salaries.[16] As *Fortune* reported, workers were "ready to make sacrifices for the war effort – *if* the other fellow will do the same, *if* the bosses don't reap new profits out of all proportion."[17]

FDR was a past master at the use of taxation to convey the image of the hour. He explained at one point that he would prefer "to see a tax which would tax all income above $100,000 at the rate of 99½%." This even shocked his budget director, but the president's joking comeback was a revealing one: "Why not? None of us is ever going to make $100,000 a year. How many people report on that much income?"[18] Roosevelt in fact went even further than this. In 1942 and again in 1943, he proposed that all income above $25,000 ($50,000 for families) be taxed away, saying that "all excess income should go to win the war." Inequities, he warned, "seriously affect the morale of soldiers and sailors, farmers and workers,

13 Keith Hutchison, "Everybody's Business: The 'New Poor,' " *Nation* 155 (28 November 1942): 574.
14 William H. Davis, in Transcript of Executive Session of National War Labor Board, 6 February 1942, pp. 1–2; Record Group 202 (National Archives).
15 "Labor Highlights," *American Federationist* 49 (July 1942): inside cover.
16 Nelson Lichtenstein, *Labor's War at Home* (New York: Cambridge University Press, 1982), p. 99.
17 "The Fortune Survey," *Fortune* 27 (February 1943): 9.
18 John Sullivan to Henry Morgenthau, Jr., 30 July 1941, "Sullivan, Daily Record July 1, 1941 – Aug. 30, 1941," box 200, Record Group 56, Records of the U.S. Department of the Treasury.

imperiling efforts to stabilize wages and prices, and thereby impairing the
effective prosecution of the war." When this income limit got nowhere in
Congress, FDR acted on his own, handing down an executive order
limiting after-tax salaries to $25,000 plus certain allowances, only to have
his action indignantly repealed by Congress.[19]

Surely more than posturing was involved here. Franklin Roosevelt
sincerely disapproved of efforts to shift the wartime tax burden away from
the rich; he played a critical role in blocking congressional efforts to
substitute a regressive federal sales tax for income-tax increases. He also
became increasingly disillusioned with what he saw as forces of petty
selfishness in the midst of a far nobler world crusade, a bitterness that
emerged most prominently in 1944 when he vetoed a loophole-ridden
tax bill as "not for the needy, but for the greedy."[20] Such factors, along
with the broader sentiment that profiting corporations should bear a heavy
burden of war support, allowed taxes on corporate profits to rise to well
over a third of the wartime tax load.[21] But what comes through just as
clearly is that taxes and other countermeasures against wartime profiteering
were an integral part of the administration's antiinflation program, not
simply to collect revenue, but also to legitimize the sacrifices that war
necessitated and to take the edge off the grievances that war engendered.

Thus, even in war, which required a vast expansion and renovation of
the tax system, the symbolic role of New Deal tax policy was prominent.
Given the prior New Deal record on taxation, this certainly comes as no
surprise. Tax policy and the rhetoric accompanying it were key components
of the New Deal's projected image of concern for the forgotten man.

This element had never been absent from New Deal tax policy, but as
seen in Part I, it clearly was subordinated in the first two years of the
New Deal. It was in that period that the New Deal had its main peacetime
impact on the actual structure of the tax system. The fact that this impact
had strong regressive elements – that taxes like the liquor tax and the
processing tax applied more harshly to poorer Americans than to affluent
ones – surely offers insight into the low place of progressive tax incidence
in New Deal priorities. It also helps call into question any contention that

19 Samuel I. Rosenman, comp., *The Public Papers and Addresses of Franklin D. Roosevelt*,
    12 (New York: Harper & Brothers, 1950), 90–3 (15 February 1943).
20 James M. Burns, *Roosevelt: The Soldier of Freedom* (New York: Harcourt Brace
    Jovanovich, 1970), pp. 434–7.
21 U.S., Department of Commerce, Bureau of the Census, *Historical Statistics*, p.
    1107.

the New Deal pushed reform to its outermost limits, for it was Congress that took the primary initiative in progressive tax reform in this period. The regressive cast of early New Deal taxes underlines the constraints on the 1930s tax system: the historical orientation of the income tax toward abnormally high incomes and the consequent limited income-tax revenue, the ambivalent commitment to budget balancing, the notion of not taxing "the people," and the requirements of Roosevelt's early policy of conciliation of business to save the capitalist system and generate growth. It obviously is no coincidence that the victims of early New Deal tax policy were unorganized, depressed, and vulnerable to the maxim that what they didn't know *could* hurt them. But it may be more important to understand early New Deal tax policy in terms of the politics of inadvertence, better revealing the New Deal's other priorities than its tax-policy commitments.

As discussed in Part II, this policy underwent a crucial shift, but less in substance than in image. The hard-hitting rhetoric of the 1935 Wealth Tax, a response to changing political circumstances, set the tone for Roosevelt's 1936 campaign. It established a kind of politics of ostracism, uniting Americans against their common – if diabolized – economic royalist enemies. As in the 1937 Revenue Act, the president had focused less on the ultimate effect of his tax policy than on the flagrancy of the abuses being attacked. Here FDR located himself in a dominant American tradition, focusing on the super-rich, rather than undertaking a more thoroughgoing effort to collect enough revenue to really redistribute income toward lower-income Americans.

It is in this sense that an essential continuity emerges from what on the surface seems a self-contradictory New Deal tax policy. The distance from proposing regressive consumer taxes in 1933–5 to advocating higher taxes on the villainous rich in 1935–7 was less than one might think (especially when considering FDR's symbolic forays into salary limitation and loophole closing in the first phase of New Deal tax policy). In terms of public image, what mattered was the spotlighting of chicanery at the top, the institutionalized oratory of FDR's income-tax proposals, not the actual financial impact of the tax system. Income redistribution was subordinated, whether in 1933–5, when the New Deal hid regressive taxes within high-visibility programs, or in 1935–7, when changes in the personal income tax added very little revenue and affected few people (the 1935 Wealth Tax's new top bracket, it will be remembered, applied only once in its first three years – to John D. Rockefeller, no less). Here again, in the late 1930s as in the middle 1930s, taxation and the polarizing atmosphere associated with it served as a New Deal safety valve. After the 1937 recession enthroned the resurgent conservative coalition, the rankling symbol of the undistributed-profits tax invited reprisal. Roosevelt had unwittingly impelled the right to cash in its power chips on a tax controversy that scarcely left an imprint on the character of the state built by the New Deal. For though tax battles took place in a symbolic realm, there were other New Deal changes more worth protecting. Although one can easily belittle, for example, the relief programs and labor policy of the New Deal for their system-preserving functions, for their sometimes halting and conservatively motivated New Deal endorsements, and for their inadequate provision for the same "forgotten men" burdened by early New Deal tax policy, one cannot deny that such legislation had a substantive impact: providing income and self-respect to relieve the suffering of millions and fundamentally altering the balance of power between business and labor. And though FDR's use of tax policy to crosscut and cement his electoral coalition was primarily symbolic, he of course also made meaningful concessions to that coalition: subsidies and loans for farmers, union rights and minimum wages for workers, old-age pensions for the elderly, and so on. In the transformed political atmosphere of the late 1930s, the durability of these changes was in question; the Works Progress Administration and the Wagner Labor Relations Act were particularly unpopular among businessmen. But the obsession with the undistributed-profits tax and all that it symbolized drained away pressure for modification of these measures and thus helped them survive the power shift toward business leadership. In New Deal tax policy, the political main events were economic sideshows, but that does not negate their importance. Taxation was the lightning rod of the New Deal, neutralizing threats from conservatives and radicals alike. It was, above all, a symbolic reform.

Index

Accountancy profession, 196
Agricultural Adjustment Act, objectives of,
   37–8, 39, 40
  see also Processing tax
Agricultural Adjustment Administration,
   reformer purge in, 122
Alcohol tax, 30–6
  budget-balancing potential of, 31, 60–1,
   63
  as by-product of legalization, 30, 32,
   183
  consensus for, 191
   business supports, 34, 234
   consumers accept, 32, 36
   economists support, 33
   left-wing supports, 34
  as "hidden tax," 192
  history of, 31
  as income-tax substitute, 31
  justifications for, 17–18, 24n
  opposition to, 33, 33n
   from alcohol industry, 34
   from prohibitionists, 31, 32
  regressivity issue and, 31–4 passim
  revenue argument for, 31–2
  revenue-bootlegger standard for, 33,
   35–6
  revenue yield of, 12, 31, 35
Altmeyer, Arthur, 277, 285
Alvord, Ellsworth, 241, 267
American Association for Social Security,
   284
American Automobile Association, 22
American Economic Association, 150
American Farm Bureau Federation, 41
American Federation of Labor, 119, 122
  conservative tax shift, 227–8
  and 1935 Revenue Act, 151, 227, 227n
  and salary publicity, 79
  sales tax, opposition to, 227
  on social security, 284, 284n
  and war sacrifice theme, 290
American Federation of Little Business,
   271
American Liberty League, 31, 134, 159,
   162

American Petroleum Institute, 22
American Taxpayers' League, 14, 163
American Telephone and Telegraph
   Company, 180
Associated Business Papers, 162
Association Against the Prohibition
   Amendment, 31, 32
Association of American Railroads, 162
Astor, Vincent, 149–50
Avery, Sewell, 209

Bailey, Josiah, Senator, 205
Bankhead, John, Senator, 268, 269
Banking, *see* Business, bankers
Barkley, Alben, Senator, 114, 117, 269
Barron's, 196, 281n
Baruch, Bernard, 49, 211, 257
Bealle, Morris, 226
Beard, Charles, 122
Berle, Adolf, 56, 166
Black, Hugo, Senator, 81, 181
Blum, John, 92
Borah, William, Senator, 100, 114, 140,
   155, 227
Borah-O'Mahoney federal incorporation
   bill, 215
Braeman, John, 89
Brandeis, Louis
  deconcentration philosophy of, 101, 132
  and FDR, 135–6, 138
  on undistributed profits tax, 174
Brookings Institution, 251, 270
Brown, J. Douglas, 285
Buckley, William, 4
Business
  on alcohol taxes, 34
  anti-FDR rigidification of, 133–4, 156–
   8, 170, 211
  argues lower taxes will raise revenues,
   231, 240, 241
  bankers, 61, 240n, 281n
  on budget balancing, 237–41, 281n
  as consumer defenders, 23–4, 24n, 34,
   41
  contradictory arguments of, 236
  and economic recovery, 66, 166–7, 236

294